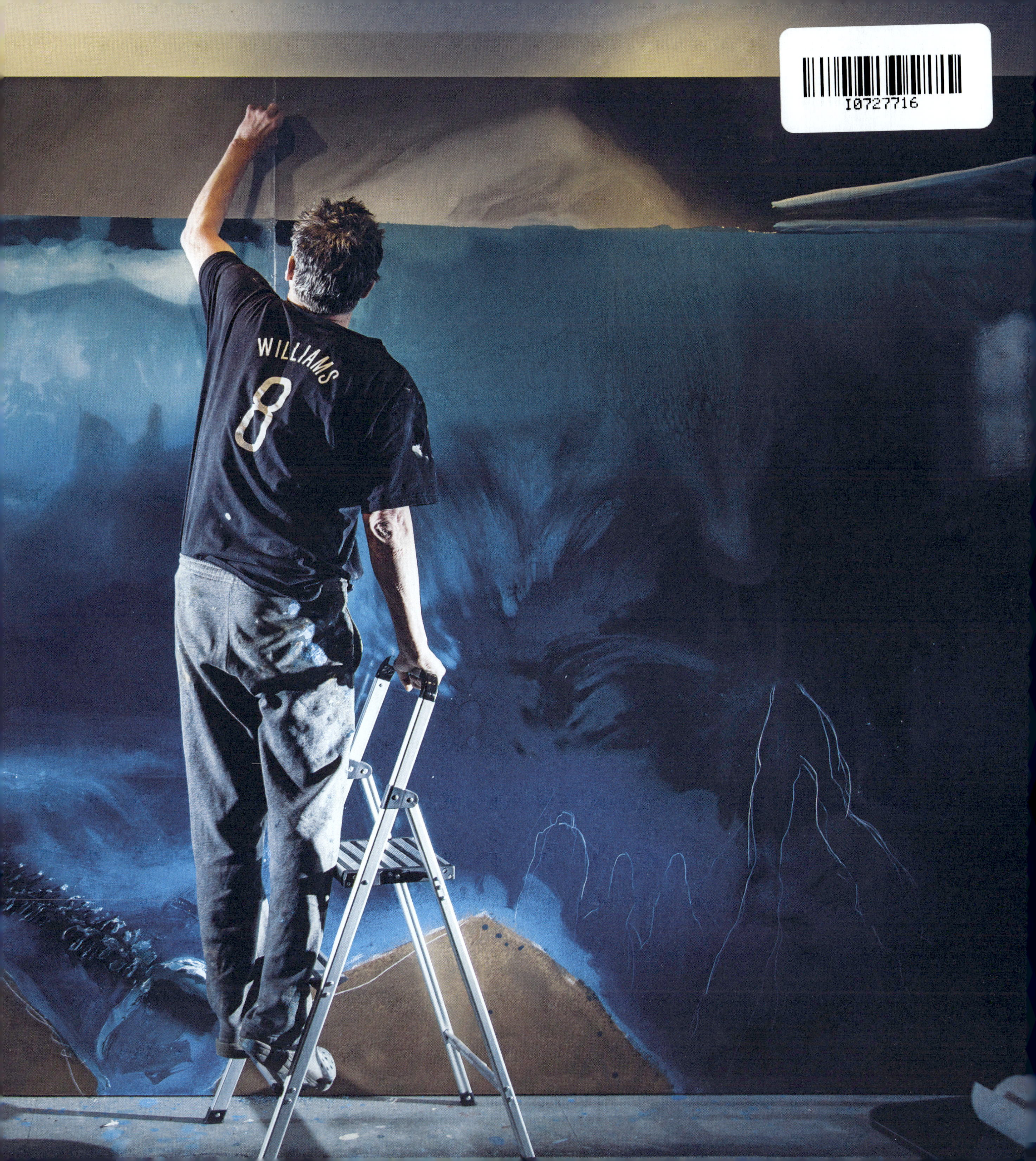

WILLIAMS
8

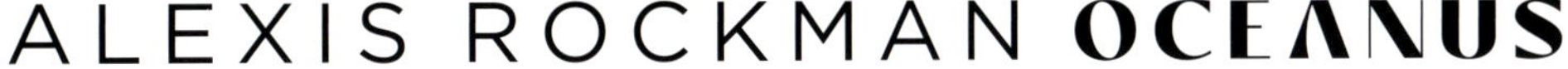

ALEXIS ROCKMAN OCEANUS

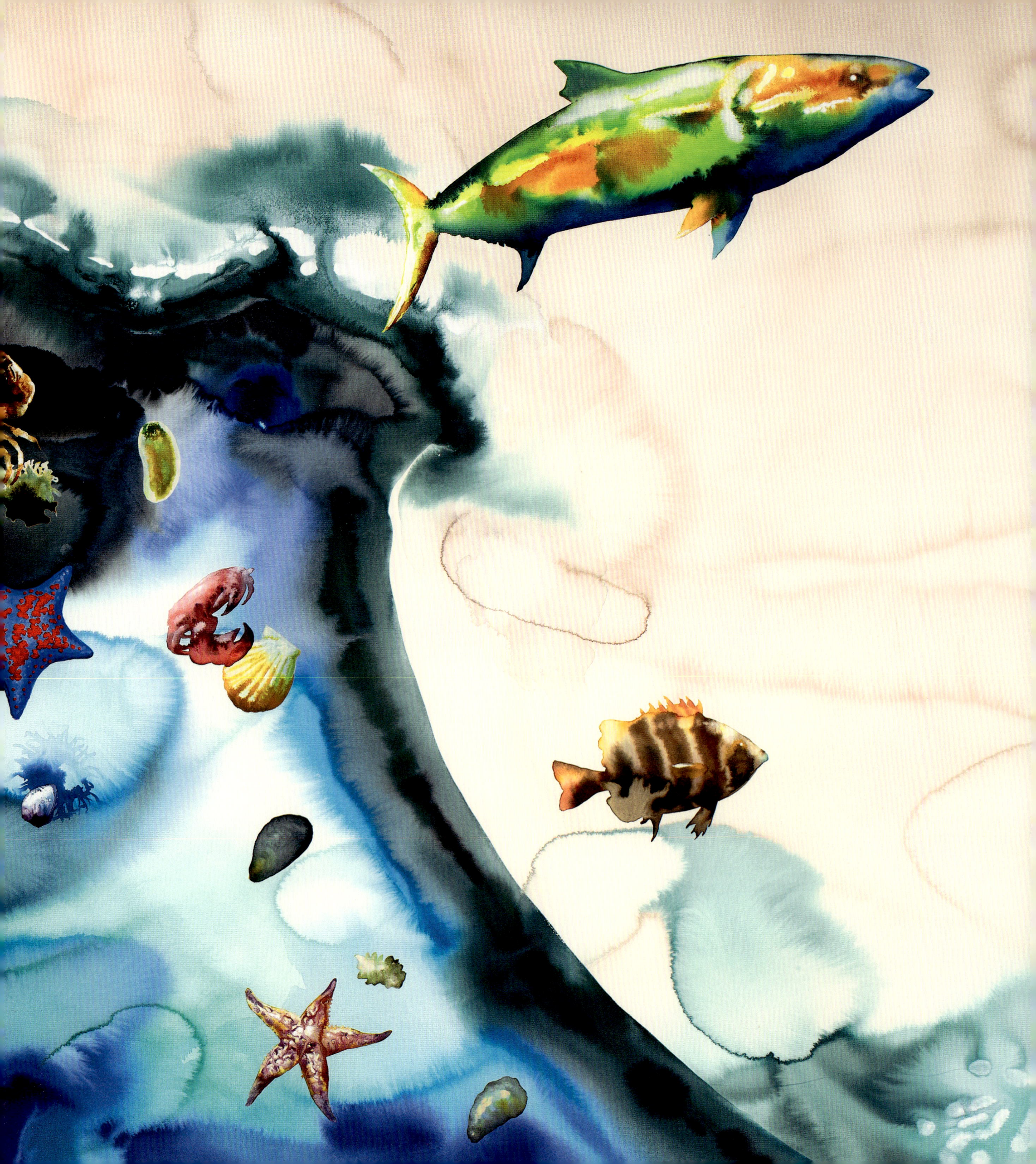

ALEXIS ROCKMAN

OCEANUS

Edited by

Christina Connett Brophy

With contributions by

Robert D. Ballard

Christina Connett Brophy

James T. Carlton

Sylvia A. Earle

Michael R. Harrison

Alexis Rockman

Helen M. Rozwadowski

Nari Ward

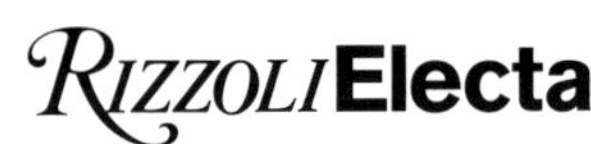

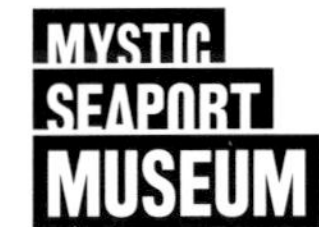

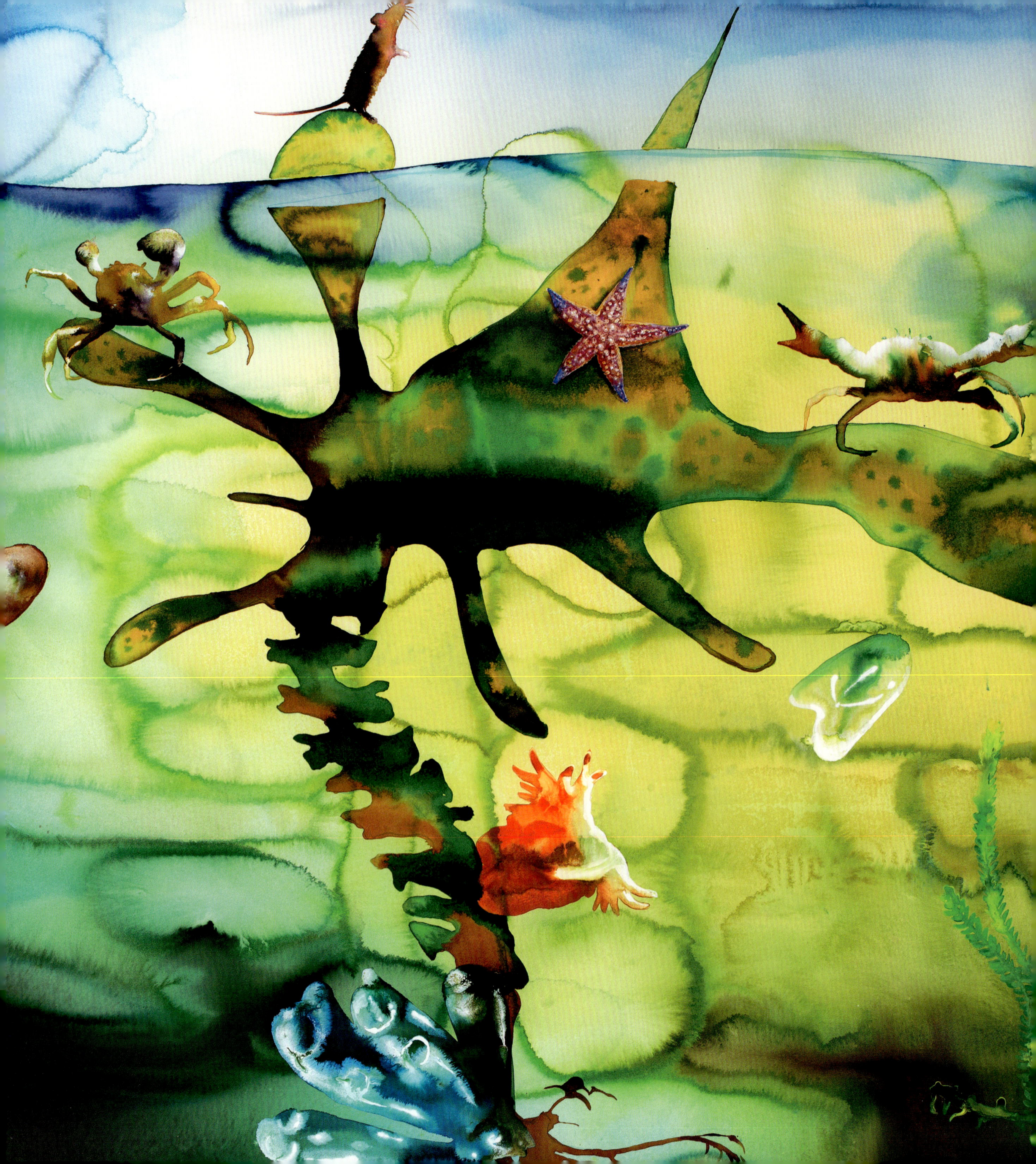

CONTENTS

REASON FOR HOPE

The real voyage of discovery consists not in seeking new landscapes but in having new eyes.

—Marcel Proust

Alexis Rockman has a rare gift. As portrayed in this elegant volume, as if in dreams, he transforms knowledge about the nature of the sea and our impact on it into inspired—and inspiring—visual poetry. His gift is seeing what others do not, then artfully sharing the view, skillfully enabling others to feel, understand, and care about what columns of numbers, clever charts, words, and even photographs cannot convey.

The message is clear. The ocean is alive and it is in trouble, and therefore, so are we. But it is not too late to find an enduring place for ourselves within the natural systems that sustain us.

It is fitting that the Mystic Seaport Museum is hosting these remarkable images. The museum not only celebrates the ingenuity of those who figured out how to build and sail seaworthy ships across vast expanses of the sea, but also highlights ongoing discoveries about the nature of life beneath the surface, even in the deepest ocean. The critical shifts in our understanding and behavior toward ocean wildlife, from killing to caring, is an underlying theme in the museum, visually expressed in Rockman's electrifying images.

"If you do not know your past you cannot know your future," says Egyptian archeologist Zahi Hawass. In the twenty-first century, as never before, we have the ability to know who we are as a species, where we have come from, and what our future could be—depending on what we do or fail to do. Throughout history, to foster our prosperity, we have consumed and displaced the ancient living systems that set Earth apart from any other place in the universe. Even thousands of years ago when our numbers were small, in the blink of a geologist's eye we altered the trajectory of life on Earth. Biologist E. O. Wilson observed that over the ages, our habit of dining on "large, slow and tasty" animals led to the extinction of many terrestrial species and diminished vulnerable sea creatures as well. Presently, the focus on taking sea life by the ton includes the small (shrimp, krill, herring, luminescent mid-water fish, squid), the speedy (tuna, swordfish, sharks, orcas), and legions of the not-so-tasty but nonetheless marketable species ground up for oil and food for pets and farmed animals.

By the 1500s, when half a billion people populated the planet, the "great age of exploration" coincided with the onset of the great era of exploitation, now enhanced by technologies that facilitate finding, killing, and marketing wildlife, especially ocean life, and domesticating all but a fraction of the wilderness that preceded our existence. As our numbers increased to a billion by 1800, trees, birds, mammals, and thousands of other species sharply declined. By 1900 a few hundred bison were all that remained from the millions that once dominated North American landscapes from coast to coast. By 1912 every last one of the billions of passenger pigeons that once existed were no more. In the sea, wars were fought over the rights to kill cod and herring and, as depicted at the Mystic Seaport Museum, the great whales were being hunted relentlessly and mercilessly far beyond coastal waters, shattering the whales' tightly knit social structures, behaviors, and ecological connections. Two billion people occupied Earth by the 1930s, and by 1980, the number swelled to four billion. Late in 2022 our numbers reached eight billion and are expected to top ten billion by 2050.

Geologists have designated the 1950s as the beginning of a new geological era, the Anthropocene, evidenced by the enduring impact humans have had on the earth, recorded in stone. Shifts in the composition of Earth's biodiversity, evidence of nuclear explosions, the occurrence of synthetic materials, and our large carbon footprint are among the enduring marks that indicate a time of significant change in the nature of the systems that underpin our existence. Alexis Rockman was born in the Holocene era that began 11,000 years ago, but he has emerged as a twenty-first-century man, living in the Anthropocene. His life as a witness to the unprecedented changes in the nature of our home planet is evident in his art, images that not only convey painful loss but also urgency and, most importantly, hope. Birds, whales, octopuses, and diaphanous jelly creatures still thrive and we can too, if we realize how our fate and theirs are inextricably connected.

In the twentieth century, at the same time that wild birds were gaining increased respect and a few special wildlands were safeguarded as parks and reserves, images of Earth from space and from the depths of the sea confirmed the miracle that life exists at all. Astrophysicist Carl Sagan called it a "pale, blue dot" embedded within the magnificent but lifeless surrounding universe. Given sufficient water and the right range of temperature and chemical composition, life may exist beyond our home planet, but Earth is the only place suitable for moss, ferns, elephants, birds, whales, tuna, and for us and for all that we care about. Never before have we known how exceptional and how fragile our existence is, and never again will there be a better chance to manage ourselves in ways that protect our life-support system, dominated by the living ocean. Whales, as intelligent as they are, cannot restore health to the planet, but we can.

Half of the sunlit tropical reefs, mangroves, marshes, and seagrass meadows have disappeared, along with 90 percent of the sharks, tuna, and numerous other commercially killed species of ocean wildlife. But some reefs and other coastal systems remain intact. With protection, some sea turtles, whales, and birds are making a comeback. While only about 3 percent of the ocean is proactively protected from fishing, mining, and the dumping of noxious things, there is a promising move to highly protect at least 30 percent of the sea by 2030. Some nations have already done so.

With knowing comes caring and with caring there is hope that we will find an enduring place for ourselves within the natural, mostly blue systems that make possible the existence of life. But knowledge alone is not enough to motivate the action needed. If it were so, we would be racing to protect nature rather than seeking to mine the deep sea, clear-cut ancient forests, and sell single tuna for more than a million dollars.

Bravo, Alexis Rockman and all who enable us to see with new eyes, to put the next century above the next quarter, and who, in seeing the juxtaposition of devastation with miracles of life, will make the right choices, while there is still time.

—Sylvia A. Earle

OCEANUS: OUR MARITIME LEGACY

American maritime heritage as historically presented at Mystic Seaport Museum (MSM) has largely focused on the surface of the world's ocean, by what is most accessible and visible to the terrestrial audiences we serve. Our collections of artifacts and over five hundred watercraft currently reflect this bias. However, the museum has begun augmenting its exhibitions, holdings, and scholarship to look toward the undersea world. One of our primary goals in this shift in perspective is to raise awareness and inspire conversations around the critical global issues that face our oceans due to the impacts of maritime activities as part of our collective cultural, social, and economic heritage. Mystic Seaport Museum recently signed a manifesto with other members of the International Council for Maritime Museums that declares our dedication to using our platform for this purpose. In addition, as an institution we are rethinking what our traditional interpretation of maritime heritage even means for the future, as blue economies, technologies, and innovations reinvent the way we relate to our oceans, to preserve and protect, exploit and explore.

One of the strategies to engage dialogue and reach a broader audience on these issues is through contemporary art. For decades, the internationally renowned artist Alexis Rockman has filtered his enormous curiosity and study of science and history into exquisitely immersive experiences that are breathtaking in technical skill and stunning in composition and color. In 2021, MSM commissioned Rockman to create *Oceanus*, a series of eleven works, including the monumental 8-by-24-foot central painting and ten large-scale watercolors (pp. 49–119). Alexis has a long history of facing tough environmental subjects in his work, from *Manifest Destiny*, 2003–4, another monumental work that gives a startling apocalyptic view of Brooklyn, to the *Great Lakes Cycle*, a sobering look at our long-range impact on these large bodies of water. To illustrate the science behind the paintings, Rockman even provides a key to the species and important content represented, in the tradition of natural history museums. Rockman had conversations with every contributor to this publication, from scientists to historians to explorers, opening his work to a credible authenticity, which forms the baseline for his works that tackle ecological issues such as climate change and species extinction. The beauty of

Rockman's approach is the circularity of his strategy: science gets creativity and art gets data, a co-creation in the shared space of imagination and knowledge, connecting emotion with facts.

Art takes science beyond the visual and the pictorial by adding imagination. In the case of Rockman it makes his paintings arresting.
—Thomas Eugene Lovejoy III

In *Oceanus*, Alexis Rockman covers themes related to the undersea world that are essential to understanding our place and role in the current and future health of our oceans. The central painting in particular is a time capsule of our legacy in this regard. He addresses critical environmental and social justice issues of our past, present, and future, including climate change and sea-level rise; both the forced and intentional ocean passages of people; dispossession of Indigenous coastal waterways; the introduction of invasive marine species through human activities, now exacerbated by climate change; maritime commerce and industry; and the cultural mystery and fascination of this last largely unknown part of our world. Using the Museum's watercraft collections and unique position on a river teeming with invasive species, this new series brings attention to our largely alien ocean and our impact upon it.

As you travel through these works, take time to appreciate Rockman's sincerity and passion, his attention to detail, which draws you into the scene but then allows a twist, a sequence of compressions that bely reality and reveal his critical interpretation. In the central work, Rockman has brought together vessels of exploitation linearly along the surface of the ocean, which culminates in a tsunami wave of epic proportions and luminescent colors. Where few of these ships were historically concurrent, in their presentation here we are able to see the succession of technologies that rendered each their respective profitable and destructive exploitation of the seas. Beneath the waves each creature has a purpose. The tuna, cod, shrimp, squid, and others have each been heavily harvested. Some species, like the oyster, have suffered terrible decimation only to be brought back by sustainable methods of aquafarming.

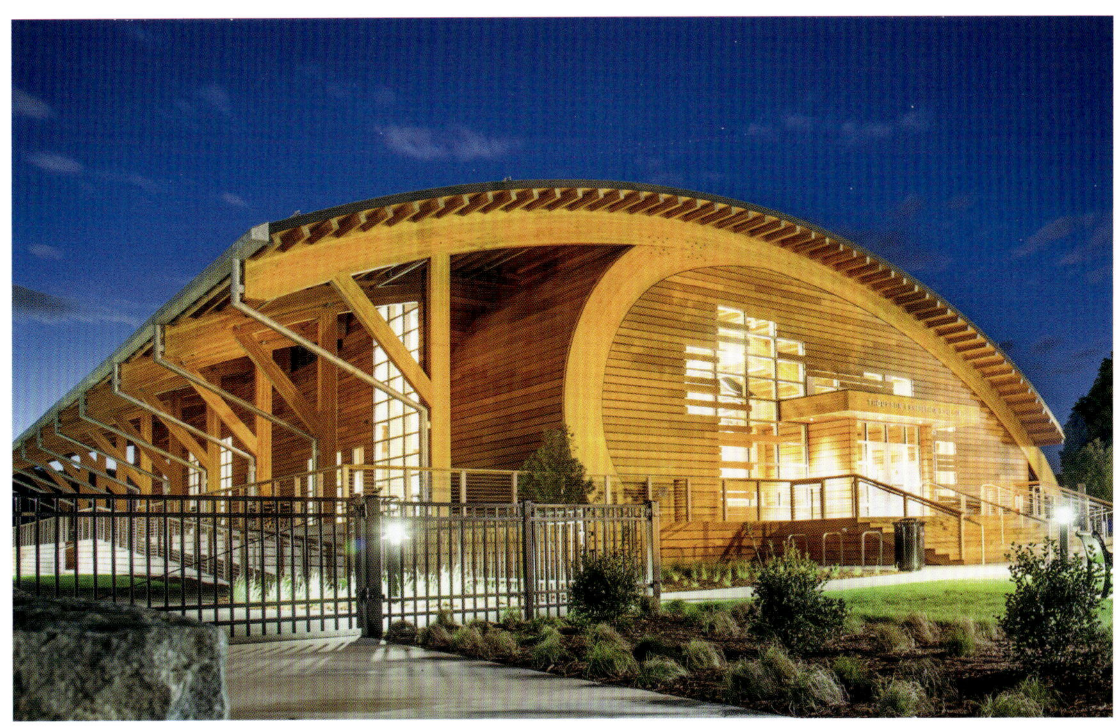

The Thompson Exhibition Building
at Mystic Seaport Museum,
Mystic, Connecticut

The whale, which has recently perished, is ravaged by various sharks, from hammerheads to great whites. However, while the whale ship to its left is probably the cause of its demise, Rockman allows us to interpret another cause, a ship strike by any number of the more modern vessels, most likely the container ship on the right. Policy changes in shipping traffic lanes to move with known migration pathways of whales, like the highly endangered North Atlantic right whale, as well as regulations on speed, have been very successful in some cases. However, ship strikes remain one of the leading causes of deaths to whales in this century. *Oceanus* opens doors to deeper conversations on these critical issues that continue to circumvent complete resolution.

Rockman's watercolors are by their nature more loosely rendered and abstracted than the oil on panel. Their juxtaposition with the central painting provides a visual shift from their immensely detailed larger companion work. They elicit an exquisite visceral response with their large swaths of intense fluid colors, engaging compositions, and oversize format. Rockman's brilliant method of creating sensorial pleasure at first glance makes the effect of the secondary response to their darker themes of biological invasions, mass extinctions, coastal destructions, loss of biodiversity, and others all the more profound. In *Transient Passage*, for example, one is drawn to the glorious oranges and greens of the composition's infrastructure of buoy and sea, followed by the sea creatures—the jewel-like yellow butterfly fish and the blue col-

ony of sea anemones. However, what the image really portrays is these animals' transit to places they are not meant to be, where they may wreak havoc on native species in a new environment, supported and protected on their journey by a man-made ecosystem of plastics.

There is hope for a sustainable and healthy ocean, thanks to thousands of solutions-based ocean health remediators and innovators, several of whom are mentioned at the end of this book. But even with these extraordinary investments in the future blue economy, the urgency and destruction that reverberate throughout Rockman's *Oceanus* series are very real. As we look to our global maritime heritage, which MSM is committed to preserving, these remarkable works will spark critical discussions on a crisis that faces us all. The discussion begins here in this volume, as our expert contributors examine Rockman's *Oceanus* through the lens of their respective disciplines. It is very much our hope that these essays and this remarkable, groundbreaking series of works inspire productive conversation and a rethinking of what has been and shall be our maritime legacy. The future is our choice to make.

—Christina Connett Brophy
Senior Vice President of Curatorial Affairs and Senior Director of Museum Galleries at Mystic Seaport Museum

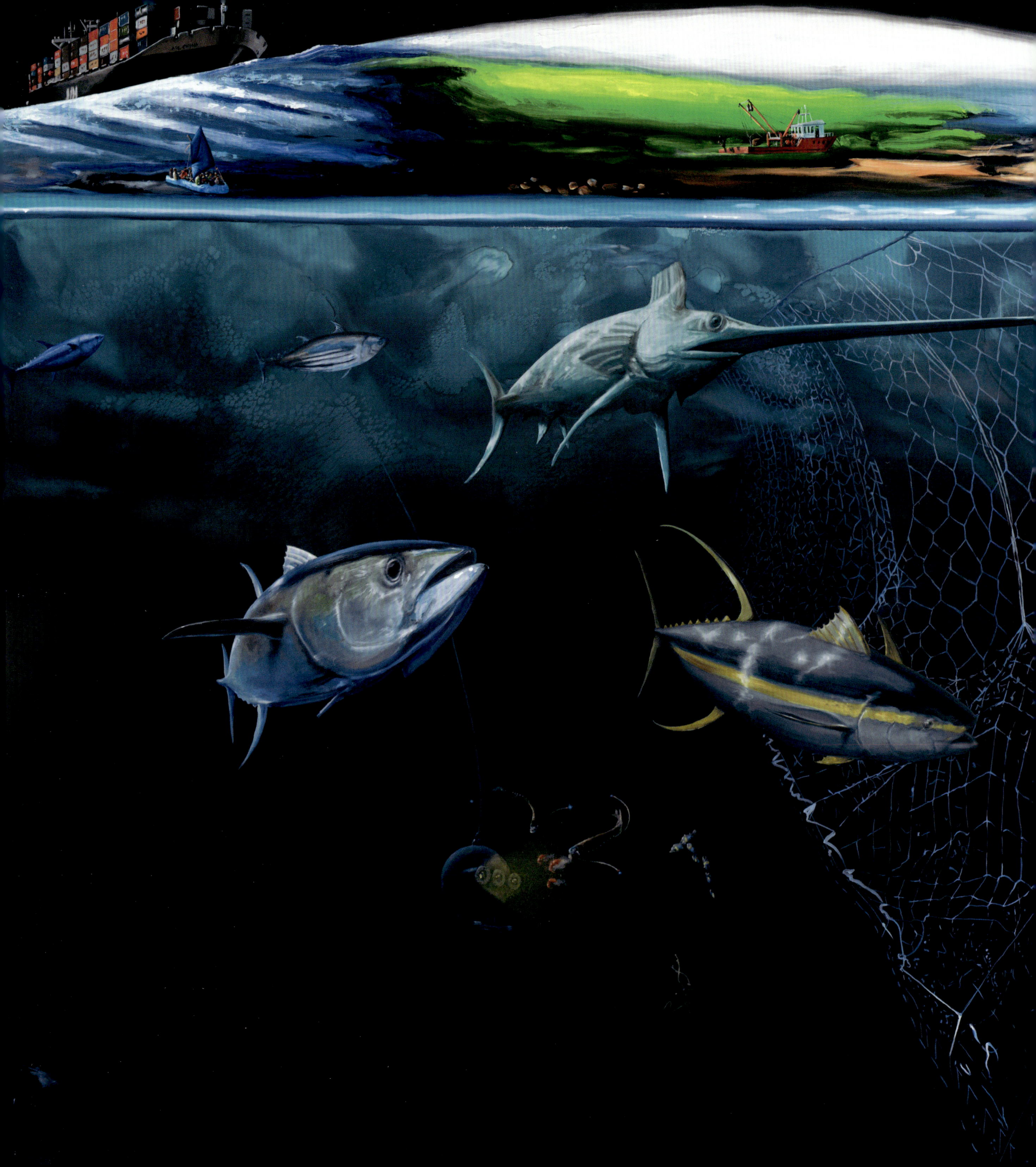

THE HISTORY AND POWER OF THE UNDERSEA VIEW

HELEN M. ROZWADOWSKI

Professor of History and founder of the Maritime Studies program at the University of Connecticut

OCEANUS OFFERS A STRIKINGLY ORIGINAL perspective on maritime heritage and legacy. Interpretation of maritime activity mostly focuses on the sea's surface, where boats bearing trade goods, cannons, or people travel from one port to another. Maritime history prominently highlights the vessels and other technologies used to sail and work at sea, such as navigational instruments, nets, or harpoons, but rarely features centrally the ocean environment itself. Ferocious storms or serendipitous winds might appear at critical moments in stories of the maritime past, yet the volumetric oceans are treated as a stage rather than an agent of history. *Oceanus*, on the other hand, crowds the normally prominent watercraft toward the top edge of the painting, where the ocean's enormous surface is dwarfed by the expansive depths, the extensive sea floor, and its three-dimensional underground. This view reflects the spatial and ecological importance of the oceans on the planetary scale; while the global ocean covers almost three-quarters of the earth, it comprises 99 percent of the available living space.[1] This focus on the undersea both reorients our approach to maritime heritage and makes visible a view that is normally not accessible to the human eye, prompting consideration of the present state and the future prospects of the worlds' oceans.

The panorama of global ocean offered by *Oceanus* is, of course, an imaginative view even as it includes realistic detail. Actual human eyes, underwater, see blurry images unless they are protected by goggles, because water touching the cornea does not allow for the refraction of light we need to see objects clearly. Turbidity caused by silt, plankton, salts, and other particles suspended in water limits visibility. That's why temperate seas, with their greater primary productivity, are more opaque than tropical waters. Furthermore, light is absorbed by water. At 10 meters (33 feet), a diver would see no reds. As the explorer William Beebe described based on his experiences diving to depths as great as 900 meters in his bathysphere in the 1930s, moving deeper, yellows disappear, then greens, and finally blues.[2] So little sunlight reaches below 200 meters that photosynthesis is impossible, and none penetrates below 1,000 meters.[3] All this points to the central role of various forms of representation, including art, in enabling us to visualize the oceans.

Historically, people around the world forged knowledge about the oceans through bodily engagement, by swimming and diving to gather food and other marine resources, and by traveling on watercraft. For many cultures, oceanic-scale water features prominently in origin stories and water beings in religious beliefs.[4] Expanding ambitions for using the volumetric oceans—for food and nonliving resources, for communication and trade, and for warfare—motivated the pursuit of knowledge about the oceans and equally depended on success in gaining it. Yet knowledge about the vast and opaque oceans is necessarily mediated through technologies and knowledge systems, both those of people in the past and equally today. The indirect nature of our knowledge of the oceans means that imagination, media, and aesthetic practices loom large in shaping our understandings of the oceans.[5] As Rachel Carson put it, "To sense this world of waters known to the creatures of the sea we must shed our human perceptions of length and breadth and time and place, and enter vicariously into a universe of all-pervading water."[6] *Oceanus* reflects the historic evolution of oceanic representations enabling vicarious entry into the sea, even as it contributes to reshaping our understanding of the imprint of human maritime activities on the volumetric oceans.

Aquariums and underwater filming and photography make views under the water's surface a familiar perspective today, but that has not always been the case. There are examples of depictions of the underwater in the distant past, such as those illustrating medieval retellings of the story of Alexander the Great visiting the sea floor in a diving bell (fig. 1).[7] Alexander's purported motives, having conquered the Persian Empire to create the world's largest empire to that date, involved curiosity to learn about the world and determination to extend his control to conquer the sea. His European successors in the so-called Great Age of Discovery of the fifteenth and sixteenth centuries similarly sought knowledge of the ocean in order to project power over it, but they were preoccupied more by the sea's surface than the depths.[8] The Portuguese and Spanish crowns built empires by trying to enforce their claims to sea routes, eastward and westward respectively, to the fabled riches of Asia. The novel Dutch and English joint stock companies, the Dutch East India Company and the East India Company of England, tied capitalism and imperialism to oceans and to the regime of free seas.[9] By the eighteenth century, science joined warfare as a tool deployed by European states to operate effectively on the seas, and states supported maritime activity including the creation and transmission of navigational knowledge.[10] Charts inspired by Enlightenment ideals gridded the oceans with lines of latitude and longitude, leaving the sea as an empty, apparently frictionless surface between land (fig. 2).[11]

Representations of the undersea surged forth in the nineteenth century, from a simultaneous scientific and cultural dis-

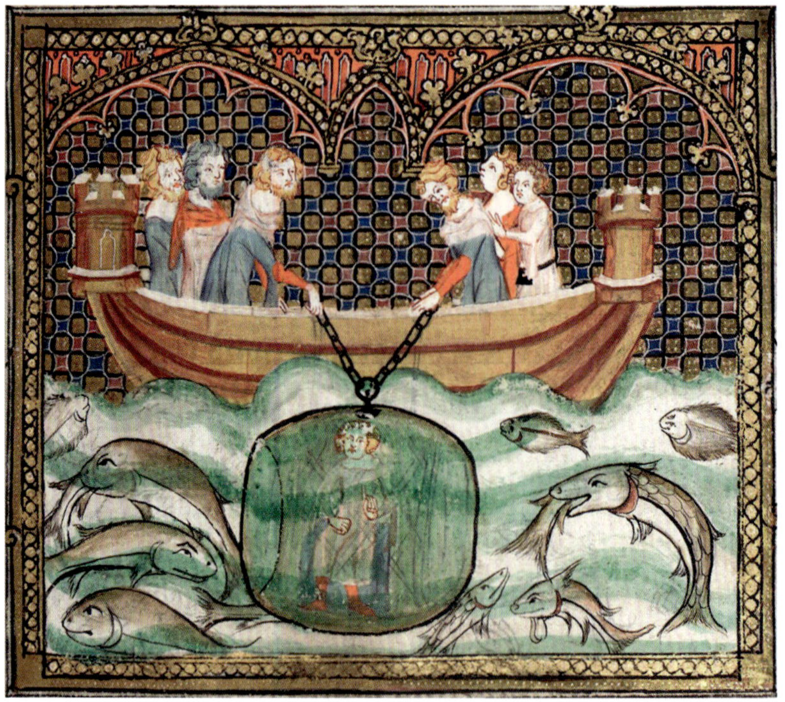

1. Jehan de Grise and his workshop, "Boat with a battlemented erection at each end, Alexander the Great in a glass diving-bell," ca. 1338–44. Miniature from the illustrated *Romance of Alexander*, by various authors including Lambert le Tort and Alexandre de Bernai (de Paris), 842–ca. 1400. Ink and gold leaf on parchment. Bodleian Library, University of Oxford, Oxford

covery of the volumetric ocean. This awakening to the sea began at its edge. Embrace of the therapeutic value of seawater and ocean bathing sparked the redefinition of the shore from an unsavory to a socially desirable place, setting the stage for the modern, recreational beach.[12] The coast also invited observers to contem-

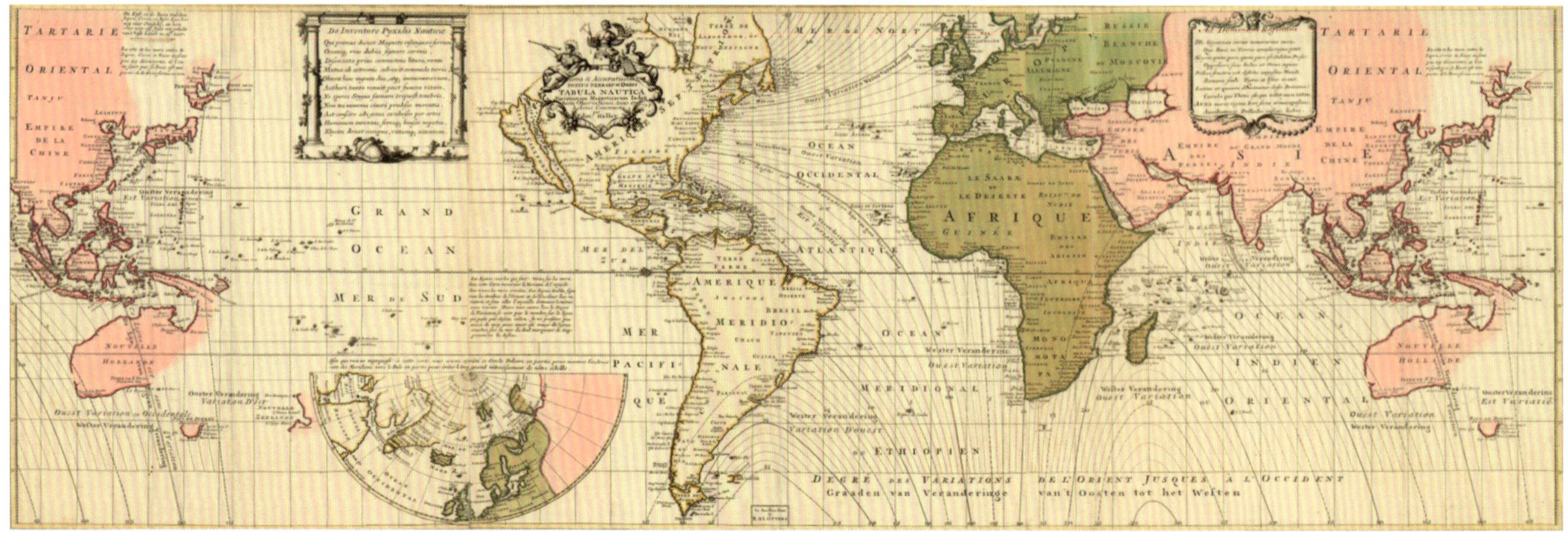

2. Reiner Ottens, Joshua Ottens, and Edmund Halley, *Nova & Accuratissima Totius Terrarum Orbis Tabula Nautica Variationum Magneticarum Index Juxta Observationes Anno 1700 Habitas Constructa per Edm*, ca. 1730. Hand-colored, 21½ × 56 inches (54.6 × 142.2 cm)

plate the new sense of deep time proposed by geologists. Observers began to view coasts as products of forces at work over vast periods of time. Cliffs offered the possibility to "browse in the archives of the earth."[13] These archives began to reveal remnants of creatures that no longer roamed the earth, unless, as some wondered, the ocean might still hide living examples. The earliest representation of deep time, an 1830 cartoon by the English geologist Henry De la Beche, depicting mostly aquatic animals, also proffered a novel view of the sea (fig. 3). Based on fossils found by the collector Mary Anning, *Duria antiquior* showed creatures from the Devonian period frolicking underwater, as if seen through aquarium glass, while at the same time including a less extensive glimpse of the sea's surface. *Oceanus* likewise provides such an aquarium view paired with a representation of the ocean's surface, placing even more scalar emphasis on the undersea. To nineteenth-century observers in the wake of Darwinian theory and the allied belief in progress, the prominence of oceans in the drama of evolution tied present oceans not only to the past but the future as well.[14]

Historians aren't sure what inspired De la Beche to employ the semi-aquarium view in *Duria antiquior*. Perhaps he had some experience with diving, but it was certainly not in imitation of actual aquariums. Those were invented at midcentury and popularized after 1854, when author, teacher, and amateur naturalist Philip Henry Gosse published *The Aquarium: An Unveiling of the Wonders of the Deep Sea* (fig. 4). The aquarium craze crested in Britain and subsequently in the United States,

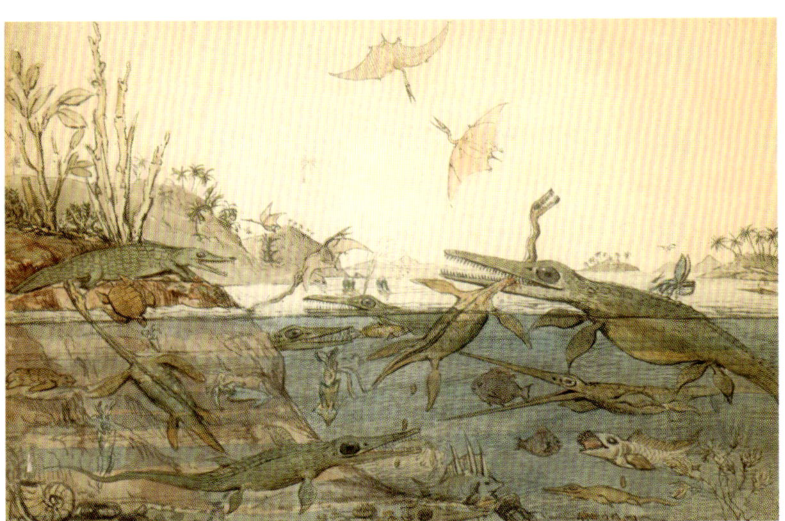

3. Henry De la Beche, *Duria antiquior* (A more ancient Dorset), 1830. Watercolor, 12½ × 8⅞ inches (31.8 × 22.4 cm). Amgueddfa Cymru, National Museum, Cardiff

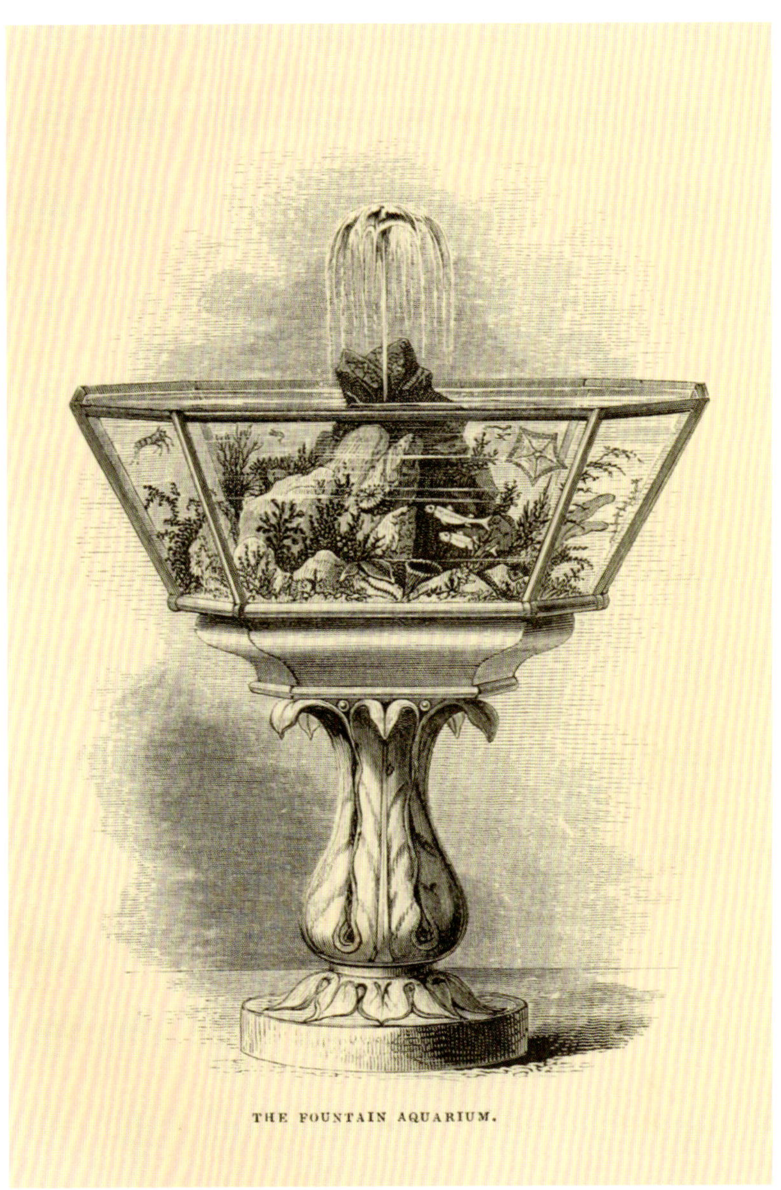

4. Illustration from Philip Henry Gosse, *The Aquarium: An Unveiling of the Wonders of the Deep Sea*, 2nd ed. (London: John Van Voorst, 1856)

then receded after a decade or so, leaving in its wake a smaller number of hobbyists, public aquariums in major cities throughout Europe and the US, and regret on the part of Gosse that amateur collectors inspired by his work had "ravaged every corner" of England's rocky tide pools.[15] Aquarium-keeping occupied one subset of enthusiastic practitioners of marine zoology and botany, fields that emerged at midcentury to draw naturalists' attention into the depths. Marine naturalists didn't themselves go underwater; rather, they modified oyster dredges, to make them easier to manage and more portable to carry with them on seaside holidays, and used them to sample the sea floor from small hired rowboats.[16] On land and sometimes aboard bigger boats, these early ocean scientists sketched, painted, dissected, and preserved the specimens they captured, developing an awareness of undersea space and what might, or might not, dwell there. Natural history illustrations of marine specimens from this time demonstrated this midcentury consciousness of the volumetric ocean, which quickly expanded from the scientific community to a much wider general public.

Depictions of the undersea grew common, appearing on sheet music on parlor pianos, in illustrated fiction and nonfiction, in newspapers and magazines, and in prints and broadsheets (fig. 5). The well-known French artist Gustave Doré illustrated Victor Hugo's *Toilers of the Sea* (1878) and Samuel Taylor Coleridge's

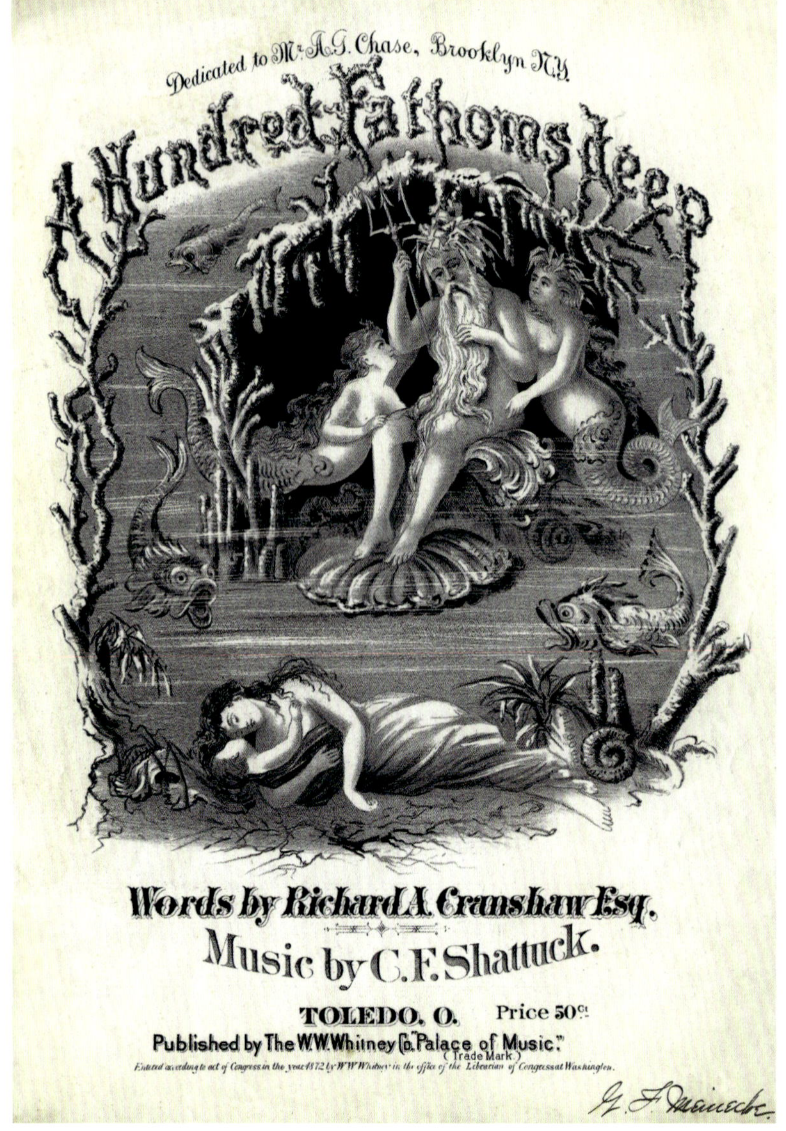

5. Sheet music illustration for "A Hundred Fathoms Deep," words by Richard A. Cranshaw, music by C. F. Shattuck (Toledo, OH: W. W. Whitney, ca. 1872). Lithograph, 14 × 11 inches (35.6 × 27.9 cm). Mystic Seaport Museum

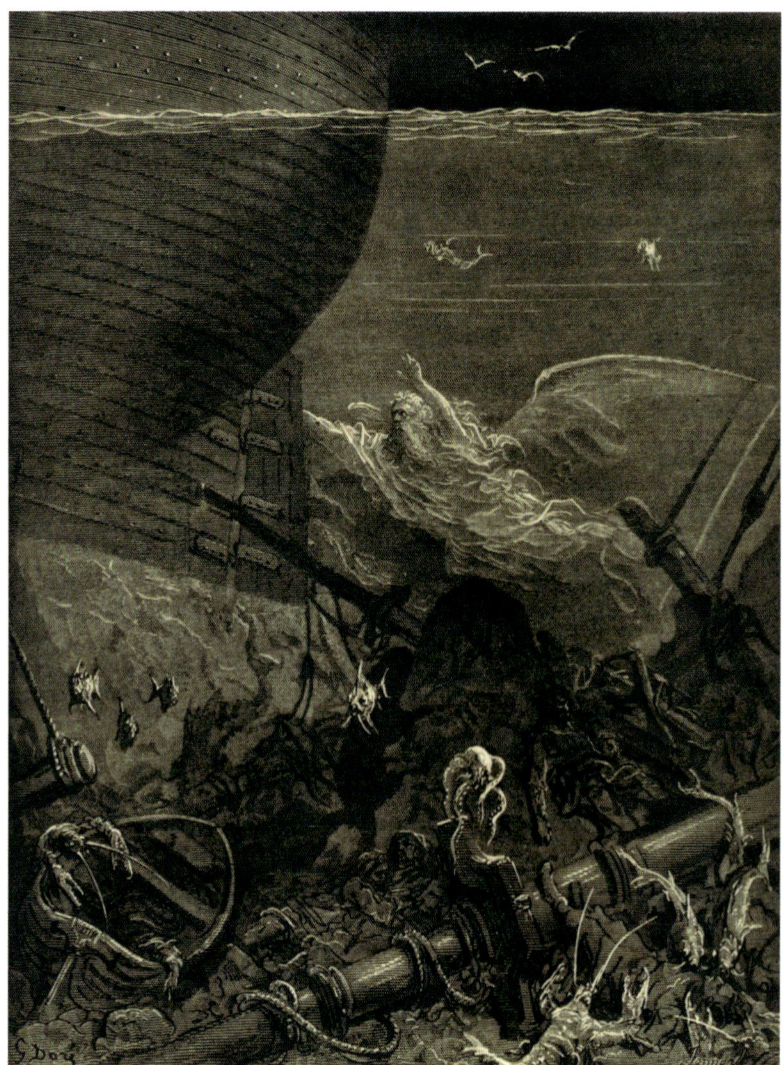

6. Gustave Doré, *Der Wassergeist verfolgt das Schiff* (The Water Spirit Follows the Ship), 1866. From *Der alte Matrose* (The Rime of the Ancient Mariner) by Samuel Taylor Coleridge, trans. Ferdinand Freiligrath (Munich: Josef Müller, 1925). 8¾ × 6⅜ inches (22.2 × 16.1 cm)

Rime of the Ancient Mariner (1876, fig. 6), while the French illustrator Édward Riou made the drawings for Jules Verne's *Twenty Thousand Leagues Under the Seas* (1871, fig. 7); all of these included undersea scenes.[17] Attempts to lay a telegraph cable across the Atlantic Ocean riveted public attention on the depths and employed representations of the undersea, ranging from the first ocean basin scale bathymetric charts to bottom profiles, showing proposed and actual cable routes.[18] The success of the 1866 Atlantic cable inspired a celebratory print titled *The Eighth Wonder of the World*, depicting the telegraph installed in the depths where Neptune could guard it (fig. 8). The scene's aquarium view transitions, like De la Beche's scene of ancient Dorset, into a view of the surface, where the North Atlantic is flanked by a lion symbolizing Britain and an eagle representing the United States. The storied steamer *Great Eastern*, the largest vessel built to that time and the only one big enough to carry the entire length of cable, floats in the center, surrounded by other vessels prosecuting maritime business. This allegory projects the pride of both nations at the great technological accomplishment and conveys confidence that the vast ocean has bent to human will by cradling the cable safely.

A different representation of a similar view by the US artist Edward Moran reveals the Atlantic seafloor as a panoramic landscape. His 1862 oil painting *The Valley in the Sea* (fig. 9, overleaf) contributes to the Hudson River School style of American

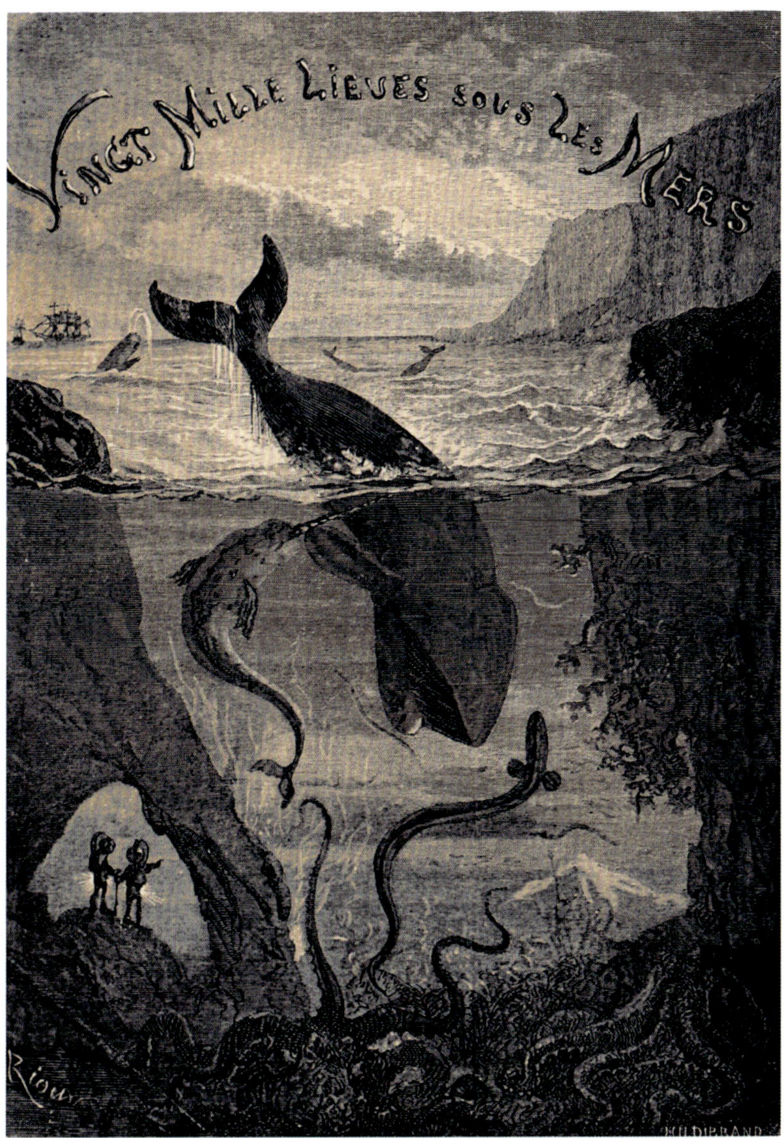

7. Jules Verne, *Vingt Mille Lieues sous les mers* (Twenty Thousand Leagues Under the Seas), frontispiece, illustrated by Alphonse de Neuville and Édouard Riou (Paris: Hetzel, 1871)

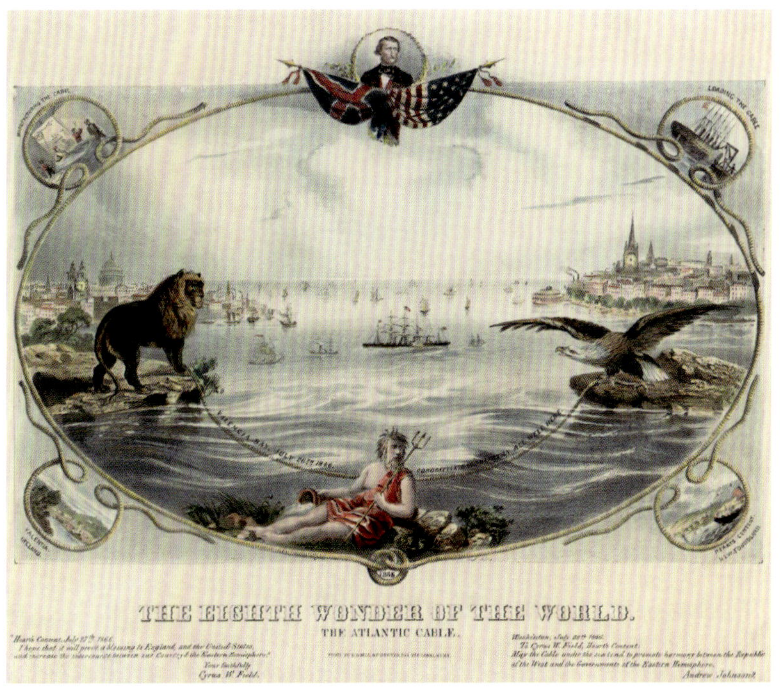

8. *The Eighth Wonder of the World: The Atlantic Cable* (New York: Kimmel & Forster, 1866). Lithograph, 12 × 16 inches (30.5 × 40.6 cm). National Museum of American History, Washington, DC

art despite its utterly unique subject matter for fine arts painting. Like other Hudson River School works, *The Valley in the Sea* reflects a romantic reaction against Enlightenment order, rationality, and control. There are strong contrasts of dark and light, and the eye is drawn around the painting following the circular framing. Like the American West scenes of his more famous brother Thomas Moran, Edward depicts a grand vista of sublime wilderness, understood by viewers as an assertion that the uniqueness and splendor of the New World landscape should be venerated as the Old World celebrated its ancient monuments and culture.[19] *The Valley in the Sea* departs from Hudson River School characteristics in other ways, however. While many contemporary landscapes convey movement, this image is still, reflecting the understanding of the deep sea as untouched by currents. The imagined quiescence of the ocean floor bolstered the idea of installing cables in the sea as it seemed to promise safety for the telegraph wires.

Moran's painting appears connected to the Atlantic cable and preparations for its installation. Commissioned in 1862 by James M. Sommerville, a Philadelphia physician, amateur artist, and naturalist-dredger, it was likely inspired by US deep-sea explorations made in the 1850s to plan for the 1857 and 1858 cable-laying attempts.[20] Moran's depiction of the undersea valley

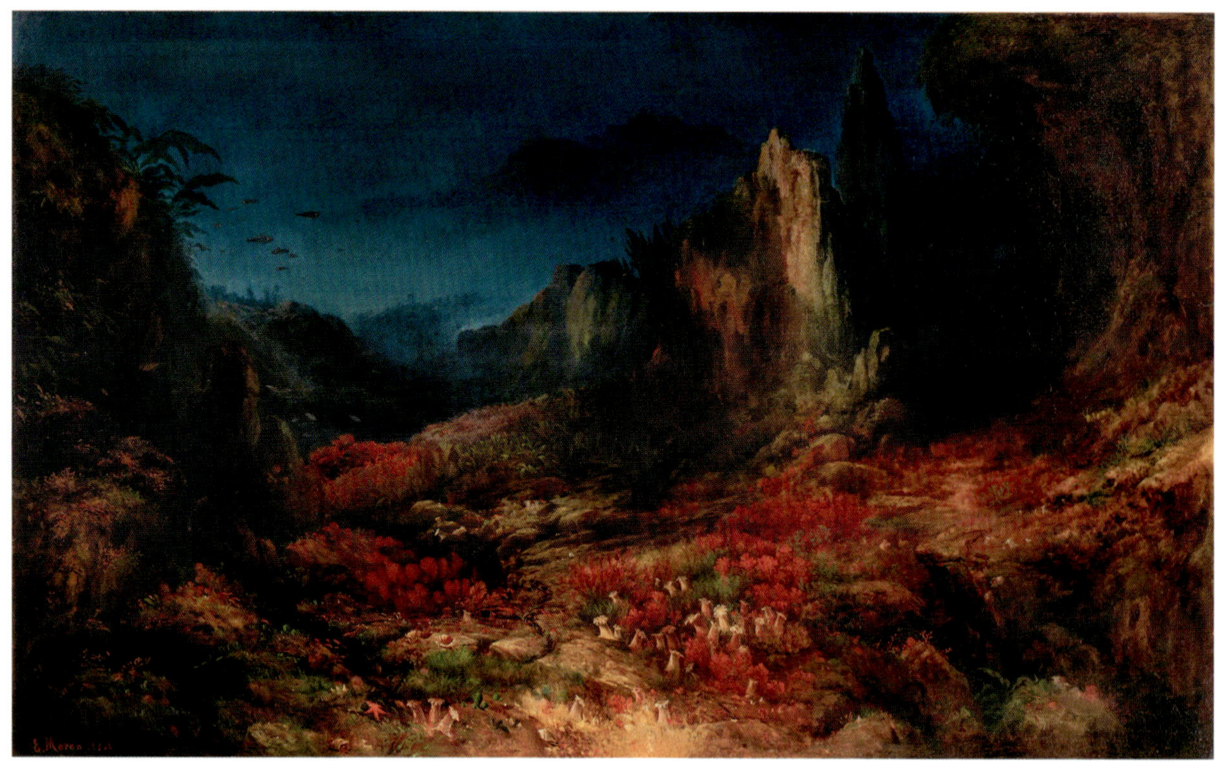

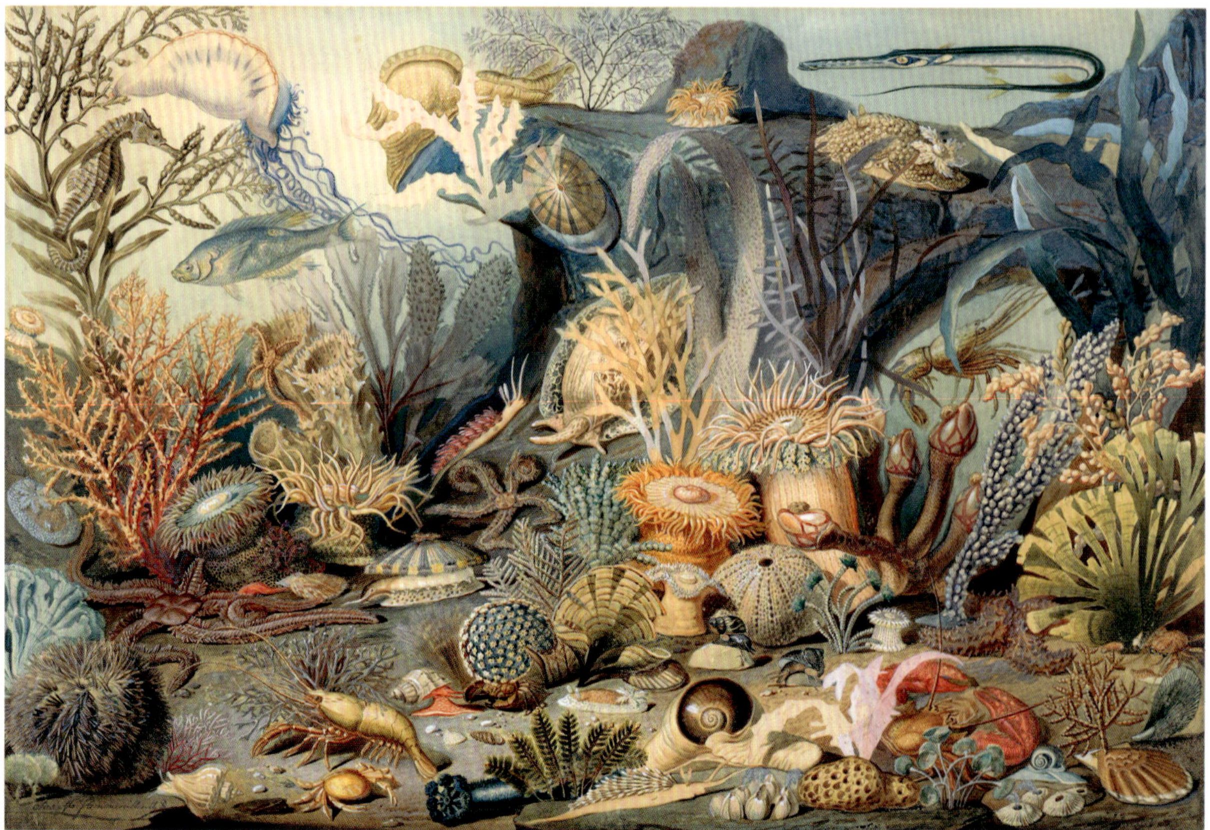

Top: 9. Edward Moran, *The Valley in the Sea*, 1862. Oil on canvas, 40½ × 64 inches (102.9 × 162.6 cm). Indianapolis Museum of Art at Newfields, Indianapolis

Below: 10. James M. Sommerville and Christian Schussele, *Ocean Life*, 1859. Watercolor, gouache, graphite, and gum arabic on off-white woven paper, 19 × 27½ inches (48.3 × 69.7 cm). Metropolitan Museum of Art, New York

brings to colorful life the shape of the North Atlantic basin described by the instigator of the seafloor explorations, Lt. Matthew Fontaine Maury. Based on the first program of regular deep-sea soundings as well as the famed naturalist Alexander von Humboldt's physical geography, Maury believed that the Atlantic basin's sides sloped regularly toward a relatively flat center. North and south of the proposed cable route, Maury found the seafloor topography to be jagged, with occasional very deep or much shallower measurements punctuating the otherwise presumed bowl-like basin shape. At the Great Circle, the shortest distance between North America and Britain and along the planned cable route, Maury found a marvelous exception he called "Telegraph Plateau," a seafloor feature "which seems to have been placed there especially for the purpose of holding the wires of the submarine telegraph, and keeping them out of harm's way."[21] Presumably based on Sommerville's marine zoology expertise (fig. 10), the creatures featured on the sea bottom of Moran's canvas are mostly recognizable species that could have been dredged in much shallower waters. Intriguingly, there appears to be a rope (which does not look like a telegraph cable but might, perhaps, be intended as such) in the foreground near the center. Like other Hudson River School paintings, which often include people or human-made objects depicted as tiny or insignificant, this rope, whether meant to be a telegraph cable or not, alludes to the reach of people into the sea, however tenuous.

Submarine cables became the first global-scale human-built infrastructure installed in the oceans. People had long built coastal structures and remade shores and littoral spaces. Wrecked ships and lost fishing gear had for eons littered oceans with evidence of maritime activities. Cables, though, were made of more durable things than wood, tar, bone, animal skins, and hemp. Their copper wires were covered in gutta-percha, a natural rubber from trees in Malaysia, and the outsides of the stretches to be laid approaching the shore were clad in other metals, to armor them. Once laid, cables were seldom removed. Soon after the Atlantic cable demonstrated the viability of long sections of oceanic telegraphs, a flurry of cable-laying, punctuated by the achievement of spanning the Pacific Ocean in 1902, culminated in the All-Red Line, a system of telegraphs that linked the global British Empire (fig. 11). Cable networks emerged from colonial empires and their security interests, which continued to shape new generations of cable systems, first in the 1950s when analog coaxial cables carried voice communications, and again from the

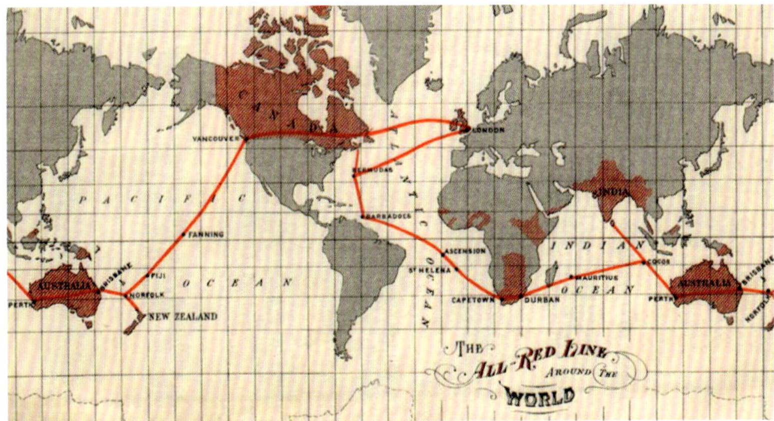

11. Map of the All Red Line, in George Johnson, ed., *The All Red Line: The Annals and Aims of the Pacific Cable Project* (Ottawa: James Hope & Sons, 1903), 10

1980s, when fiber-optic cables disrupted the anticipated ascendancy of satellite communications.[22] Today undersea fiber-optic cables carry virtually all transoceanic digital communications, enabling the functioning of governments, militaries, and economies, but remaining largely invisible to the general public.

The invisibility of submarine cables throughout the twentieth century reflects a more general failure to appreciate the extent to which the vast and deep ocean became an important site for industrialization and capitalism in the twentieth century. Most of the consumer goods we buy are shipped across oceans in containers. Tankers carry oil and other liquid cargoes, while bulk carriers transport coal, ores, food grains, and other dry cargoes. The fleet of dedicated shipping vessels carried four hundred times more cargo in the early twenty-first century than in the mid-nineteenth, while transport costs for key commodities such as coal and oil hardly rose in the second half of the twentieth century. Efficiencies enabled by mechanization reduced the number of maritime laborers. Since the 1950s, in part stimulated by the container revolution, ports moved away from their traditional locations: Manhattan was abandoned in favor of Port Elizabeth, NJ, San Francisco in favor of Oakland, CA, London in favor of Felixstowe and Rotterdam. Despite the increasing scale of global shipping, it tends to remain invisible, attracting attention only when pirates attack, ships wreck, or supply chains falter. Once transoceanic cargoes were loaded on docks in cities, where urbanites witnessed ships and maritime activity every day. Fenced in for security, modern ports insulate maritime activity from the lives of the terrestrial consumers who benefit from global shipping.[23]

Fishing, too, expanded dramatically in the post–World War II period, causing enormous changes to the ocean environment that have nevertheless remained inconspicuous. The northwest Atlantic cod fishery, which began when Vikings and Basques crossed from Europe, was prosecuted continuously from the sixteenth century, spurred by depletions of fish in European waters and resulting in ecological transformation of coastal waters even before mechanized harvesting. Adoption of trawls in the nineteenth century transformed fishing from a passive to an active pursuit of fish.[24] Giant factory fleets serially exhausted fish stocks around the world starting in the 1950s, masking overfishing as fishers continually targeted new populations and species.[25] Soviet fleets, for example, almost eradicated *Sebastes*, or Pacific Ocean perch, off the Oregon coast in the 1960s. Recovery proved challenging, a fact better understood when scientists discovered that these fish can live for over 200 years.[26] Alaskan pollock, a species of cod and the one used for fish sticks, became the target of industrial fisheries in the last decades of the twentieth century as other commercial stocks were severely depleted.[27] The tiny anchoveta, found off the coasts of Peru and Chile, has supported greater catches than any other single wild species in the world but its numbers fluctuate dramatically in response to El Niño events.[28] Anchoveta catches peaked in 1971 and global fish catches peaked in the mid-1990s. The Atlantic cod fishery collapsed in that decade and global fisheries have declined since then. Today, a third of global fish stocks are overexploited or fished to the limit, according to the United Nations Food and Agriculture Organization.[29] New postwar technologies such as sonar, nylon for nets,

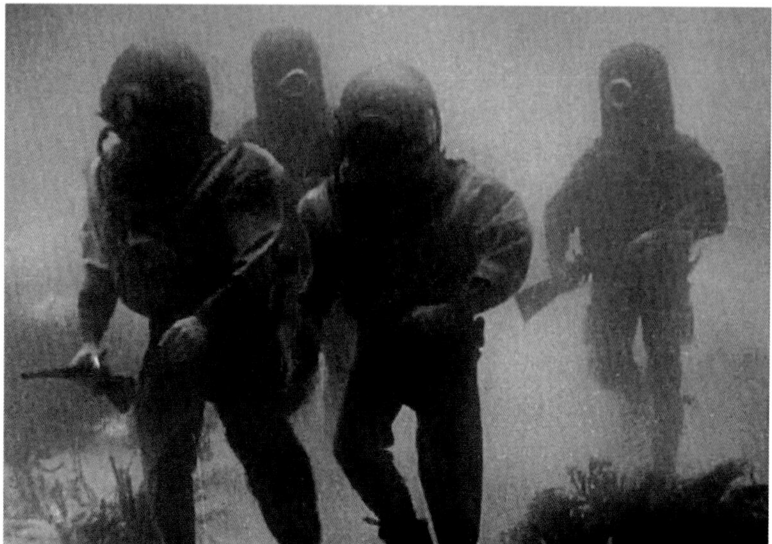

12. Still from the 1916 silent film *20,000 Leagues Under the Sea*, directed by Stuart Paton and made with the assistance of underwater photography pioneers John Ernest and George M. Williamson

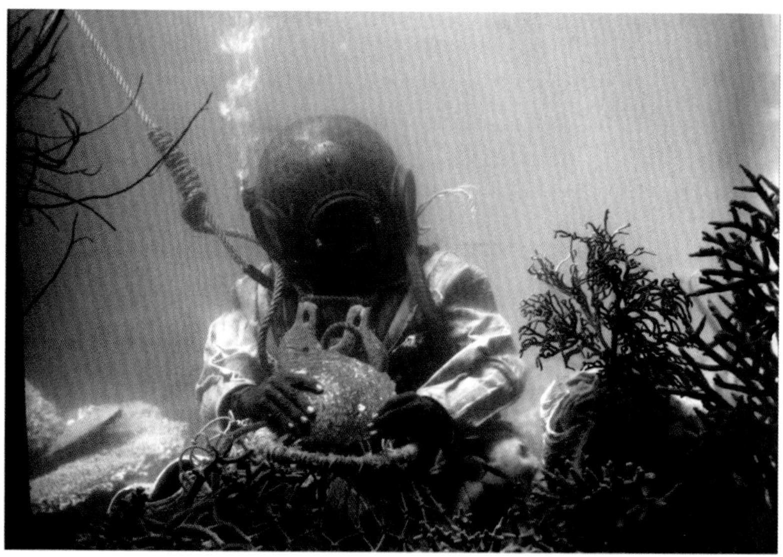

13. Still from Frank Hurley's 1921 documentary about Papua New Guinea, *Pearls and Savages*

and power blocks to haul in catches, contributed to unsustainably rising catches. With the shift from natural materials to plastics for nets and traps, lost or "ghost" gear continues killing animals as it drifts out of sight, not rotting away. Overcapitalization of fishing fleets has resulted in far too many boats, and thus too much fishing capacity, for the number of fish in the sea, so that industrialized fishing nations take fish upon which small inshore fishers and their communities depend.[30] Scientists have come to understand that removal of commercial fish populations has not just reduced the number of commercially valued fish but has profoundly changed entire ecosystems.[31] While aquaculture has expanded, much is not sustainable. Salmon and other finfish, after all, eat other fish. Oceanic environmental concern during the terrestrial environmental movement of the 1960s and '70s focused on coastal areas endangered by oil spills and the great whales targeted by industrial whaling, not the open oceans and their depths, which seemed at the time resilient or even impervious to human activities.[32] The organization that became Ocean Conservancy in 2001, for example, formed in the 1970s to save whales.[33] Environmental concern for the global oceans lagged until the twenty-first century, emerging from the dawning awareness of the massive scale of overfishing as well as the profound role of the oceans in the global climate.[34]

One central contributor to today's waxing ocean environmentalism has been the rising visibility of the volumetric ocean, made possible through the intersection of developments in aquarium tanks, underwater filming, and scuba technology.

An early innovator in filming underwater, John Ernest Williamson, and his brother George M. Williamson, built a contraption they called a photosphere to get a photographer, in a dry space, onto the seafloor to film underwater action from behind a plate glass window. The Williamsons took inspiration from Jules Verne, who himself was inspired to write *Twenty Thousand Leagues Under the Seas* in part by a visit to an aquarium.[35] Williamson's 1916 silent film version of *Twenty Thousand Leagues* attracted attention from audiences newly conscious of the oceans' depths from the menacing submarine warfare of the First World War (fig. 12). While others experimented with waterproof housings for cameras, so that photographers themselves could go underwater, many creators of so-called underwater images in the middle decades of the twentieth century actually worked with aquarium tanks, which allowed for better control of light, composition, ani-

mal subjects' behaviors, and other factors. Famously, undersea sequences of the Australian explorer Frank Hurley's 1921 film *Pearls and Savages*, purportedly made in the waters of the Torres Strait, were actually filmed ashore, in aquariums whose sides were carefully excluded from the camera's view (fig. 13).[36] In 1938, Marine Studios opened in northern Florida as a studio for filming underwater scenes, although it also served as a popular attraction and hosted some research as well.[37] Even today tanks remain the preferred site for capturing undersea action, including in such movies as *The Abyss*, *Free Willy*, and *The Life Aquatic with Steve Zissou*, although today the photographers are submerged rather than filming from outside the tank.[38]

Scuba technology, starting with the Aqua-Lung co-invented by Jacques Cousteau and first marketed in North America starting in 1949, multiplied the number of activities that ordinary people

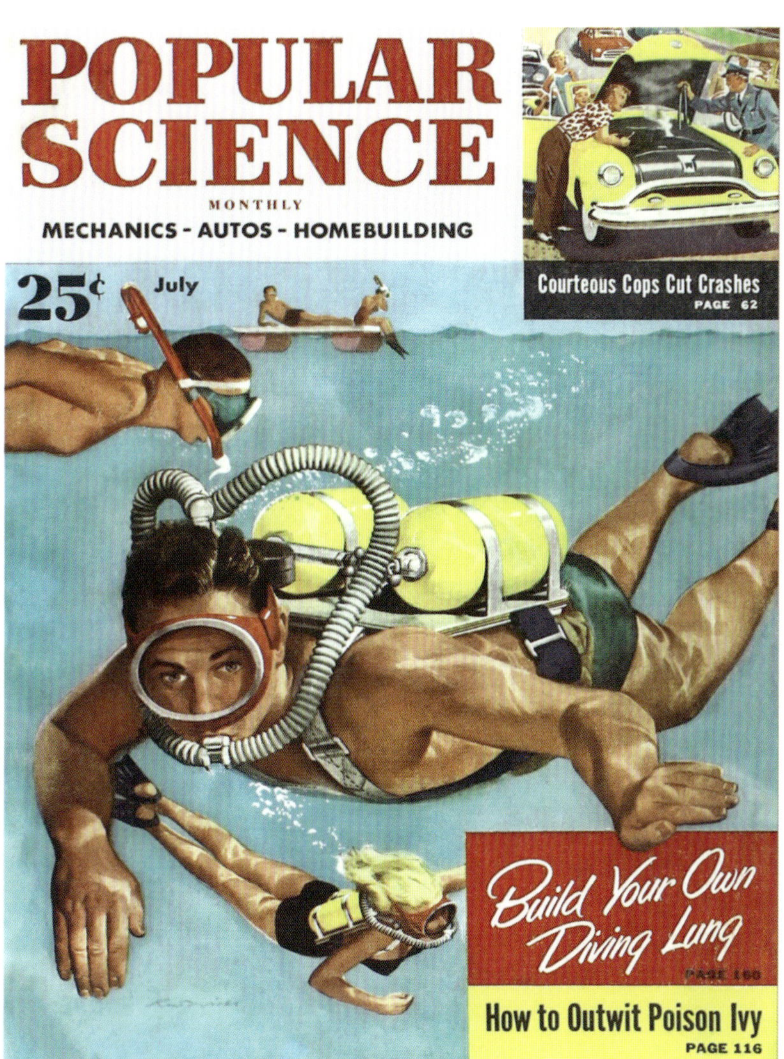

14. *Popular Science* magazine cover, July 1953

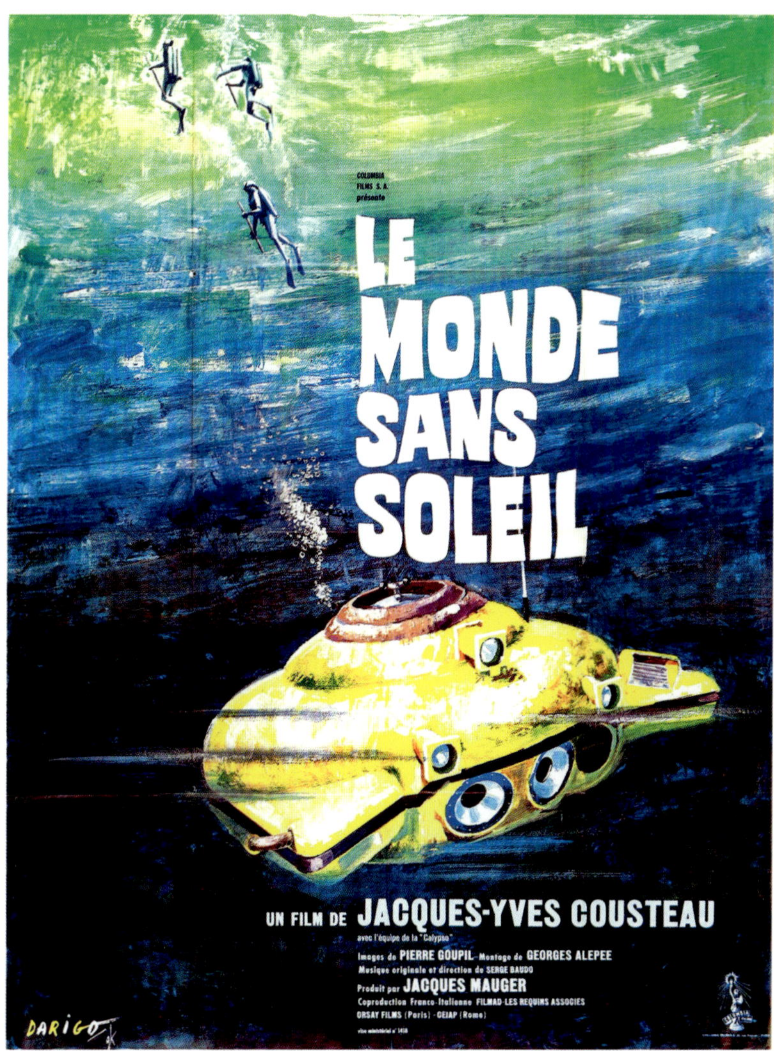

15. Poster for *Le Monde sans soleil* (World Without Sun), directed by Jacques-Yves Cousteau, 1964

could do underwater. Previous diving technologies were more challenging to use and employed mainly for military, salvage, and construction work, but a wide range of users embraced scuba for spearfishing, recreation, science, archaeology, and photography (fig. 14, previous page).[39] Cousteau himself invented waterproof housings for cameras and created the well-received films *Silent World* (1956) and *World Without Sun* (1964, fig. 15, previous page).[40] A spate of exciting television shows and movies with underwater scenes transformed the undersea into grist for popular culture. This cultural discovery of the depths contributed to a wider sense in the post–World War II period of the oceans as the anticipated source of virtually endless raw materials and foodstuffs. Widely viewed as a "frontier" akin to the US West in the nineteenth century, the oceans' depths and seafloor promised space for industrial development and possibly even future living space for people.[41] Futuristic visions for uses of ocean space, such as the anticipated undersea oil industry illustrated by Reynolds Metals Company, intersected with plans for outer space.[42] Both were fueled as much by dystopian fears of disappearing resources in the context of global overpopulation as by optimistic technological enthusiasm.[43]

The 1950s and '60s futuristic visions for using the ocean's depths did not fulfill their extravagant promises but they did leave enduring legacies. The offshore oil industry represents the most well-developed instance of the intended industrialization of the seafloor, although today's industry does not rely as much on human bodies undersea as originally envisioned. The entirely unexpected discovery of prolific life around hydrothermal vents in 1977 happened aboard what was at the time a small but rapidly growing fleet of small submersibles with deep-diving capacity, built with the expectation that industrial uses would follow military and scientific applications of deep submergence.[44] The appeal of wealth flowing from the "ocean frontier" powerfully shaped negotiations over international law of the sea, contributing to the expansion of control of large swaths of ocean space by coastal nations in the 200-mile exclusive economic zones that were formally accepted in 1982 with the United Nations Convention on the Law of the Sea.[45] While anticipated mining of manganese nodules and other deep-sea minerals did not happen in the wake of the enthusiastic predictions made in the 1960s, this dream has revived, to the delight of those who envision profit flowing from deep-sea mining and insist on its necessity for green energy, and to the dread of environmentalists who fear devastation to a part of the planet that is still so unknown.[46]

The persistence of unrealized plans for deep-sea mining threatens to distract us from the true extent to which the oceans' depths have already become a human environment. The giant seafloor mining machine depicted in *Oceanus* jars the viewer because we are accustomed to thinking about the oceans, particularly their deepest recesses, as an untouched wilderness.[47] In reality, coastal oceans are filled with oil rigs, wind turbines, and aquaculture facilities, competing for marine space with commercial fishing, shipping routes, and recreational boating. Networks of buoys and cables throughout the world's oceans support both commercial data transmission and military surveillance, and increasingly, scientific surveillance of the marine environment.[48] Abandoned infrastructure such as oil rigs are left in some places to become artificial reefs, a practice advertised to the aquarium-going public as an environmentally friendly aspect of offshore oil production.[49] Plastics of varying size accumulate on the shores of islands far distant from where they are produced and consumed, as well as in the middle of ocean gyres and throughout the water column. Anthropogenic climate change is increasing the acidity and temperature of ocean waters and the intensity of storms, as well as causing sea levels to rise.

The oceans' scale, opacity, and fluidity present challenges to communicating the extent of the human imprint there. Artists employ their craft and creativity to call attention to realities such as the extent of marine plastic pollution and the projections of sea-level rise, among other changes the oceans are undergoing. Media of all kinds, including scientific illustrations and film but equally importantly art, play a central role in helping us comprehend—and believe—what is happening under the sea's surface or far away from the shores where we live, work, and recreate.[50] The BBC documentaries *Blue Planet* (2001) *and Blue Planet II* (2017) illustrate the growing attention paid to oceans in the present century, including recent urgency to call out anthropogenic changes.[51] Organizations have created image banks of coral reefs and other marine environments to enable free access to high-quality underwater images to help conservationists tell compelling stories (fig. 16, overleaf).[52] Representations of the oceans, perhaps especially artistic ones, reveal the profound connections between people and oceans, encompassing the economic, the political, the cultural, and the historical. Ideally, they help us see the oceans as Alexis Rockman does through *Oceanus*, as a marvelous natural place tightly connected to humanity and in need of our respect, gratitude, and stewardship.

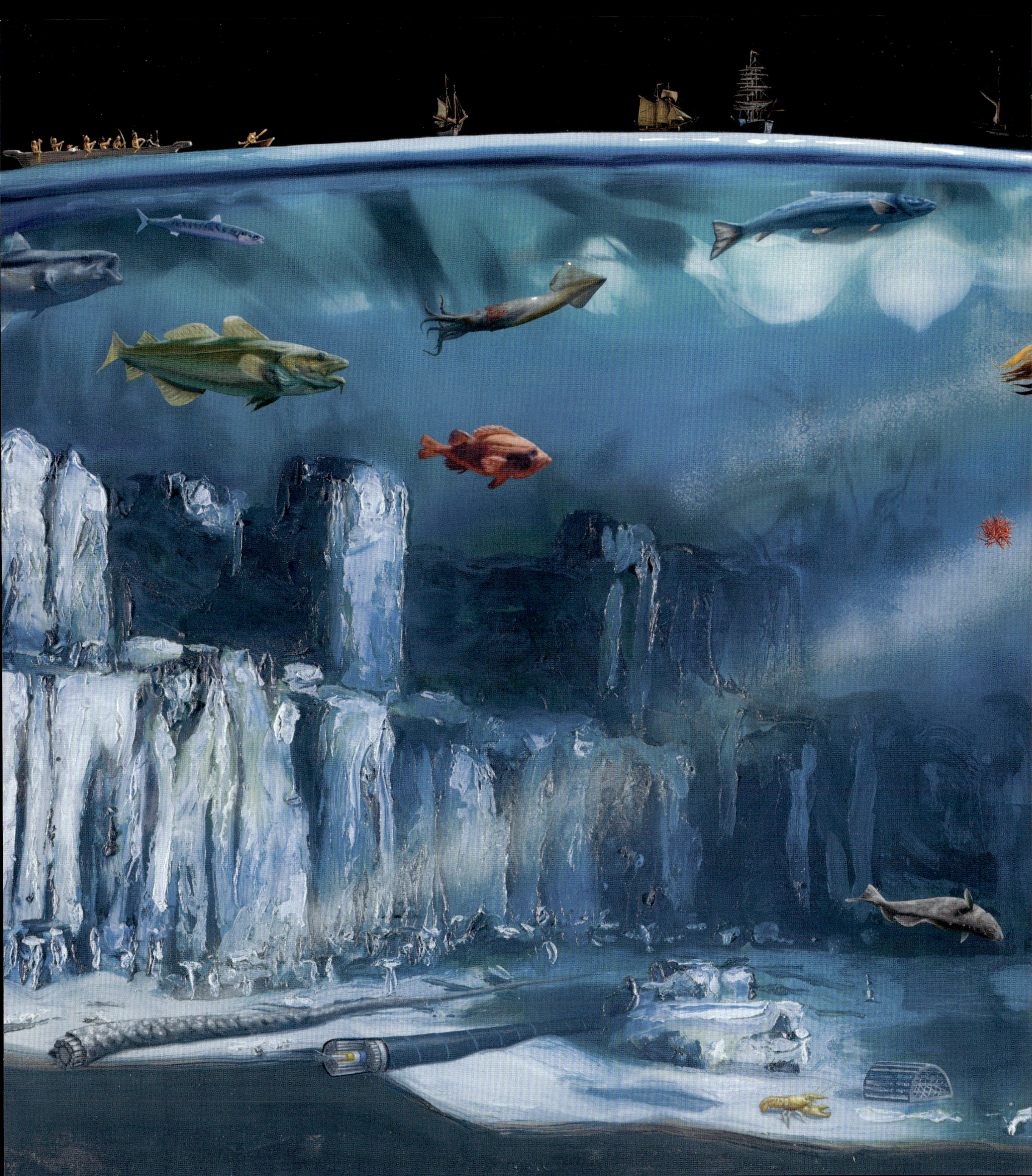

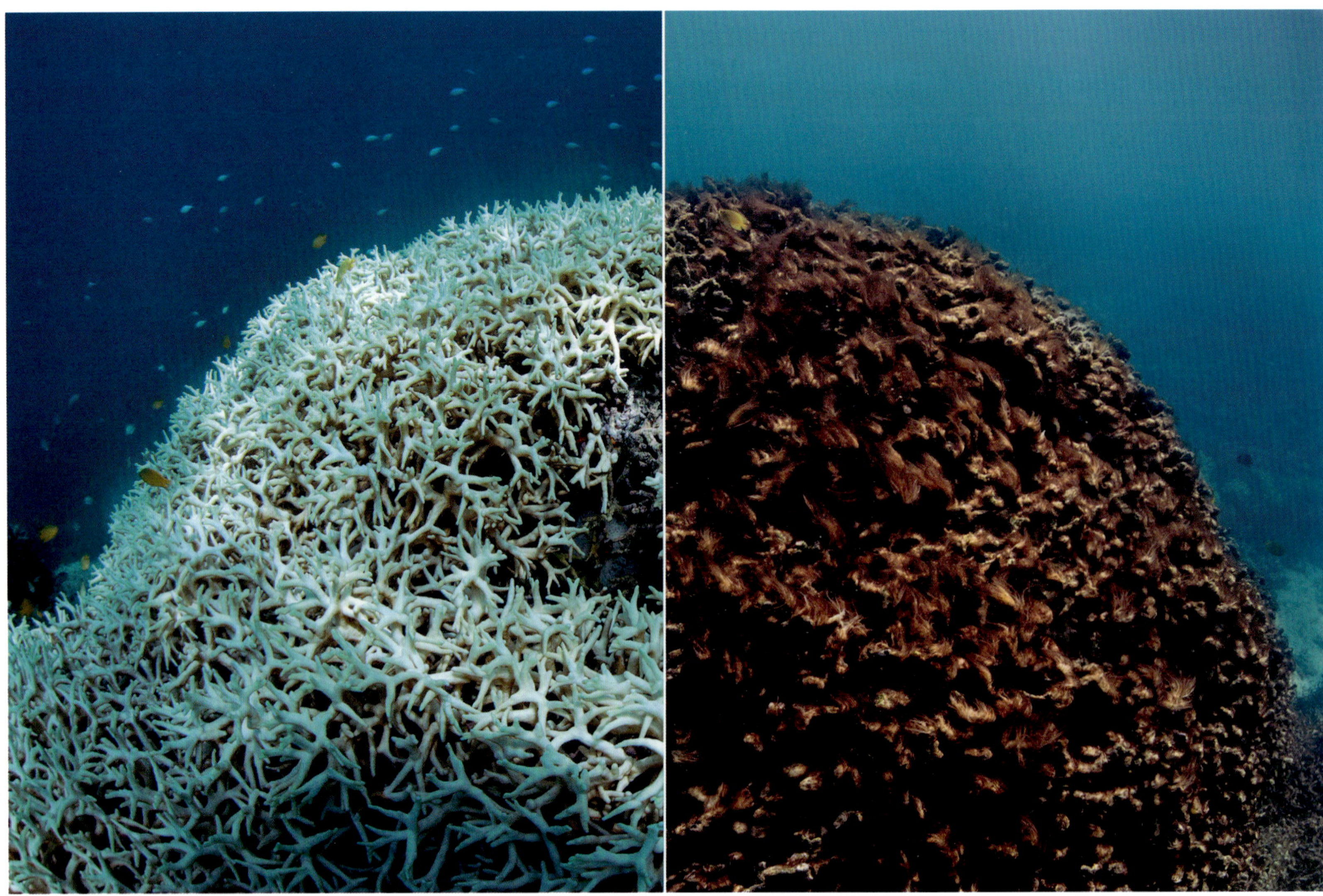

16. Photographs of a reef before and after oil pollution, from the Coral Reef Image Bank, created by Kate Sutter and gifted to the collection of the Ocean Agency Image Bank

1. Peter G. Brewer, ed., *Oceanography: The Present and Future* (New York: Springer-Verlag, 1983), 129.

2. William Beebe, "Descent into Perpetual Night," *New York Times Magazine*, October 19, 1932, SM1.

3. See John A. Adolfson and Thomas E. Berghage, *Perception and Performance under Water* (New York: Wiley, 1974); "How far does light travel in the ocean?," National Ocean Service, last updated November 5, 2021, https://oceanservice.noaa.gov/facts/light_travel.html#:~:text=A%20full%20transcript%20is%20available,on%20depth%20and%20light%20level.

4. See, for example, Paolo Villa et al., "Neandertals on the Beach: Use of Marine Resources at Grotta dei Moscerini (Latium, Italy)," *PLoS ONE* 15, no. 1 (2020): https://journals.plos.org/plosone/article?id=10.1371/journal.pone.0226690; Kevin Dawson, *Undercurrents of Power: Aquatic Culture in the African Diaspora* (Philadelphia: University of Pennsylvania Press, 2018); Karen Eva Carr, *Shifting Currents: A World History of Swimming* (London: Reaktion Books, 2022); and Helen M. Rozwadowski, *Vast Expanses: A History of the Oceans* (London: Reaktion Books, 2018), 38–70.

5. See Rozwadowski, *Vast Expanses*; and Keith R. Benson, David K. van Keuren, and Helen M. Rozwadowski, "Introduction," in *The Machine in Neptune's Garden*, ed. Rozwadowski and van Keuren (Canton, MA: Science History Publications/USA, 2004), xiii–xxviii.

6. R. L. Carson, "Undersea," *Atlantic Monthly* 160, no. 3 (September 1937): 4.

7. Josho Brouwers, "Alexander's Underwater Adventure: A Medieval Story about Alexander the Great," Josho Brouwers (website), June 15, 2021, https://www.joshobrouwers.com/articles/alexanders-underwater-adventure/.

8. See J. H. Parry, *The Discovery of the Sea* (New York: Dial Press, 1974); and Michael S. Reidy, *Tides of History: Ocean Science and Her Majesty's Navy* (Chicago: University of Chicago Press, 2008).

9. See William Dalrymple, *The Anarchy: The East India Company, Corporate Violence, and the Pillage of an Empire* (London: Bloomsbury, 2019); and Lauren Benton and Lisa Ford, *Rage for Order: The British Empire and the Origins of International Law, 1800–1850* (Cambridge, MA: Harvard University Press, 2016), 117–47.

10. See Margaret Schotte, *Sailing School: Navigating Science and Skill, 1550–1800* (Baltimore: Johns Hopkins Press, 2019); and Harold L. Burstyn, "Seafaring and the Emergence of American Science," in *The Atlantic World of Robert G. Albion*, ed. Benjamin W. Labaree (Middletown, CT: Wesleyan University Press, 1975), 76–109.

11. See Michael S. Reidy and Helen M. Rozwadowski, "The Spaces in Between: Science, Ocean, Empire," *Isis* 105, no. 2 (2014): 338–51; and Rozwadowski, *Vast Expanses*, 71–103.

12. See Alain Corbin, *The Lure of the Sea: The Discovery of the Seaside in the Western World, 1750–1840*, trans. Jocelyn Phelps (Berkeley: University of California Press, 1994).

13. See ibid., 97–120 (97); and Martin J. S. Rudwick, *Scenes from Deep Time: Early Pictorial Representations of the Prehistoric World* (Chicago: Chicago University Press, 1992).

14. See Natascha Adamowsky, *The Mysterious Science of the Sea* (London: Routledge, 2015), 10–12; Antony Adler, *Neptune's Laboratory: Fantasy, Fear, and Science at Sea* (Cambridge, MA: Harvard University Press, 2019); Helen M. Rozwadowski, "'Bringing Humanity Full Circle Back into the Sea': *Homo aquaticus*, Evolution, and the Ocean," *Environmental Humanities* 14, no. 1 (March 2022): 1–28, available at https://www.environmentandsociety.org/sites/default/files/key_docs/1rozwadowski.pdf;

and Rosalind Williams, *Notes on the Underground: An Essay on Technology, Society and the Imagination* (Cambridge, MA: MIT Press, 1990).

15. See Bernd Brunner, *The Ocean at Home: An Illustrated History of the Aquarium* (Princeton: Princeton Architectural Press, 2005); Philip Henry Gosse, *The Aquarium: An Unveiling of the Wonders of the Deep Sea* (London: J. Van Voorst, 1854); Edmund Gosse, *Father and Son* (London, 1907), 125–26; and Samantha Muka, *Oceans under Glass: Tank Craft and the Sciences of the Sea* (Chicago: University of Chicago Press, 2023).

16. See Helen M. Rozwadowski, *Fathoming the Ocean: The Discovery and Exploration of the Deep Sea* (Cambridge, MA: Harvard University Press, 2005); Eric L. Mills, "Edward Forbes, John Gwyn Jeffreys, and British dredging before the *Challenger* expedition," *Journal of the Society for the Bibliography of Natural History* 8, no. 4 (May 1978): 507–36; and Philip F. Rehbock, "The Early Dredgers: 'Naturalizing' in British Seas, 1830–1850," *Journal of the History of Biology* 12, no. 2 (Autumn 1979): 293–368.

17. See Jules Verne, *Vingt Mille Lieues sous les mers*, illus. by Alphonse de Neuville and Édouard Riou (Paris: Pierre Jules Hetzel, 1871) (first English publication 1872); Victor Hugo, *The Toilers of the Sea* (New York: Harper and Brothers, 1878); Samuel Taylor Coleridge, *The Rime of the Ancient Mariner* (New York: Harper and Brothers, 1876); and Rozwadowski, *Vast Expanses*, 104–29.

18. See Rozwadowski, *Fathoming the Ocean*, 67–96.

19. See Charles C. Eldredge, "Wet Paint: Herman Melville, Elihu Vedder, and Artists Undersea," *American Art* 11, no. 2 (1997): 106–35. Edward Moran, *The Valley in the Sea*, object information and provenance: http://collection.imamuseum.org/artwork/56245/.

20. See James M. Sommerville, *Ocean Life* (Philadelphia: Barnard & Jones, 1859).

21. Matthew Fontaine Maury to James C. Dobbin, February 22, 1854, quoted in Jaquelin Ambler Caskie, *Life and Letters of Matthew Fontaine Maury* (Richmond, VA: Richmond Press, 1928), 110–12. See also Rozwadowski, *Fathoming the Ocean*, 67–96; and Penelope K. Hardy and Helen M. Rozwadowski, "Maury for Modern Times: Navigating a Racist Legacy in Ocean Science," *Oceanography* 33, no. 3 (September 2020): 8–13.

22. See Nicole Starosielski, *The Undersea Network* (Durham, NC: Duke University Press, 2015); and Simone M. Müller, *Wiring the World: The Social and Cultural Creation of Global Telegraph Networks* (New York: Columbia University Press, 2016).

23. See Rose George, *Deep Sea and Foreign Going: Inside Shipping, the Invisible Industry that Brings You 90% of Everything* (London: Granta, 2018); *The Forgotten Space*, directed by Allan Sekula and Noël Burch (Brooklyn, NY: Icarus Films, 2012); and Rozwadowski, *Vast Expanses*, 152–54.

24. See W. Jeffrey Bolster, *The Mortal Sea: Fishing the Atlantic in the Age of Sail* (Cambridge, MA: Harvard University Press, 2014).

25. See Carmel Finley, *All the Fish in the Sea: Maximum Sustainable Yield and the Failure of Fisheries Management* (Chicago: University of Chicago Press, 2011).

26. Carmel Finley, "All the Science in an Ear Stone," *Carmel Finley* (blog), December 31, 2016, https://carmelfinley.wordpress.com/2016/12/31/all-the-science-in-an-ear-stone/.

27. See Kevin M. Bailey, *Billion-Dollar Fish: The Untold Story of Alaskan Pollock* (Chicago: University of Chicago Press, 2013).

28. See Gregory Cushman, *Guano and the Opening of the Pacific World: A Global Ecological History* (Cambridge: Cambridge University Press, 2013).

29. See "The State of World Fisheries and Aquaculture 2020: Sustainability in Action," Food and Agriculture Organization of the United Nations (website), accessed August 2022, https://www.fao.org/3/ca9229en/online/ca9229en.html.

30. See Carmel Finley, *All the Boats on the Ocean: How Government Subsidies Led to Global Overfishing* (Chicago: University of Chicago Press, 2017).

31. See Jeremy B. C. Jackson, Karen E. Alexander, and Enric Sala, eds., *Shifting Baselines: The Past and The Future of Ocean Fisheries* (Washington, DC: Island Press, 2011); and Daniel Pauly, "Anecdotes and the Shifting Baseline Syndrome of Fisheries," *Trends in Ecology and Evolution* 10, no. 10 (October 1995): 430.

32. See Wesley Marx, *The Frail Ocean* (New York: Coward McCann, 1967); Frank Zelko, *Make it a Greenpeace!: The Rise of Countercultural Environmentalism* (Oxford: Oxford University Press, 2013); and Helen M. Rozwadowski, *The Sea Knows No Boundaries: A Century of Marine Science under ICES* (Seattle: University of Washington Press, 2002), 212–44.

33. See Gary Kroll, *America's Ocean Wilderness: A Cultural History of Twentieth-Century Exploration* (Lawrence: University Press of Kansas, 2008), 1, 189–94.

34. Rozwadowski, *Vast Expanses*, 214–28.

35. See John E. Williamson, *20 Years Under the Sea* (Boston: Ralph T. Hale, 1936); Trevor Norton, *Stars Beneath the Sea: The Pioneers of Diving* (New York: Carroll & Graf, 2000), 176–97; and Ann Elias, *Coral Empire: Underwater Oceans, Colonial Tropics, and Visual Modernity* (Durham, NC: Duke University Press, 2019), 49–116.

36. See Elias, *Coral Empire*, 117–84; and Samantha Muka, "Imagining the Ocean: Marine Artists and Our Visions of the Marine World," in *Soundings and Crossings: Doing Science at Sea 1800–1970*, ed. Katharine Anderson and Helen M. Rozwadowski (Sagamore Beach, MA: Science History Publications, 2016), 245–76.

37. See Gregg Mitman, *Reel Nature: America's Romance with Wildlife on Film* (Cambridge, MA: Harvard University Press, 1999), 157–79.

38. See Laura Tretheway, *The Imperiled Ocean: Human Stories from a Changing Sea* (New York: Pegasus Books, 2019), 1–22.

39. See Helen M. Rozwadowski, "From Danger Zone to World of Wonder: The 1950s Transformation of the Ocean's Depths," *Coriolis: the Interdisciplinary Journal of Maritime Studies* 4, no. 1 (September 2013): 1–20.

40. See Brad Matsen, *Jacques Cousteau: The Sea King* (New York: Vintage Books, 2009); Axel Madsen, *Cousteau: An Unauthorized Biography* (New York: Beaufort Books, 1987); and Jon Crylen, "Living in a World without Sun: Jacques Cousteau, Homo aquaticus, and the Dream of Dwelling Undersea," *Journal of Cinema and Media Studies* 58, no. 1 (Fall 2018): 1–23.

41. Rozwadowski, *Vast Expanses*, 161–87.

42. See Helen M. Rozwadowski, "Arthur C. Clarke and the Limitations of the Ocean as a Frontier," *Environmental History* 17, no. 3 (July 2012): 578–602. Connections between oceans and outer space are common; see, for example, Melody Jue, *Wild Blue Media: Thinking through Seawater* (Durham, NC: Duke University Press, 2020); and Stefan Helmreich, *Alien Ocean: Anthropological Voyages in Microbial Seas* (Berkeley: University of California Press, 2009).

43. See Sam Robinson, "Scientific Imaginaries and Science Diplomacy: The Case of Ocean Exploitation," *Centaurus* 63, no. 1 (February 2021): 150–70. https://doi.org/10.1111/1600-0498.12342; and Helen M. Rozwadowski, "Wild Blue: The Post–World War Two Ocean Frontier and Its Legacy for Law of the Sea," *Environment and History* (January 2021), doi: 10.3197/096734021X16245313029949.

44. See Gardner Soule, *Undersea Frontiers: Exploring by Deep-Diving Submarines* (Chicago: Rand & McNally, 1968); Cindy Lee Van Dover, *The Octopus's Garden: Hydrothermal Vents and Other Mysteries of the Deep Sea* (New York: Basic Books, 1996); and Cindy Lee Van Dover, *Deep Ocean Journeys: Discovering New Life at the Bottom of the Sea* (New York: Basic Books, 1997).

45. See Rozwadowski, "Wild Blue"; and Robinson, "Scientific Imaginaries and Science Diplomacy."

46. See John Hannigan, *The Geopolitics of Deep Oceans* (Cambridge, MA: Polity, 2015); and Shaine Scarminach, "Diving into the History of Seabed Mining," *Edge Effects*, last updated October 12, 2019, https://edgeeffects.net/seabed-mining/.

47. See Kroll, *America's Ocean Wilderness*.

48. See Starosielski, *The Undersea Network*; and Jeffrey Marlow, "Undersea Internet Cables Can Detect Earthquakes—and May Soon Warn of Tsunamis," *New Yorker*, July 26, 2022, https://www.newyorker.com/science/elements/undersea-internet-cables-can-detect-earthquakes-and-may-soon-warn-of-tsunamis.

49. See Dolly Jørgenson, "Mixing oil and water: naturalizing offshore oil platforms in American aquariums," in *Oil Culture*, ed. D. Worden and R. Barrett (Minneapolis: University of Minnesota Press, 2014), 267–88.

50. See Syma A. Ebbin, "Humanizing the Seas: A Case for Integrating the Arts and Humanities into Ocean Literacy and Stewardship," *Parks Stewardship Forum* 36, no. 3 (2020): 361–64, doi: 10.5070/P536349840.

51. Jue, *Wild Blue Media*, 15.

52. See, for example, the Coral Reef Image Bank created by Kate Sutter (https://katesutter.com/image-bank), now part of the Ocean Agency's Ocean Image Bank, https://www.theoceanagency.org/ocean-image-bank.

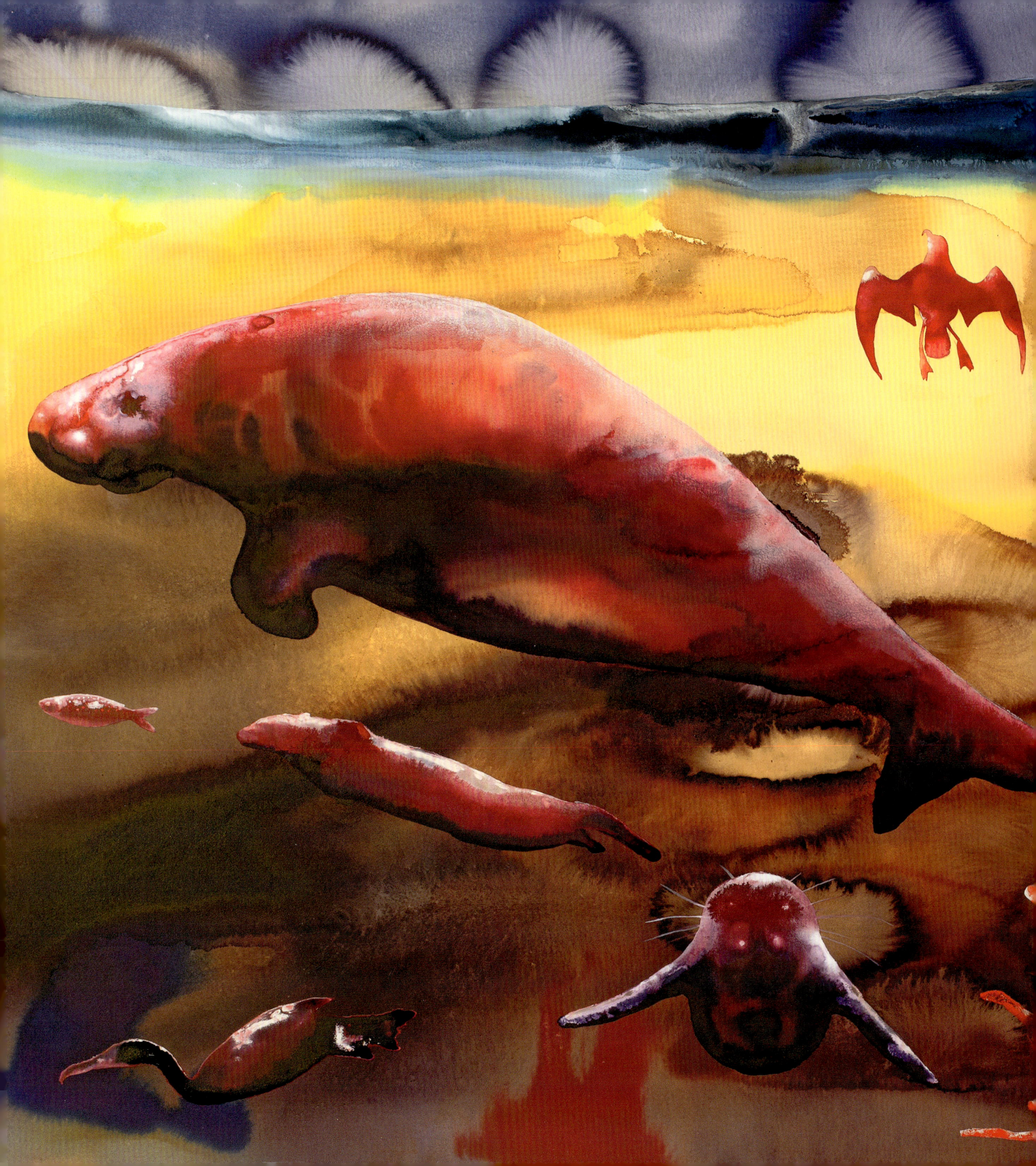

DELETIONS AND ADDITIONS IN THE SEA

JAMES T. CARLTON

Professor of Marine Sciences Emeritus, Williams College and Director Emeritus,
The Coastal & Ocean Studies Program of Williams College & Mystic Seaport Museum

IT MAY COME AS A SURPRISE TO YOU, OUR reader, that we have no idea how many species of marine life have disappeared from the world's oceans in the past three hundred years—the period of time over which the heavy footprints of humans began to sink deeper and deeper into the sea.

It may also come as a surprise that the number of species that have been moved around the world by human activity is similarly not known.

At the beginning of the twenty-first century, we have only coarse-grained estimates of the number of species deletions (extinctions) and additions (introductions) from and to marine ecosystems in modern times. In contrast, our ability to robustly and effectively tackle pressing issues of ocean conservation, preservation, and restoration rely on a fine-grained understanding of how and why marine biodiversity changes over time and space.

Biodiversity changes in three ways. Species populations may decrease or increase, species may disappear, or new species may arrive. Wherever you grew up, all of these processes were (and continue to be) in play. Dynamic changes in biodiversity have been occurring naturally for eons. But only in recent centuries have the scale and novelty of change been profoundly altered. These changes lay, not surprisingly, at the doorstep of humans, the dominant species on Earth.

According to United Nations estimates, the global human population will reach eight billion in 2022. Eight billion. In 1950, there were 2.5 billion people. With another billion people here, and another billion there, there is less and less room for other species. In turn, there is more movement of people, and the goods they require, than ever before, and there is thus more and more opportunity to spread species to new corners of the world.

Marine extinctions happen at different scales. *Local* extirpation involves the destruction of a population from one site. *Regional* extinction involves the removal of a species from many sites. Population destruction may occur, for example, by filling in coastal waters, such as salt marshes and shallow bays, to create land for agriculture, urban development, industrial sites, and airports. Marine populations may also be obliterated by the opposite—by dredging out shallow waters to create ports, harbors, and marinas. We know little about the diversity and abundance of many species along our coastlines prior to the vast urbanization and industrialization that commenced hundreds of years ago.

Global extinction is, of course, more fundamental, and involves those species that are most sincerely dead. In the sea, our knowledge of extinction is almost entirely limited to large animals.

Perhaps the most famous marine animal extinction is the Arctic Steller's sea cow, which disappeared sometime soon after 1768 on the Командо́рские острова́—the Commander Islands —taken out by Russian hunters. A marine mammal related to manatees, an adult sea cow reached ten tons and was nine meters long. Gone too is the West Indian monk seal, last reliably seen in the early 1950s. Also hunted into oblivion, they once commanded much of the Caribbean Sea by the millions. Only two more marine mammals are on the extinct list: the Japanese sea lion and the poorly known sea mink, which once lived on the Maine coast.

Nine or so sea and coastal marine birds are gone. The most notable of these was the extraordinary North Atlantic great auk, flightless and penguin-like (but not related). It stood nearly three feet tall. The last two, when discovered on June 3, 1844, on a small island off Iceland, were shot.

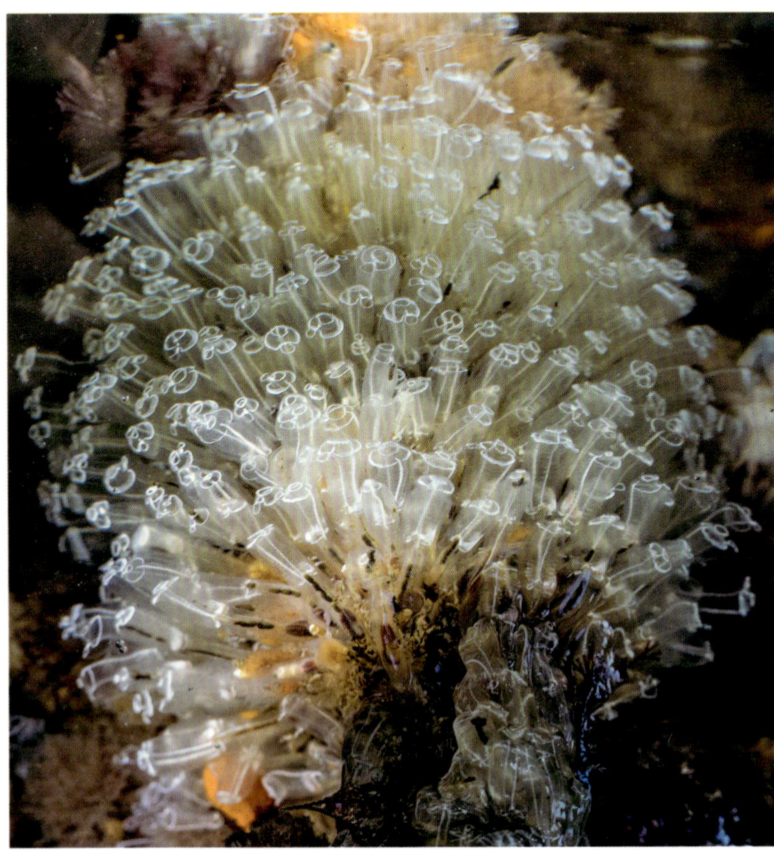

European lightbulb sea squirt, *Clavelina lepadiformis*, Stonington Harbor, Connecticut, 2021

Three snail species, one seastar, one seaweed, and perhaps one fish make up the rest of the list.

The list is not long—less than twenty species. The names are not hard to remember and not hard to teach in a classroom. But most people have never heard of any of these animals or plants.

And what of the rest of the life in the sea? The tens of thousands of species of fish and seaweed? The millions of species of marine invertebrates? The reports of the demise of only a few ocean species might lead to a conclusion that extinctions in the sea are not only rare but that perhaps the seas are largely immune to extinctions. But the evidence weighs heavily to another conclusion. The few recorded marine extinctions are more likely due to a remarkable gap in our knowledge: extinction in the sea has not been a subject of extensive study in marine biology. In fact, many marine invertebrates have not been seen since the 1700s, 1800s, or early 1900s. A general explanatory default is that we simply need to search more, and they may yet be found.

Or not.

As we began losing species, we also began, over about the same time period of the past three hundred years, globally rearranging the distribution of thousands of marine species. While vessels had been moving within ocean basins for thousands of years, and while long-distance global exploration commenced five hundred years ago, it was not until the 1700s that hundreds of wooden sailing vessels were sailing across the Atlantic, Pacific, and Indian oceans. On the hulls of these ships were hundreds of species of marine life—sea anemones, sponges, barnacles, mussels, seasquirts, seaweeds, and many more. Burrowing into these ships were wood-boring organisms, including wormlike bivalve mollusks called shipworms; the holes and tubes and caverns in the wood so created then provided homes to many other species, such as snails, crabs, and small fish that would otherwise get washed away from a vessel's hull. And without fail these same ships had to load solid ballast for stability and trim—ballast that often consisted of shore rocks, sand, and debris, laden with hundreds of other species.

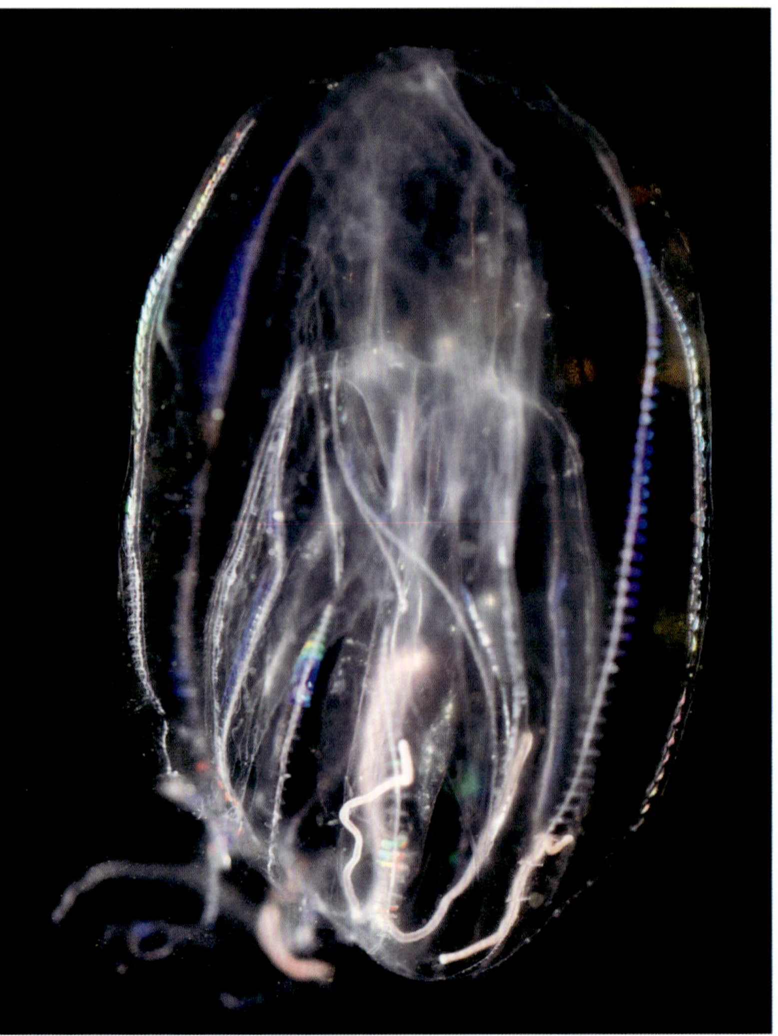

American comb jelly, *Mnemiopsis leidyi* (introduced to the Black Sea and Europe), Stonington Harbor, Connecticut, 2021

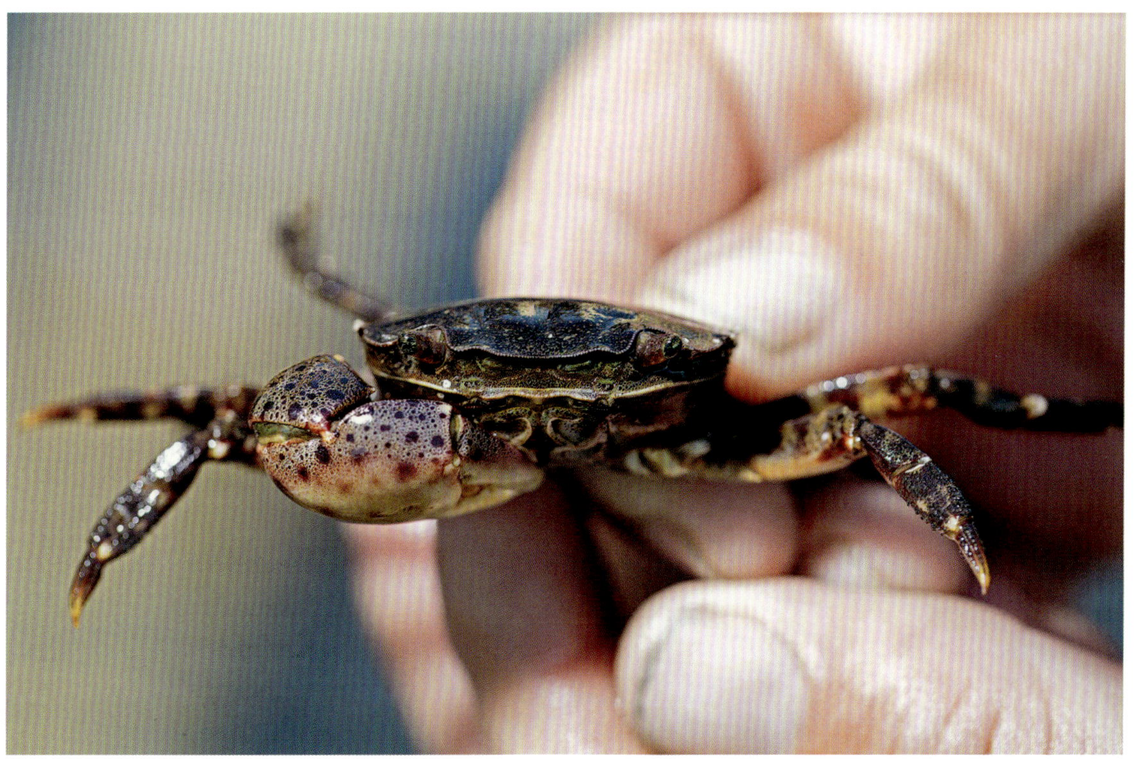

Asian shore crab, *Hemigrapsus sanguineus*, Stonington Harbor, Connecticut, 2021

And so set in motion was a phenomenon never seen before in the history of the earth: floating biological islands began cruising the seas, from the British Isles to Australia, from the coasts of Asia to the Caribbean, from North American western shores to eastern shores, and every conceivable crisscrossing route in between, picking up and dropping off species worldwide. These voyages—these accidental zoos and botanical gardens—sailed the seas for centuries before marine biologists began documenting ocean biodiversity. And, despite the fact that the first marine biologists to explore the world sailed on ships to get to exotic locations, they largely assumed that all the species they found had been where they were since time immemorial—a classic example of what's known as the shifting baseline.

By the end of the nineteenth and beginning of the twentieth century, wooden ships had been largely replaced by iron ships. Rock and sand ballast then gave way to water ballast. And with the water ballast came entire new fleets of transported marine life.

The most common shore snail and the most common shore crab of New England hail from Europe and Asia, respectively. A crab from the Yangtze River is abundant in European rivers. An American comb jellyfish now occurs from the Baltic Sea to the Caspian Sea. One of the most abundant clams in San Francisco Bay has its home port in the Amur River. The story repeats a thousand times on a thousand shores. The repercussions of biological invasions in the sea have been uncountable economic, environmental, cultural, human welfare, and food security impacts.

Attempts to consider how to reduce invasions by ships began only in the 1990s, focused on ballast water and later on hull fouling. Despite these efforts to reduce invasions through maritime traffic, yet another species vector unexpectedly emerged in the twenty-first century. Not surprisingly, this, too, is linked to humans.

On March 11, 2011, a massive earthquake struck Japan. The ensuing tsunami took more than twenty thousand lives and destroyed hundreds of thousands of buildings and coastal facilities. Millions of household, industrial, and maritime objects were ejected into the North Pacific Ocean. Often colonized by Japanese coastal species, these objects, made of wood, metal, glass, and plastic, began drifting eastward. One year later this debris field began arriving in North America and the Hawaiian Islands. After a few years, however, the wood, glass, and metal were largely gone—leaving, predictably, mostly plastic debris. Nonbiodegradable and lasting for years, plastic became the major fraction of marine debris conveying Asian species across the Pacific. Remarkably, the biofouled debris continued to arrive for over ten more years with living Asian species, seeding both the American Pacific coast and the Hawaiian Archipelago with more than four hundred species.

Before the tsunami, we already knew there was a huge amount of plastic debris in the North Pacific, in a region popularly dubbed the "garbage patch." The 2011 tsunami added to the patch a significant debris fraction, but in this case carrying living Western Pacific species. For a long while it was assumed that this debris—and the species aboard—were simply passing through the ocean. But a discovery in 2018 in the patch dramatically changed this picture: the species sent to sea by the Japanese tsunami were found to be colonizing non-tsunami debris, and, in fact, were reproducing on the high seas!

Coastal species were long assumed to not be able to survive for long periods in the open ocean, a low-productive environment poorly suited to species that came from richly productive continental margins. But we now realize the reason coastal species were not previously found to be permanently living on the high seas may be that there was relatively little place to live—

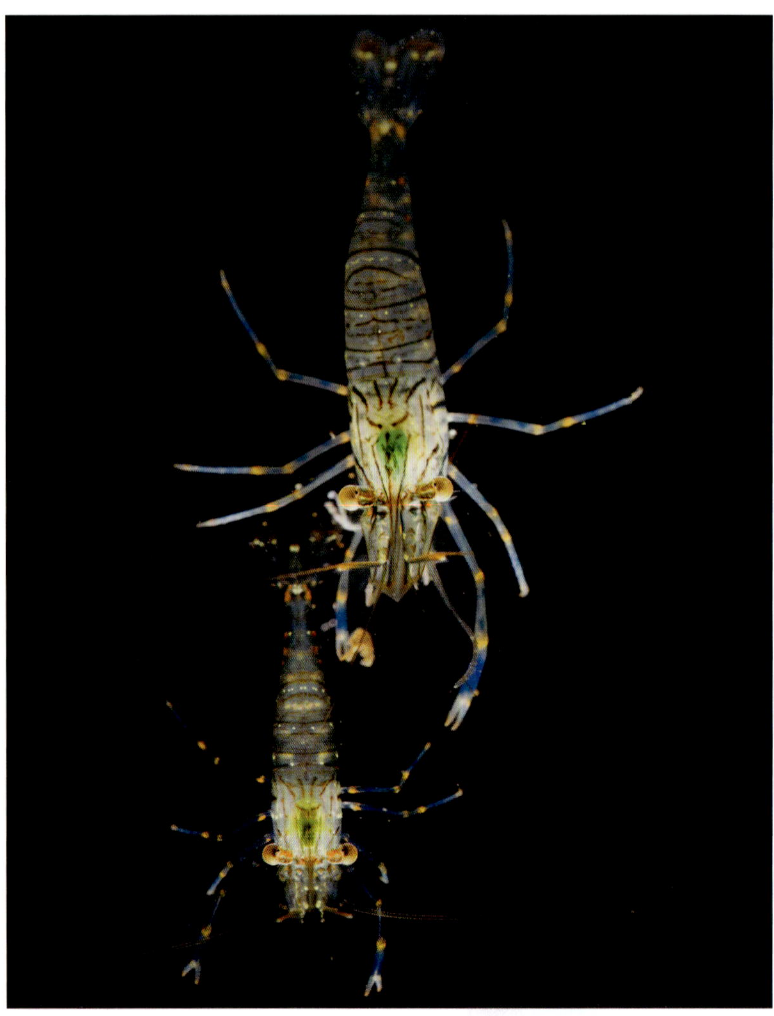

European rock pool shrimp, *Palaemon elegans*, Stonington Harbor, Connecticut, 2021

the occasional log, perhaps, or highly ephemeral (in the Pacific Ocean) drifting seaweed.

But by the middle to end of the twentieth century, we had changed all that: we had inserted into the sea vast fields of hard, semipermanent, floating substrate—a habitat that had never existed before. And then, when an event of unprecedented scale carried a tsunami of species into this plastic sea, the unforeseen happened: coastal species living on the high seas. In 2021 scientists dubbed this new regime the neopelagic community. The stage had been inadvertently set to change what had long been viewed as one of the last pristine environments on Earth—the open seas.

"The Oceans" is not a required course in university curricula. Most students graduating from university hear nothing formally about the oceans, which occupy nearly 75 percent of the surface of the earth. The oceans, which feed hundreds of millions of people. No required college course mentions this. The oceans, which regulate the world's climate on a planet of rapid climate change. No required college course mentions this. The oceans, upon which ships carry 90 percent of all world goods. No required college course mentions this. Nothing is mentioned in any required college course that the oceans are inexorably rising to inundate coastal lands, occupied in many regions of the world by peoples who have no resources to move.

Nothing.

Still, there are reasons for hope and optimism.

Fifty years ago there would have been no exhibition blending ocean art and ocean science and highlighting invasions, extinctions, and the role of plastics as an unexpected dispersal agent in the sea, nor the fate of coral reefs and the deeply integrated roles of climate change. Fifty years ago there were invasions, extinctions, and plastics were appearing in the oceans. Coral reefs were in trouble, and climate change was well known. But now we are more aware than ever before of the scale of attention and research that are required and must be invested to address these issues.

And perhaps most importantly, more and more students are now deeply engaged in ocean issues (garnered perhaps more from media than university)—students who have grown up in a world where addressing critical environmental issues is a career choice, rather than simply something to read about.

In our students, and in the paths they take, lie some of the greatest hopes for the world's oceans.

Opposite: Alexis Rockman, *Tsunami*, 2021. Detail

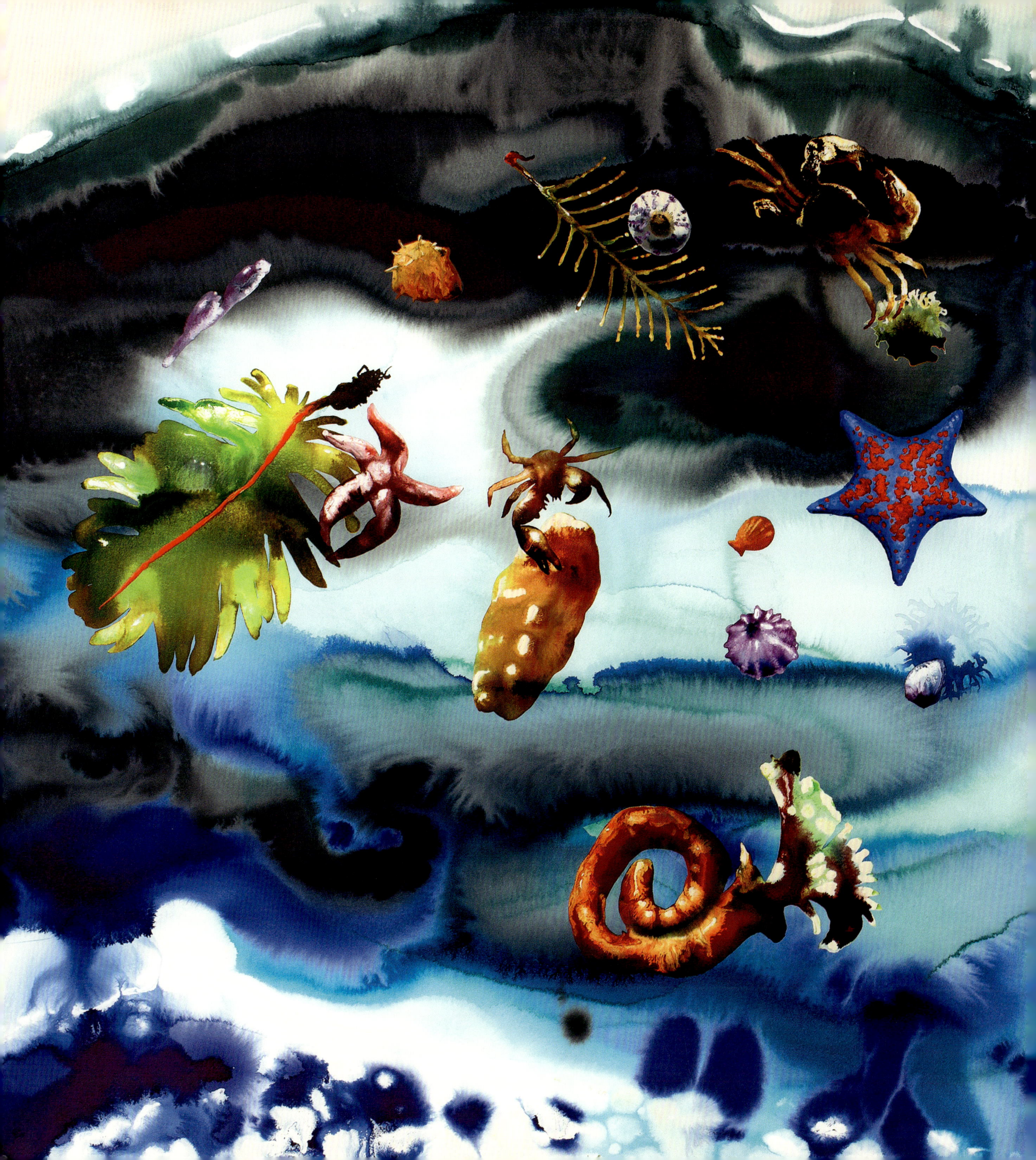

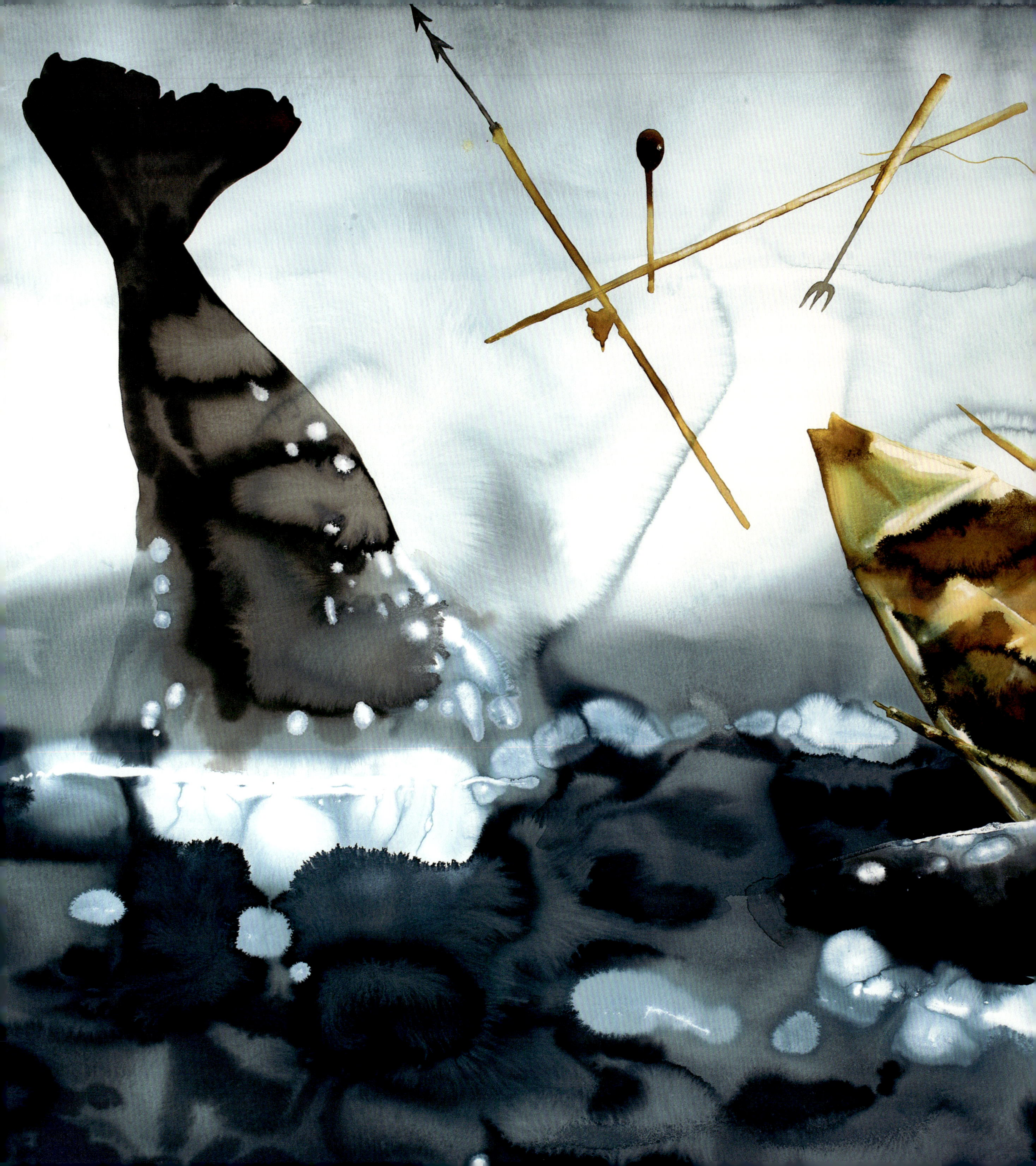

THE WATERCRAFT
OF *OCEANUS*

MICHAEL R. HARRISON

Chief Curator, Obed Macy Research Chair, Nantucket Historical Association

THE PAINTINGS AND WATERCOLORS THAT make up Alexis Rockman's *Oceanus* project explore aspects of human interaction with the sea. For millennia, humankind has looked to the water for food and transport. Human ingenuity has found ways to harvest the sea's natural bounty, reach new horizons, and connect peoples. We celebrate this human ability to meet the challenges of the deep and turn the water from a barrier into an opportunity. At the same time, Rockman's paintings acknowledge how often maritime enterprise has led to exploitation, from the decimation of species and destruction of marine ecosystems to the conquest and colonization of distant lands, the crimes of the slave trade, and the human toll of modern refugee displacement. The vessels that cut across the surface of Rockman's central painting, *Oceanus* (pp. 49–65), represent key aspects of this ingenuity and exploitation. All but four were inspired by a model or craft in the Mystic Seaport Museum collection. Because of this, the vessels in *Oceanus* are mostly American examples, but the stories they tell represent global patterns and reveal many of the complexities of what Rockman calls "humanity's indelible relationship with the ocean."

The world's waters are rich with fish and shellfish, although these resources have in many places been diminished or destroyed by overfishing, pollution, and ecological change. The desire to reach these rich sources of protein has inspired centuries of boat and equipment experimentation and refinement. The first vessel depicted in *Oceanus* is a dugout canoe, a type found in many forms across the globe. The example in *Oceanus* is a *mishoon/ muhshoon*, a boat of the Algonquin-speaking peoples of the Northeast. Historically, the Native peoples who lived in North America's coastal and riparian regions had deep maritime knowl-

edge and skills that supported their daily lives. The Lenape, Pequot, and Wampanoag, to name just three groups in the region of present-day Mystic Seaport Museum, made mishoons from tree trunks in a variety of sizes, from small one- or two-person vessels suited to fishing, to larger craft able to carry twenty or more rowers plus substantial cargo.[1]

In contrast, the Indigenous peoples of the Arctic, stretching from Siberia and Alaska through Northern Canada to Labrador and Greenland, developed light, maneuverable skin boats to fish and to hunt fowl, caribou, and marine mammals. Each Inuit, Inupiat, and Yupik group developed its own distinctive *qajaq* designs to suit the materials available and the conditions in which the boats needed to operate. As Charles Arnold once commented, outsiders studying these craft "risk failing to appreciate that the traditional wood, sinew, and skin kayaks used by Inuit … represent a high-water mark in creating watercraft suited to local needs, using preindustrial technologies and the limited materials at hand in the Arctic."[2]

Fishing in Europe's American colonies was also carried on in a variety of vessels designed to suit the particular conditions where fish were sought. In seventeenth- and eighteenth-century New England and Canada, small shallops and sloops dominated the inshore fisheries, while larger schooners were developed to exploit George's Bank and the Grand Banks, which were of central economic importance to the colonies. In 1731 the New England fisheries employed perhaps three to four thousand men afloat, and they produced about twenty-three million pounds of dried fish a year, valued at £138,000 in European markets. Uncounted thousands more men and women worked in the shoreside aspects of fishing. In 1741 the Massachusetts colony had four hundred

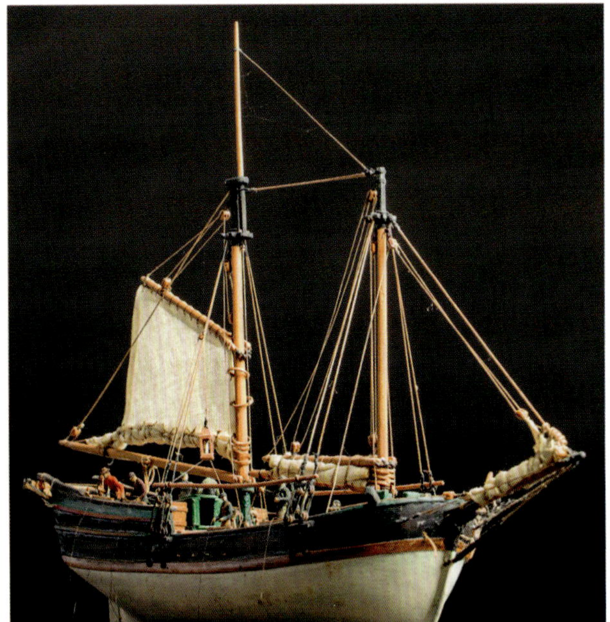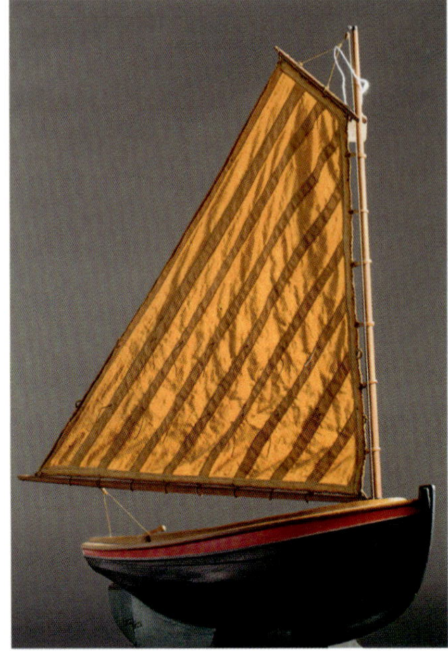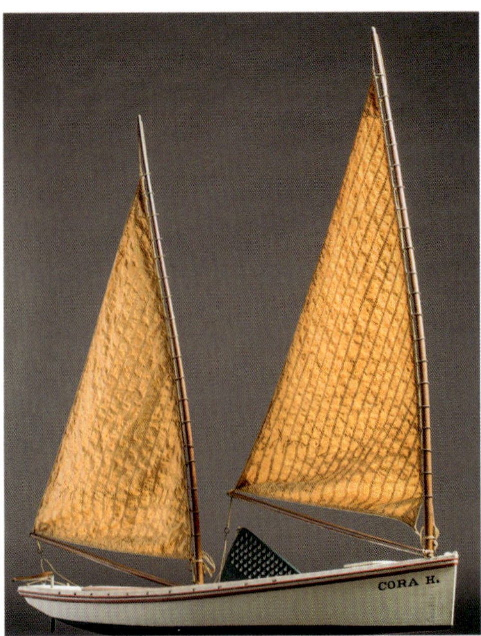

From left: 1. Colonial heeltapper. Model by Mystic Seaport Museum staff, 1964. Mystic Seaport Museum Collection, 2019.34.1;

2. Newport fish and lobster boat. Model by unidentified maker. Mystic Seaport Museum Collection, 1956.886;

3. New Haven sharpie *Cora H*. Model by unidentified maker. Mystic Seaport Museum Collection, 1954.1511

schooners and a similar number of smaller fishing vessels employed in inshore and offshore fishing. The swift-sailing Marblehead schooner was developed to carry on offshore fishing at a time when foreign commerce raiding and piracy were common dangers. Although derided by a later generation as "heeltappers" (fig. 1) for their supposed resemblance to floating shoes, these craft were known in their day for their good sailing qualities and speed. When General George Washington needed vessels to attack British supply ships during the siege of Boston in 1775, he chartered Marblehead schooners for the job. The seventy-eight-ton fishing schooner *Hannah* (fig. 4) thus became the Colonies' first armed military vessel, and captured the Patriots' first prize at sea.[3]

A century later, salt cod from the Banks remained a staple in the American diet. Population growth in the country's cities—enabled by emigrant ships crossing the Atlantic Ocean—and expanding railroad networks enlarged the market for both preserved and fresh fish. Ship owners and builders responded by developing faster schooners to speed the catch to shore. The *Nimbus* (fig. 7, overleaf), built at Bath, Maine, in 1876–77 for the Gloucester, Massachusetts, fishing fleet, represents the type of extreme clipper-schooner that came to dominate the New England fisheries. These were dangerous craft, prone to tripping in heavy seas or going adrift if a gale struck the fishing grounds. Many fishermen drowned working them. The *Nimbus* itself lasted

little more than a year before wrecking in a gale on the coast of Nova Scotia in December 1878. Two of the crew were lost.[4]

Many types of smallcraft were developed over the centuries to extract fish from America's varied regional waters. In the painting we see the Newport fish and lobster boat (fig. 2) of the 1870s and 1880s, which was a small, dinghy-like cat-rigged keelboat once popular for lobster trapping and hook-and-line fishing in the calm waters at the head of Narragansett Bay in Rhode Island. We also see a New Haven, Connecticut, oyster sharpie (fig. 3). This type of boat developed as a platform for oyster tonging, where, according to naval architect and historian Howard Chapelle, "steadiness, reasonable carrying capacity, low building cost, and good sailing qualities were desired—and the boat had to row well." Large sharpies of the 1880s measuring thirty-five feet in length could be worked by two men and carry between 150 and 175 bushels of oysters.[5]

The otter trawler *Surf* (fig. 5) represents efforts to introduce labor-saving steam-powered trawling into the New England deep-sea fisheries. The *Surf* was built for the Bay State Fishing Company in 1911. Worked by a crew of eighteen, this ship deployed trawl nets 130 feet long and about 110 feet wide at their mouth, which were towed across the seafloor to catch fish. A steam trawler with an otter trawl could catch six to eight times the amount of fish a sailing trawler could, and many times more

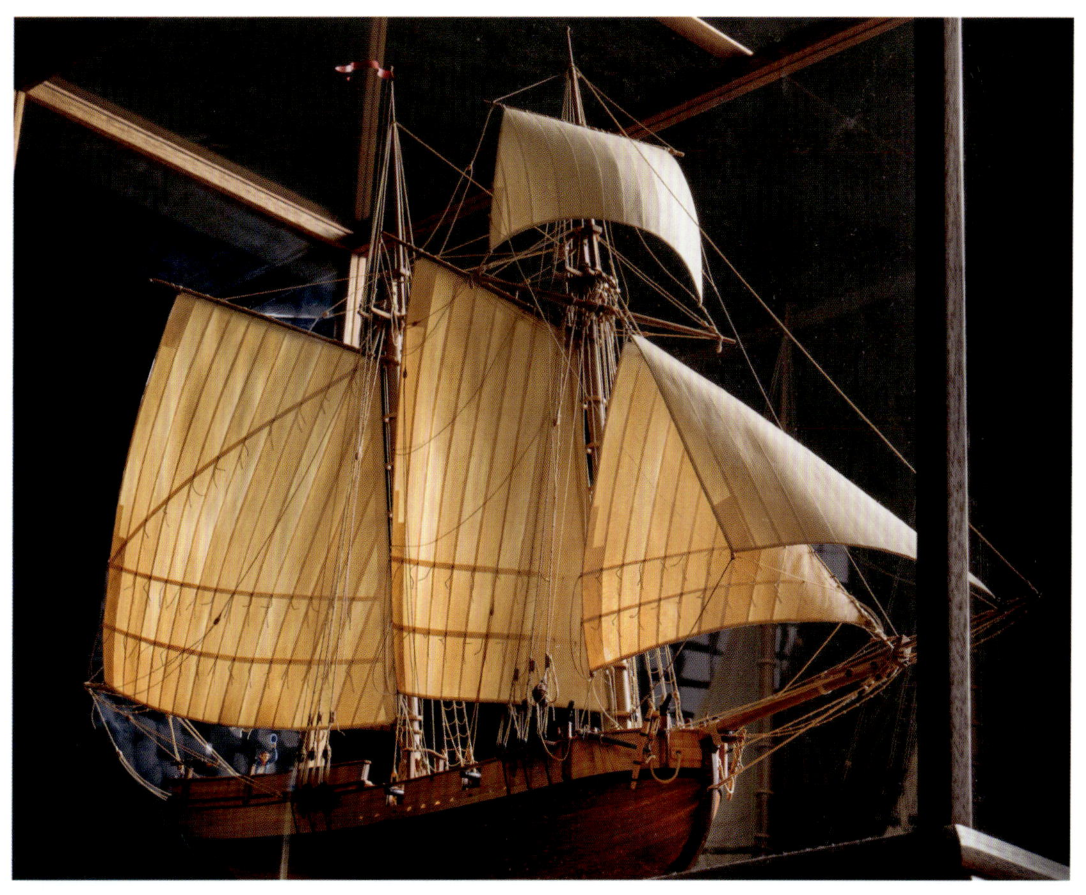

4. Schooner *Hannah*.
Model by William F. Wiseman, 1987–88.
Mystic Seaport Museum Collection,
2012.36.12

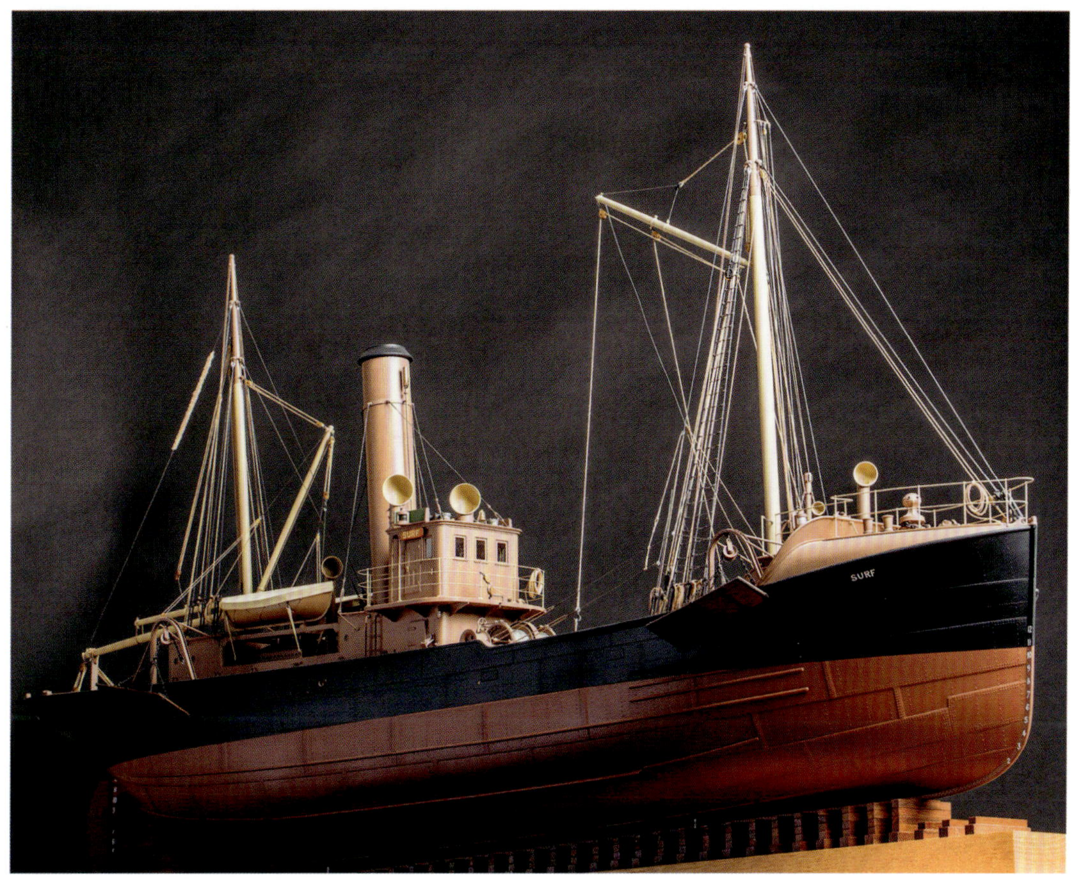

5. Steam trawler *Surf*.
Model by Erik A. R. Ronnberg Jr., 1987–90.
Mystic Seaport Museum Collection,
1989.100.12

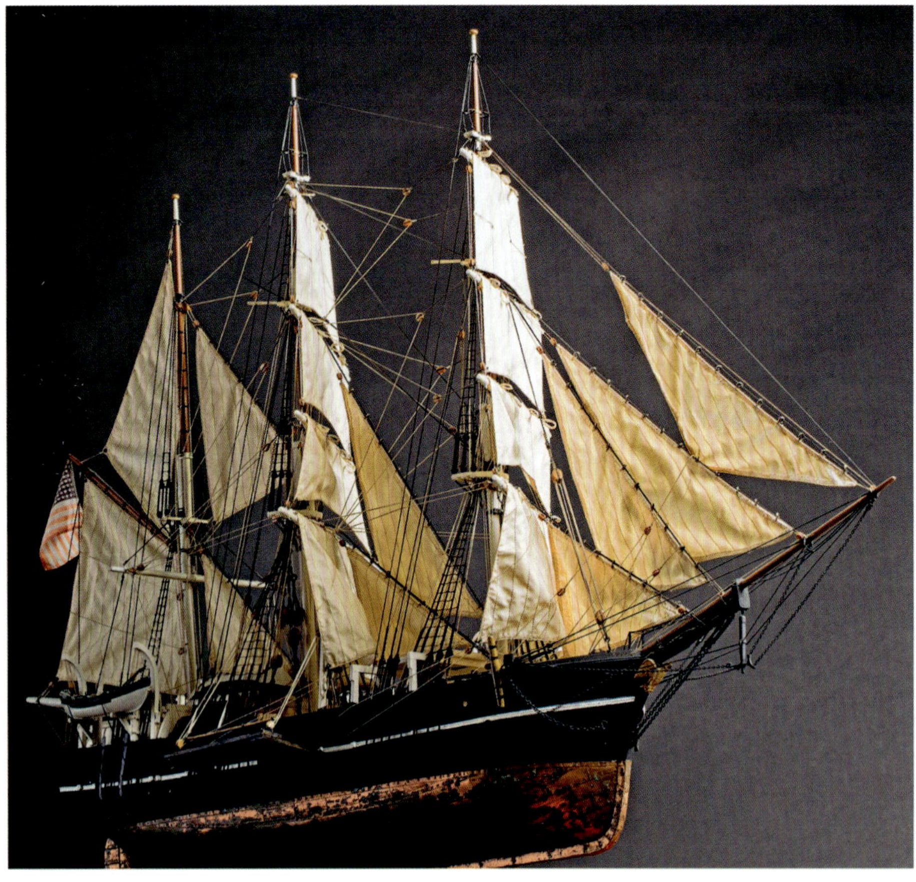

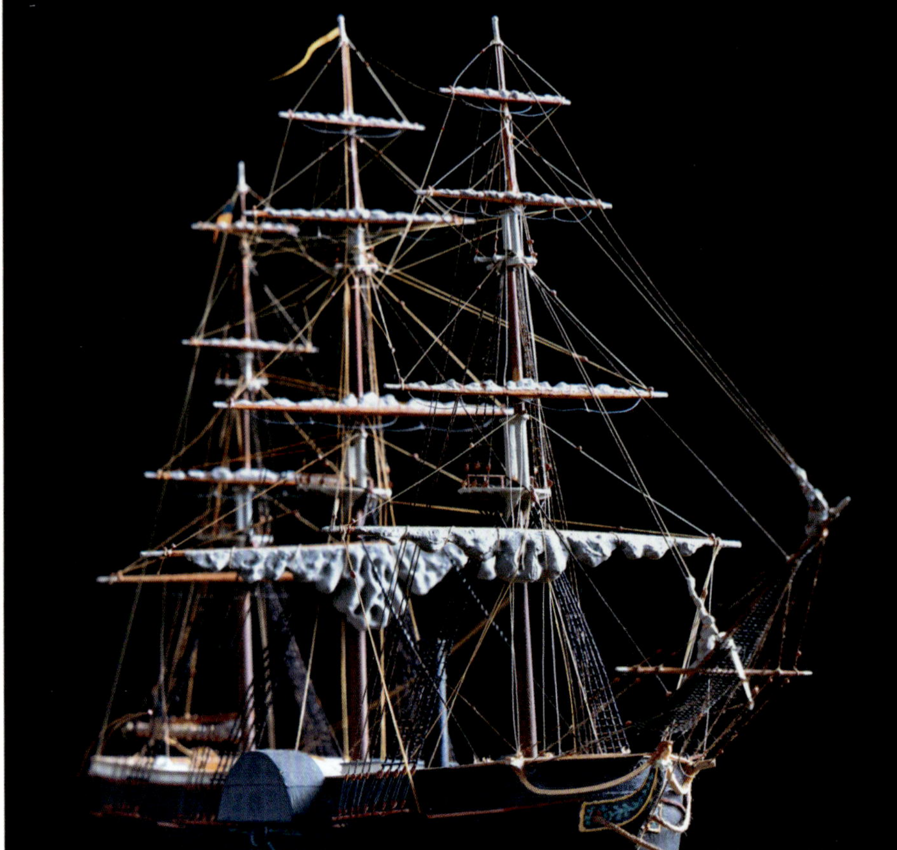

Clockwise from top left:

6. Whaling bark *Wanderer*. Model by unidentified maker. Mystic Seaport Museum Collection, 1941.625

7. Clipper-schooner *Nimbus* (with dory detail). Model by Mystic Seaport Museum staff, 1964. Mystic Seaport Museum Collection, 2019.34.2A

8. Steam packet *Savannah*. Model by Alexander Law, ca. 1959. Mystic Seaport Museum Collection, 1966.317

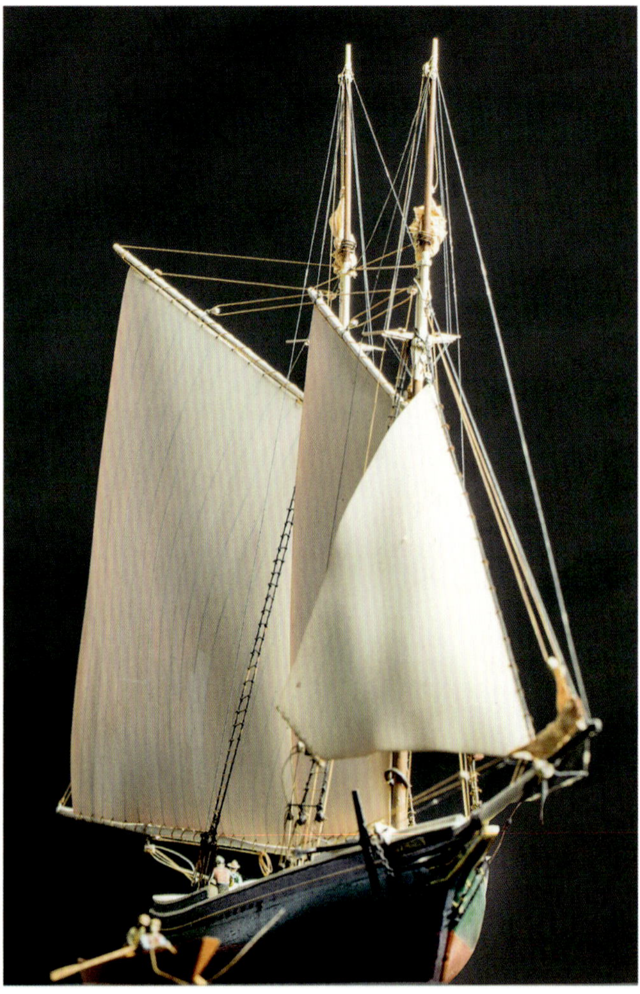

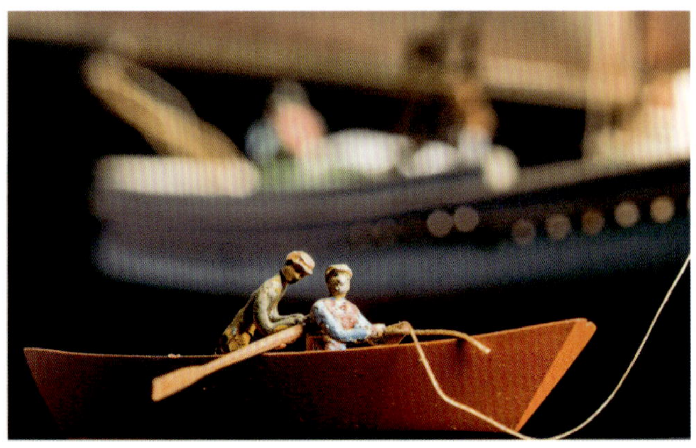

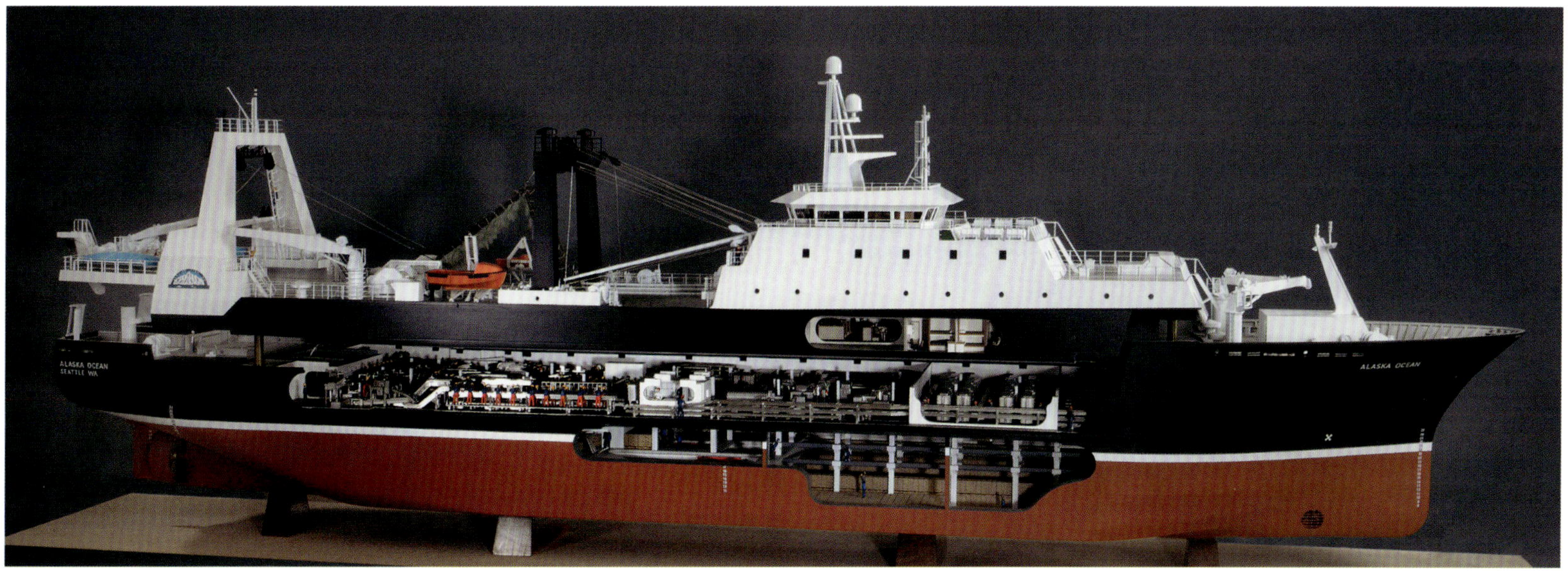

9. Catcher-processor vessel *Alaska Ocean*. Cutaway model by Erik A. R. Ronnberg Jr., 2009. Smithsonian National Museum of American History

than traditional schooner-launched dory fishing was capable of—but steam trawling also increased bycatch, the accidental capture of species the fishermen were not after. Trawling also created opportunities for overfishing and destroyed large numbers of marine mammals, turtles, and noncommercial fish at the same time. Only in the 1960s did bycatch begin to attract serious attention, and scientific, economic, and political solutions to its challenges continue to be worked on today.[6]

The 376-foot factory trawler *Alaska Ocean* (fig. 9) is one of the largest fishing vessels operating under the American flag today. With a crew of up to 150, it works the North Pacific and the Bering Sea, trawling for "white fish"—pollock and hake. Capable of harvesting about 300 metric tons of fish a day, this vessel also processes the catch into fillets and minced fish. The fish are caught and immediately butchered, flash frozen, and packaged. Unregulated large trawlers decimated the Atlantic cod in the twentieth century, but in the North Pacific where the *Alaska Ocean* operates, regulation and cooperation among fishing companies has led to more sustainable and safer practices.[7]

Alongside fishing, whaling was a core economic activity in eighteenth- and nineteenth-century New England. In 1844, at Yankee whaling's height, the industry employed 696 vessels and nearly 12,000 sailors. It extracted 405,677 barrels (about 12.8 million gallons) of sperm and whale oils and 1,508 tons of baleen, products considered essential to the nation's industrial progress.[8] Whale oil, boiled out of the blubber of right and bowhead whales, was the standard industrial lubricant of the day and an important source of illumination. Sperm oil, from sperm whales, was the highest quality lubricating oil available to industry and oiled everything from fine timepieces to cotton-mill spindles. It also burned brightly and cleanly and found wide use in lighthouses and upper-class parlors. Spermaceti candles, made from a wax from the sperm whale's head, were a luxury good that commanded high prices, while ambergris, a rare secretion occasionally found in sperm-whale digestive tracts, was used as a fixative in perfumes and was more valuable ounce for ounce than gold. Baleen, from the filter plates in the mouths of right and bowhead whales, was widely used for umbrella frames, whips, and clothing stays.

American whalers sailed across the globe, launching six-man rowboats to capture and kill the earth's largest animals. It was backbreaking, gory work. The bark *Wanderer* (fig. 6) hunted whales on more than two dozen voyages across forty-six years. It is remembered as the last wooden sailing vessel to depart a US port on a whaling voyage, wrecking on Cuttyhunk Island mere hours after leaving New Bedford, Massachusetts, in August 1924. Even as *Wanderer* broke up on the rocks, the introduction of industrial processes to whaling—engines, gun-fired harpoons, and mechanical processing—was already leading to devastating exploitation of whale populations. The innovations of twentieth-century whaling far outstripped any damage done to whale populations in the age of sail. Where whaling crews of all nations killed an estimated 300,000 sperm whales across the entire eighteenth and nineteenth centuries, industrial whaling killed that number between 1900 and 1962, then did so again between 1962

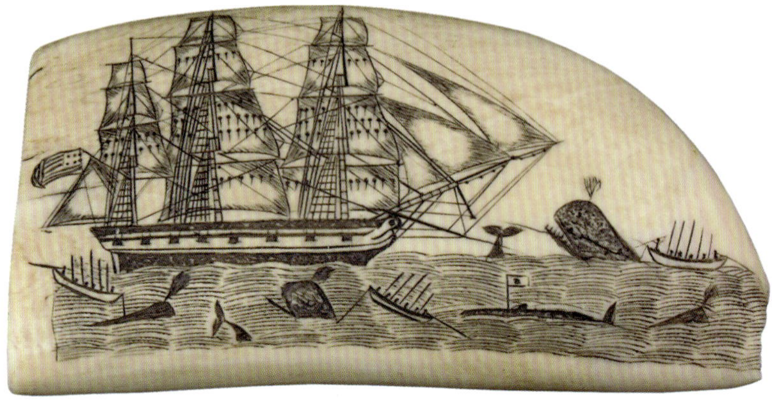

10. Whaling scene on a sperm whale tooth, ca. 1820s. Engraving by Edward Burdett. Ivory, 5⅛ × 2⅝ inches (13 × 6.7 cm). Nantucket Historical Association Collection, gift of the Friends of the NHA, 1989.126.4

and 1972. All told, at least 2.9 million whales of all species were harvested from the world's oceans in the twentieth century. The impacts of this slaughter on individual species and ecosystems are still being realized.[9]

A byproduct of American whalers' globe-trotting activities was the movement of people and ideas across the globe, creating connections between coastal New England and the islands of the Pacific. The world's sea-lanes have long formed networks for communication, trade, migration, and immigration—watery highways with world-altering consequences. Consider the Spanish treasure fleets, which knit Spain's global empire together for more than two hundred years, enriching a European power with the inbound products of three continents while sending religion and other ideas out. Or the transatlantic slave trade: across nearly four hundred years, approximately twelve million people from Africa were forcibly transported to the Americas by European enslavers; around one million of them were brought to North America. The overcrowded, squalid, suffocating conditions in the hold of a slave ship constituted a horrific and inhuman ordeal; yet, enslaved people claimed what control they could, refusing to eat or throwing themselves overboard rather than remain captive. And they carried with them their African cultural traditions—languages, music, foodways, beliefs—which influenced and enriched the cultural development of the Americas. The touchstone for these people's stories in Rockman's work is *La Amistad* (fig. 11). In 1839 a group of captive Mende people, illegally transported from West Africa, seized control of this vessel, a coastal-trading schooner that was carrying them along the Cuban coast. Eventually brought to New Haven, Connecticut, these people finally gained their freedom in a case brought before the US Supreme Court.

More benign aspects of ocean commerce are represented by HMS *Beagle*, the *Savannah*, and the ocean liner *Imperator*. The *Beagle* (fig. 14, overleaf) was one of 110 brig-sloops launched for the British Royal Navy between 1808 and 1834. These vessels frequently carried passengers and mail among far-flung outposts of the British Empire, or served as survey and scientific vessels. The *Beagle* was one of the latter and made three hydrographic survey voyages between 1826 and 1843, contributing to Western understanding of the physical world. Famously, Charles Darwin was aboard the *Beagle*'s globe-circling second voyage.[10]

Beginning in 1818, New York merchants pioneered the idea of scheduling commercial voyages, adding an element of predictability to the uncertainties of wind-powered travel. Their packet ships immediately became the preferred ocean conveyances for wealthy travelers and high-value cargo. The idea was soon extended to transporting immigrants and developed into a lucrative, large-scale business. At the same time, on America's rivers, inventors and entrepreneurs successfully introduced steam propulsion, which allowed traffic to run both down and up stream on set schedules. In 1818–19 the *Savannah* (fig. 8, previous page), a ship built to be an ocean packet, was fitted with an auxiliary steam engine and made the first experimental steam-assisted crossing of the Atlantic.[11] From this very modest beginning, ocean steamship service began. By the 1870s steamship lines crisscrossed the world, and more than 90 percent of the immigrants who arrived in the United States came by steamship. Between 1880 and 1930, more than twenty-seven million people immigrated to

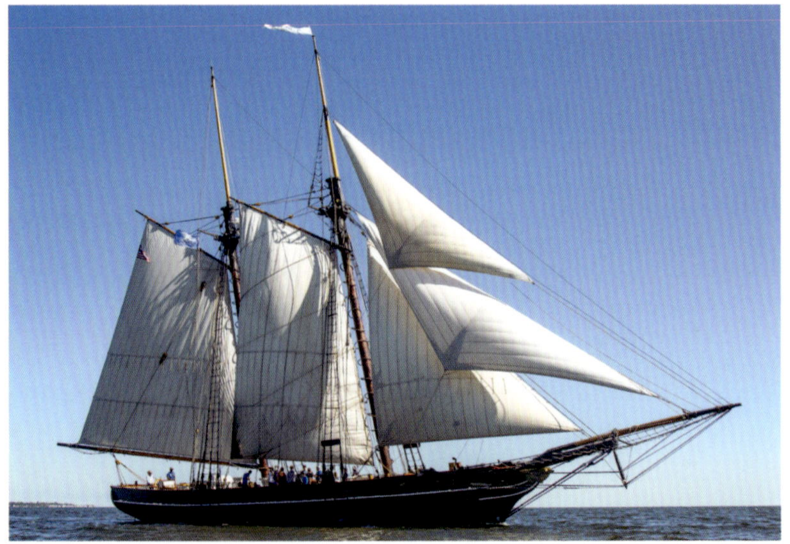

11. Two-masted schooner replica *Amistad*, built between 1998 and 2000, by shipwrights at Mystic Seaport Museum, Mystic, Connecticut

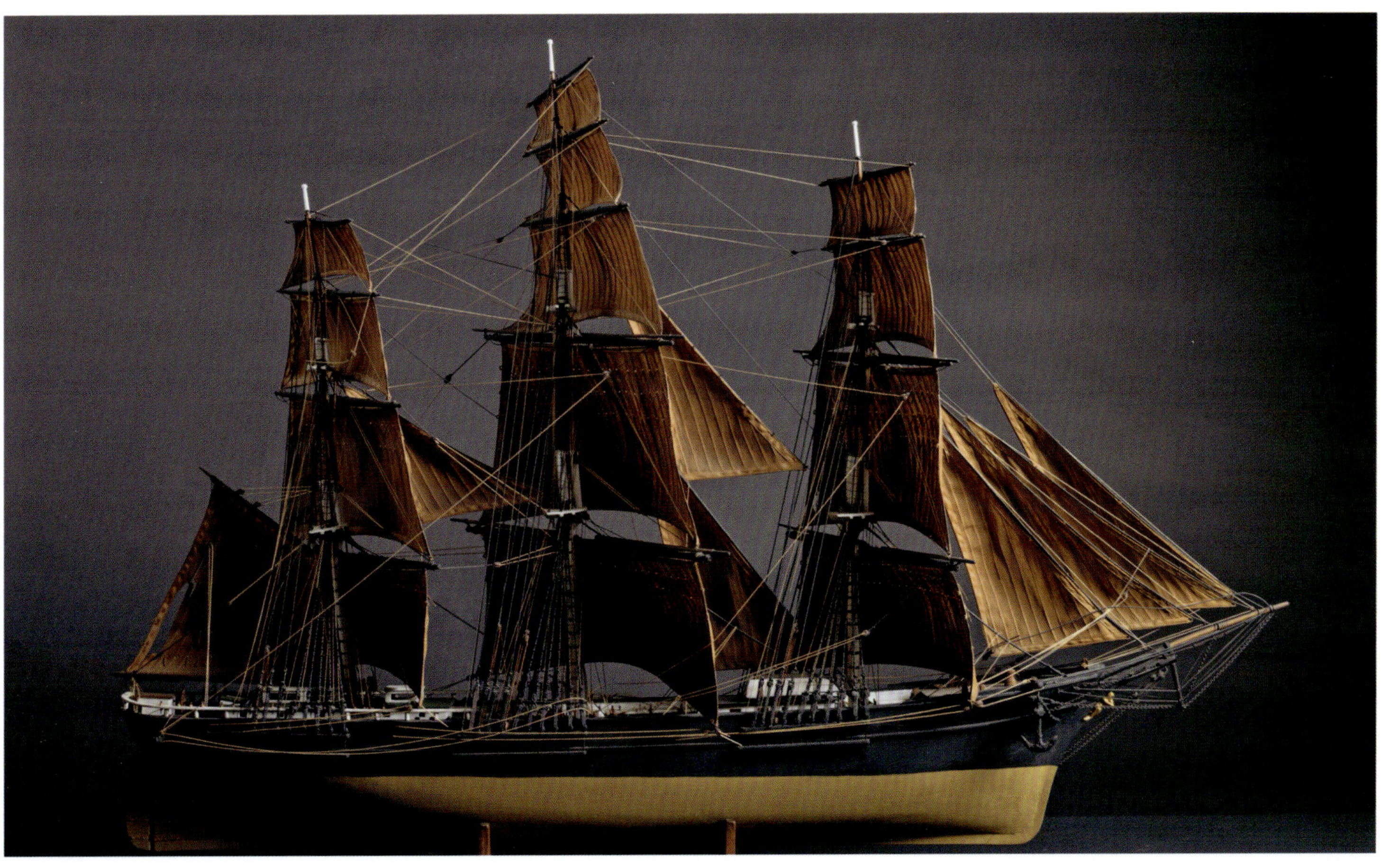

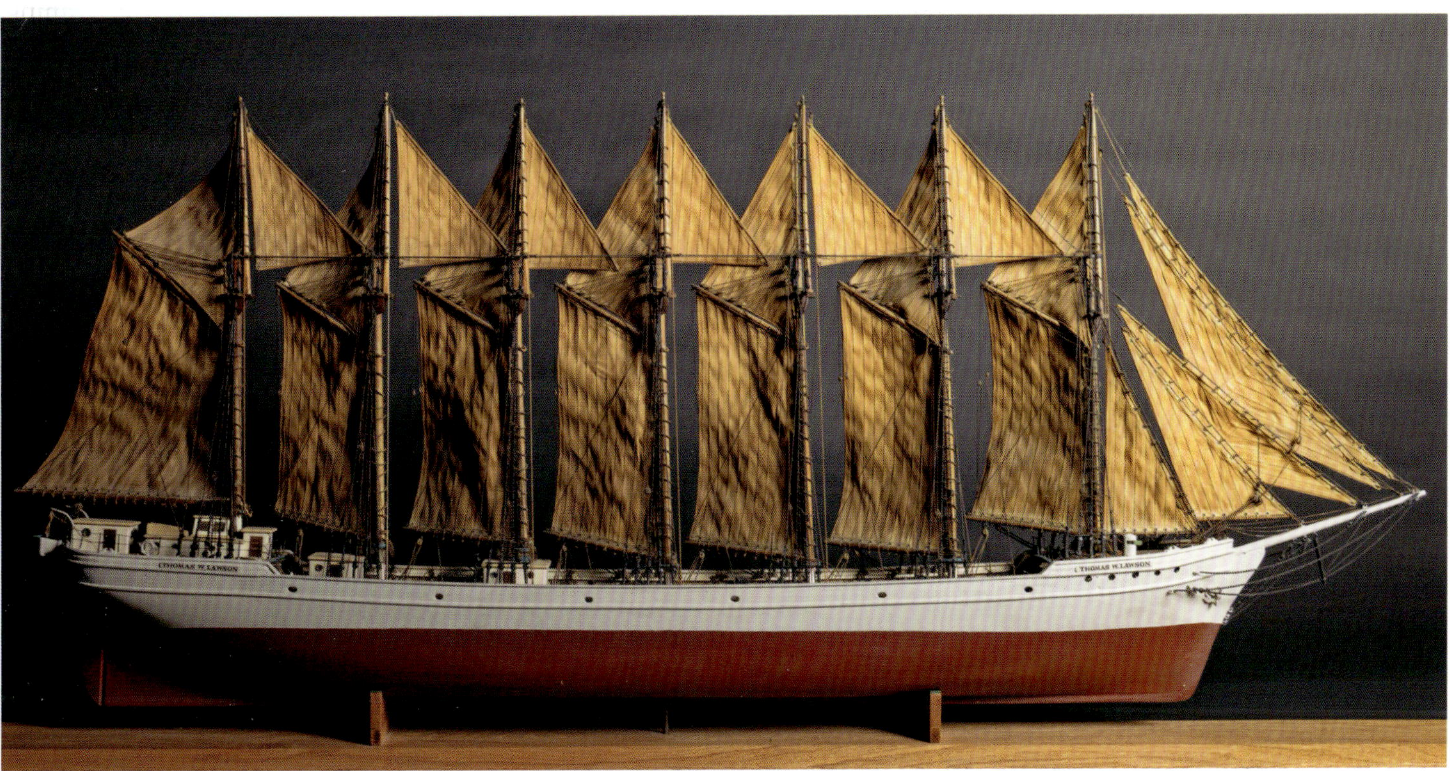

Top: 12. Clipper *Sovereign of the Seas*. Model by Thomas Rosenkvist, date unknown. Mystic Seaport Museum Collection, 1953.85
Below: 13. Schooner *Thomas W. Lawson*. Model by Thomas Rosenkvist, ca. 1923. Mystic Seaport Museum Collection, 1954.1591

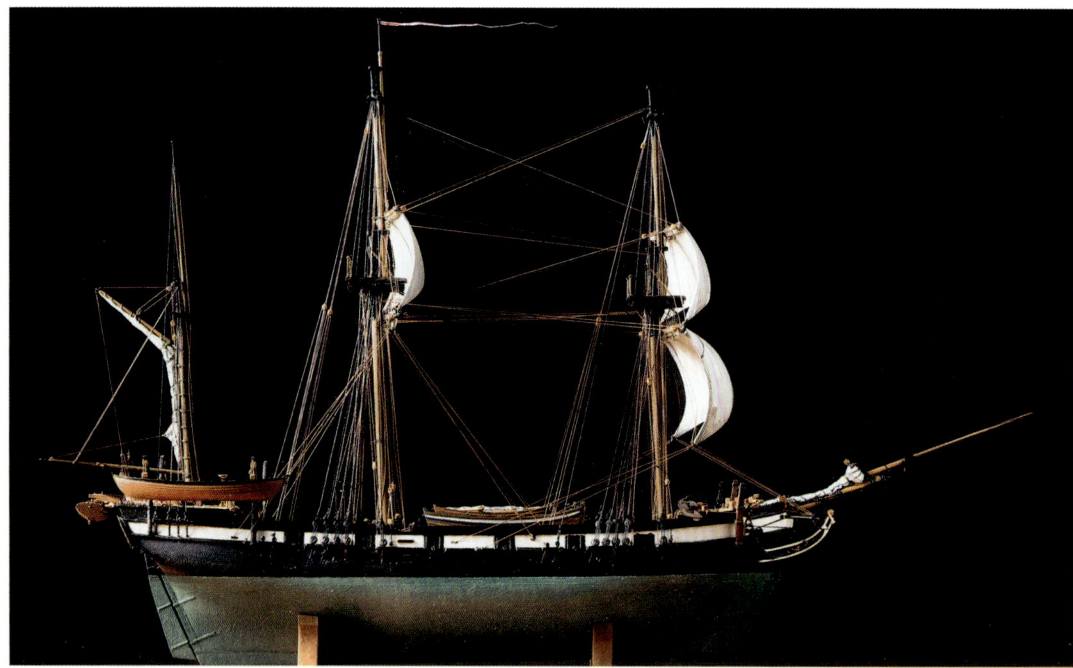

14. HMS *Beagle*.
Model by Lois Darling, 1959.
Mystic Seaport Museum Collection,
1991.108.3

the United States from around the world, seeking economic opportunities or to escape from political and social upheaval in their native countries. Steamship companies competed with each other to develop ever larger ships to carry this immigrant business, providing at the same time ever more luxurious accommodations for a substantially smaller number of wealthy business and leisure travelers. The steamship *Imperator* (fig. 15), seen in the painting, represents this international competition. Launched in 1912 for the express passenger service between Hamburg, Germany, and New York City, it was for a brief time the largest ship in the world, with capacity for 4,235 passengers and more than 1,300 crew. After World War I the ship was given to the Cunard Line and became the *Berengaria*, reparation for the torpedoed *Lusitania* (fig. 16).[12]

The long history of international cargo shipping under sail is represented in the painting by the 1852 clipper ship *Sovereign of the Seas* (fig. 12, previous page), which made a record-setting eighty-two-day run from Honolulu to New York in 1853. Clippers enjoyed a brief heyday in the mid-nineteenth century, when the money to be made in the Chinese tea trade and in supplying the California Gold Rush justified the construction and operation of ships that sacrificed cargo capacity for speed. They were the fastest commercial sailing vessels ever built.[13]

Coastal shipping was as vital to the growth of America as international shipping. In Colonial and early Federal America, fleets of small sloops and schooners connected coastal settlements and cities, carrying commodities and passengers. Even in 1900, big coastal schooners still carried the nation's bulk cargoes of construction materials, fuel, and food, including lumber, bricks, grain, coal, ore, and ice—items whose value did not justify the expense of shipping under steam. The shipyards of New England and the Pacific Northwest turned out ever larger wooden schooners: three masts, four masts, then on to five and even six masts by 1900 on the East Coast. In 1902, Fore River Ship & Engine Company launched the only seven-masted schooner ever built, the *Thomas W. Lawson* (figs. 13, previous page, 17, overleaf). Designed and built to sail between the Philippines and the US Pacific Coast, perhaps to capitalize on the demand for coal that America's new naval presence there demanded, the schooner was employed instead by the Coastwise Transportation Company of Boston in the New England coal trade due to difficulties with US

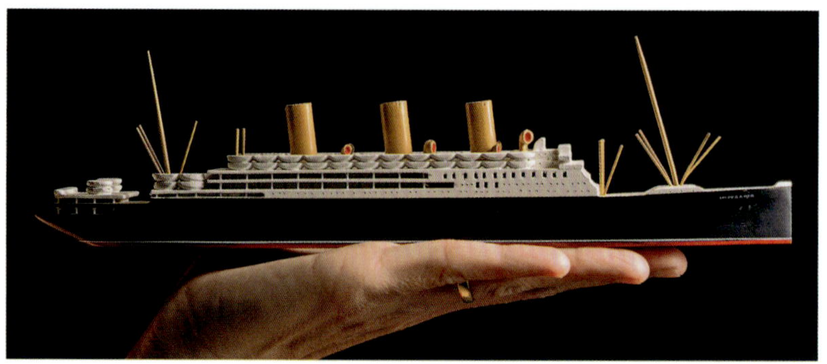

15. Ocean liner *Imperator*. Model by Charles Van Ryper, date unknown. Mystic Seaport Museum Collection, 1965.924

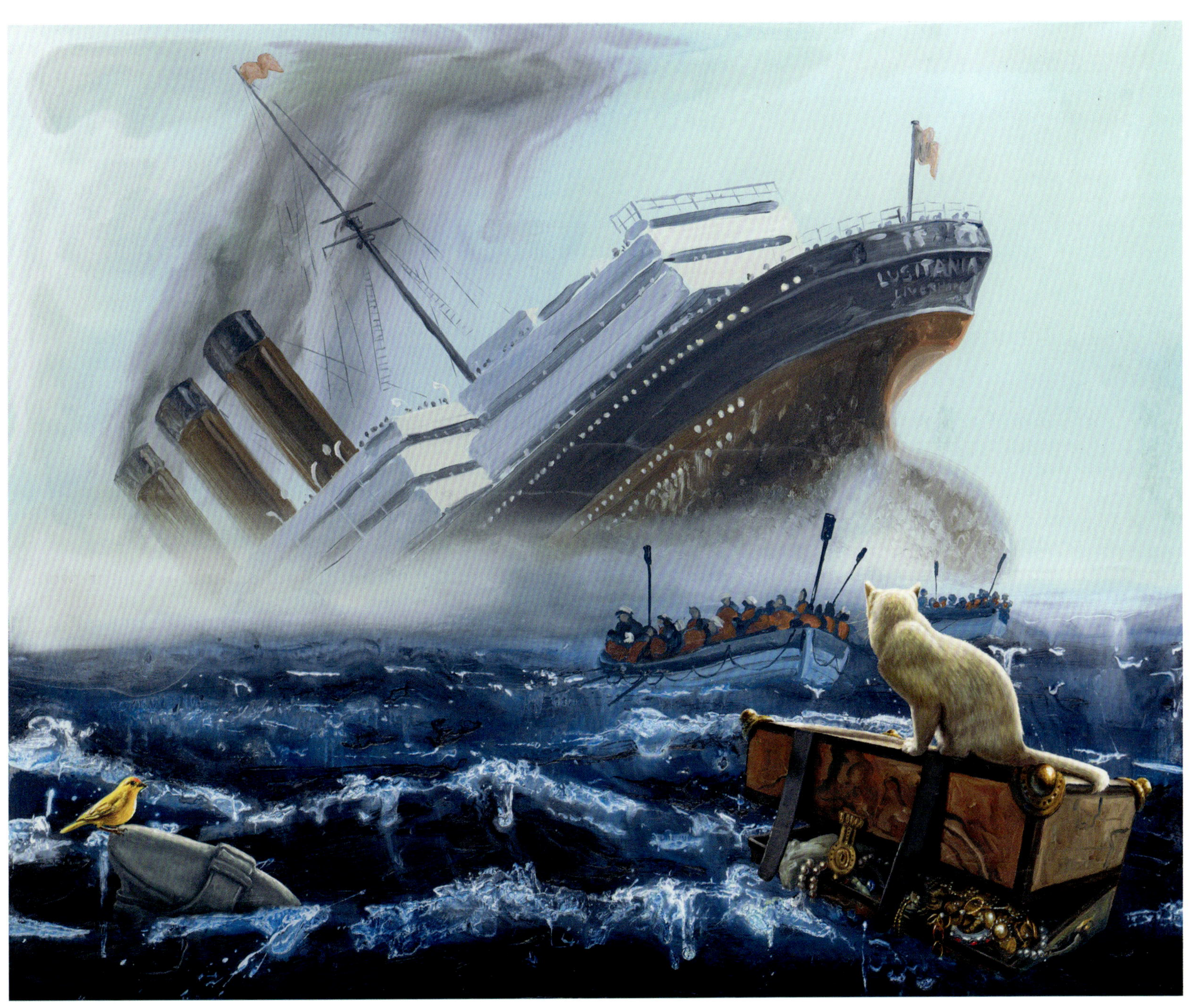

16. Alexis Rockman, *Lusitania*, 2020. Oil on wood, 40 × 48 inches (101.6 × 121.9 cm)

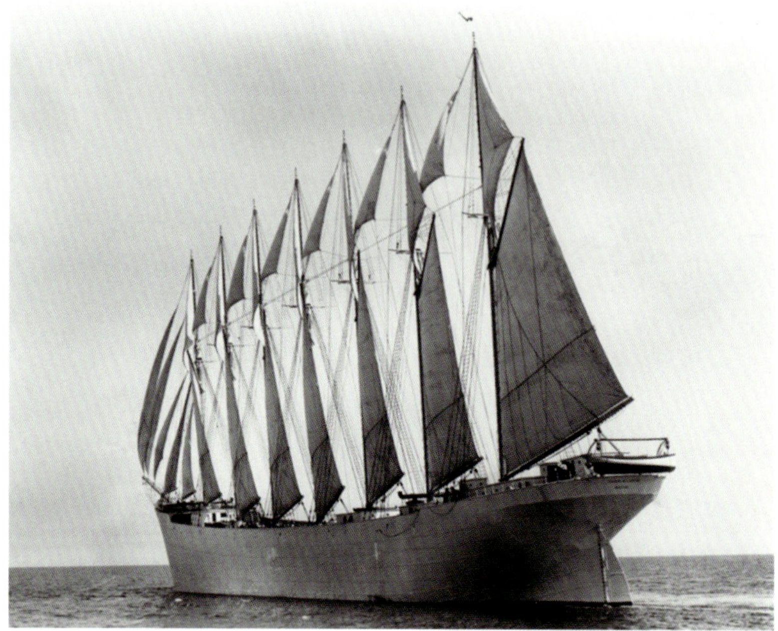

17. Schooner *Thomas W. Lawson*. Photograph by Nathaniel L. Stebbins, 1902

shipping regulations. Operated by a crew of sixteen, the vessel's steel construction allowed for a high cargo capacity. As Erik Ronnberg has noted, "*Lawson*'s cavernous interior was a far cry from the congestion of keelsons, sister keelsons, riders, deck beams, clamps, knees, and the sheer bulk of frames and ceiling which impinged on the hold space of a wooden schooner. What we see by contrast is the economy and efficiency of a steel warehouse in a hull that was stiffer, drier, and far more durable than any wooden structure this size."[14] The *Lawson* could carry 11,000 tons of coal, but that made the schooner too deep for any East Coast harbor except Newport News, limiting loads to around 7,000 tons. The owners converted the vessel to a bulk tanker in 1906. It wrecked in the Isles of Scilly during a December 1907 storm, while on a charter voyage to the UK, killing all aboard except Captain Dow and engineer Edward L. Rowe. The wreck released more than two million barrels of paraffin oil into the Celtic Sea. Although it evaporated quickly, the oil killed birds and small mammals on adjacent Annet Island. "It was a horrible time," a local wrote, "Everything seemed to reek of the oil. The very spray on the windows ran down in oily blue streaks for long after …" This was the first recorded petroleum-cargo spill from a ship.[15]

The steam schooner *Barbara C* (originally the *Pacific*) (fig. 18) carried lumber between Washington State and San Pedro, California, from 1920 to 1941. Requiring a crew of twenty-seven, the *Barbara C*, like other steam schooners, was manned predom-

inantly by Scandinavian immigrants and carried general cargo and passengers as a side business. Immense demand for wood to build America's cities led to the development of vast lumbering operations to exploit the old-growth forests of Oregon and Washington in the second half of the nineteenth century. The sea was the quickest—and sometimes the only—way to get this wood to market, and entrepreneurs built fleets of sailing schooners to transport timber down the coast to San Francisco and San Pedro. Steam schooners, the special steamships developed to advance this trade, became prevalent in the early twentieth century. Lumber companies frequently built both sailing schooners and steam schooners for their own freight service. Furthermore, these vessels were constructed from the same immense old-growth timber they were designed to transport—some of the planks of the steam schooner *Wapama*, which survived as a museum ship into the 2010s, were over seventy feet in length. These ships and their cargoes demonstrate the magnificence of the trees available to shipbuilders in the early twentieth century, and Americans' eagerness to use them.[16]

Today, the vast majority of the world's trade goods travel by ship from their country of origin to country of use. Giant tankers move oil and refined petroleum products; bulk carriers transport grain, coal, ores, and other unpackaged cargo. Manufactured goods cross the world in containers, twenty- and forty-foot-long steel boxes that are loaded in large numbers aboard container ships. Containers can be easily moved from truck to train to ship, creating an intermodal shipping system that reduces handling costs and helps make modern globalized manufacturing

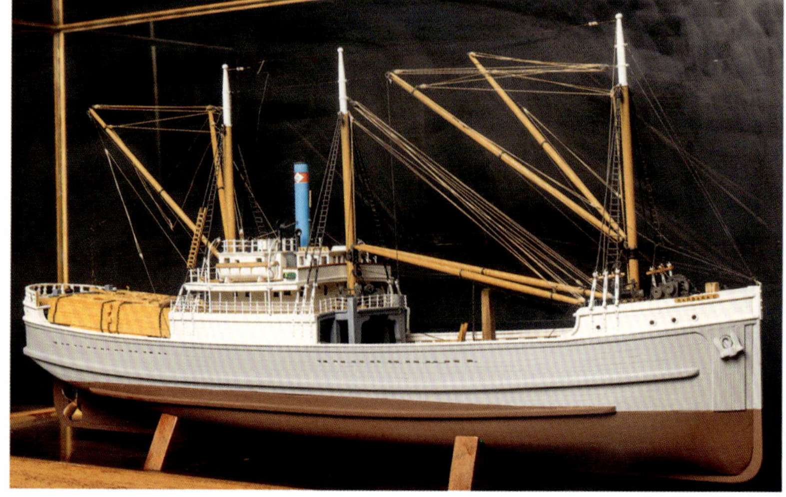

18. Steam schooner *Barbara C*, ex-*Pacific*. Model by Robert E. Stewart, 1991. Mystic Seaport Museum Collection, 1993.43

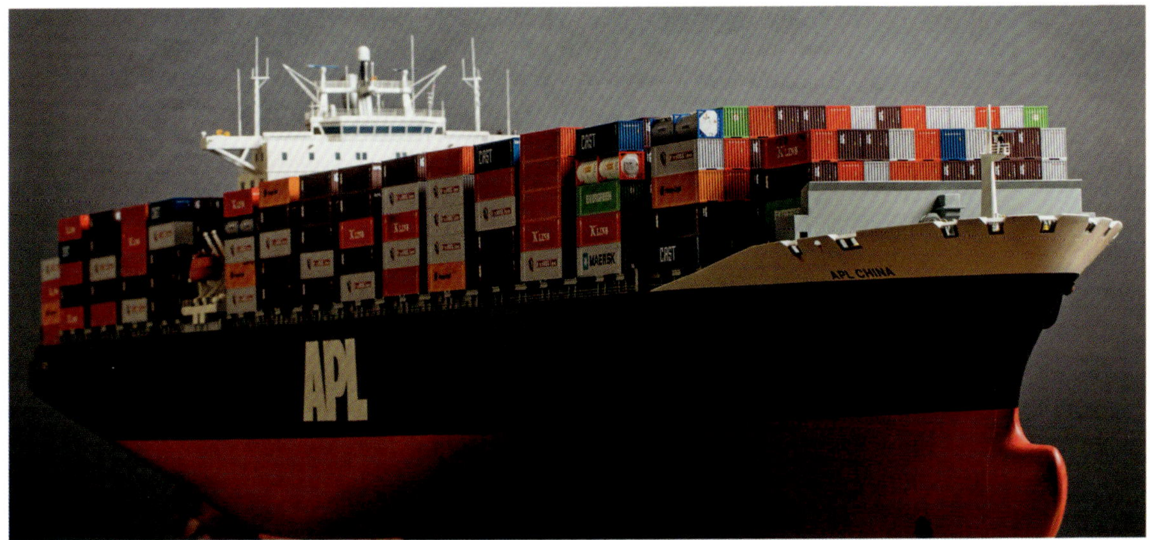

19. Container ship *APL China*. Model by Greg McKay, 2002. Mystic Seaport Museum Collection, 2002.57

possible. The container ship *APL China* (fig. 19), represented in *Oceanus*, was built in 1995 with a capacity of 4,832 TEU (twenty-foot equivalent units, the volume of a twenty-foot-long container). By comparison, the MV *Ever Given*, built in 2015, which famously grounded in the Suez Canal in March 2021, can carry 20,124 TEU. And what's in those containers? A typical modern forty-foot container might carry one hundred refrigerators from Mexico, or four hundred mattresses from Poland, or twenty thousand pairs of jeans from China, or even 6.4 million cashews from Ghana.

In October 1998, *APL China*, en route to Seattle from Taiwan, was caught in Typhoon Babs. In seventy-five-foot waves and high winds, it lost hundreds of containers overboard. Scientists use cargoes lost from container ships to study drift patterns and the spread of pollution in the world's oceans.[17]

Around the world, maritime museums such as Mystic Seaport Museum gather and preserve the artifacts of the seafaring past in order to make sense of that past and to suggest ways to more deeply understand the present. In an introductory gallery at the National Maritime Museum in Greenwich, England, the curators acknowledge the complexities of the water in human history: "Through science, trade, conflict, work, and leisure, the sea has dominated the history of mankind and shaped our understanding of the world and our place within it. The sea has offered opportunities for glory but can also be a place of great loss." Alexis Rockman has woven the threads of science, trade, work, glory, loss, and more into *Oceanus*, creating a work that challenges us to consider the many aspects of the human relationship with the maritime world, which remains as promising and perilous today as it ever has been.

1. See Andrew C. Lipman, "Murder on the Saltwater Frontier: The Death of John Oldham," *Early American Studies* 9, no. 2 (Spring 2011): 277–79.

2. Charles D. Arnold, "Review of *Qayaq: Kayaks of Alaska and Siberia*," *Arctic* 55, no. 1 (March 2002): 94.

3. See Adam Anderson, *An Historical and Chronological Deduction of the Origin of Commerce* (London: J. Walter, 1787), III:172; Howard Chapelle, *The National Watercraft Collection*, 2nd ed. (Washington, DC: Smithsonian Institution Press, 1976), 162–63, 178–79; Walter B. Norris, "Who is the Father of the American Navy?," *Current History* 27, no. 3 (December 1927): 355–56; and Paul H. Silverstone, *The Sailing Navy, 1775–1854* (New York: Routledge, 2006), 13.

4. See *List of Vessels Belonging to the District of Gloucester*, August 1878 (Gloucester, MA: John S. E. Rogers, 1878), n.p.; and "Maine Seamen Drowned," *Portland Daily Press*, December 24, 1878, 2.

5. See Howard I. Chapelle, *American Small Sailing Craft* (New York: W. W. Norton, 1951), 110, 242–44, quote from 105; and Maynard Bray et al., *Mystic Seaport Watercraft* (Mystic, CT: Mystic Seaport, 2001), 18.

6. See Erik A. R. Ronnberg Jr., "Steam Trawlers Come to the Boston Fishing Fleet," *Nautical Research Journal* 39, no. 4 (1994): 199–213; and Martin A. Hall, Dayton L. Alverson, and Kaija I. Metuzals, "By-Catch: Problems and Solutions," *Marine Pollution Bulletin* 41, nos. 1–6 (2000): 204–19.

7. "Fishing for World Markets," *On the Water: Stories from Maritime America*, National Museum of American History, accessed July 12, 2022, https://americanhistory.si.edu/on-the-water/modern-maritime-america/global-connections/fishing-world-markets.

8. *Statistics of the United States in 1860* (Washington, DC: Government Printing Office, 1866), 547.

9. See Daniel Cressey, "World's Whaling Slaughter Tallied at 3 Million," *Scientific American*, March 11, 2015; and Robert C. Rocha Jr., Phillip Clapham, and Yulia Ivashchenko, "Emptying the Oceans: A Summary of Industrial Whaling Catches in the 20th Century," *Marine Fisheries Review* 76, no. 4 (March 2015): 37–48.

10. James Taylor, *The Voyage of the Beagle: Darwin's Extraordinary Adventure in Fitzroy's Famous Survey Ship* (Annapolis, MD: Naval Institute Press, 2008), 36–38.

11. See Howard I. Chapelle, *The Pioneer Steamship Savannah: A Study for a Scale Model* (Washington, DC: Smithsonian Institution, 1961).

12. C. R. Vernon Gibbs, *Passenger Liners of the Western Ocean* (London: Staples, 1957), 80–81.

13. Octavius T. Howe and Frederick C. Matthews, *American Clipper Ships, 1833–1858* (New York: Dover, 1986), II:598.

14. Erik A. R. Ronnberg Jr., "Stranger in Truth than in Fiction: The American Seven-Masted Schooners," *Nautical Research Journal* 38, no. 1 (March 1993): 13–15, 17.

15. W. J. Lewis Parker, *The Great Coal Schooners of New England 1870–1909* (Mystic, CT: Marine Historical Association, 1948), 79; Gary Shigenaka, "The Wreck of the Thomas W. Lawson: The 'First' Large Oil Spill," *Oil Industry History* 18, no. 1 (2017): 1–6, quote from 4.

16. See *Merchant Vessels of the United States*, 1921, 147; and Michael R. Harrison, "Addendum to Steam Schooner Wapama," HAER No. CA-67, Historic American Engineering Record (HAER), National Park Service, US Department of the Interior, 2011, 38.

17. See Steve Ginsberg, "Lawsuits Rock APL's Boat," *San Francisco Business Times*, November 20, 1998, and "Ship Disaster Leaves APL Lost in Sea of Legal Woes," *San Francisco Business Times*, March 19, 1999.

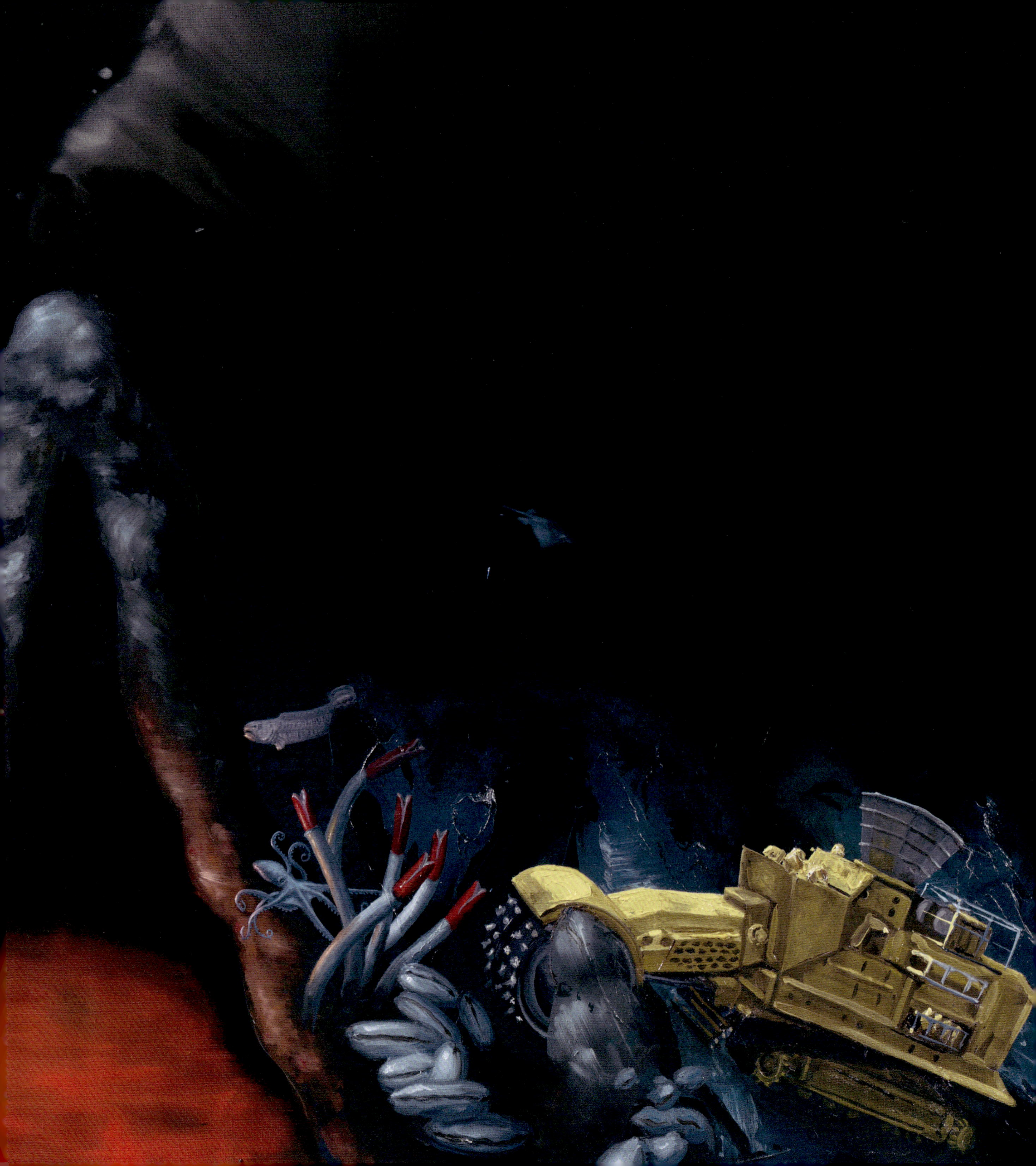

EXPLORING
THE NEW AMERICA

ROBERT D. BALLARD

President of the Ocean Exploration Trust

AS WE LOOK AT THE CENTRAL WORK OF ALEXIS Rockman's *Oceanus* series, the artist's references to the historic impact of destructive exploitation of the undersea world is evident, but there is opportunity to positively change the nature of our use of the seas as a sustainable economic resource through twenty-first-century scientific exploration. While the terrestrial assets of the United States have been well mapped and evaluated, due to significant developments in new technologies, we have exciting new possibilities to better understand the potential of the exclusive economic zone (EEZ) of the ocean floor that surrounds our nation.

On April 11, 1803, Napoleon Bonaparte offered to sell what was then called Louisiana to the United States: a vast piece of land stretching from New Orleans north up the Mississippi and Missouri rivers to the Bitterroots mountains of western Montana, containing over 827,000 square miles (fig. 1). The price tag was $15 million, and President Thomas Jefferson agreed to the terms.

Jefferson sent forth Captain Meriwether Lewis and Second Lieutenant William Clark and their Corps of Discovery on a two-year journey of exploration to discover what America now claimed, an expedition that would go down in history as the "Lewis and Clark Expedition," and which began on the banks of the Missouri River in St. Charles, Missouri, on May 14, 1804. Modern historian Douglas Brinkley, director of the Eisenhower Center for American Studies, stated, "With the Declaration of Independence and the Constitution, this is one of the three things that created the modern United States."[1]

Prior to the Louisiana Purchase, 90 percent of America's economy was based upon local farming practices. Cities were growing rapidly but they did not produce a large proportion of the national economic output. Given the rocky soil and poor weather in the northern colonies, large-scale farming was not possible, so the colonizers focused on the abundance of fish and lumber to drive their economy. The middle colonies—better known as the "bread colonies"—produced corn, wheat, and oats as exports to England. Trading with Native Americans for fur was also common practice. In the southern colonies, a plantation-based economy using slaves produced tobacco, rice, and indigo, which were also shipped in large measure back to England. This would all change after the Louisiana Purchase, which was rich in gold, silver, and other ores, huge forests, and endless lands for grazing and farming. This purchase would make America immensely wealthy and completely change the economy of the country.

The economic impact of the Louisiana Purchase was massive, transforming this newly acquired land into vast farmlands

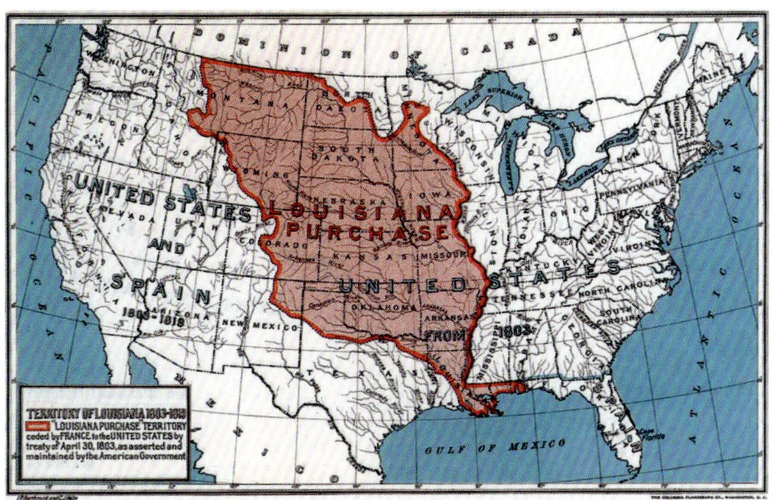

1. Map of "Louisiana" and the Louisiana Purchase. Washington, DC: Government Printing Office, 1912

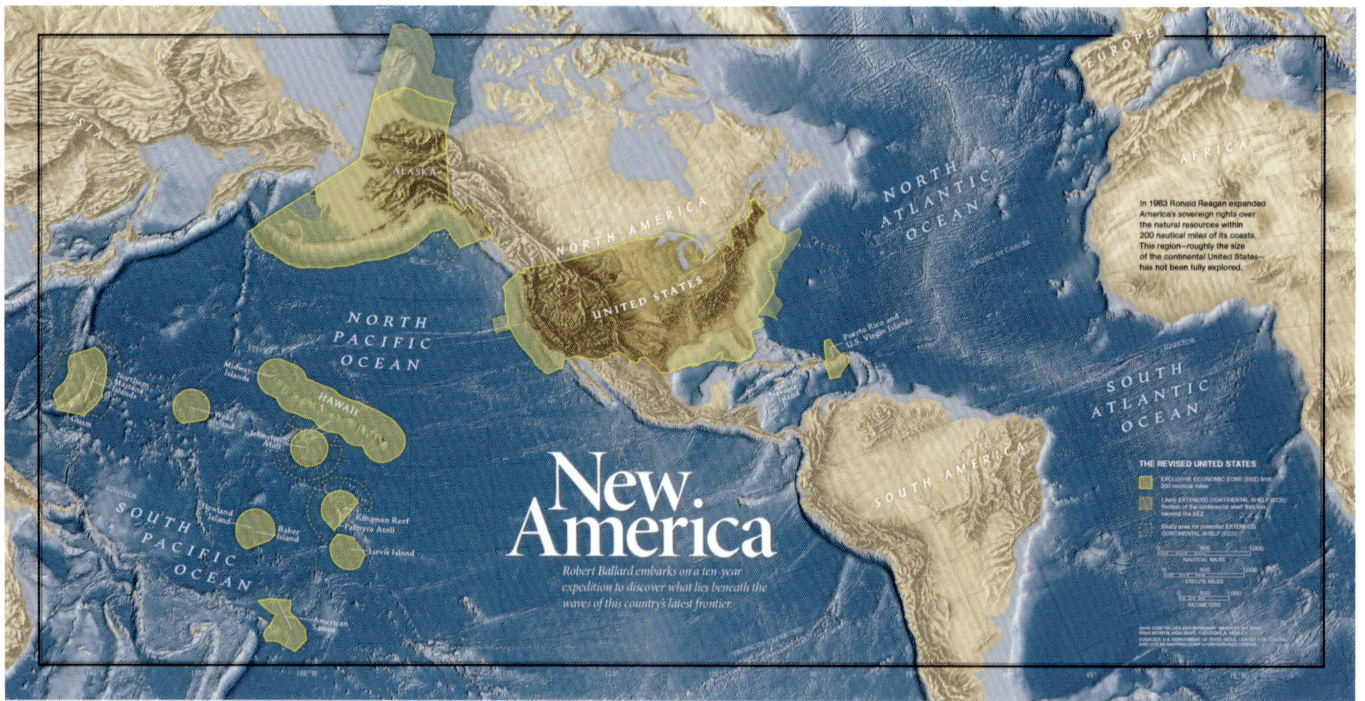

2. The exclusive economic zone (EEZ), otherwise known as "New America," lies beneath the sea and represents 52% of America's landmass

covered by seas of corn and wheat, cattle ranches that stretched for miles, and valuable ore mines, followed by the discovery of major oil and gas deposits. Equally important was the creation of more National Parks, which would grow even larger in size as the boundaries of the nation expanded further west and south.

Jump forward 181 years, to 1984, when President Ronald Reagan recognized that a nation could claim rights to the ocean floor 200 nautical miles from its shores. In so doing he created America's exclusive economic zone (EEZ) covering more than 4,383,000 square miles, five times the size of the Louisiana Purchase. This "New America" now represents 52 percent of our nation, yet we have better maps of Mars than of what we own off our own shores (fig. 2). An assessment of these largely unknown undersea "territories" was in order, a new Lewis and Clark expedition for the modern age, but this time requiring the greatest technological advances in deep-sea exploration and mapping.

In 2018 the US government announced a nationwide competition to create the Ocean Exploration Cooperative Institute (OECI), which would conduct a ten-year expedition to help map and characterize the "New America."

In response to Reagan's announcement, I formed a consortium of oceanographic institutions including the Woods Hole Oceanographic Institution, the University of New Hampshire, the University of Southern Mississippi, the University of Rhode Island, and the Ocean Exploration Trust. The E/V *Nautilus* was to become the flagship for this new effort, and in 2019 the Ocean Exploration Cooperative Institute came into existence with a mission to explore our EEZ "for the purpose of commerce." This multiyear exploration program would be carried out in that part of the submerged America that has never been mapped or explored.

In the past, when an important discovery has been made, it might take one or more years before a follow-up expedition could be organized to better understand and characterize the discovery, since the experts required to do so were more than likely not aboard ship when the discovery was made. Fortunately, our team had pioneered the use of "tele-presence" technology in 1989 when we installed a high bandwidth satellite system aboard our ship to transmit the underwater imagery our remotely operated vehicles (ROVs) were collecting through a fiber-optic cable to the ship's command center, and from there, via satellite to shore.

During the intervening years, tele-presence technology has continued to evolve, including the construction of the Inner Space Center at the University of Rhode Island's Graduate School of Oceanography, which serves as the telecommunications hub for the E/V *Nautilus* when it is at sea (fig. 3). It now takes a matter of minutes to access a network of experts in a broad range of disciplines, all of whom are willing to be contacted as soon as a new discovery is made.

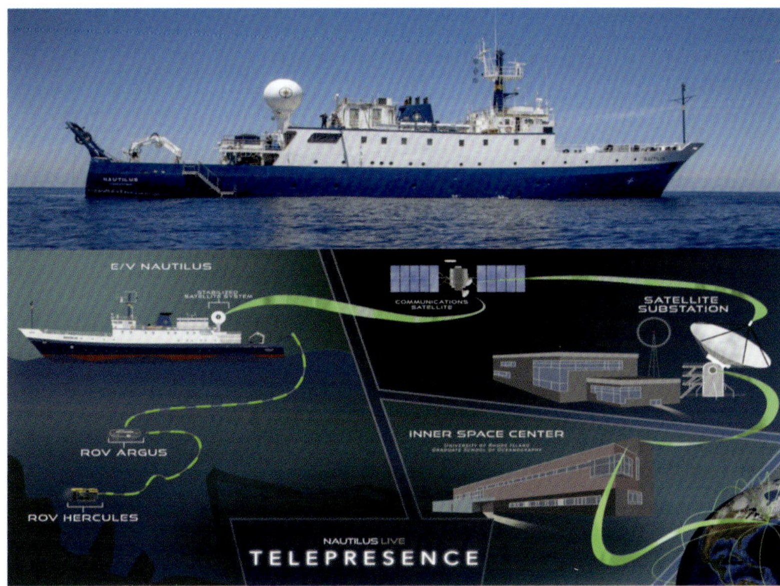

3. E/V *Nautilus* and its satellite link to the shore-based Inner Space Center and from there to the outside world in real time

To make this possible, we initially focused on the development of the ROVs Argus and Hercules, which are deployed on a fiber-optic cable so they can remain on the bottom of the ocean floor for long periods of time, working around the clock for days on end. Most recently we have begun putting additional vehicles in the water at the same time, to expand our exploration footprint. These include an autonomous surface vehicle (ASV) named Dri-x, which can collect high-resolution bathymetric data and also serve as a second "mother ship" to a series of other ASVs (figs. 4, 5).

Once these vehicles are deployed, they can travel long distances away from the E/V *Nautilus* with Dri-x monitoring their work through an acoustical modem and then via a microwave link back to the *Nautilus*. One ASV called Mesobot explores the "twilight layer" or mid-water zone where 40 percent of all marine life in the ocean lives (fig. 5, center). At the same time, another ASV called Sentry (fig. 5, upper right) explores the ocean floor far away from the *Nautilus*. Should any of these vehicles make an important discovery, it can relay what it finds to Dri-x and from there to the command center on the *Nautilus*. The scientists aboard or ashore can review the data and develop a follow-up investigation by Sentry.

As the far as the future is concerned, there will be a greater emphasis placed upon the deployment of multiple autonomous vehicles, much like the military is doing with aerial drones, using "swarming technology" to increase our exploration footprint. Ulti-

mately, exploration will be done with a fleet of crewless surface ships such as Ocean Infinity's *Armada*, now coming online.

One can only imagine what our Corps of Exploration will discover in the four million square miles that make up the "New America," but, just as the Lewis and Clark Expedition changed the economic engine of our nation, so too will this second expedition. More than likely, America's EEZ will become a tapestry like the exploration of the Louisiana Purchase, as America's new blue economy begins to emerge within this submerged landscape, driven by the depletion of our natural resources on land.

Harvard sociobiologist E. O. Wilson predicts that, by 2050, land-based agriculture will no longer be able to feed the world, even if everyone becomes a vegetarian. As the world population grows, the amount of farmland needed to feed it increases, while our cultivation practices lead to further loss of topsoil and our changing climate results in droughts and forest fires worldwide. This will place mounting pressure on the ocean's wild marine life to feed the world. Unfortunately, over 90 percent of all the large fish in the sea are gone due to overfishing. As a result, the hunting of wild fish stocks needs to be replaced by open ocean aquaculture on a global basis.

One unique approach, called the Velella Project (fig. 6), involves taking a highly desired fish called Hamachi or Kona Kampachi, a top predator in tropical reefs, and converting it to a herbivore. The fish are raised in pens ashore then taken out into

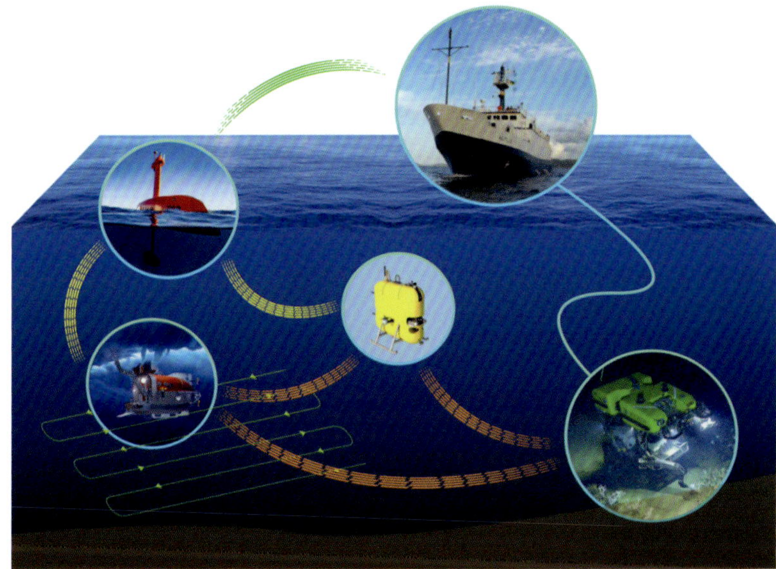

4, 5 (overleaf). The size of *Nautilus*'s exploration "footprint" is increased with the addition of autonomous surface vehicles (ASVs) as well as autonomous underwater vehicles (AUVs) operating at the same time

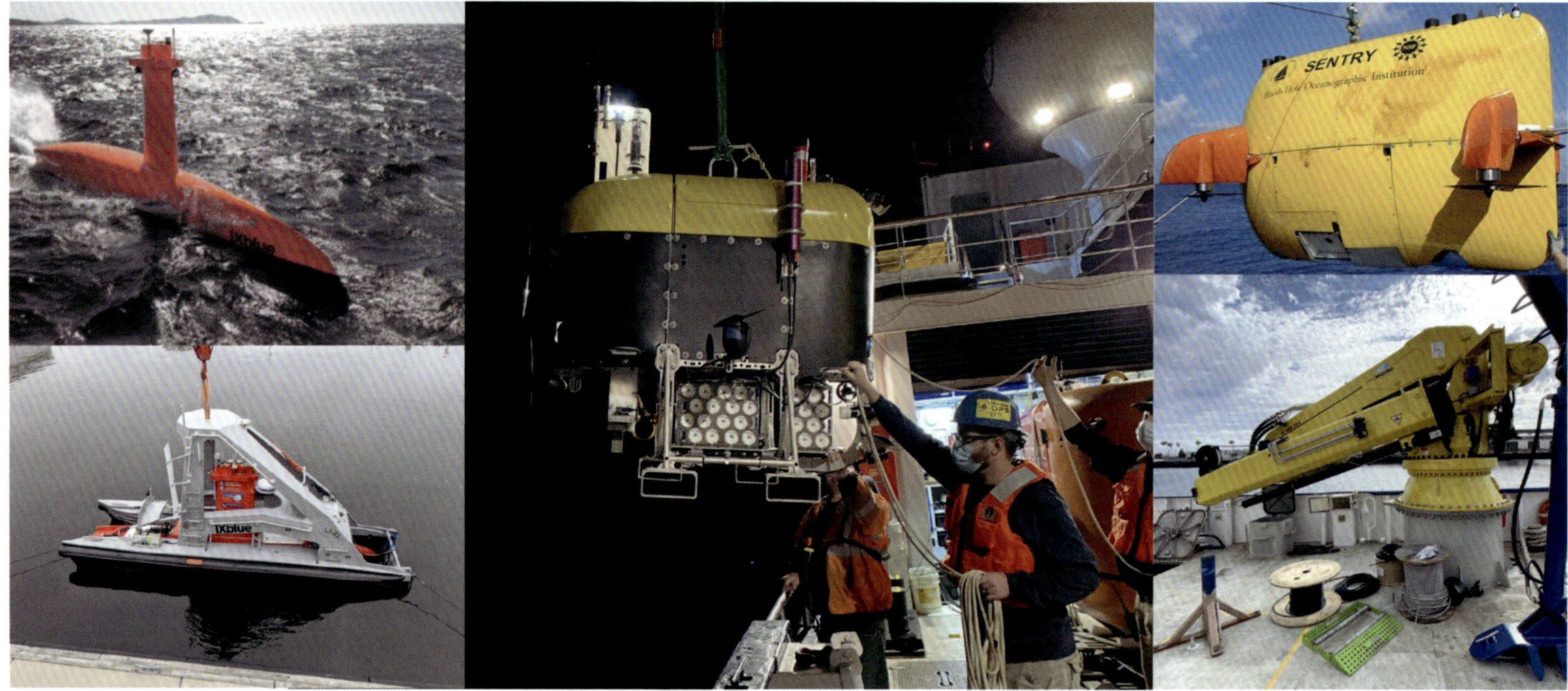

5.

deep water in the tropics and placed in floating cages deep enough to avoid posing a navigational hazard to passing ships.

The cages have remotely controlled flotation units which can raise the cage back to the surface where the fish are fed soybean as well as algal pellets. Equally important, the cages are placed in rotating eddies on the down current side of the Big Island of Hawaii, so they don't wander further out to sea. They are placed in 12,000 feet of water so any waste the fish generate falls to great depths, resulting in carbon sequestration. The fish come to market after five months. Such open ocean aquaculture can be done in many parts of the world and will take the pressure off wild species, which are so heavily overfished.

Another aspect of the future blue economy will be the expansion of marine protected areas in our EEZ that act as nurseries for wild species, further expanding tourism for scuba divers. These marine sanctuaries also include our Great Lakes, which contain numerous lost chapters of human history.

One very controversial aspect of the blue economy is the subject of deep-sea mining, which must be taken very seriously. There are three classes of mineral deposits that are of particular interest: manganese nodules of the abyssal plains of the Pacific; polymetallic sulfide deposits created by high-temperature "black smokers" along the axis of the mid-ocean ridge; and cobalt-rich crusts that, over time, precipitate out of the water column on exposed hard-rock surfaces, in particular the thousands of undersea seamounts in the Western Pacific, many of which are located within America's EEZ.

A major concern of scientists is the impact mining operations could have on ecosystems on the ocean floor and throughout the entire water column, since the various extraction methods being proposed involve resuspending vast amounts of the bottom sediment into the water column. This could have a significant negative impact on marine organisms, especially those species that are filter feeders living at the base of the ocean food chain. Several countries, including Russia and China, have applied to the United Nation's International Seabed Authority for permission to mine polymetallic nodules in the Clarion-Clipperton Fracture Zone in the Central Pacific—this before we really understand the environmental impact such mining could have. America's exploration of its EEZ has also resulted in the discovery of thousands of methane seeps along the continental margins of the East, West, and Gulf Coasts. The Defense Department recently funded a research program to convert the methane coming out of these seeps into electrical energy.

When I was growing up, I never missed a single episode of *The Underwater World of Jacques Cousteau* and I was fascinated by Cousteau's Conshelf projects—attempts to live for long periods of time beneath the sea. These were followed by a US Navy program called SEALAB, in which teams of divers perfected the science of "saturation diving." Dr. George Bond discovered that when you dive underwater your blood accumulates gases within the bloodstream, requiring you to "decompress" as you return to the surface. Pausing several times during your ascent—taking "decompression stops"—allowed your body to slowly release the gas within the bloodstream. If you come up too fast, gas bubbles follow in your bloodstream and accumulate in your joints, causing decompression sickness ("the bends"), which is extremely painful and can be fatal.

The deeper you go and the longer you stay at that depth, the longer it takes to "decompress" on the way back to the surface. But Dr. Bond also discovered that at some point your bloodstream becomes saturated with gas and your decompression "penalty" becomes constant, no matter how much longer you remain underwater. So, if you live underwater, you can work during the day, live in an underwater habitat at night, and go back to work the next day. This makes it possible for you to continue working until your task is complete and then you only have to pay your decompression penalty once when you return to the surface.

This led others to begin dreaming about creating underwater cities of the future. Unfortunately, seawater is highly corrosive and marine life quickly begins to grow on everything, requiring constant maintenance. The high costs of living underwater have made living in or on the ocean impossible on any large scale. What we need to be thinking about is not living *in* the ocean but living *with* the ocean as it begins to take over our world on land.

Global warming is a fact. If all the ice sheets and glaciers on Earth melt and the water flows back into the sea, sea level will rise 195 feet or 60 meters, adding another 5 percent of the earth's surface to the sea, making the sea 75 percent of the total surface area of Earth. This won't happen overnight, but most of Earth's ice will melt in less than eighty years, so we need to plan accordingly.

Getting the word out to the general public in creative and engaging ways—like the *Oceanus* project—is key to raising awareness. Likewise, linking people with science and exploration of the deep sea through robust virtual programming, live feeds, and beautiful images via organizations like Ocean Exploration Cooperative Institute, inspires fascination and connection. As Jacques Cousteau once said, "People protect what they love. A lot of people attack the sea, I make love to it."

1. Douglas Brinkley, quoted in Joseph A. Harriss, "How the Louisiana Purchase Changed the World," *Smithsonian Magazine*, April 2003, https://www.smithsonianmag.com/history/how-the-louisiana-purchase-changed-the-world-79715124/.

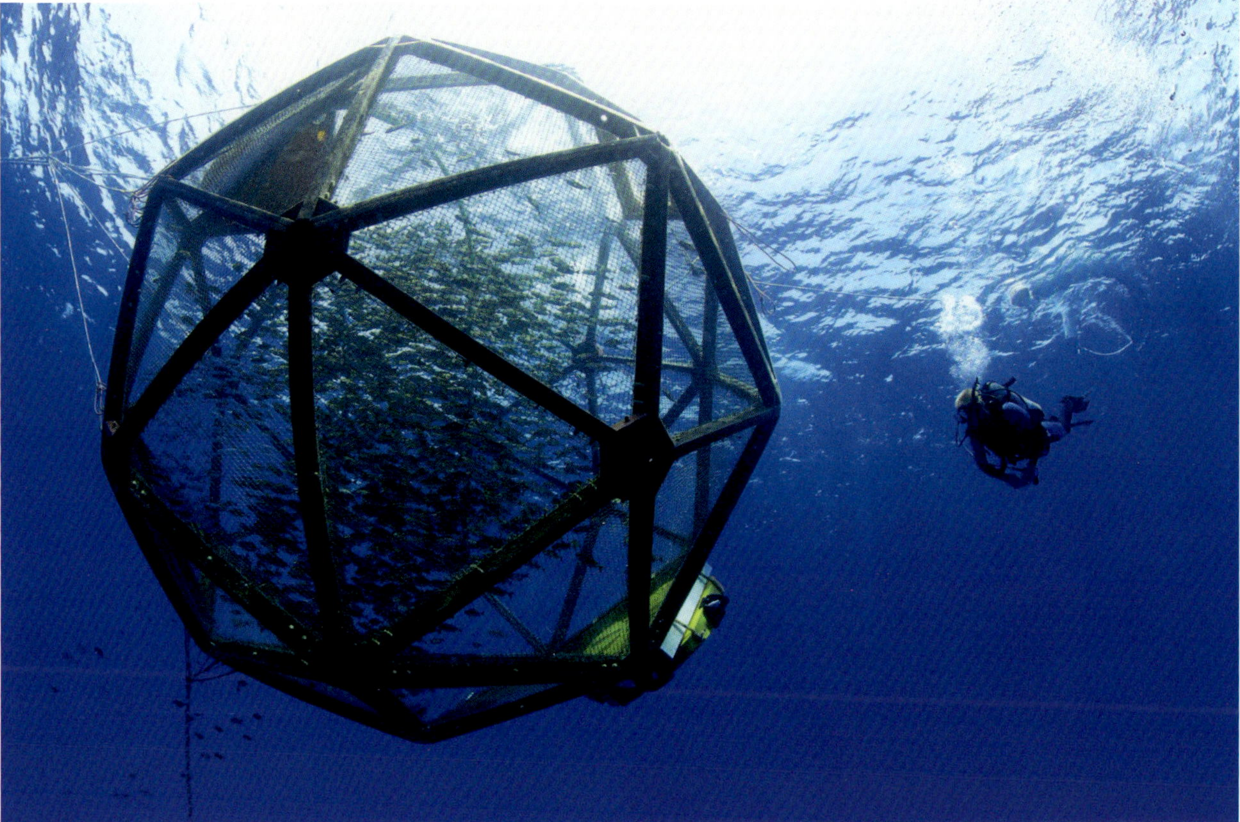

6. The Velella Project aquapods turn top predators into herbivores

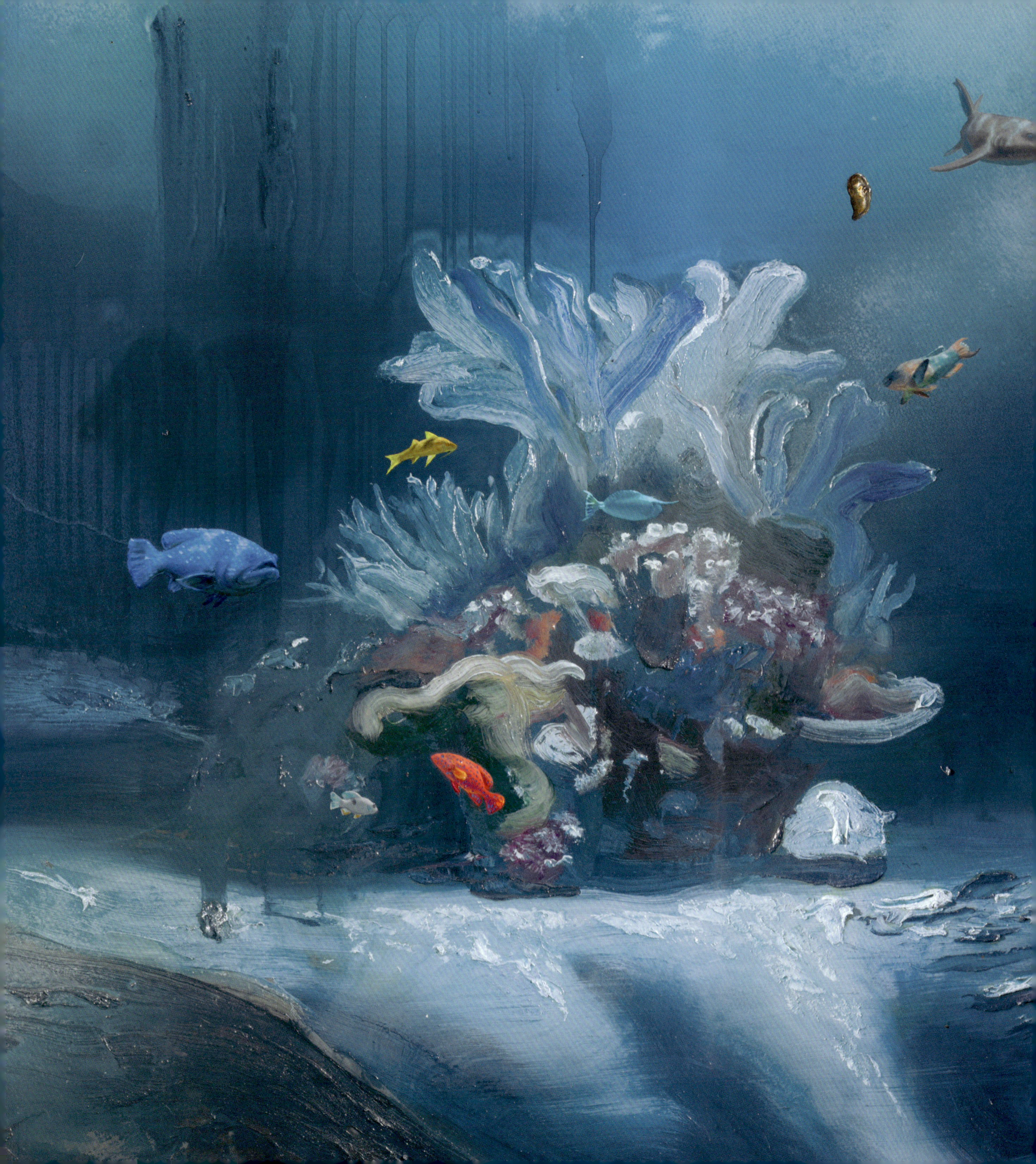

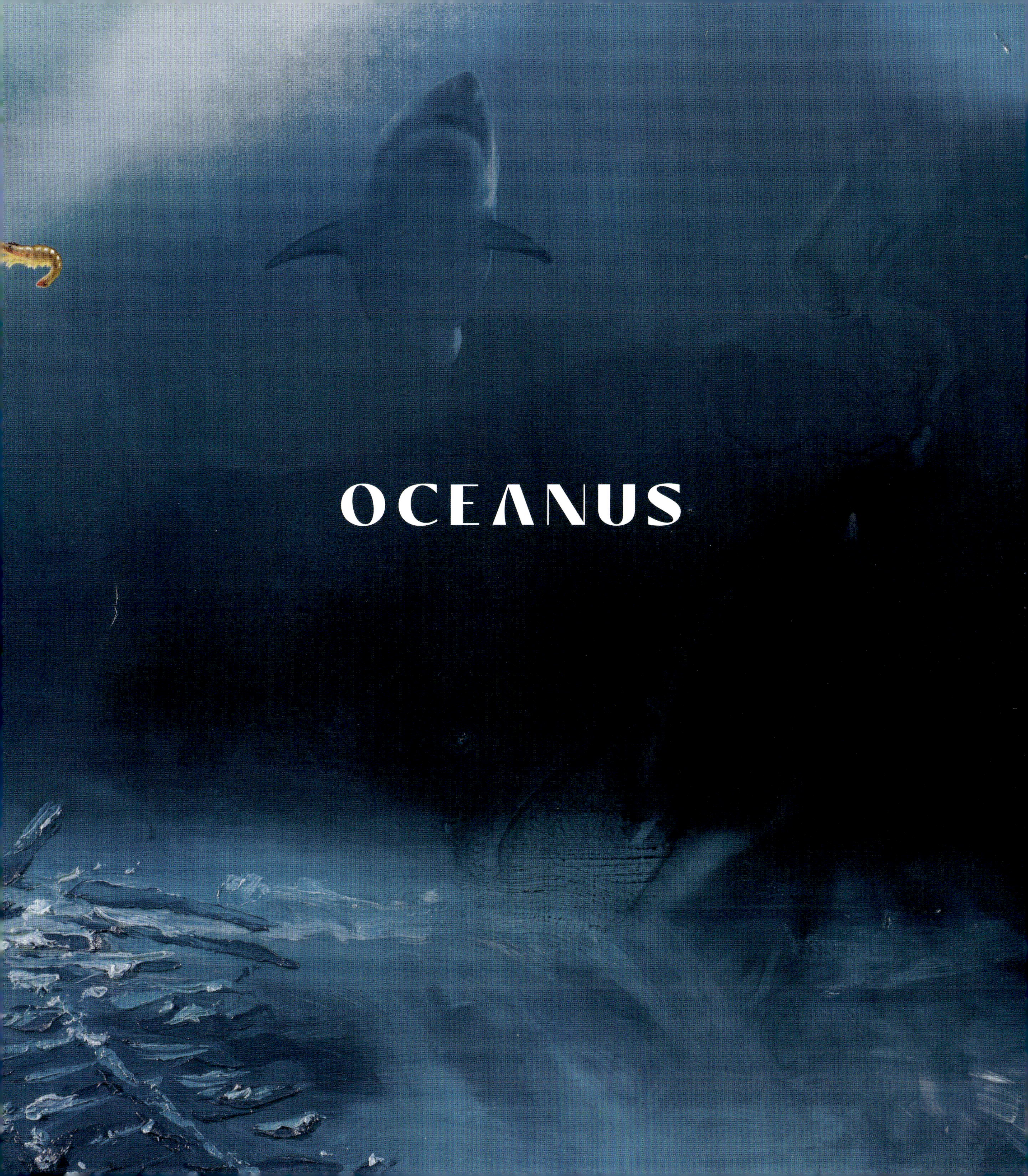
OCEANUS

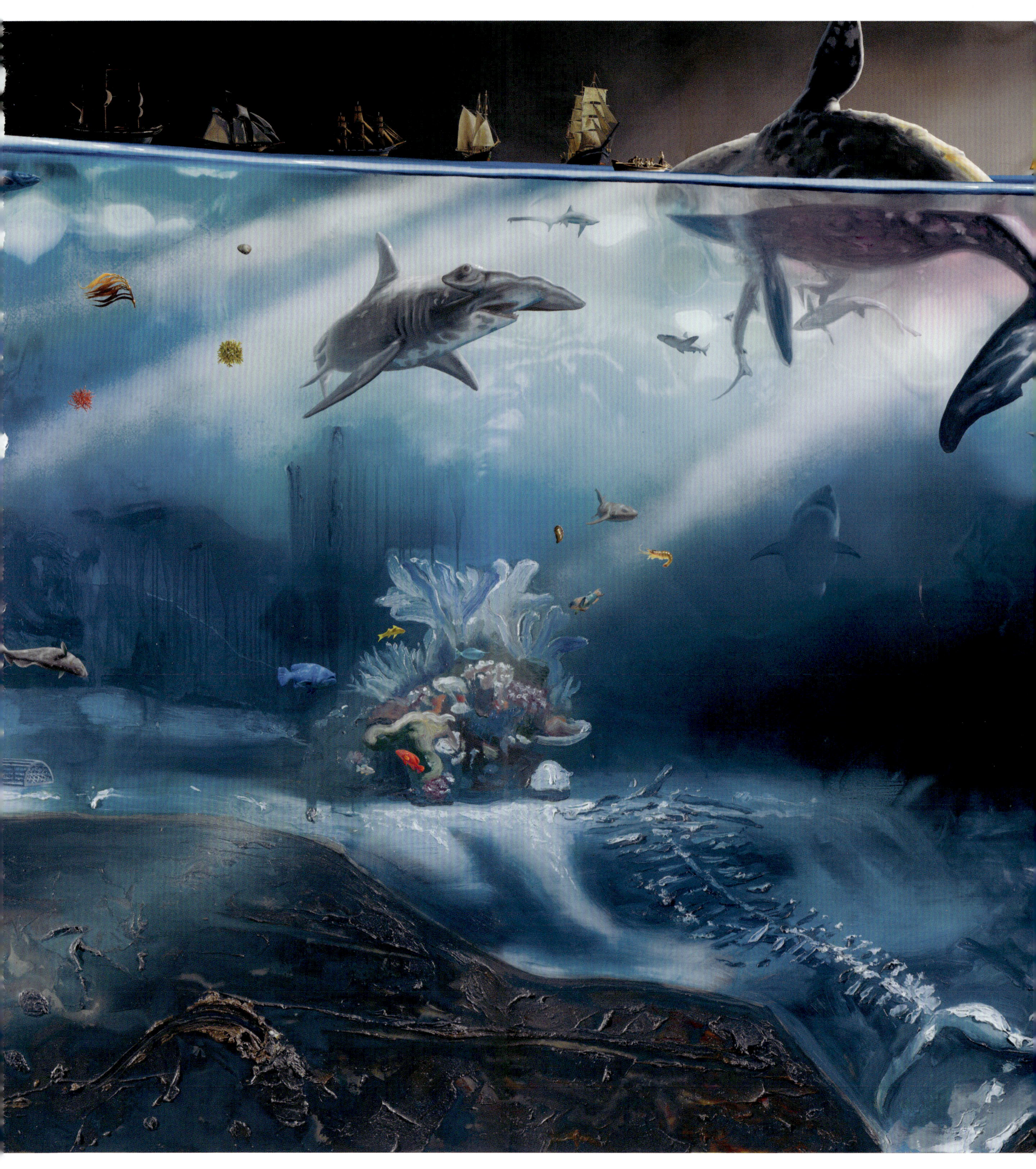

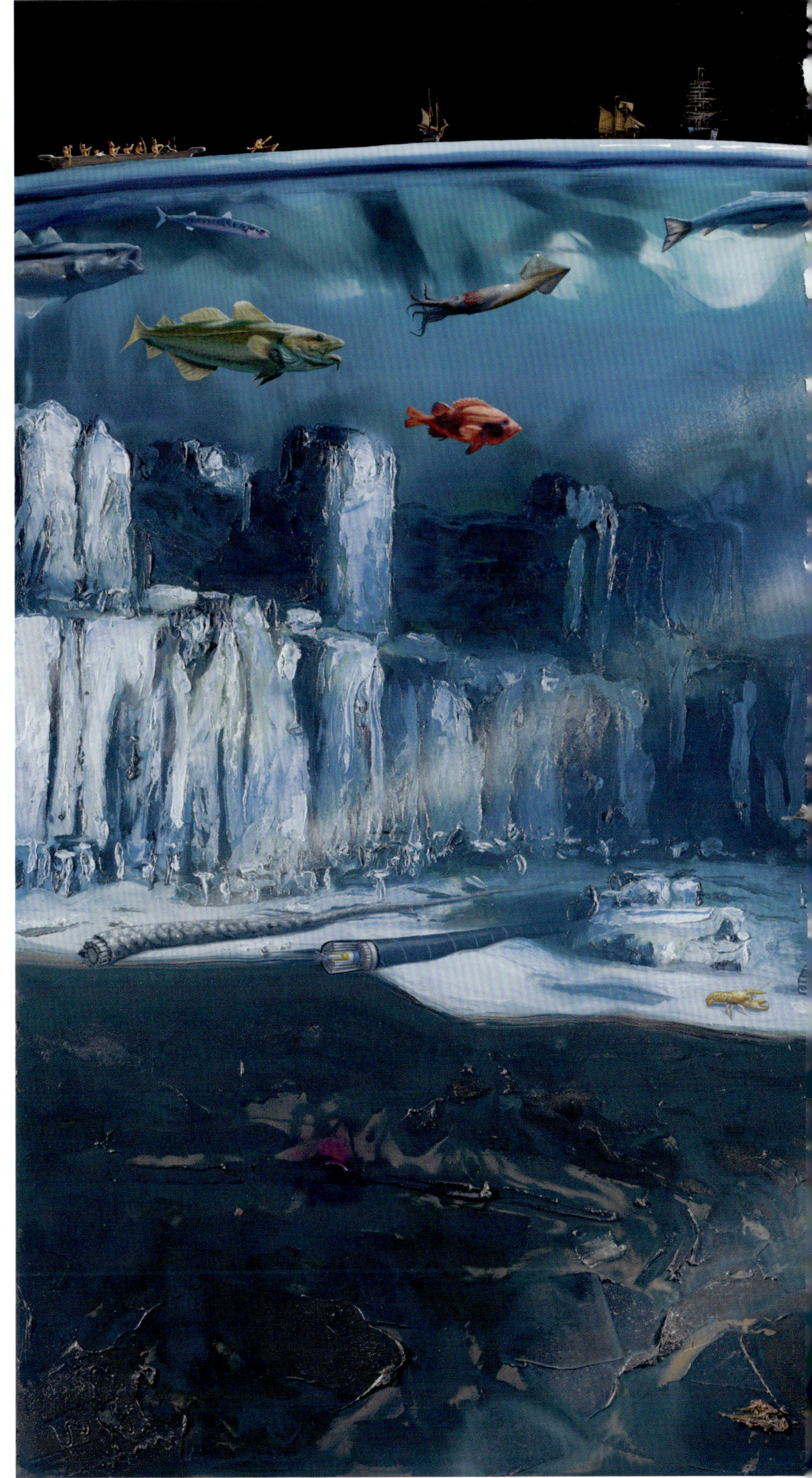

OCEANUS

Oceanus is a history painting that juggles many paradoxes—describing the vastness of our many oceans and what was its incredibly rich biodiversity and humans' complex and mixed relationship to it.

The work examines our collective maritime heritage through the lens of the Watercraft Collection at Mystic Seaport Museum and the related industries and activities—fishing and whaling—that are associated with the exploitation of natural resources, as well as the transportation of goods, human migration and slavery, invasive marine species, pollution, the biodiversity crisis, extinction, and climate change—the most pressing issues of our time.

As a painting *Oceanus* synthesizes aspects of multiple pictorial genres that aren't often seen together: visceral, Ab Ex–like intuitive painting; poured paint; maritime genre ship painting; and natural history illustration. Through this combination, the painting tells a unique and mysterious story of humankind's indelible relationship with the ocean and the connections between the sea and our own survival. The painting evokes many simultaneous perspectives of the world, both above and below the waterline. Viewed on the surface of the water are twenty-one vessels, sixteen of which are based on models in the MSM collection, organized in chronological order to create a timeline for exploring complex stories that aren't often privileged in the Western and human-centric versions of history, including non-homocentric views through the lens of ecology and our impacts on the open ocean, coasts, islands, reefs, and the deepest parts of the ocean. Virtually all ocean habitats have been affected in some ways by mining, dredging, pollution, and overfishing.

Oceanus takes us on a global journey of discovery beneath the world's changing seas, weaving natural history, archeology, adventure, political analysis, and science into a story about the ocean and the human condition.

—Alexis Rockman

Oceanus, 2022. Oil and cold wax on Dibond on aluminum substrate, 95¾ × 282 inches (243.2 × 716.3 cm)

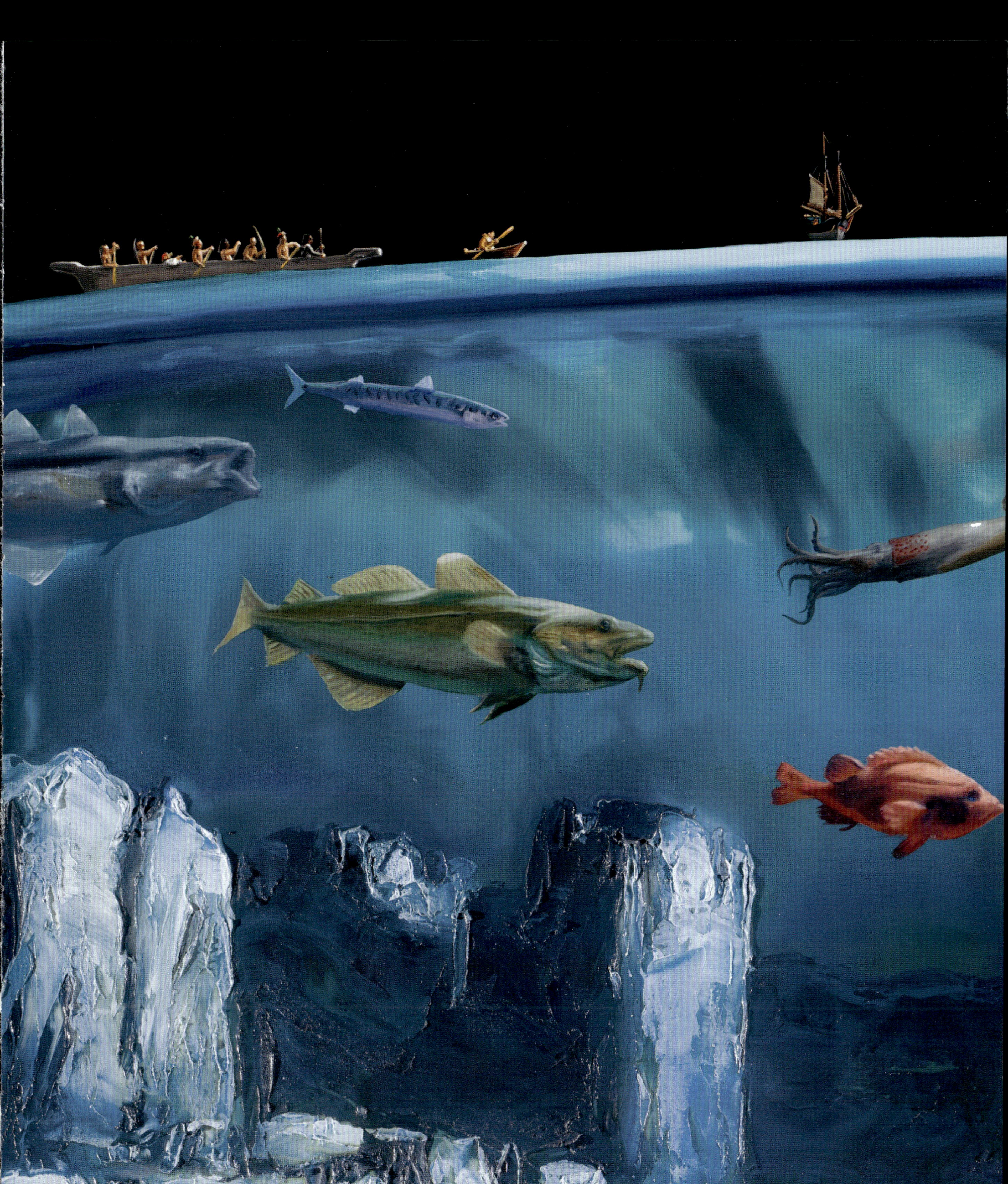

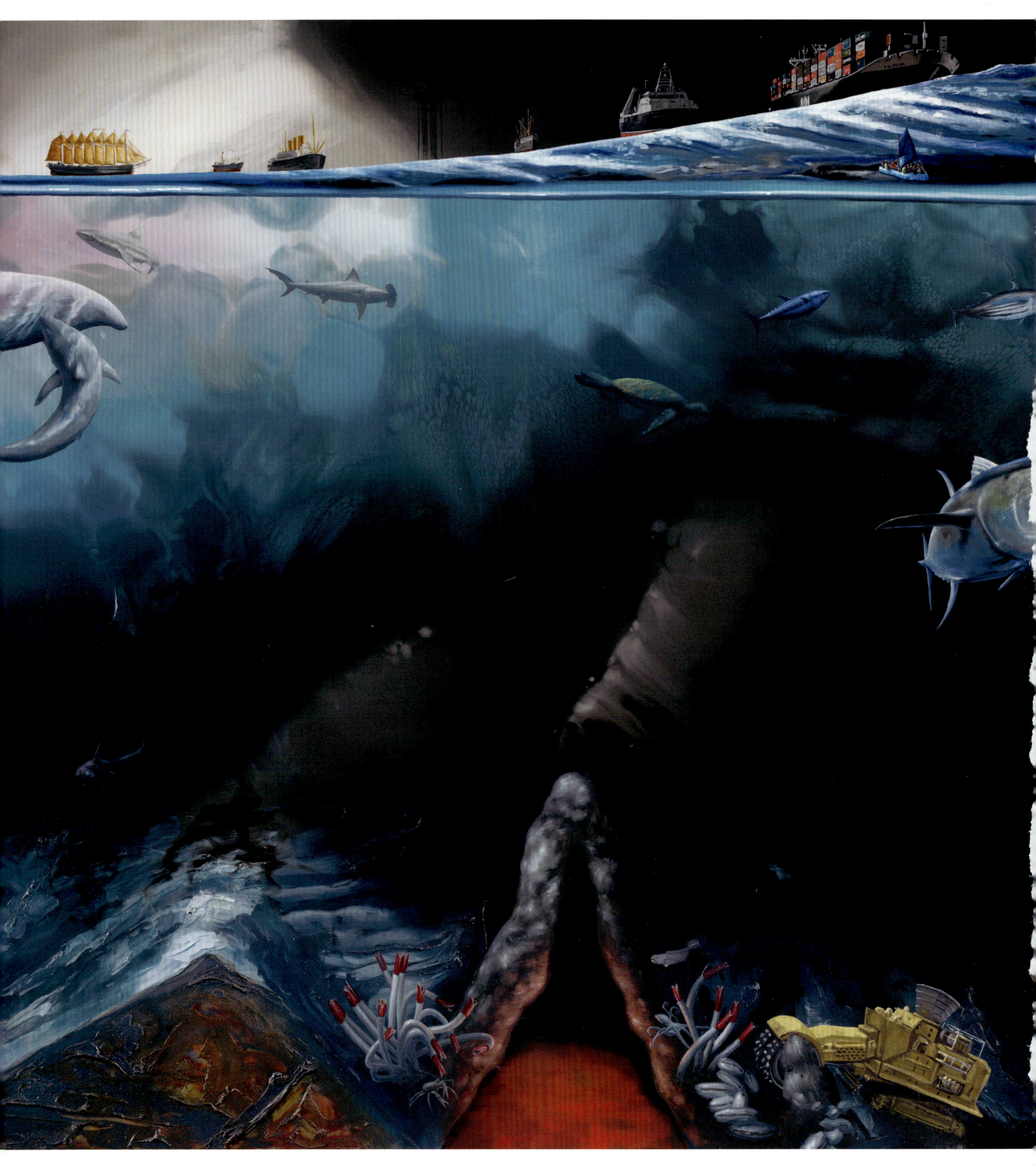

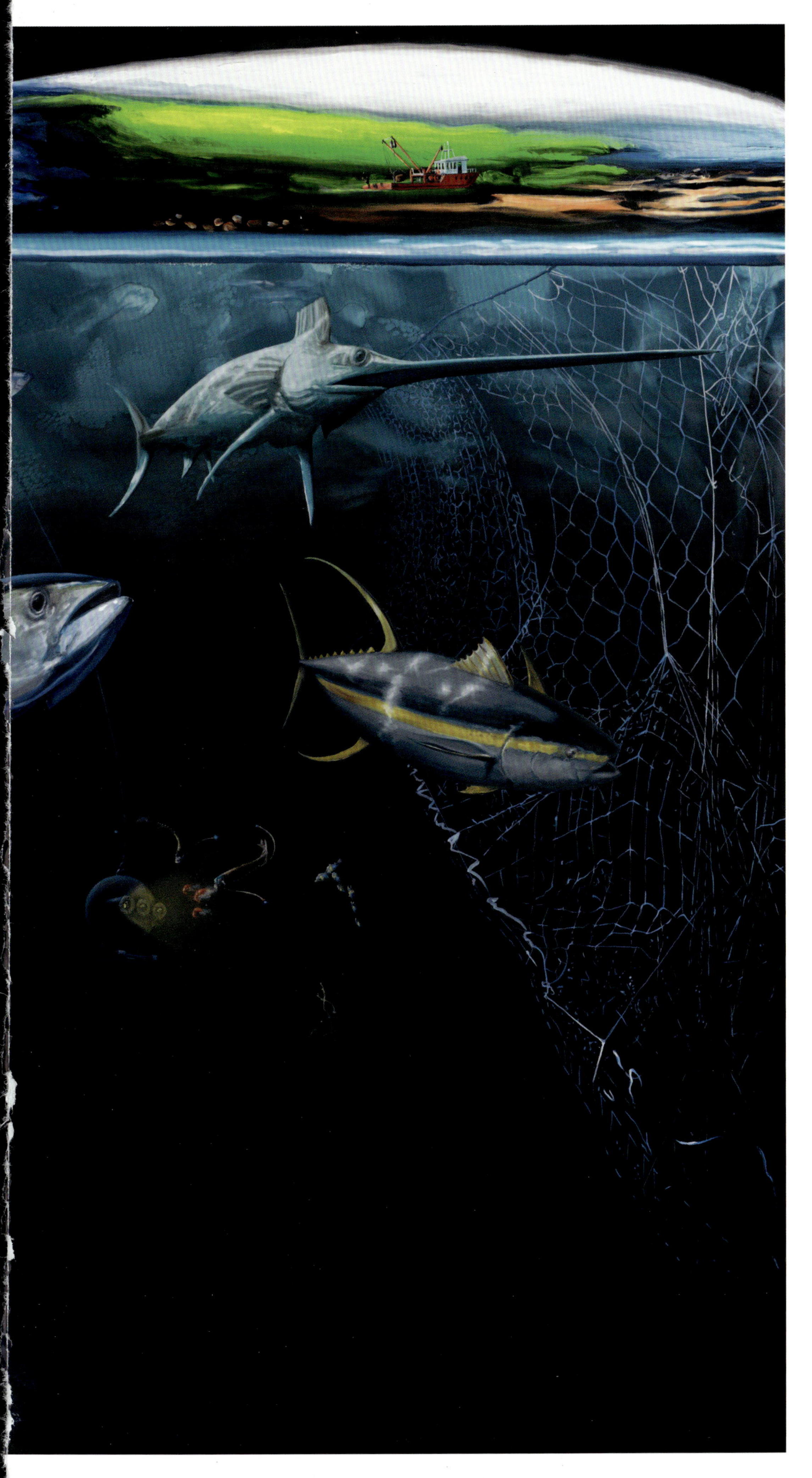

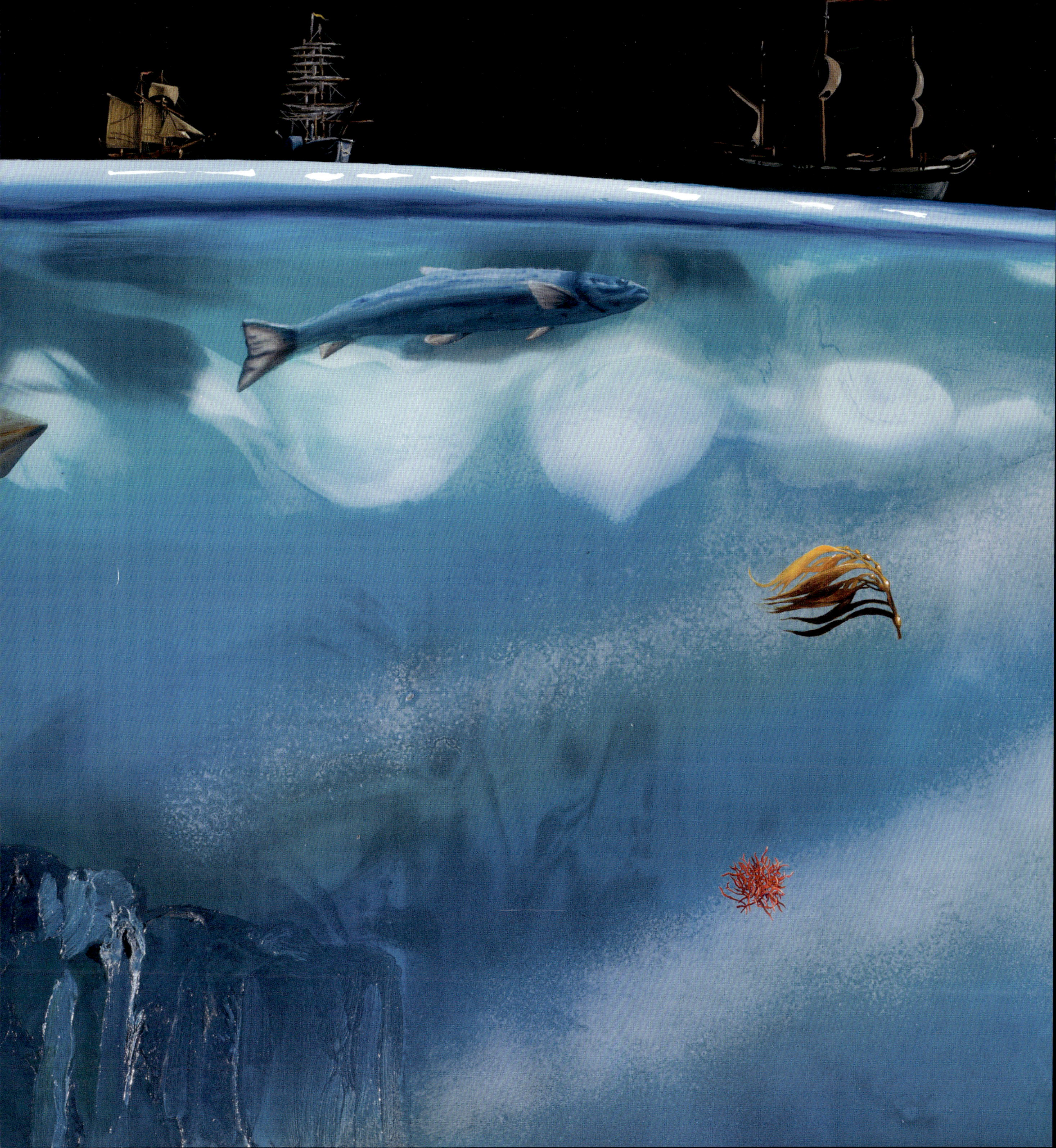

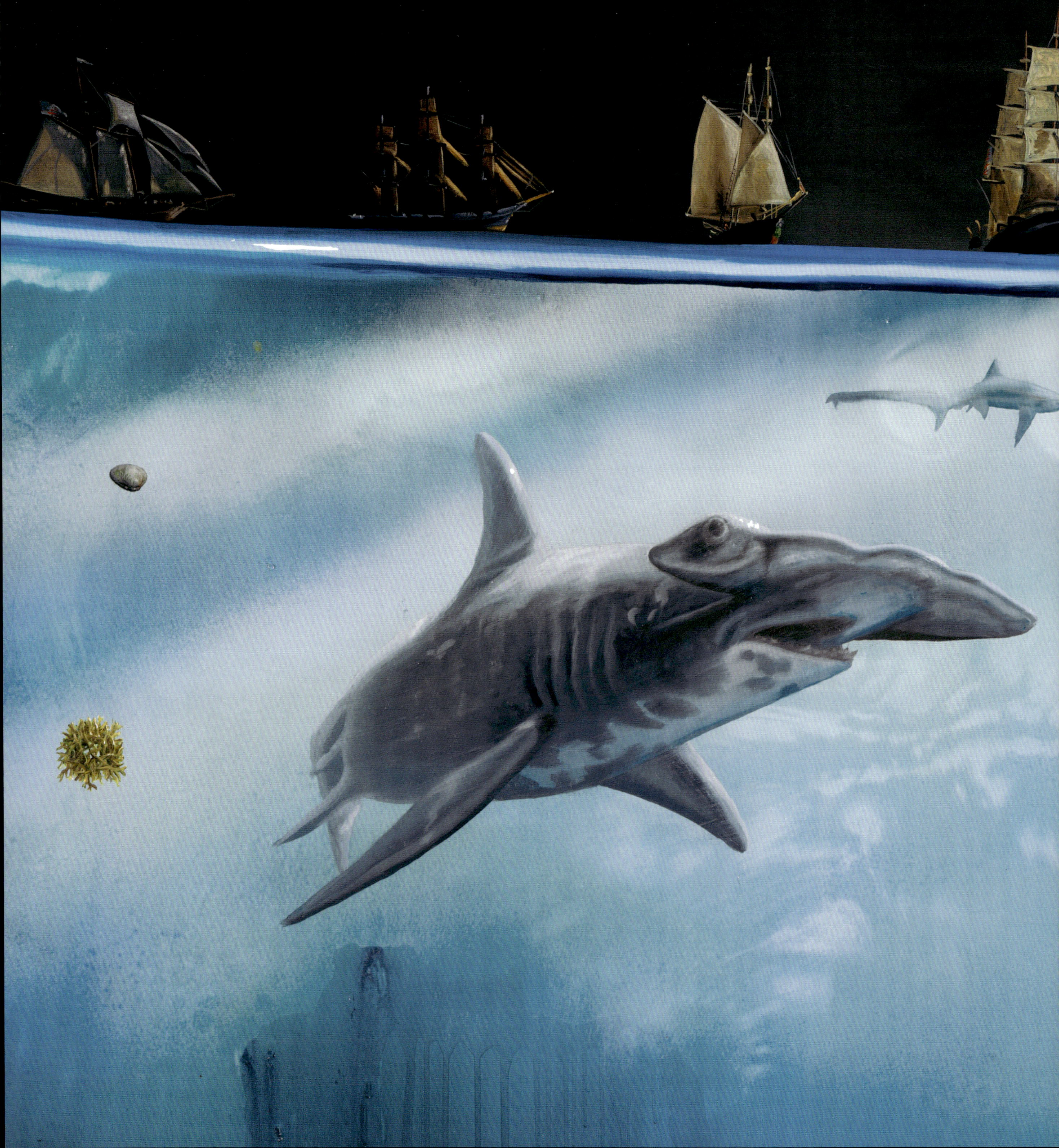

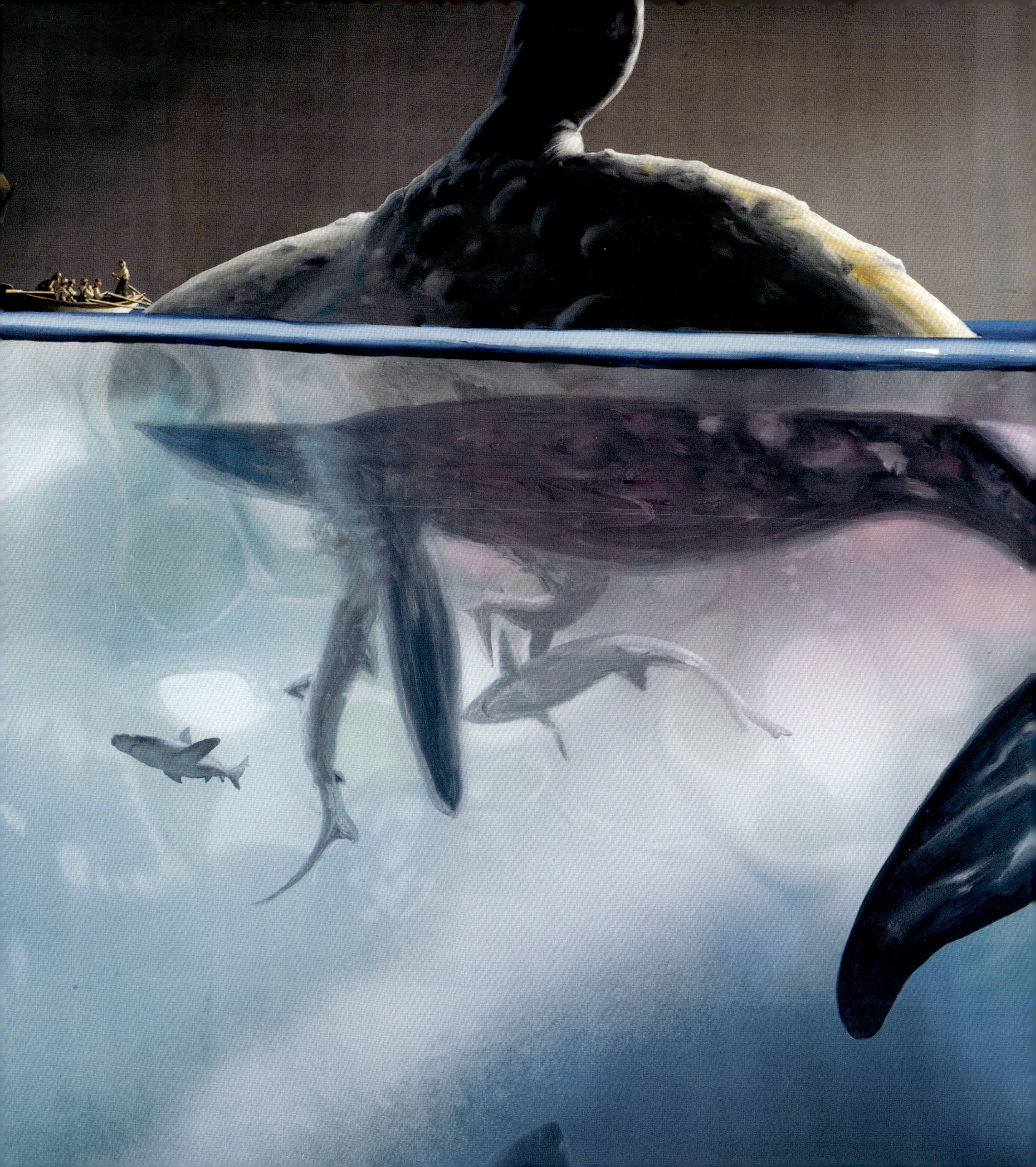

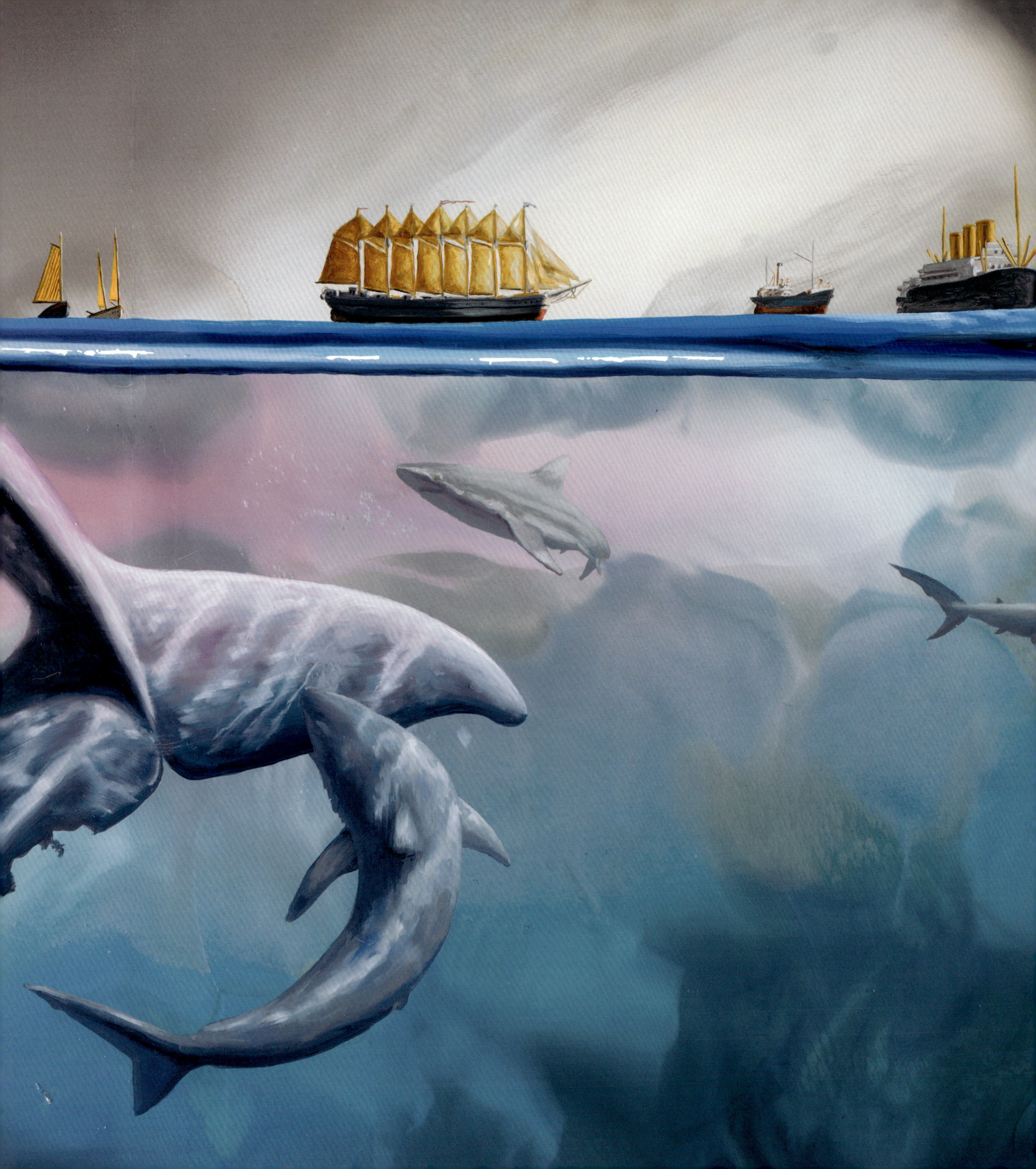

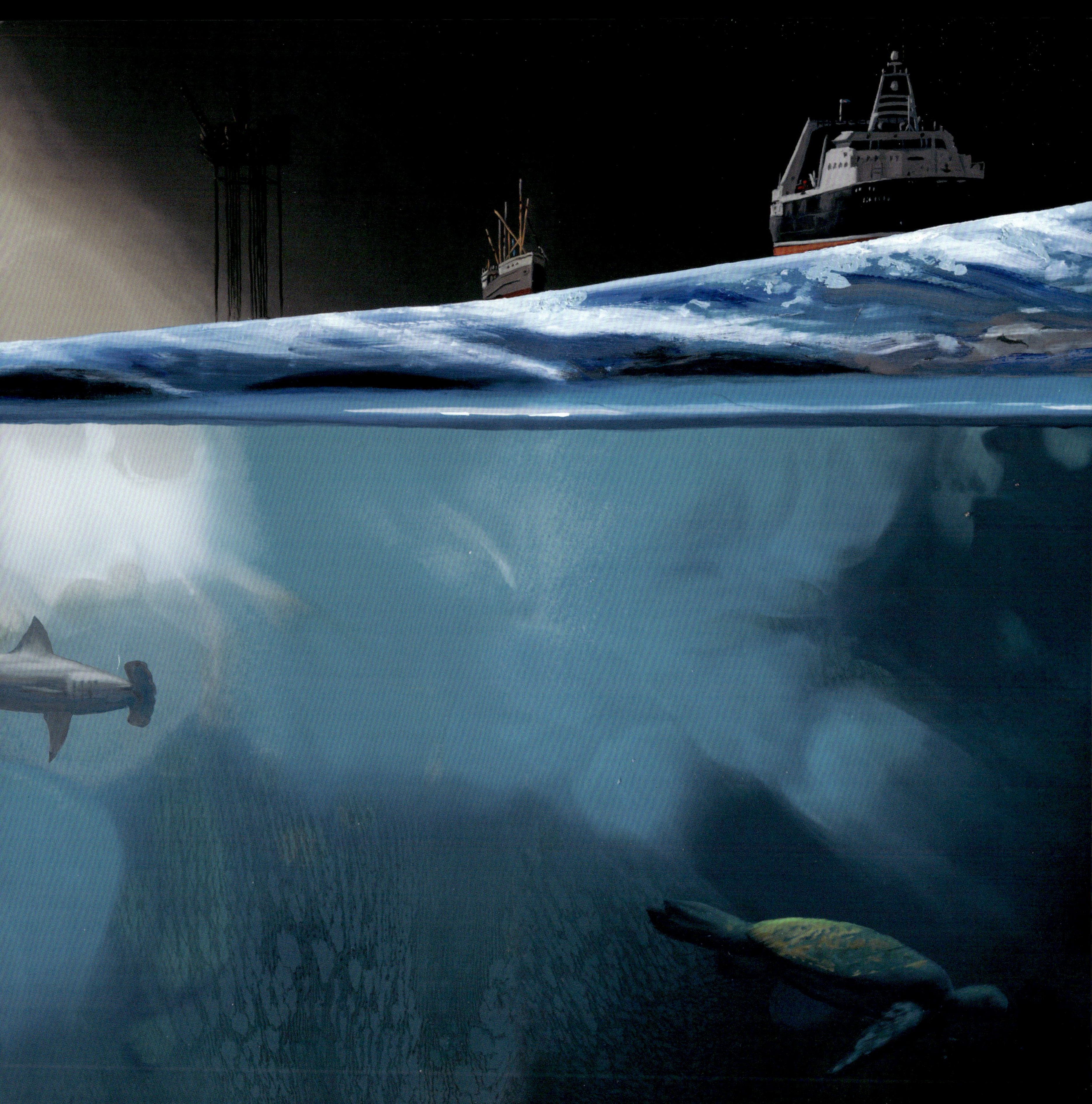

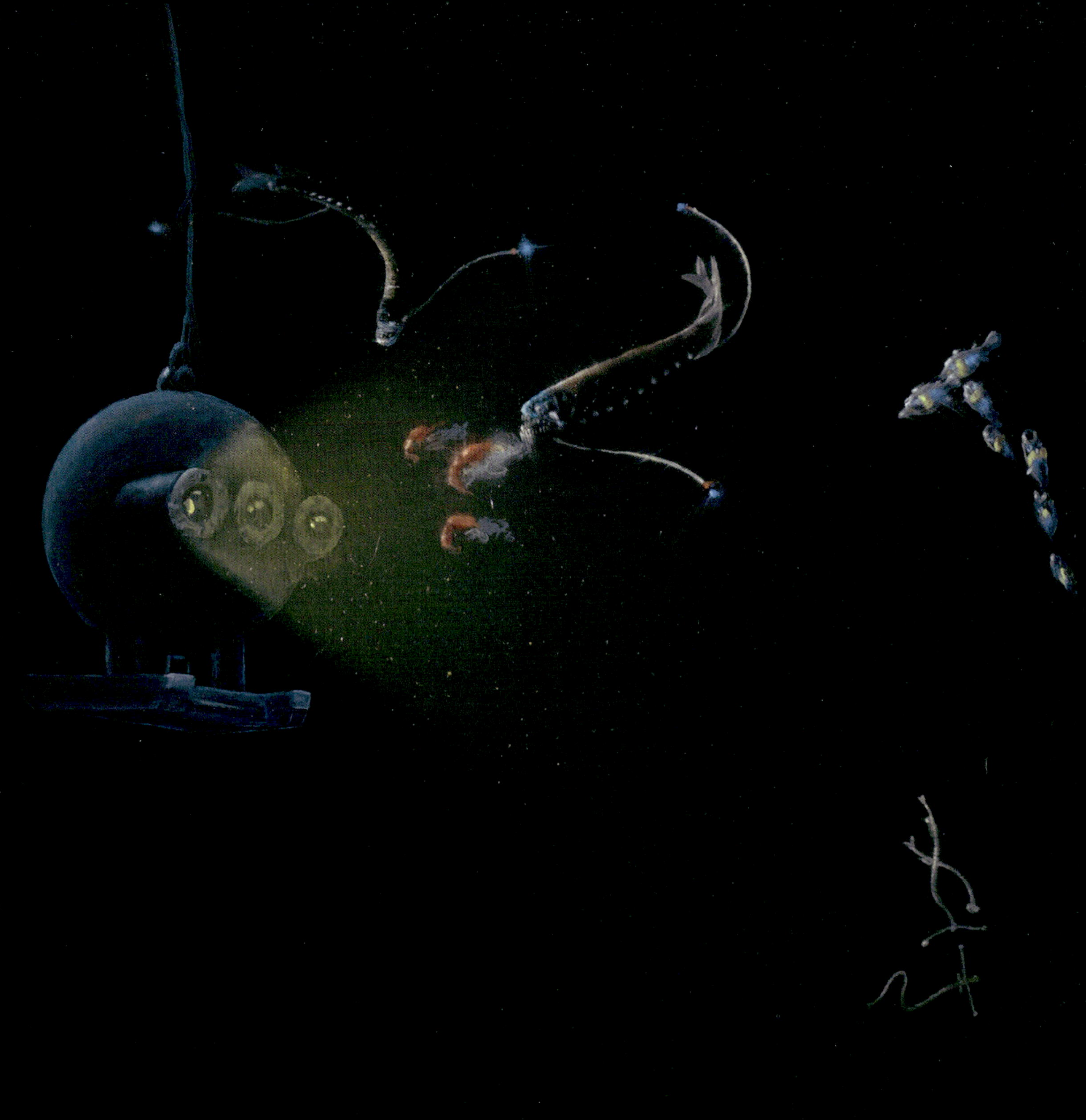

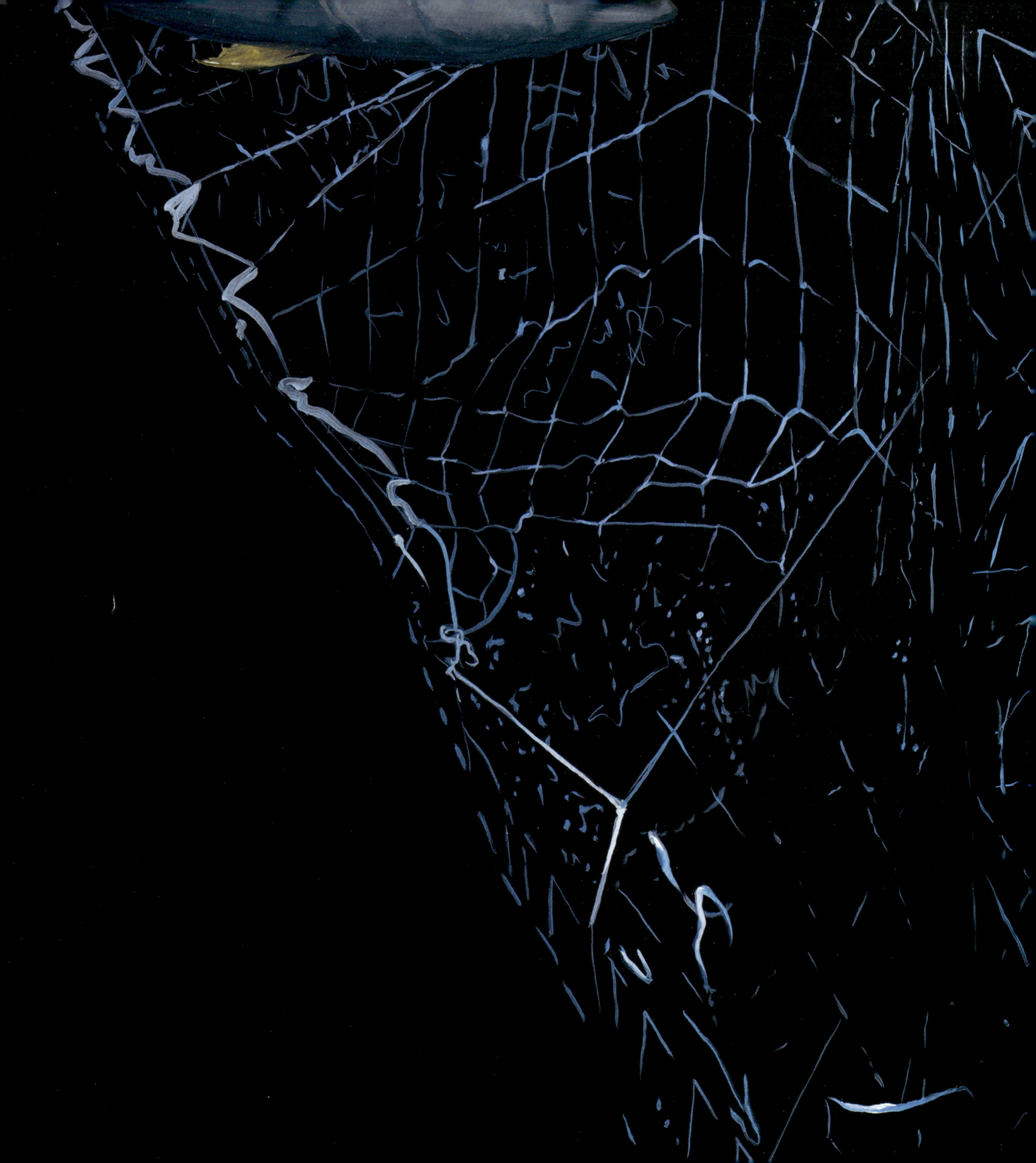

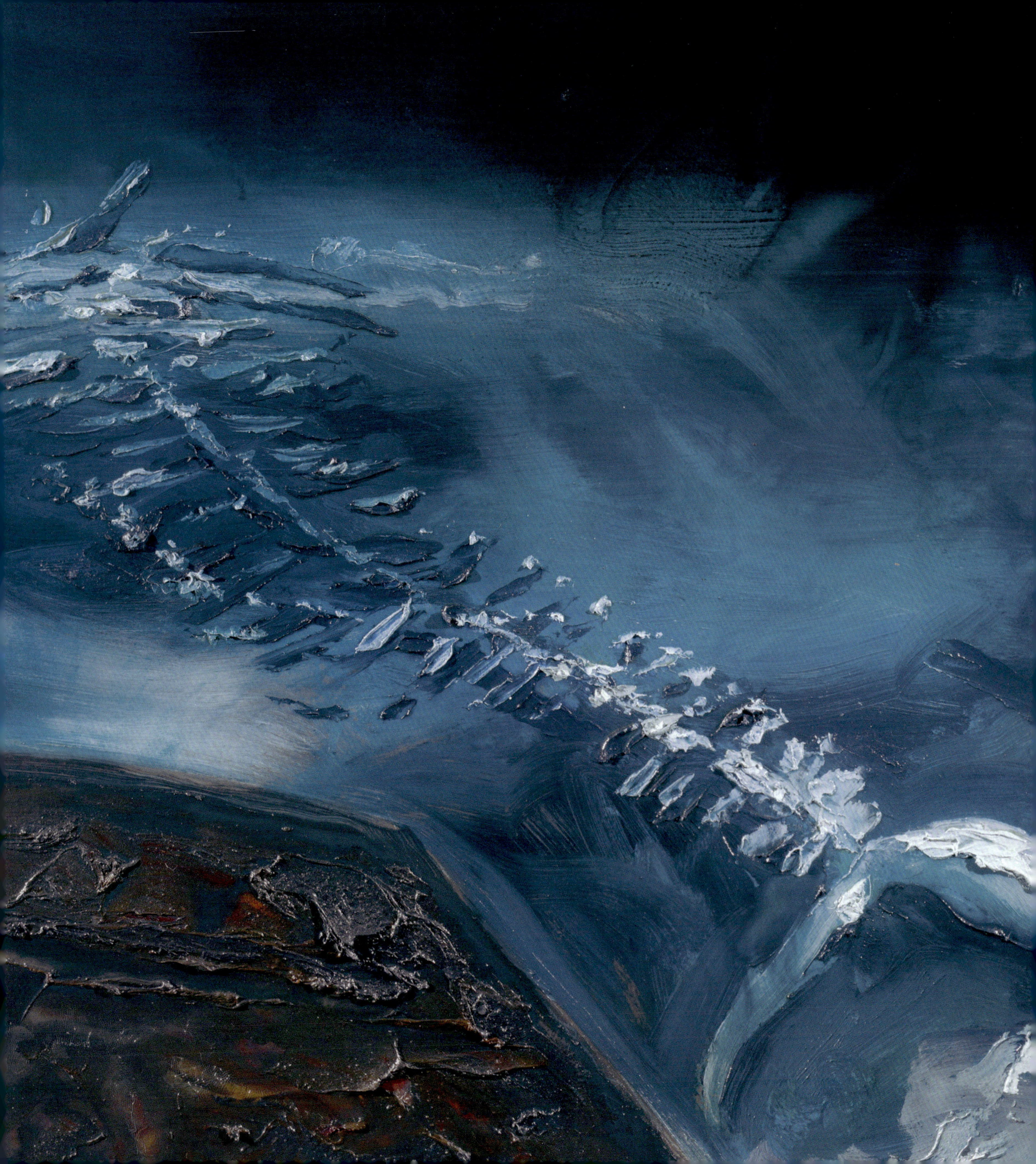

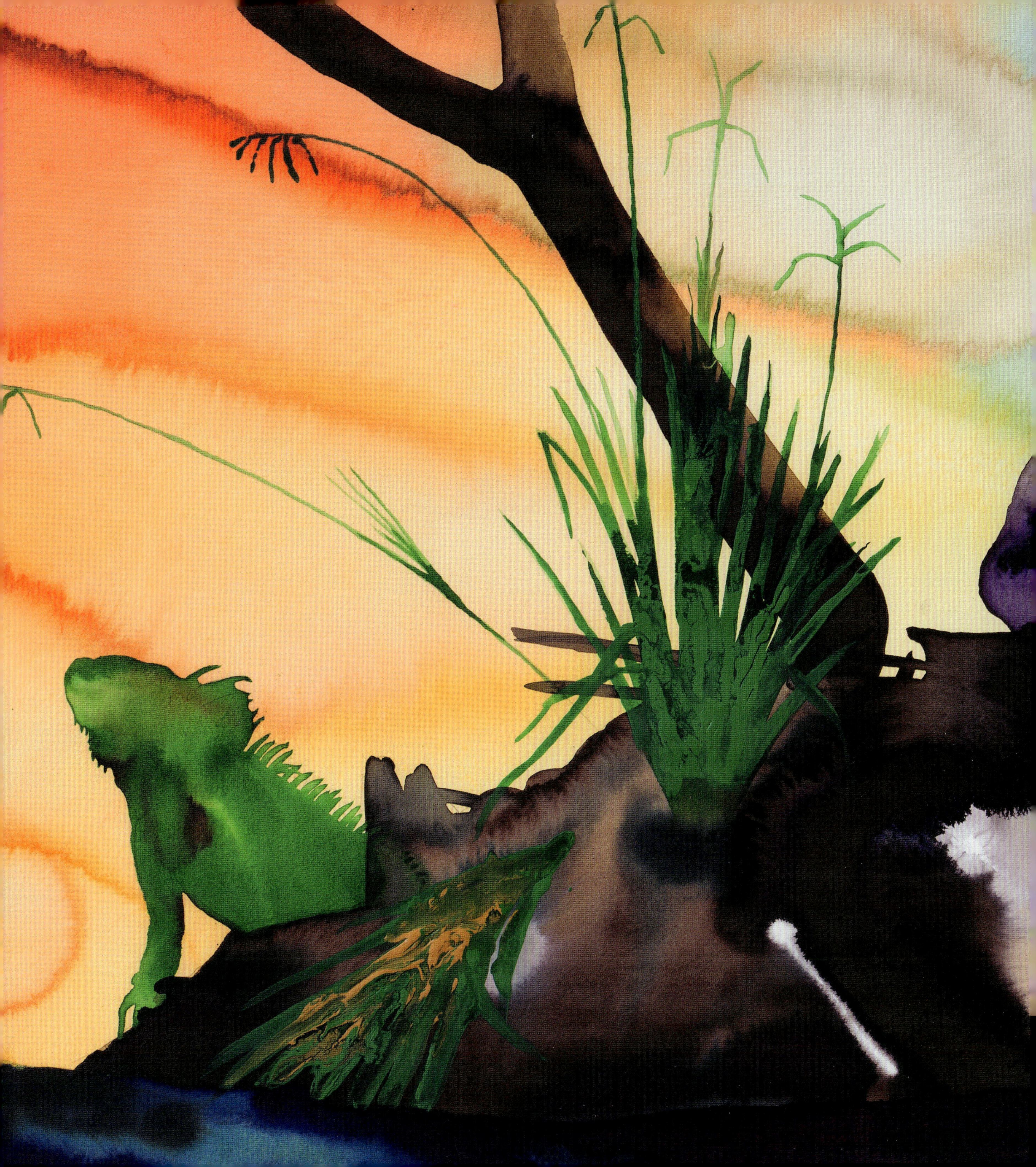

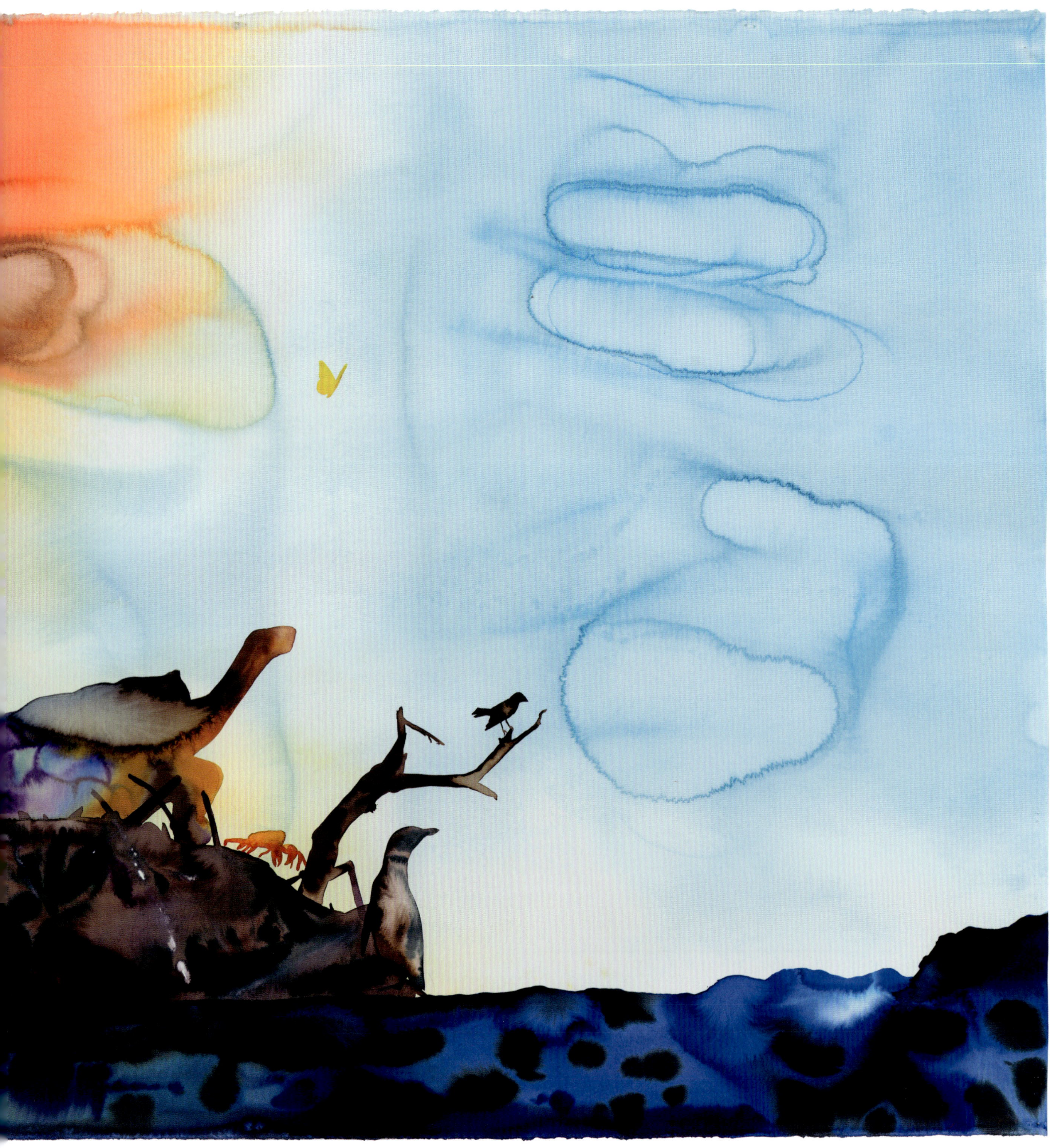

RAFTING THE HUMBOLDT CURRENT

The miraculous biodiversity of remote volcanic islands usually
has a common origin—the "rafting" of species from a distant
mainland. In *Rafting the Humboldt Current*, a group of hopeful-
type specimens including a tortoise, finch, penguin, booby, and
an iguana float on an immigrant's raft of debris, blown out to
sea from the South American mainland to Galápagos. This scenario describes the likely method by which plants and animals
find ways to colonize newly available habitat, in this case the
Galápagos Islands, a series of volcanic archipelagos, probably no
more than five million years old. Not unlike an animal immigrant version of Emanuel Leutze's triumphal 1851 painting
Washington Crossing the Delaware, and perhaps more than the
other watercolors in this series, this work has a romantic, cine-
matic, and narrative feel as these individuals look off toward
their bright future.

—AR

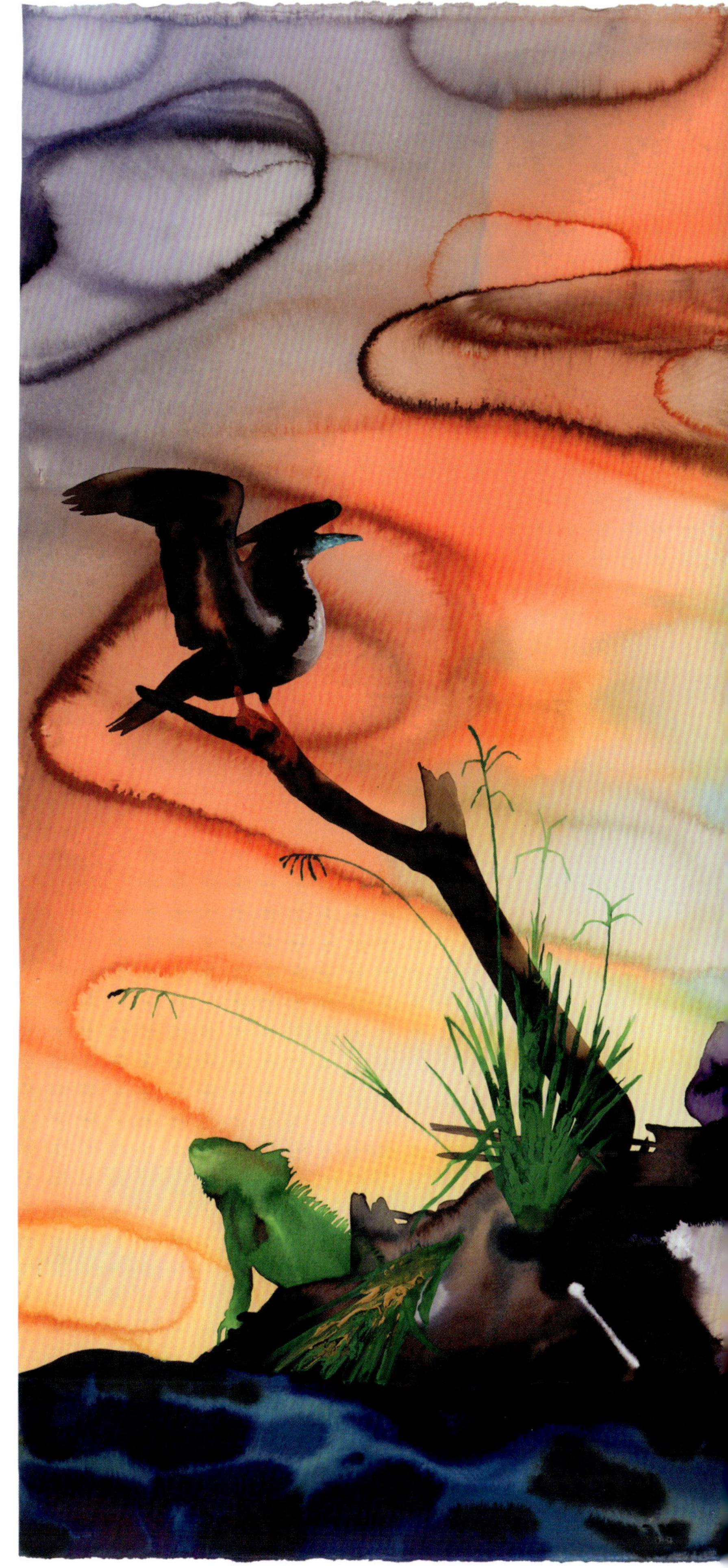

Rafting the Humboldt Current, 2022. Watercolor and acrylic
on paper, 52 × 74½ inches (132.1 × 189.2 cm)

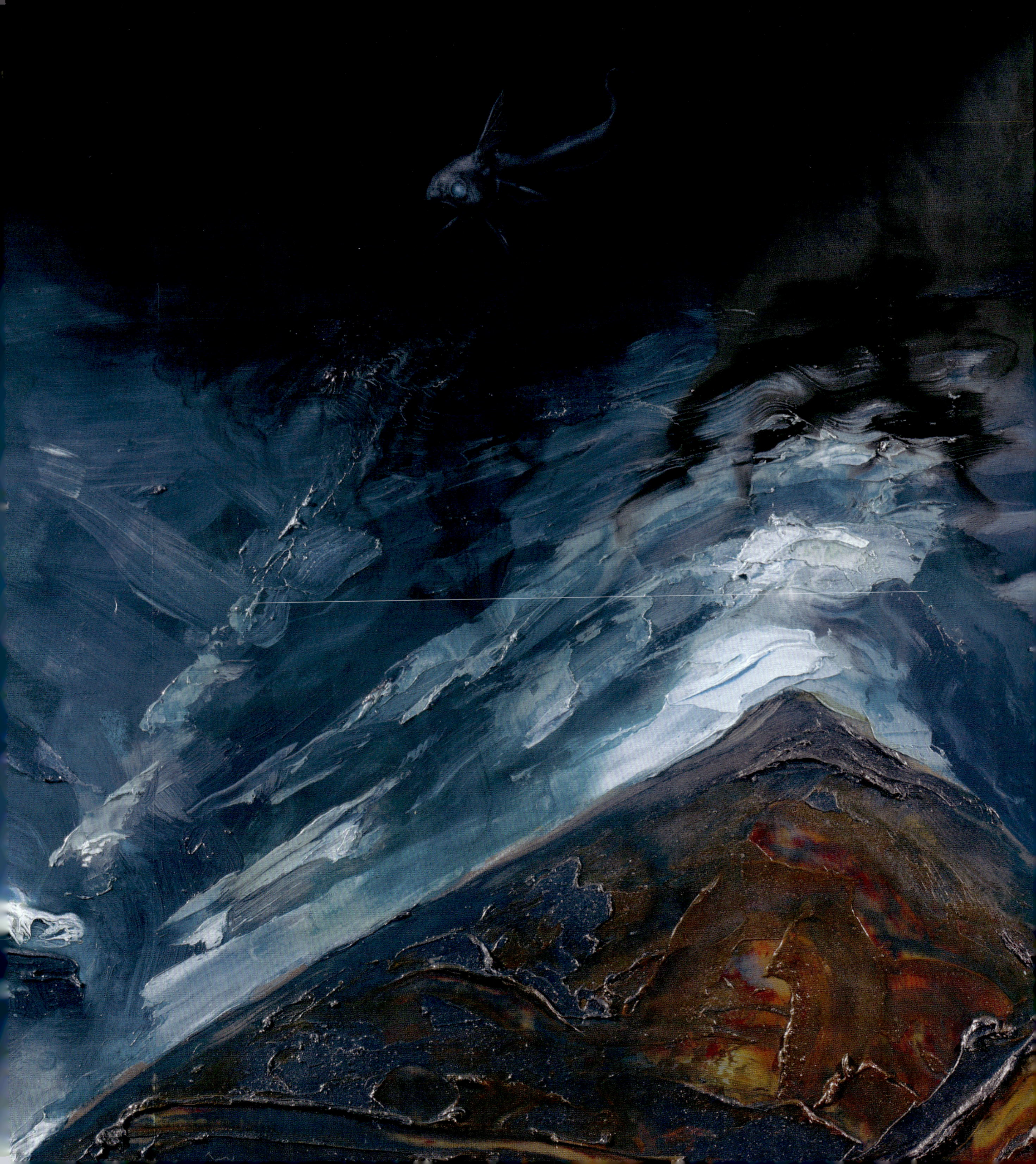

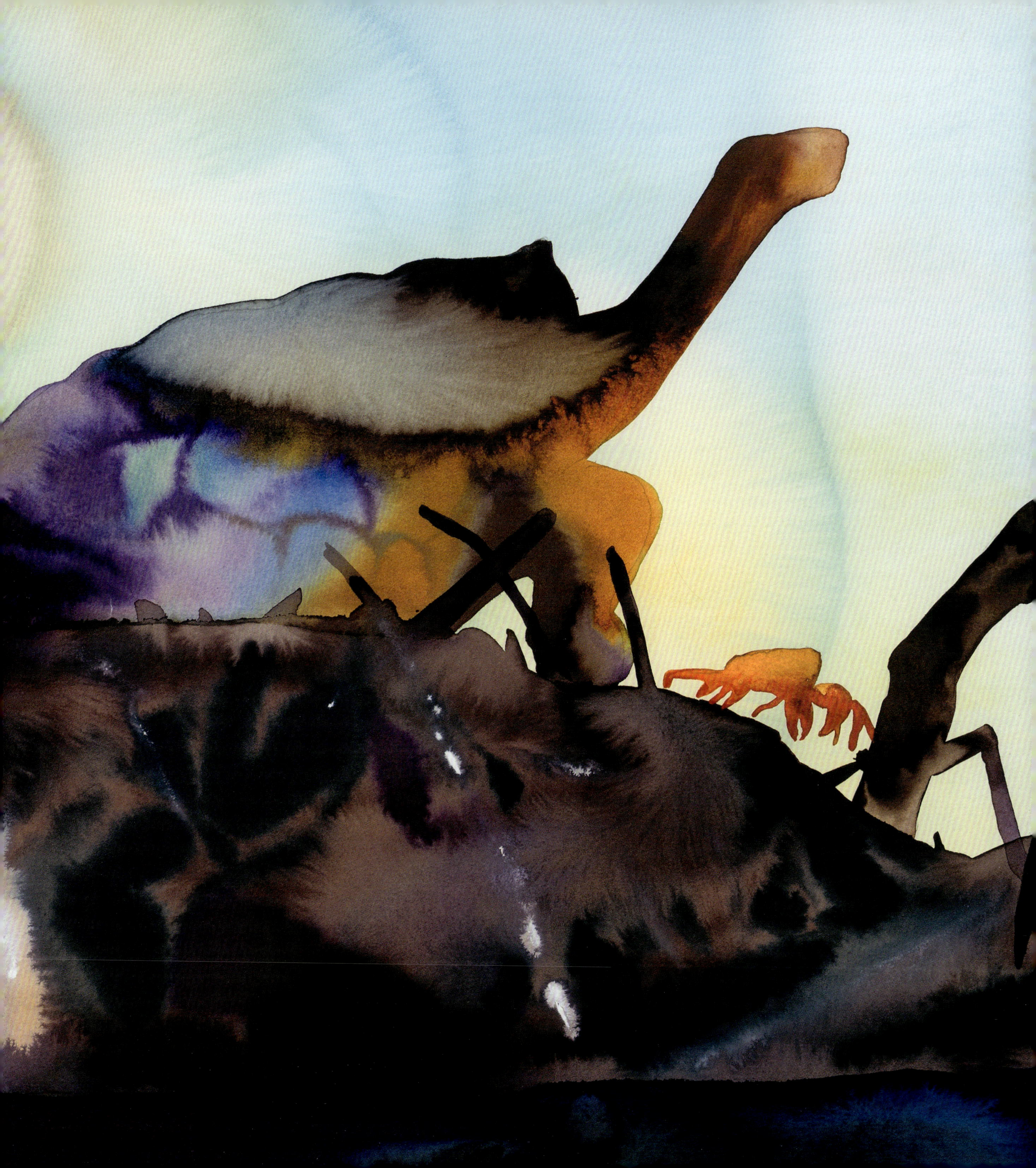

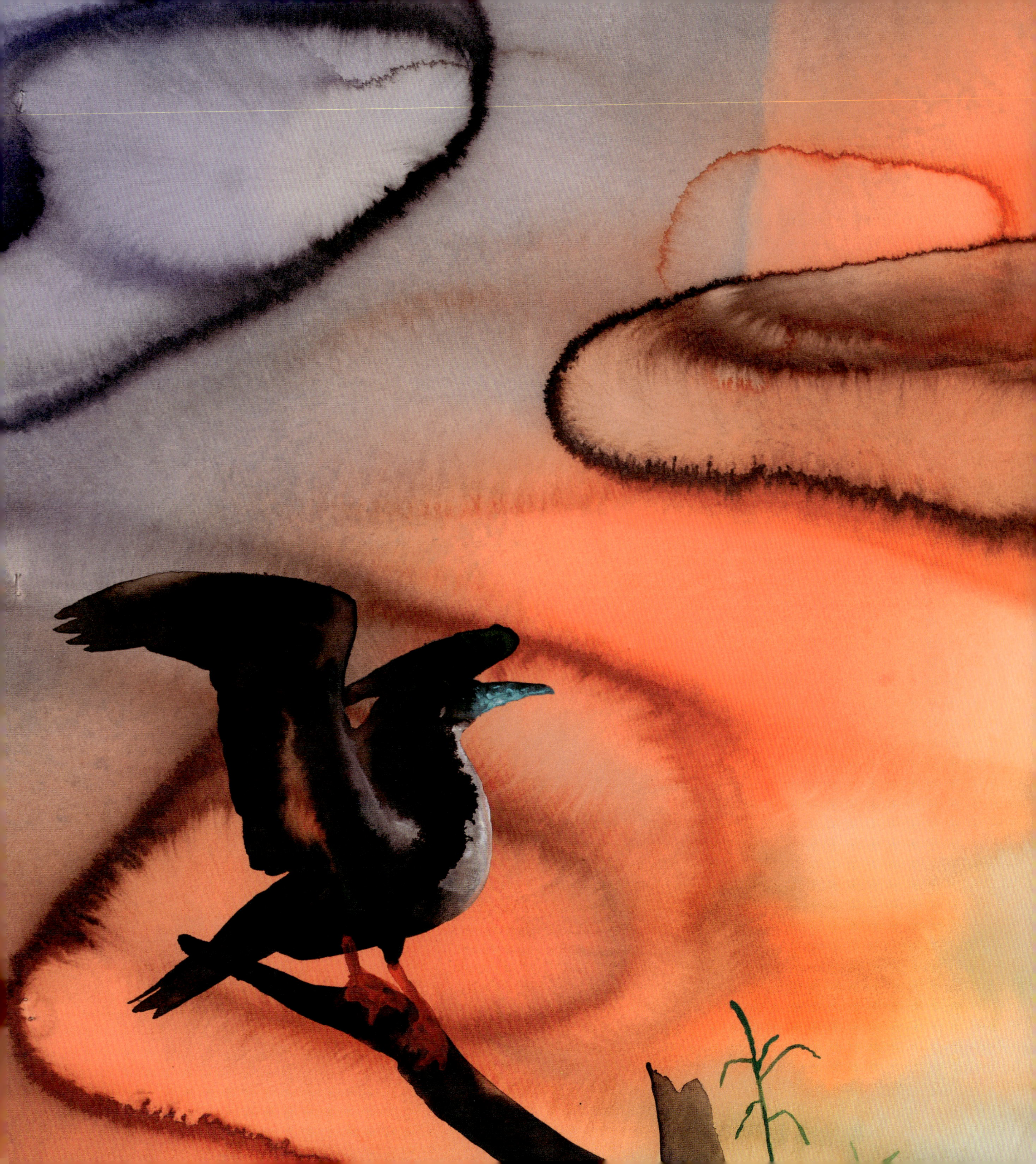

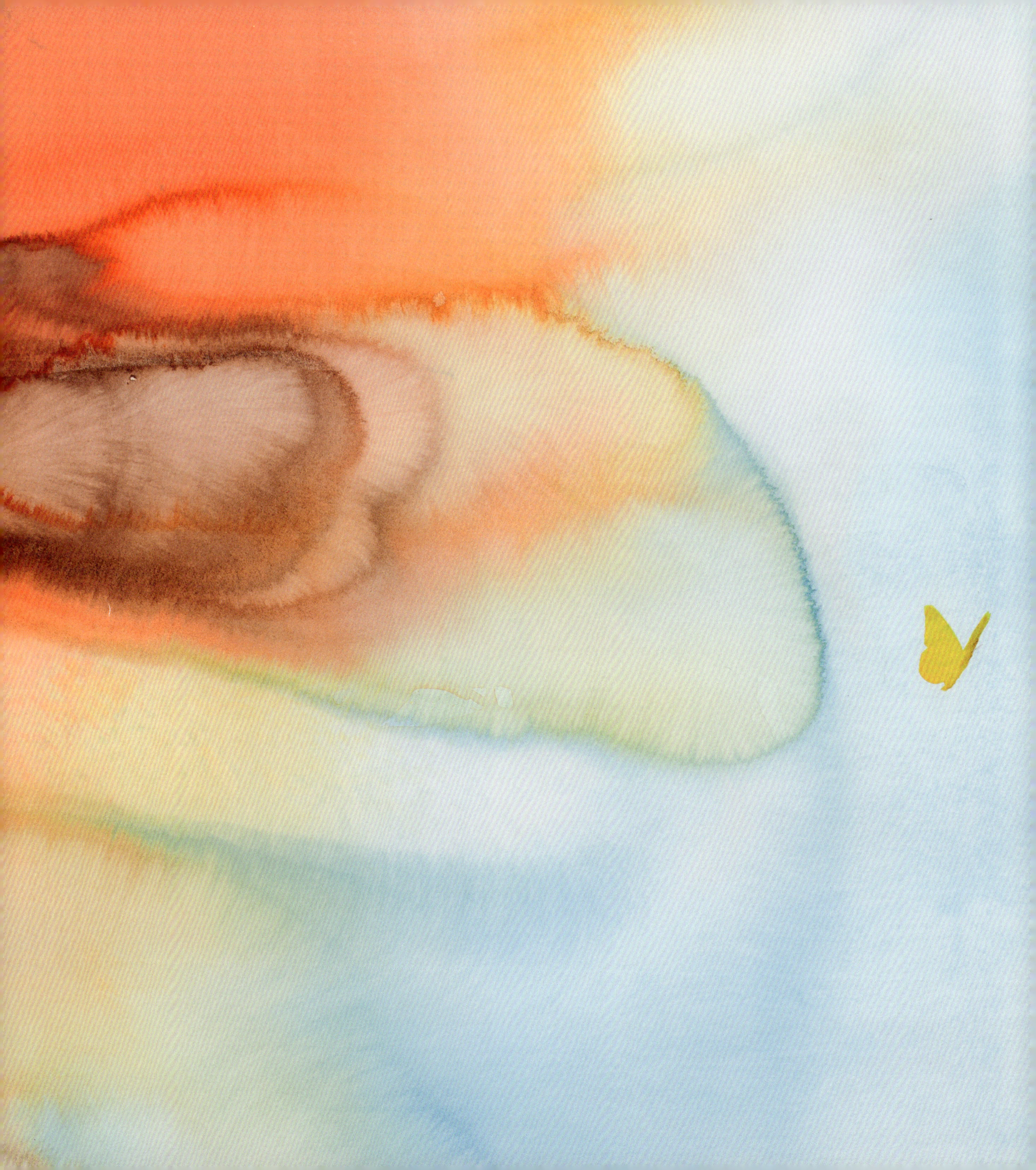

TROPHIC WEB

A spiral can be an elegant way to describe a succession of organisms in an ecological community that are linked to each other through the transfer of energy and nutrients, as well as a way of describing a food chain, which, in this case, is frequently seen on both sides of the North Atlantic. In *Trophic Web*, cetaceans, such as the humpback whale and the bottlenose dolphin, chase striped bass, bluefish, and menhaden, which in turn eat the crucial plants and animals at the base of the food chain. When planning this image, I imagined the point of view as either free diving or scuba diving and looking toward the sky. There is a long tradition in Western art history of using this formal device to reference notions of heaven, transcendence, and the cosmos; in this way, the work nods to the elegiac cosmographies of artists throughout history such as William Blake, Hieronymus Bosch, Antonio da Correggio, and Giovanni Battista Tiepolo.

—AR

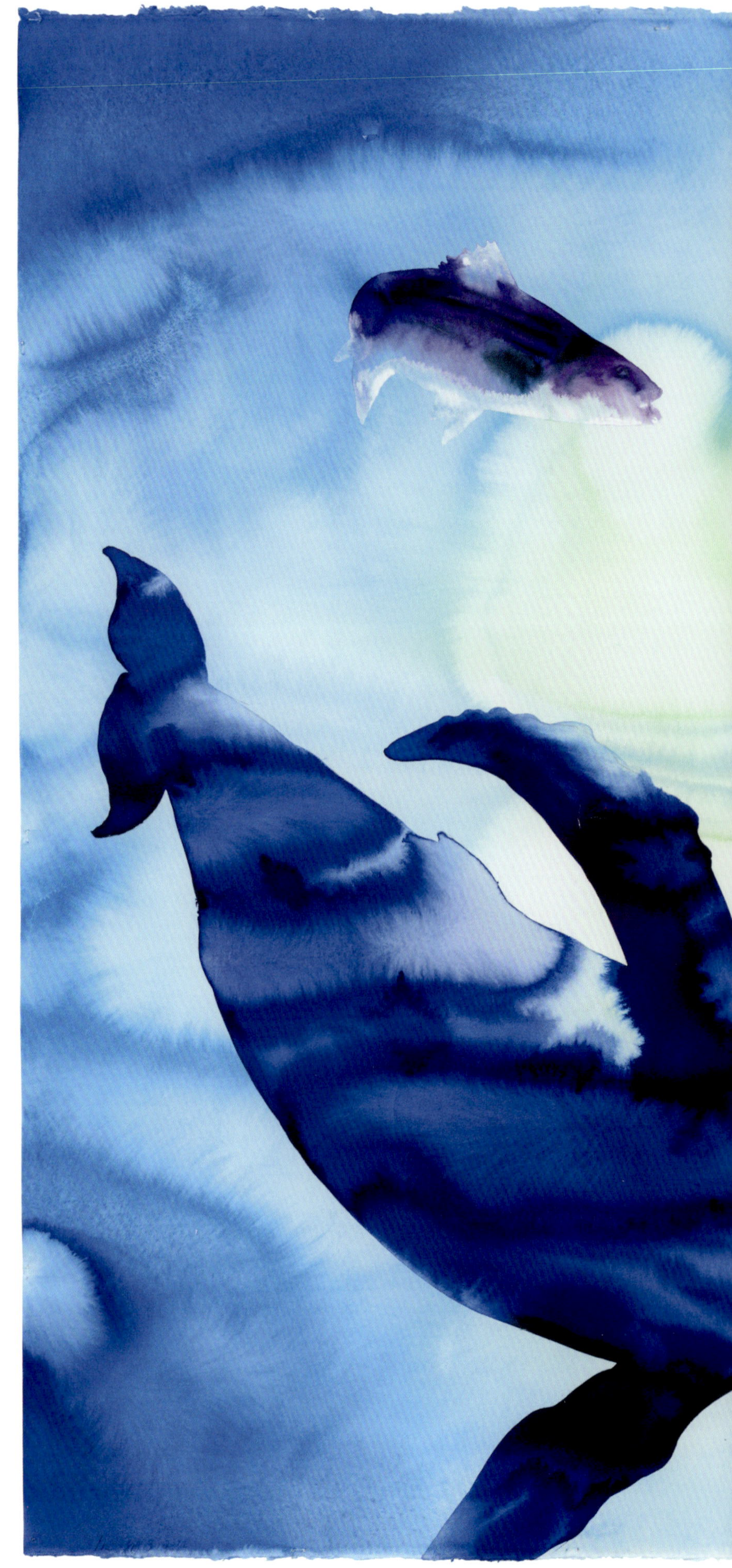

Trophic Web, 2022. Watercolor and acrylic on paper,
52 × 75¼ inches (132.1 × 191.1 cm)

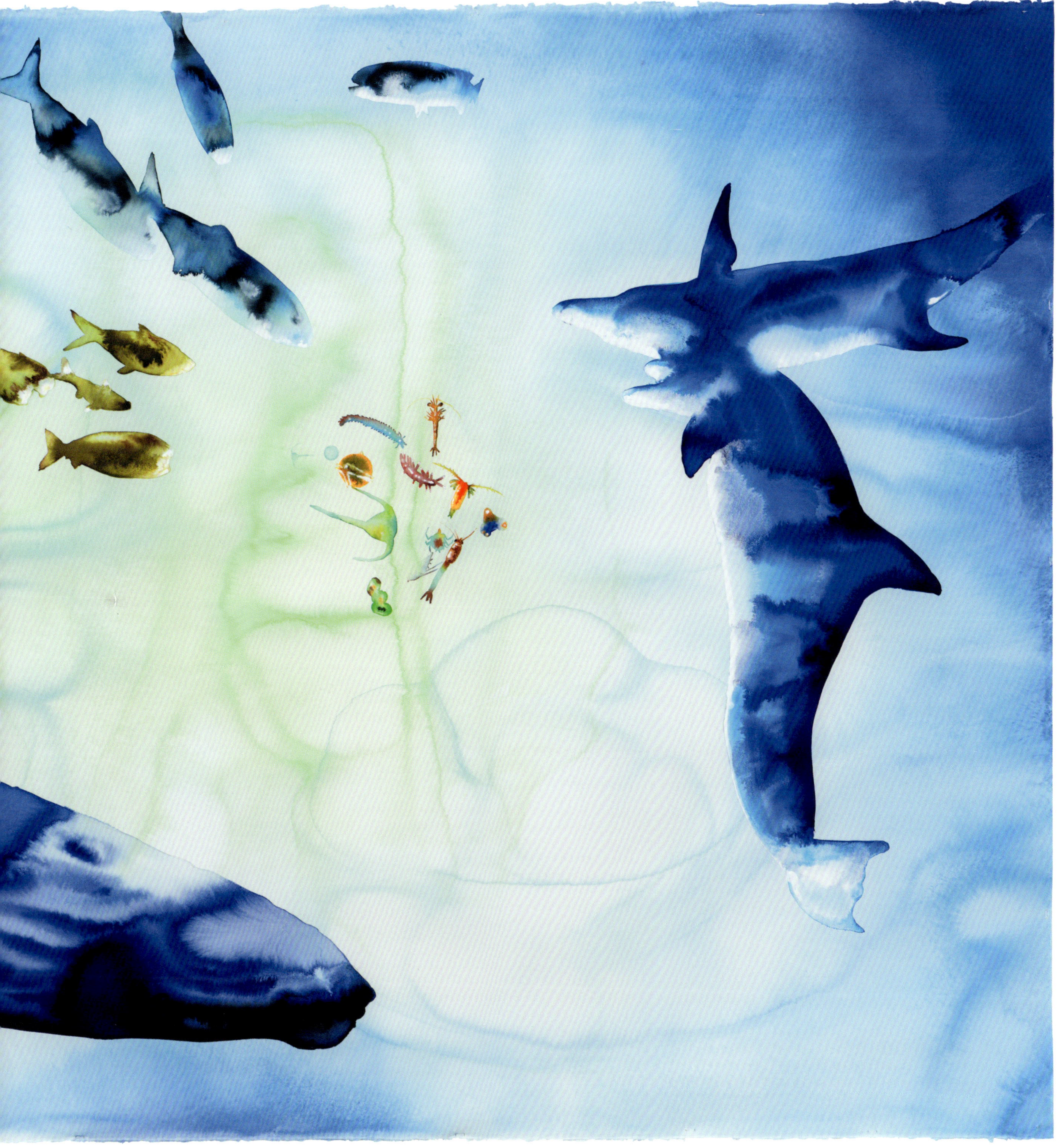

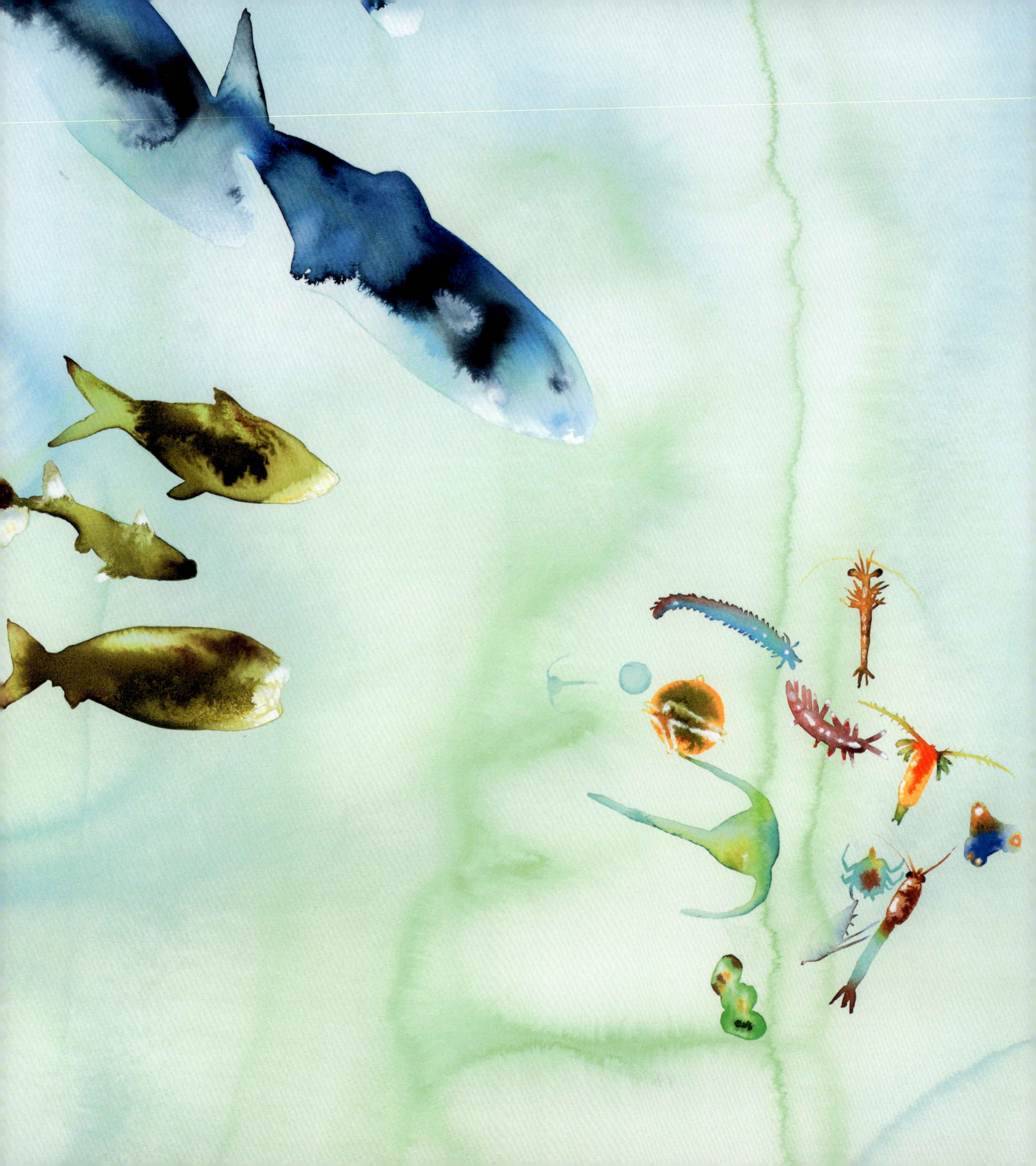

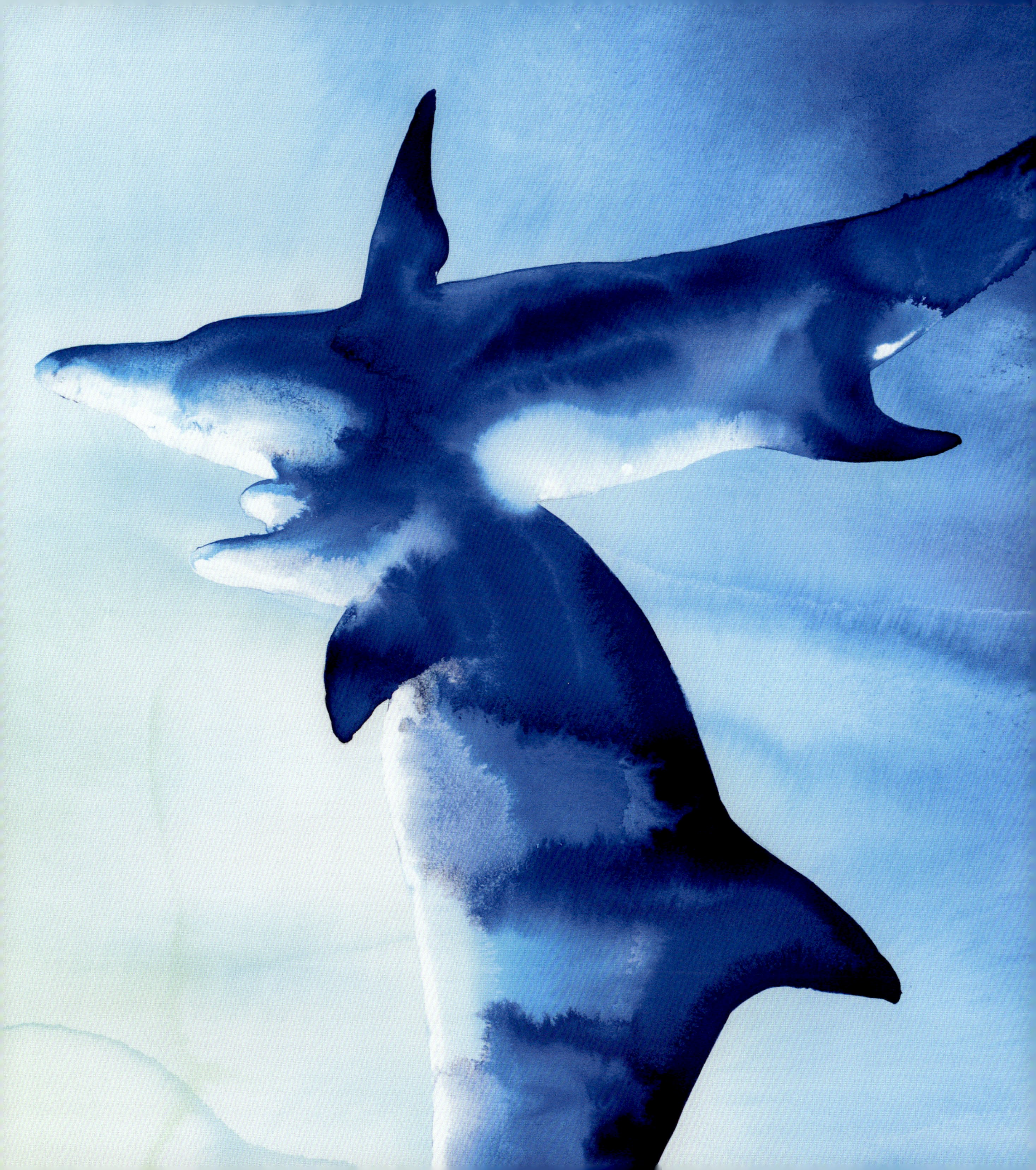

REVERSAL OF FORTUNE

Reversal of Fortune presents a rare scenario in the genre of whaling pictures—a happy ending for the sperm whale—while also playing on the genre of nineteenth-century whaling painting itself. Whaling pictures usually present triumphal scenarios in which the human protagonists prevail in successfully bagging the whale with few consequences, no matter the life-threatening perils a whaler faces. By the mid-nineteenth century these whales had very little chance once the whalers got a harpoon or two into their bodies. My depiction plays off paintings such as Charles S. Raleigh's *Stove Boat, Smashed* (1877) and Percy Elton Cowen's *Sperm Whale Upsetting a Whaleboat* (ca. 1920), as well as Raleigh's 1887 drawing of whaleboat gear from George Brown Goode's *The Fisheries and Fishery Industries of the United States*. The specificity of the whaler's implements and equipment, such as the Provincetown toggle, the tail knife, the small blubber knife, and the sailor's palm, adds to the authenticity and credibility of the scenario.

—AR

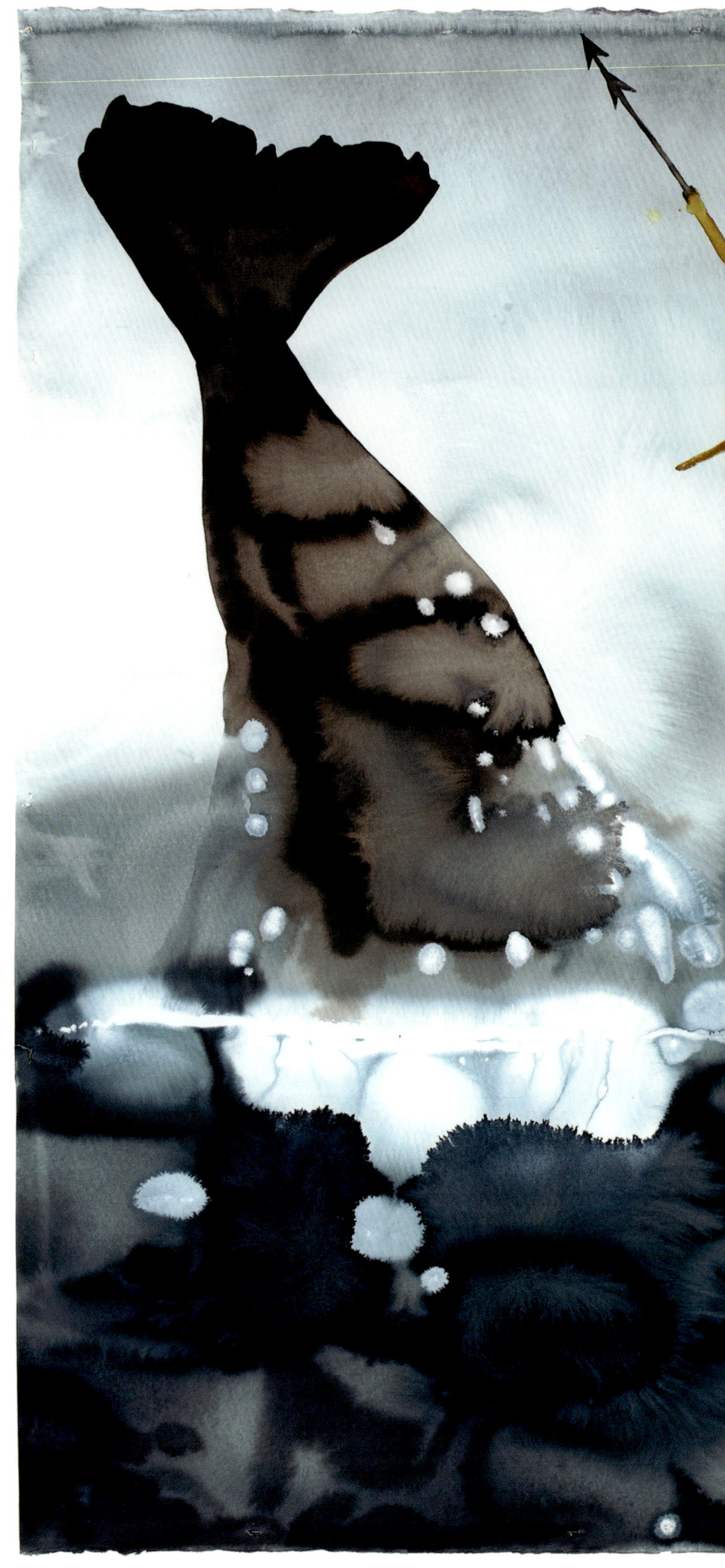

Reversal of Fortune, 2021. Watercolor and acrylic on paper,
52 × 74 inches (132.1 × 188 cm)

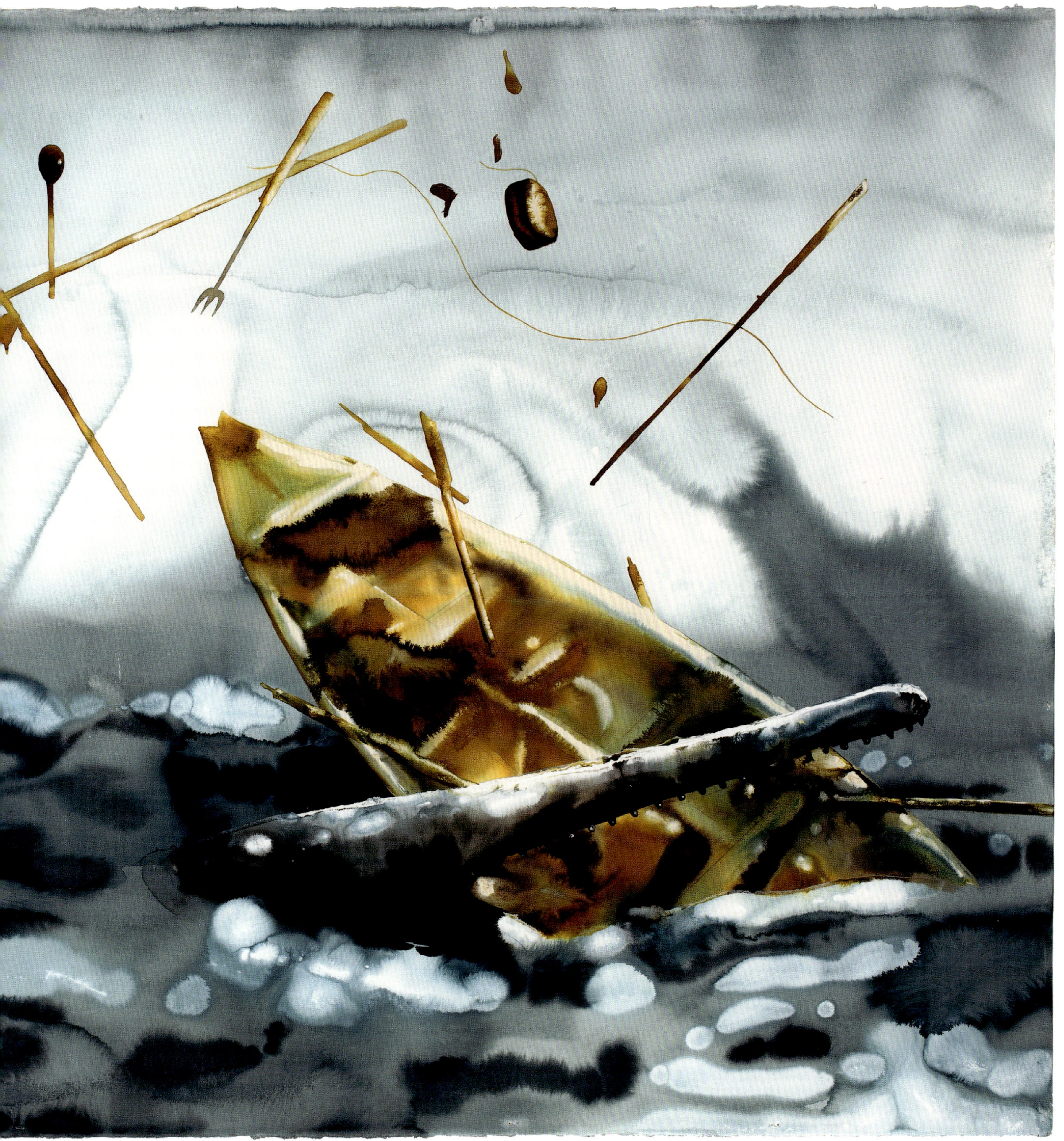

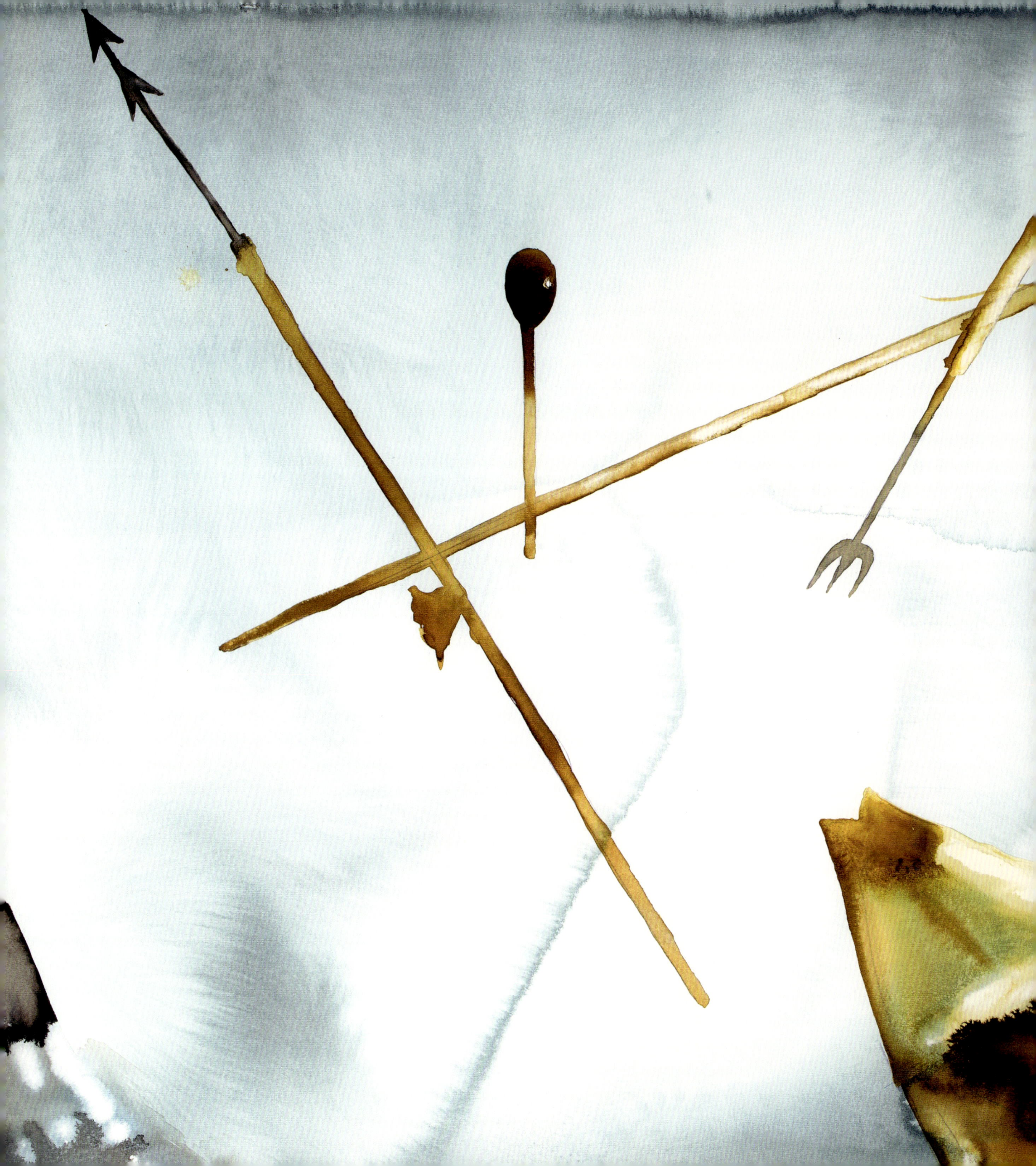

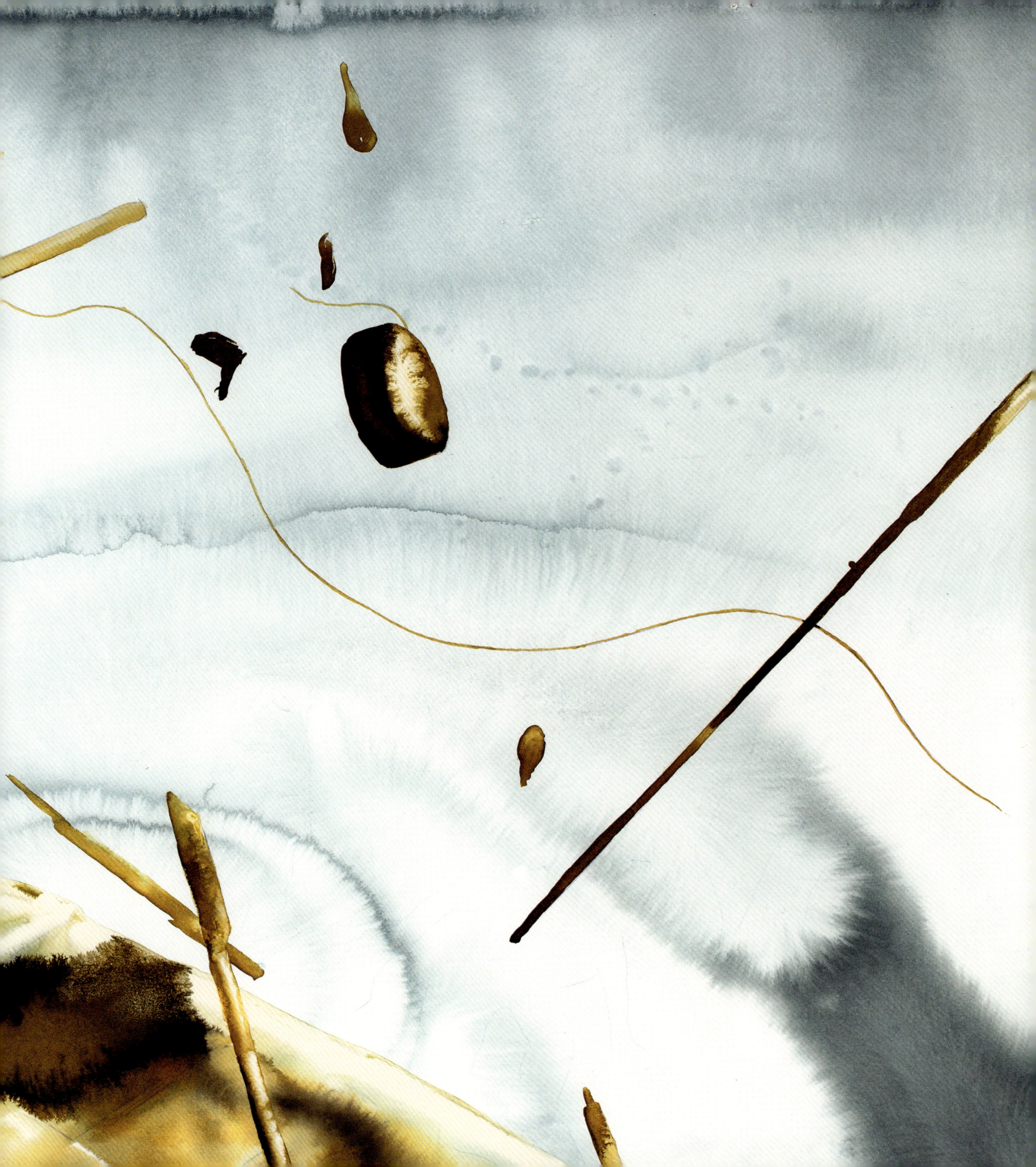

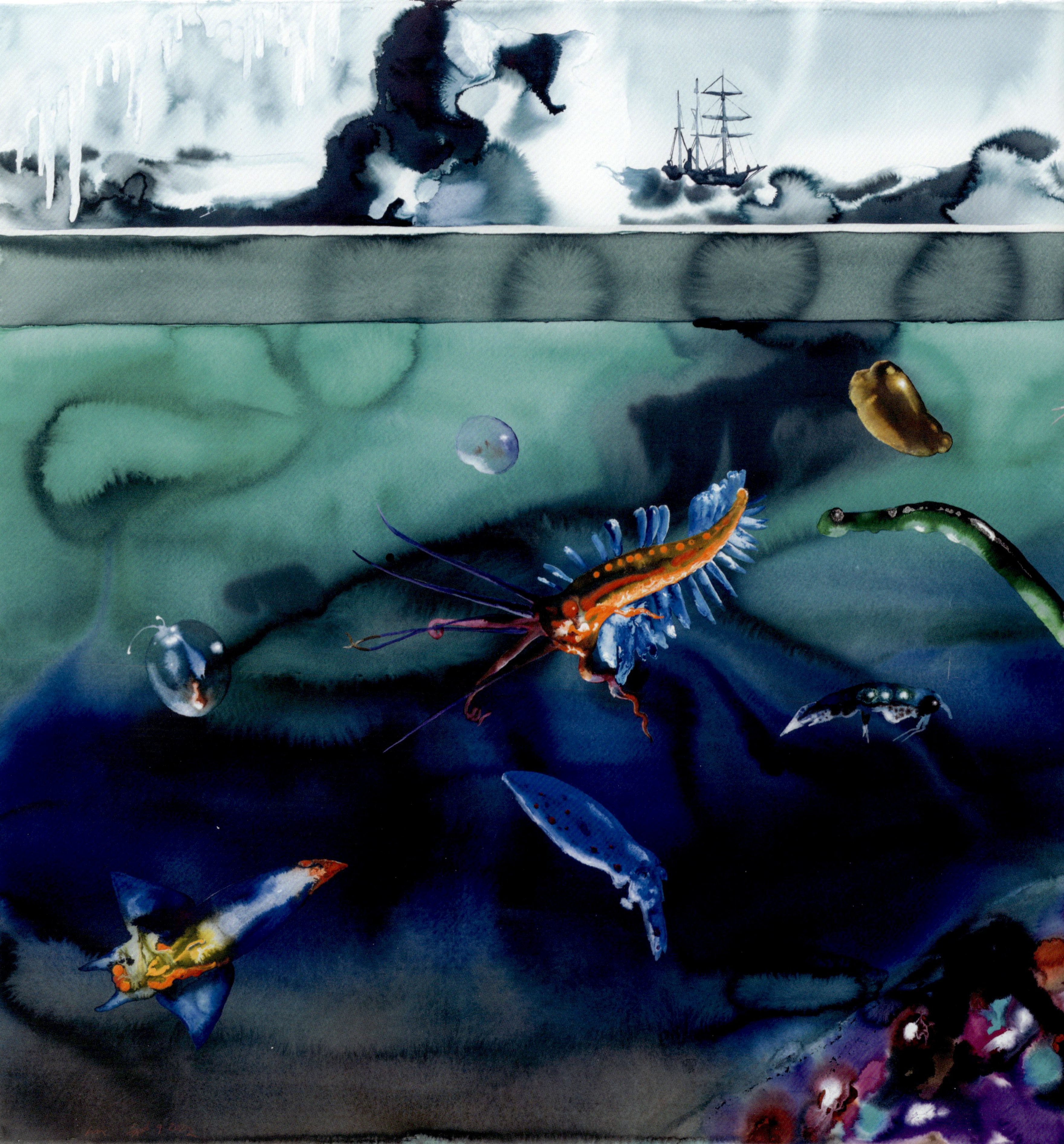

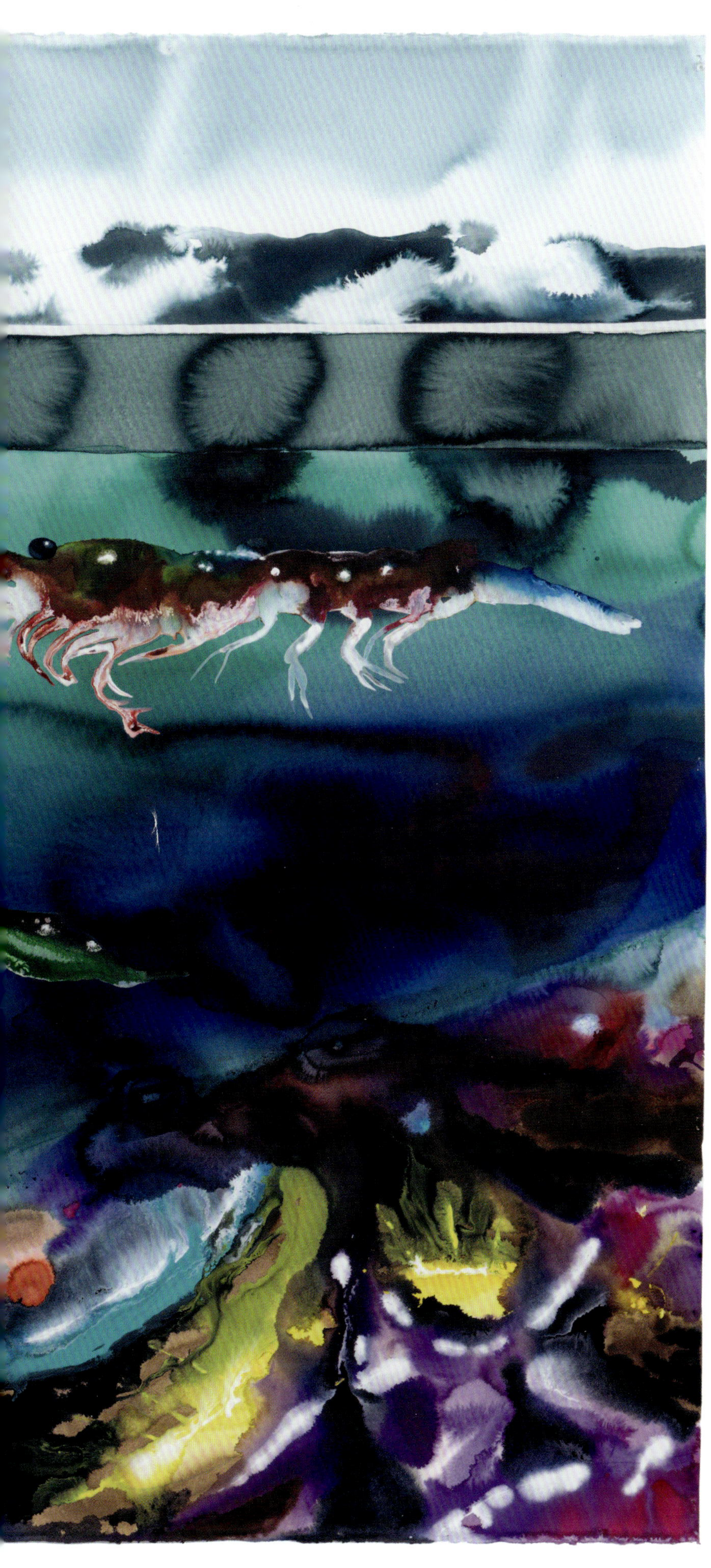

ENDURANCE

While crossing the Drake Passage on the Lindblad Expeditions–National Geographic ship *Endeavor* on a trip to Antarctica in November 2007, my wife, Dorothy Spears, and I witnessed the sinking of the MS *Explorer*, a Canadian ecotourism cruise ship, fondly known in the maritime world as "the little red ship." This ship happened to be on the "Spirit of Shackleton" tour; the passengers stopped at the Falkland Islands and South Georgia Island before heading for the tip of Antarctica when the ship struck ice and sank. I remember imagining what the animals below the surface of the icy waters were doing while this human drama unfolded on the surface of the ocean. So much has been scrutinized about Ernest Shackleton's extraordinary adventure on the *Endurance* in Antarctica. His ship was crushed by sea ice and sank in 1915, forcing Shackleton and his men to make an astonishing escape on foot and in small boats. Then there's the subsequent discovery of the wreck in March 2022. It's fascinating to ponder how life under the ice was going about its daily business, indifferent to the struggles of humans above. In *Endurance*, and continuing in the tradition of my recent body of work called *Shipwrecks*, I have framed Shackleton's tiny ship off in the distance as it struggles, locked in ice by the freezing sea while the local ecology goes about its daily life below the ice.

—AR

Endurance, 2022. Watercolor and acrylic on paper,
52 × 75¼ inches (132.1 × 191.1 cm)

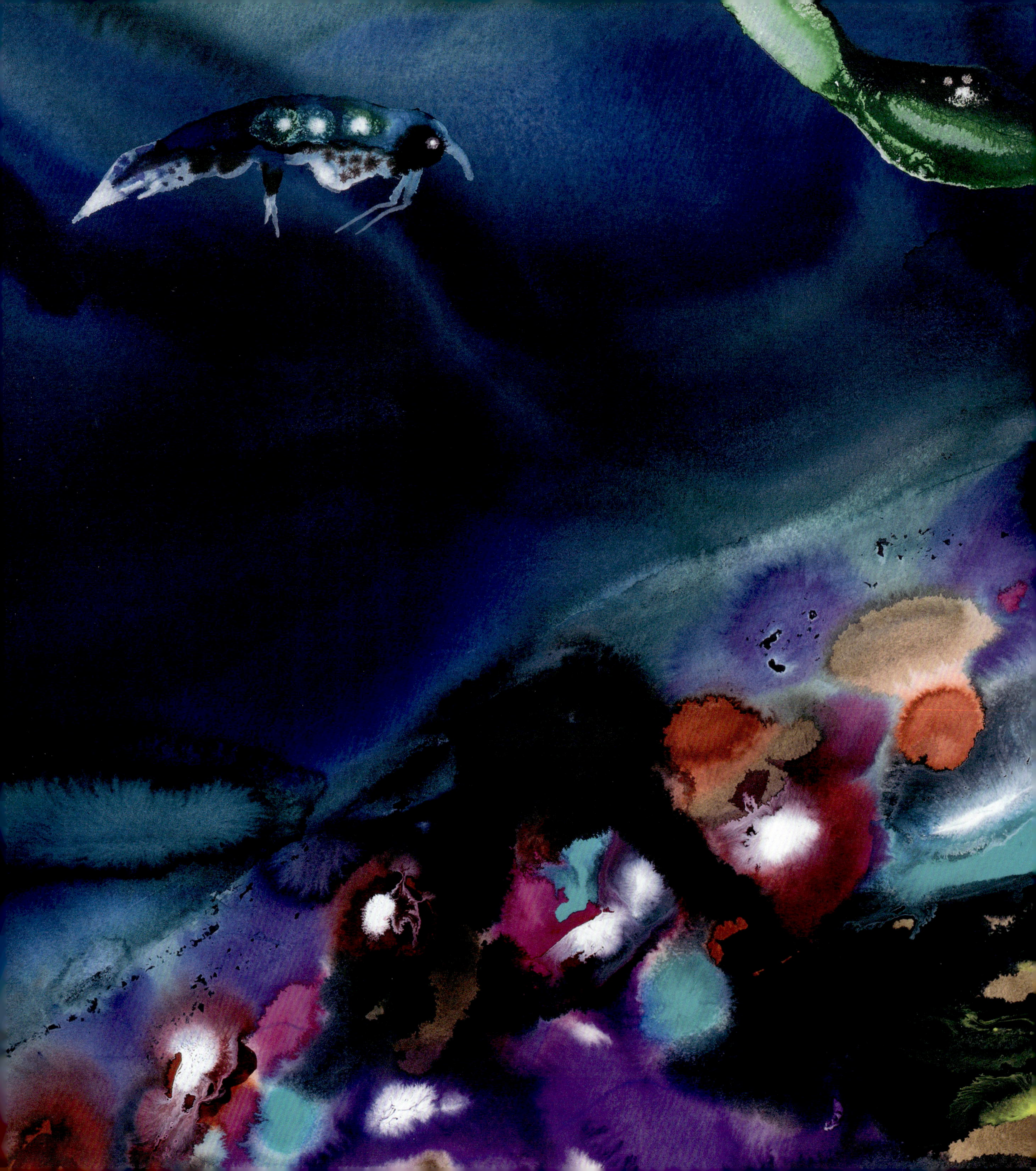

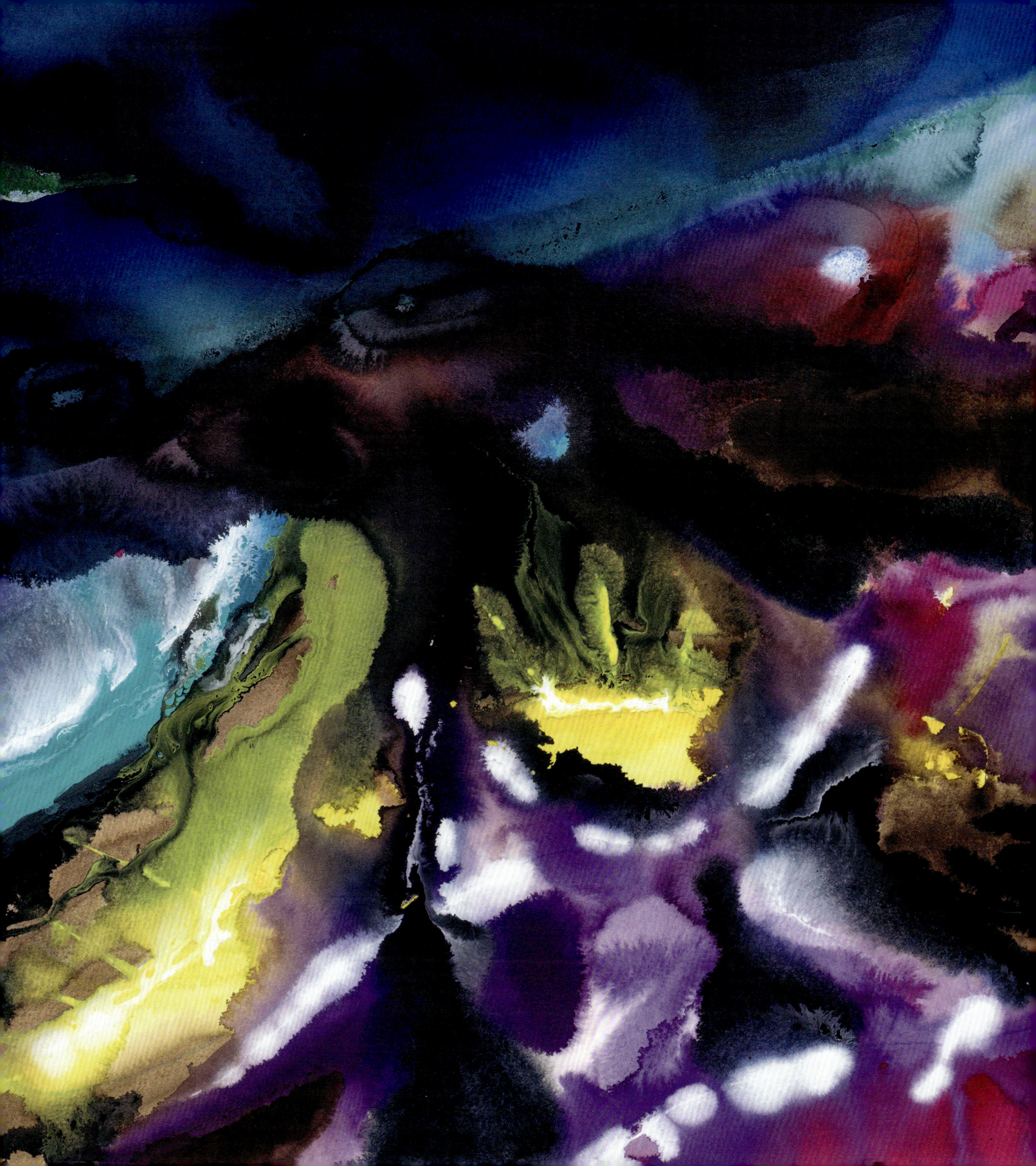

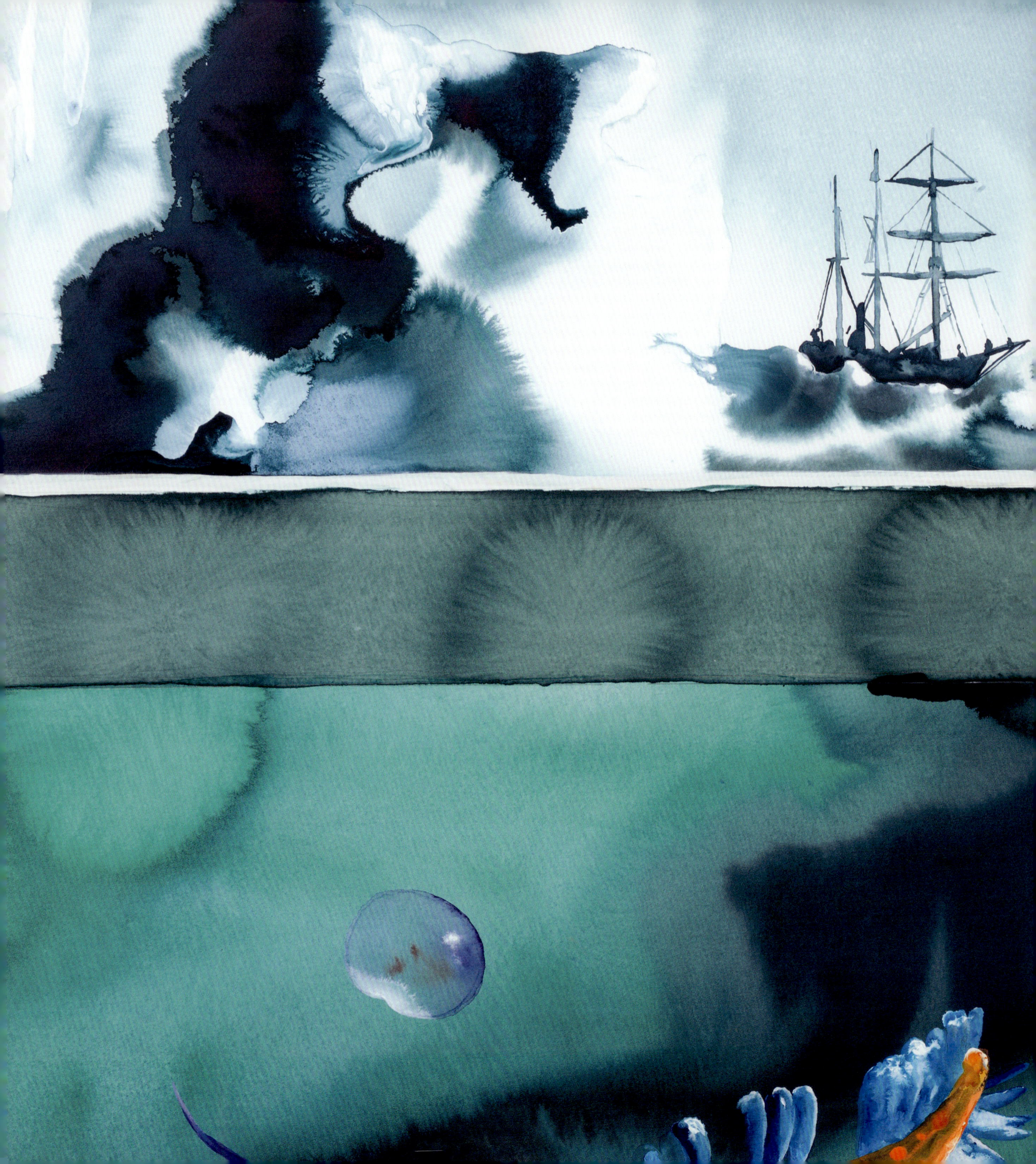

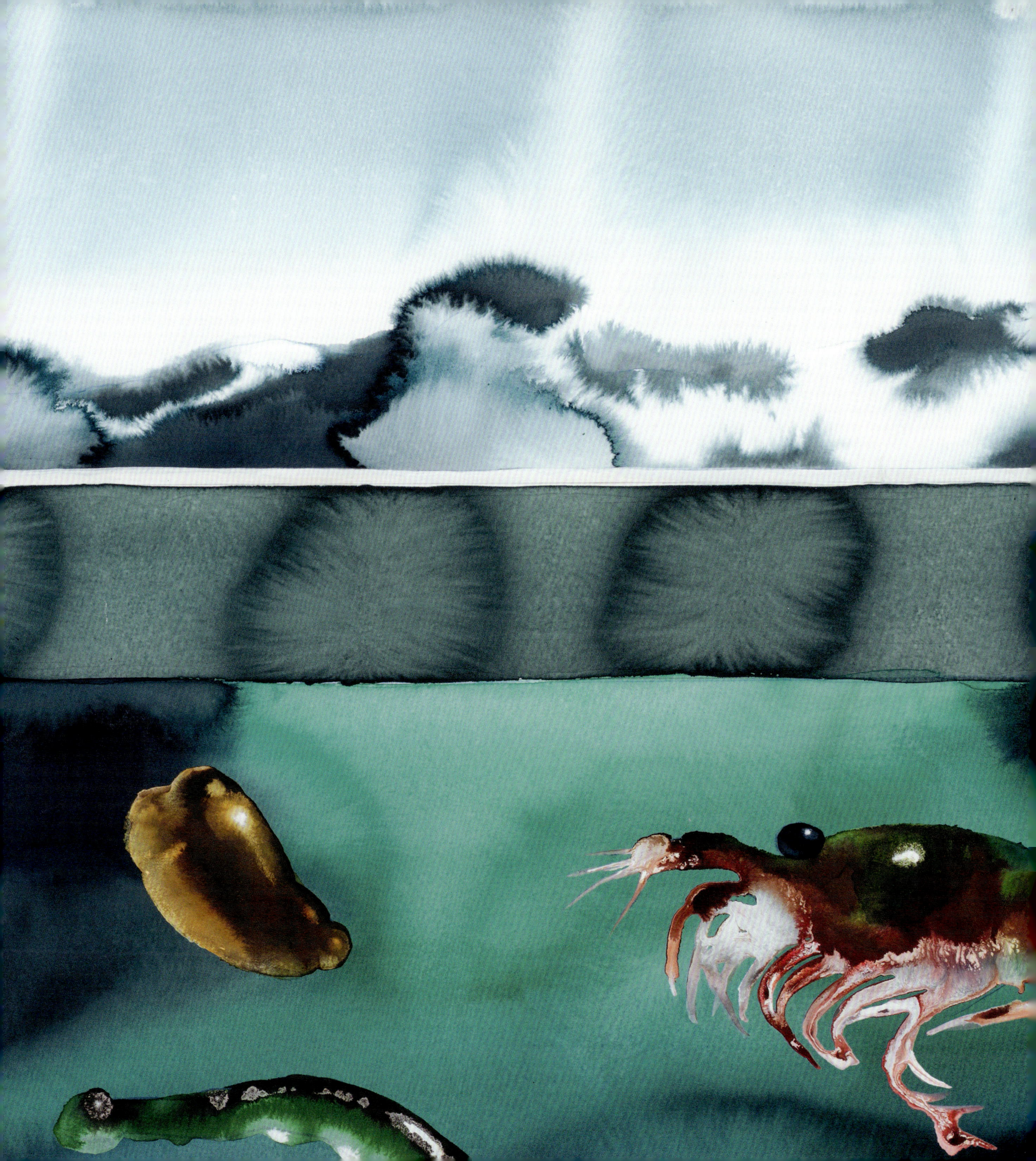

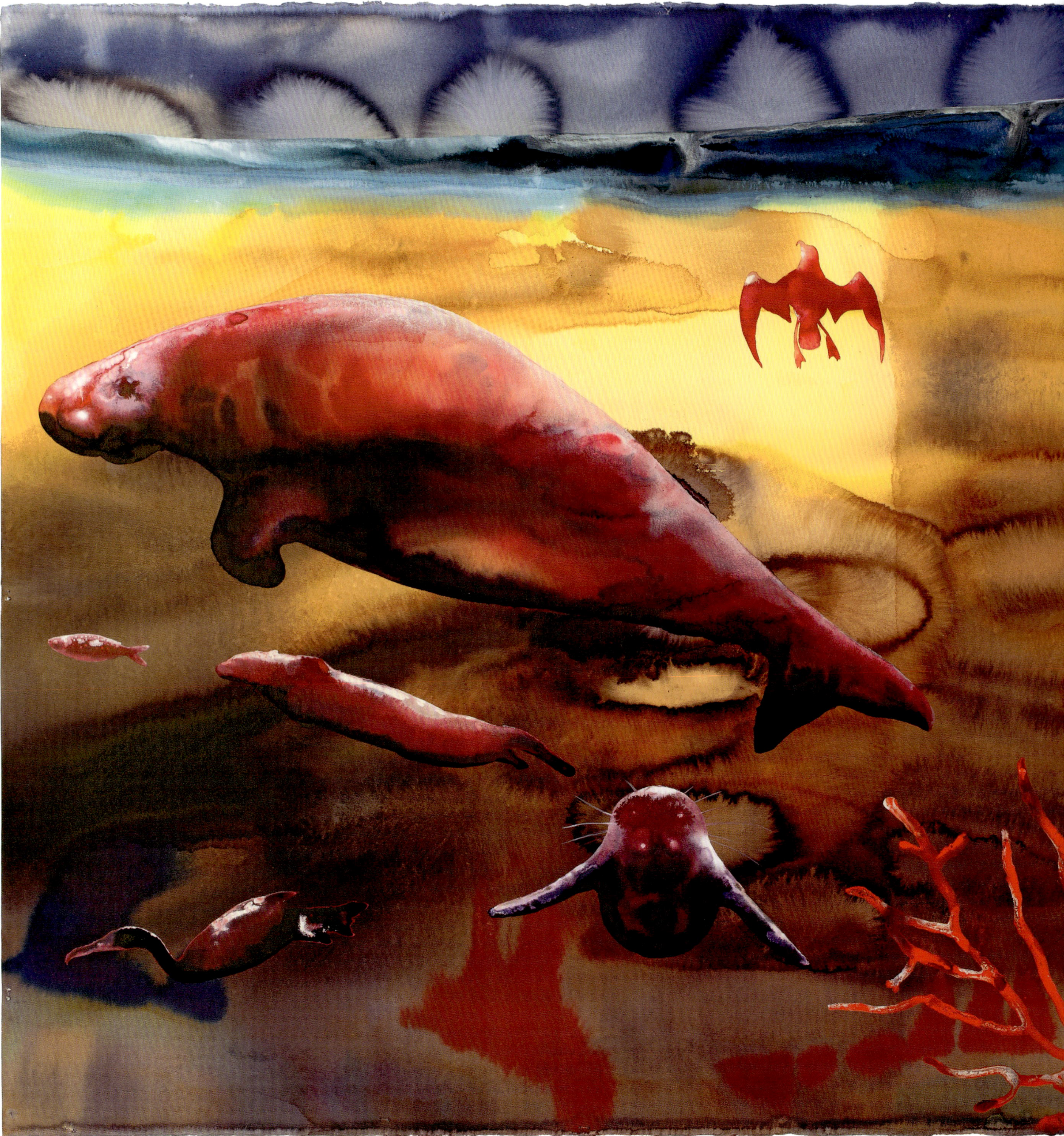

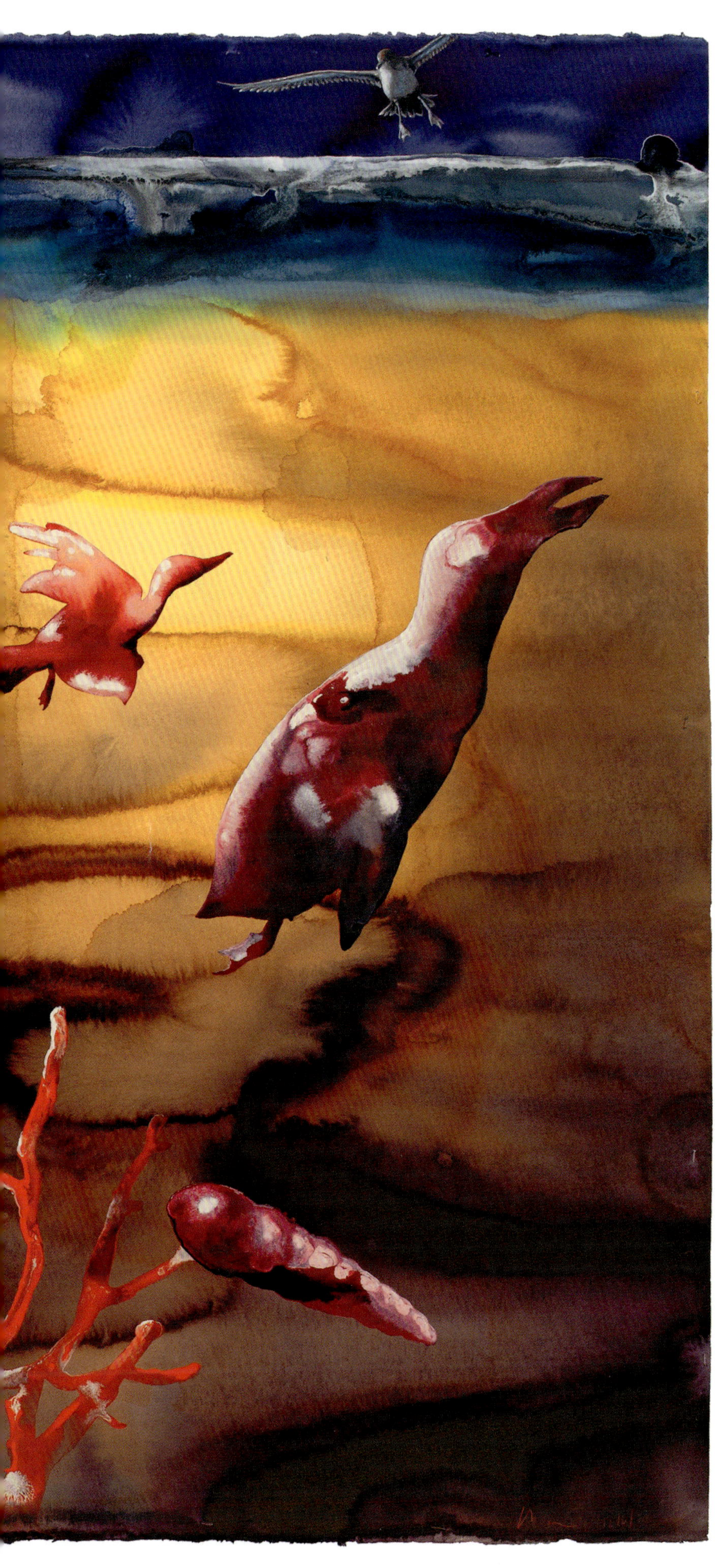

LEGACY

Human history is sown with heartbreaking and terrible stories of animal extinction. None is more infuriating than the story of the Steller's sea cow. When I first read about them some thirty-five years ago, I was in disbelief that they were annihilated within twenty-seven years of their discovery in 1741. In *Legacy*, the tree of life becomes a tree of extinction. This and the decidedly unnatural, unoceanic palette describe the nether-worldly limbo of extinct animals—the great auk, the Caribbean monk seal, and other sad stories. My way into this image was a chance visit to Frederic Edwin Church's house at Olana, where I saw the painting *Sunset Jamaica* (1865), which is a very small study for his painting *The After Glow* (1867), and decided that, if I turned the image upside down, I could use it as a springboard for the emotional tone of the work. Though this image describes the ten verified marine extinctions, there are only a handful of ways to verify extinctions, and it's suspected that hundreds more species have disappeared from our oceans forever.

—AR

Legacy, 2021. Watercolor and acrylic on paper,
52 × 75 inches (132.1 × 190.5 cm)

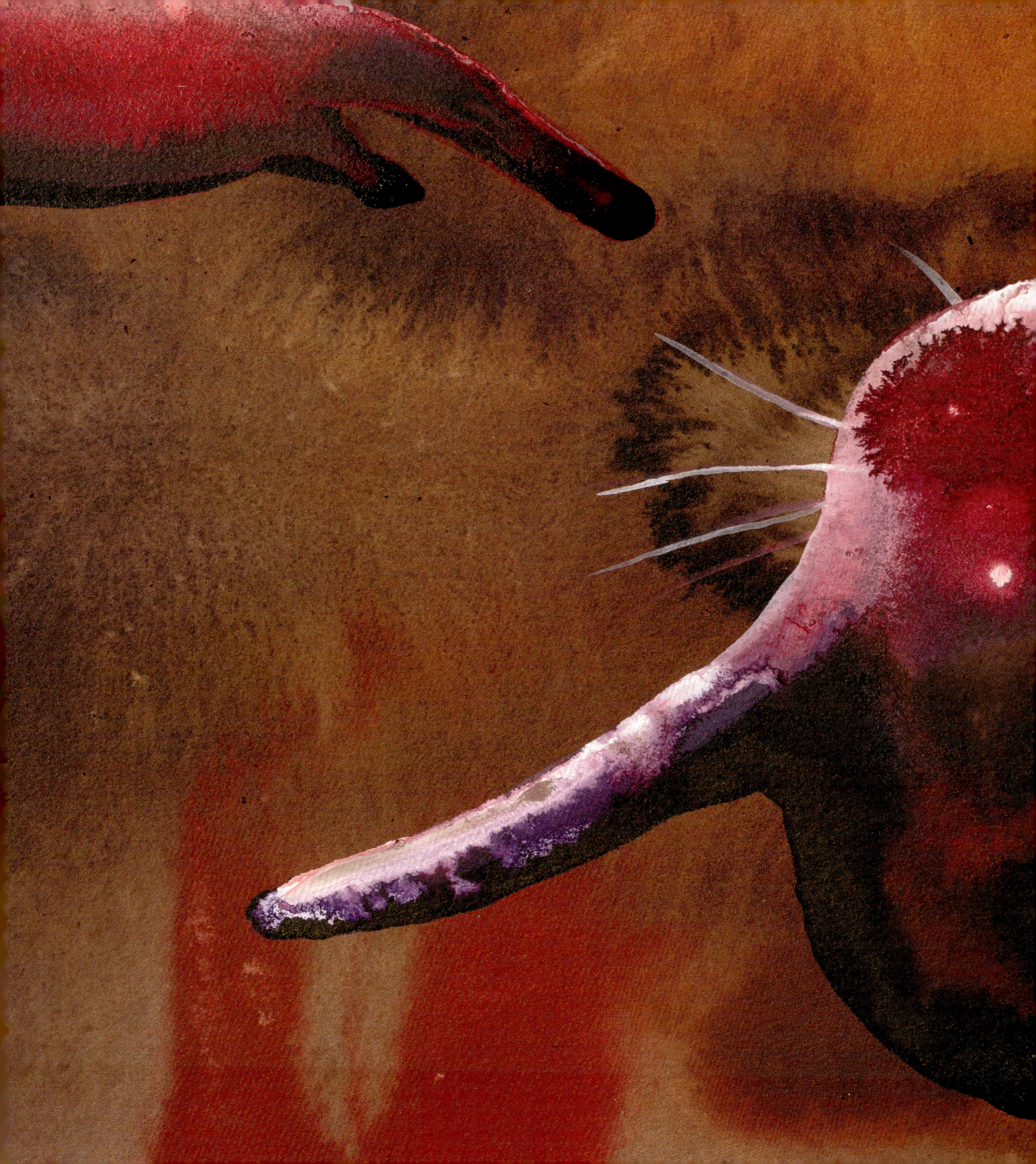

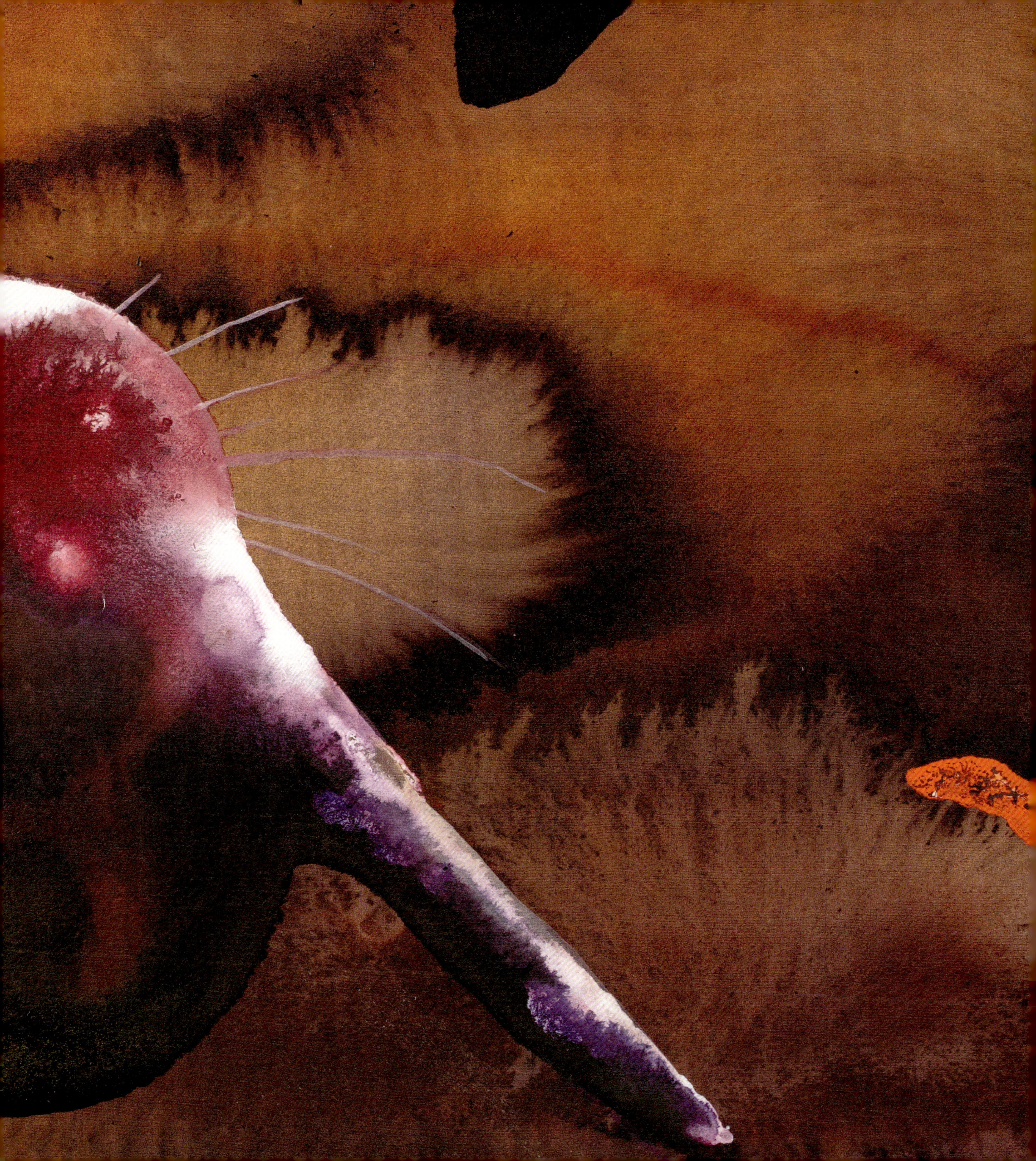

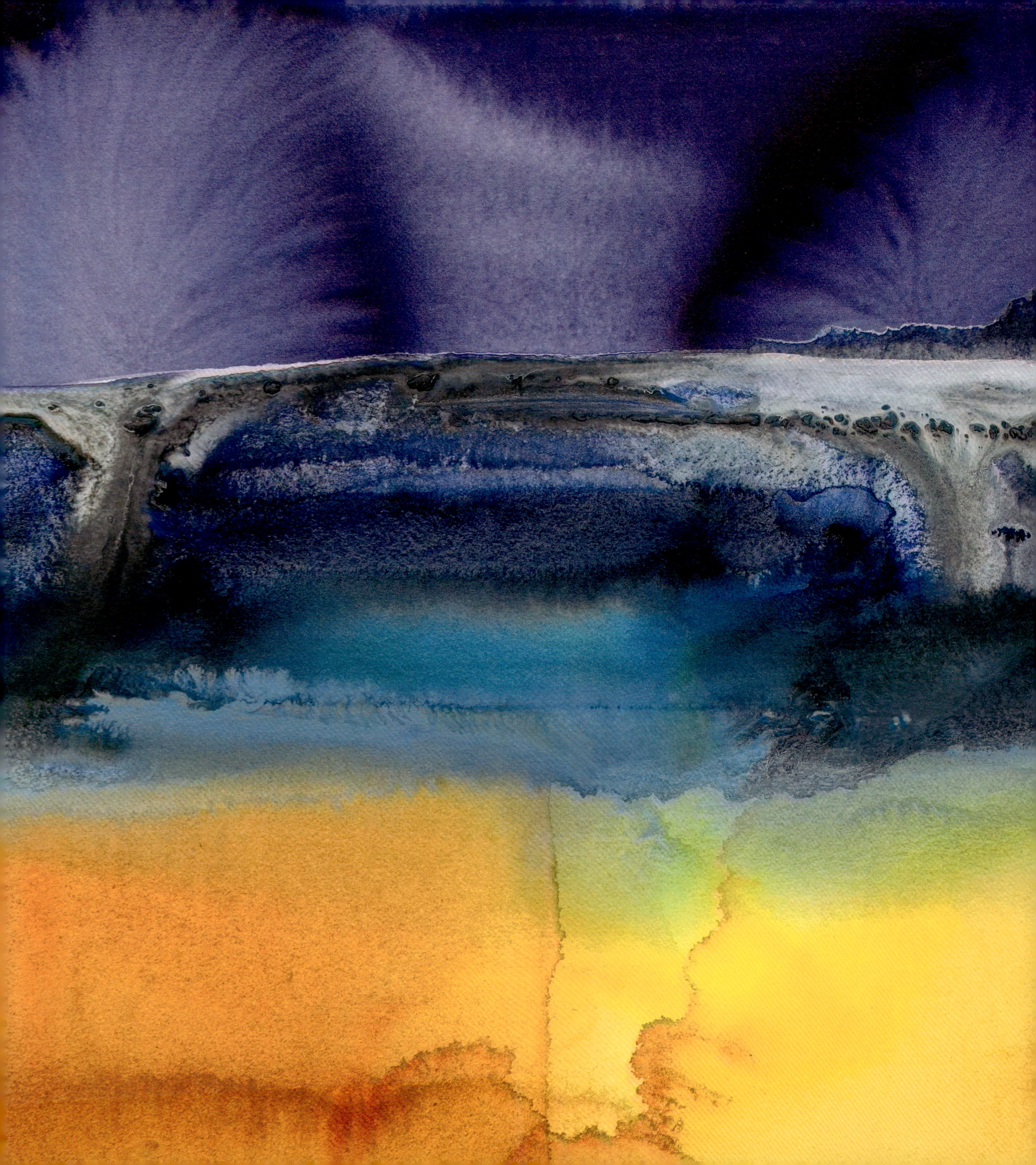

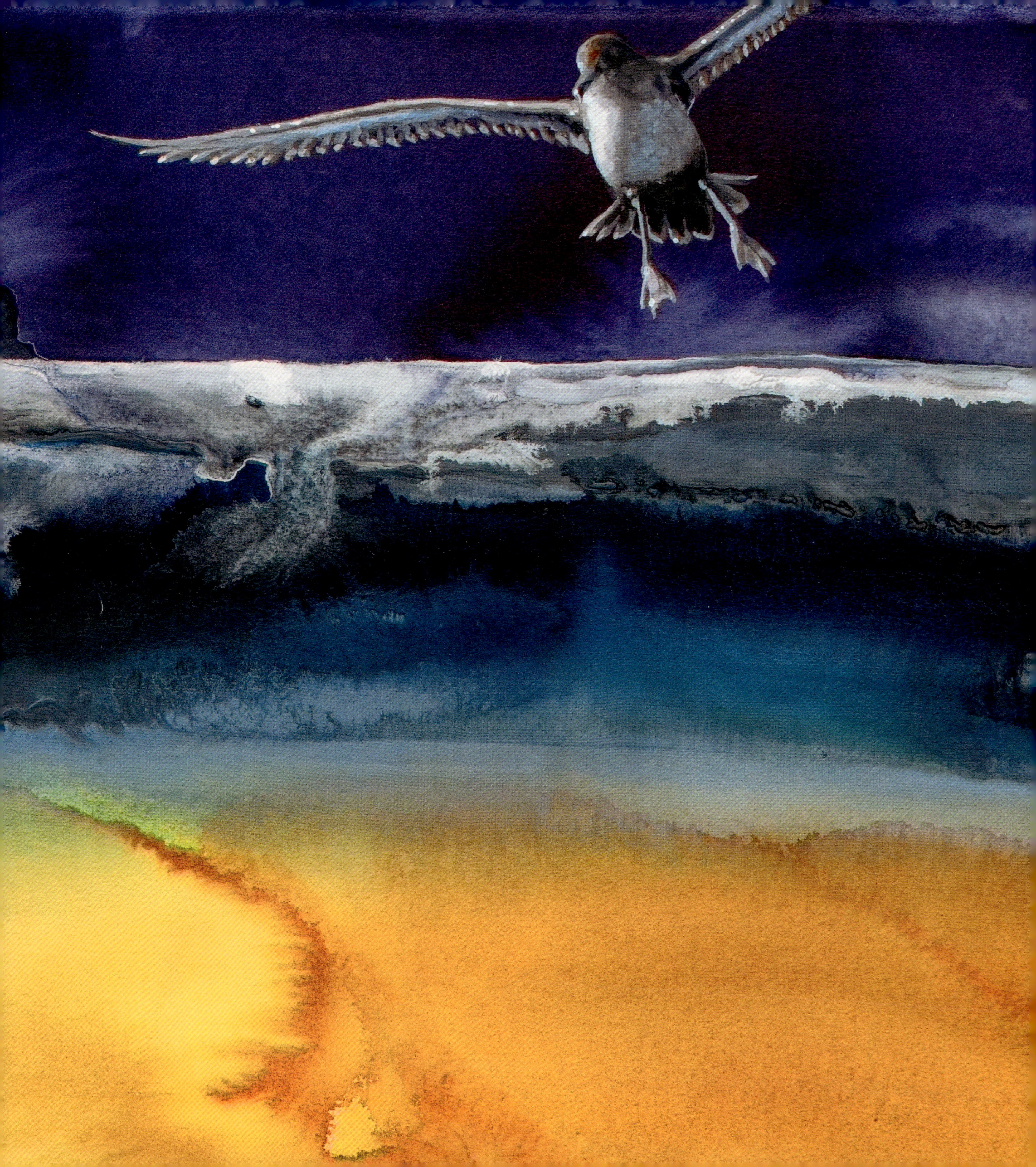

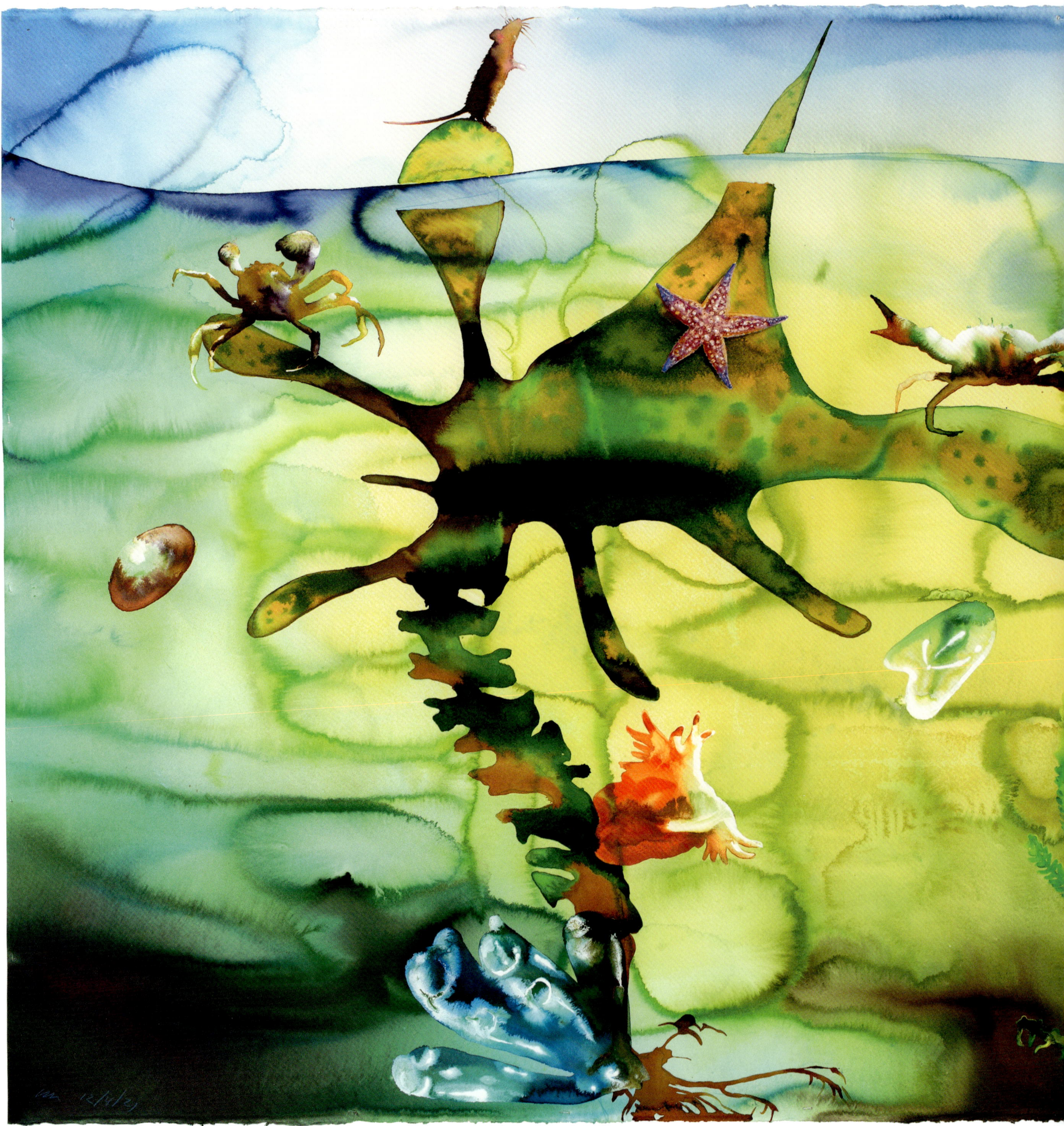

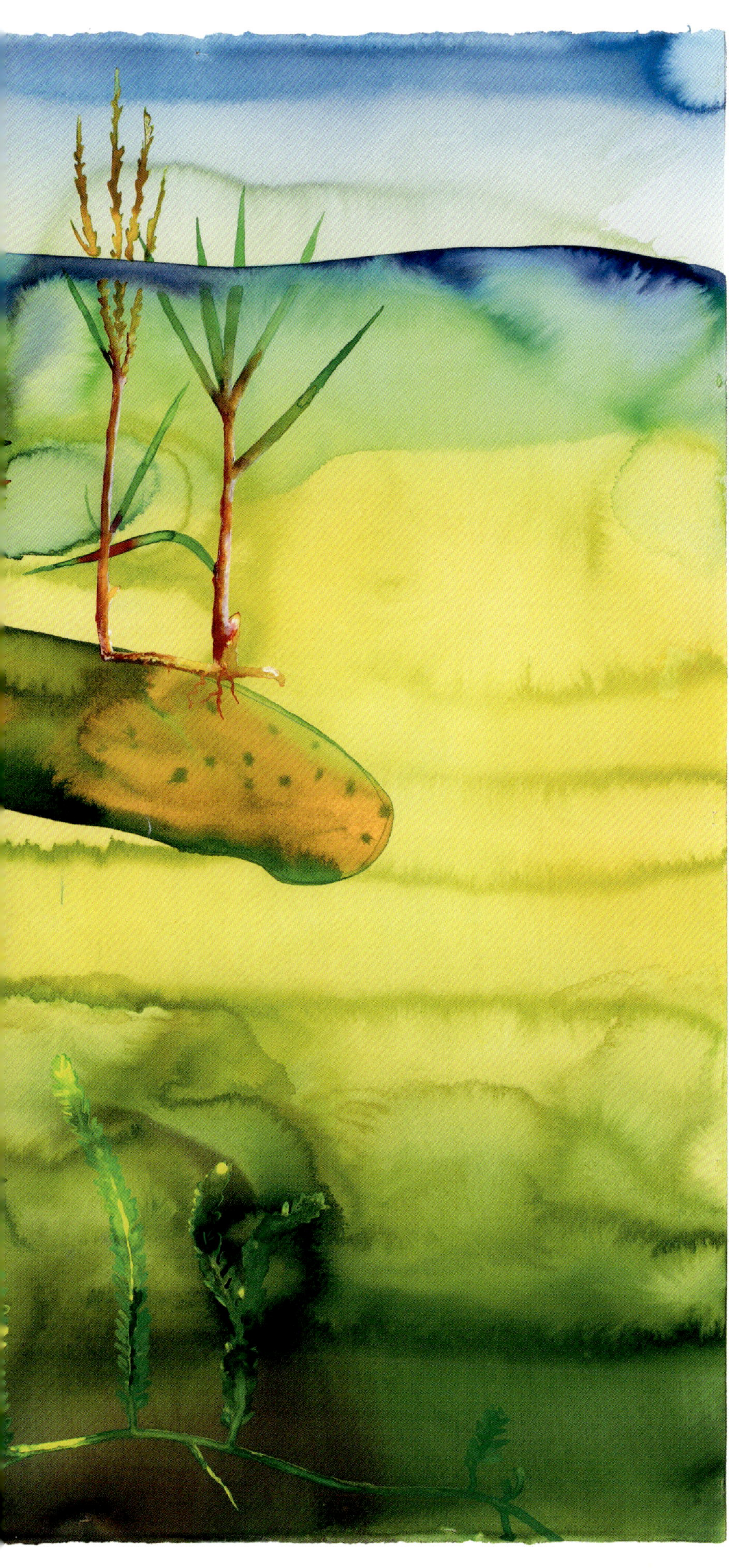

Vectors and Pathways, 2021. Watercolor and acrylic on paper, 52 × 76 inches (132.1 × 193 cm)

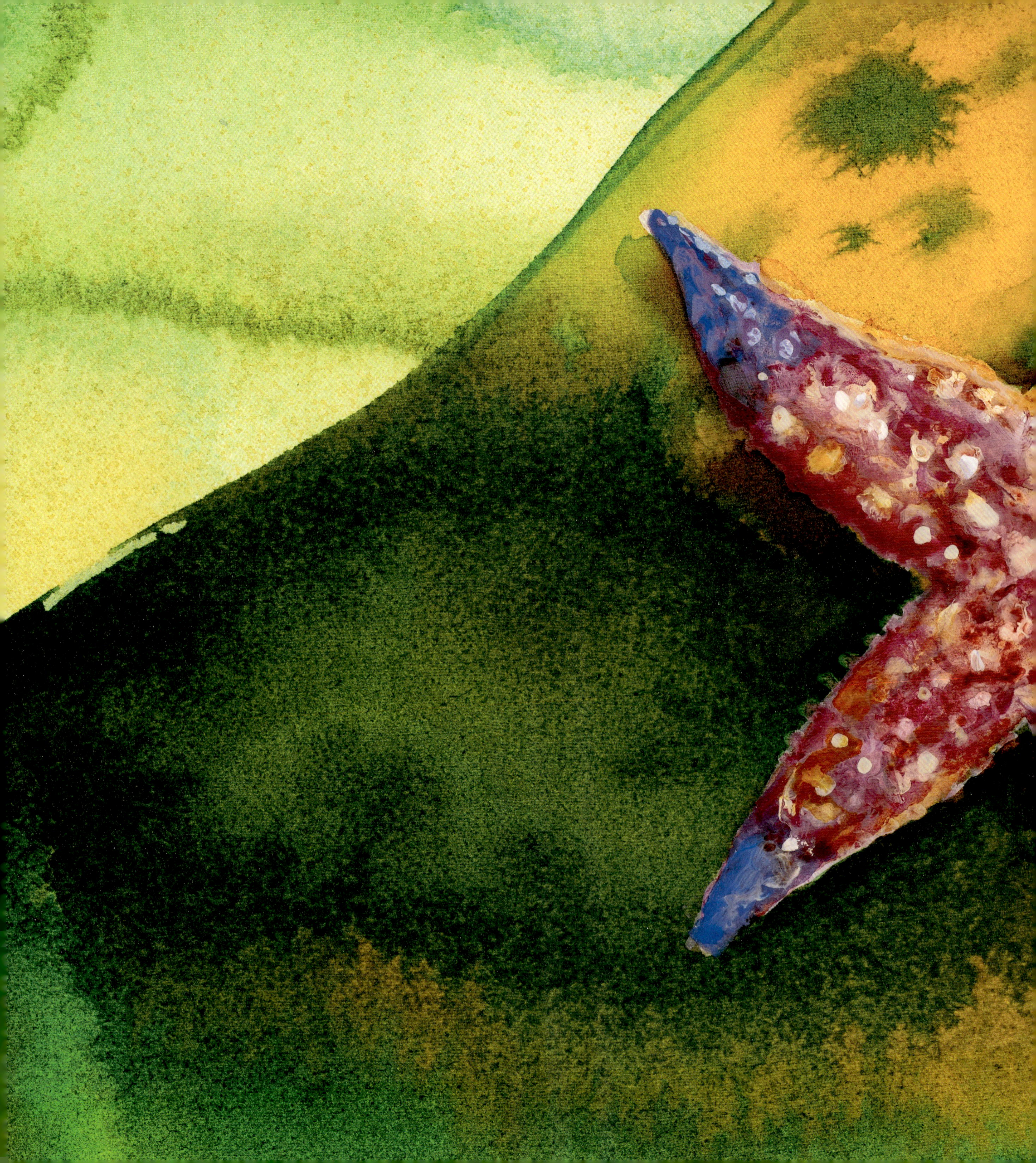

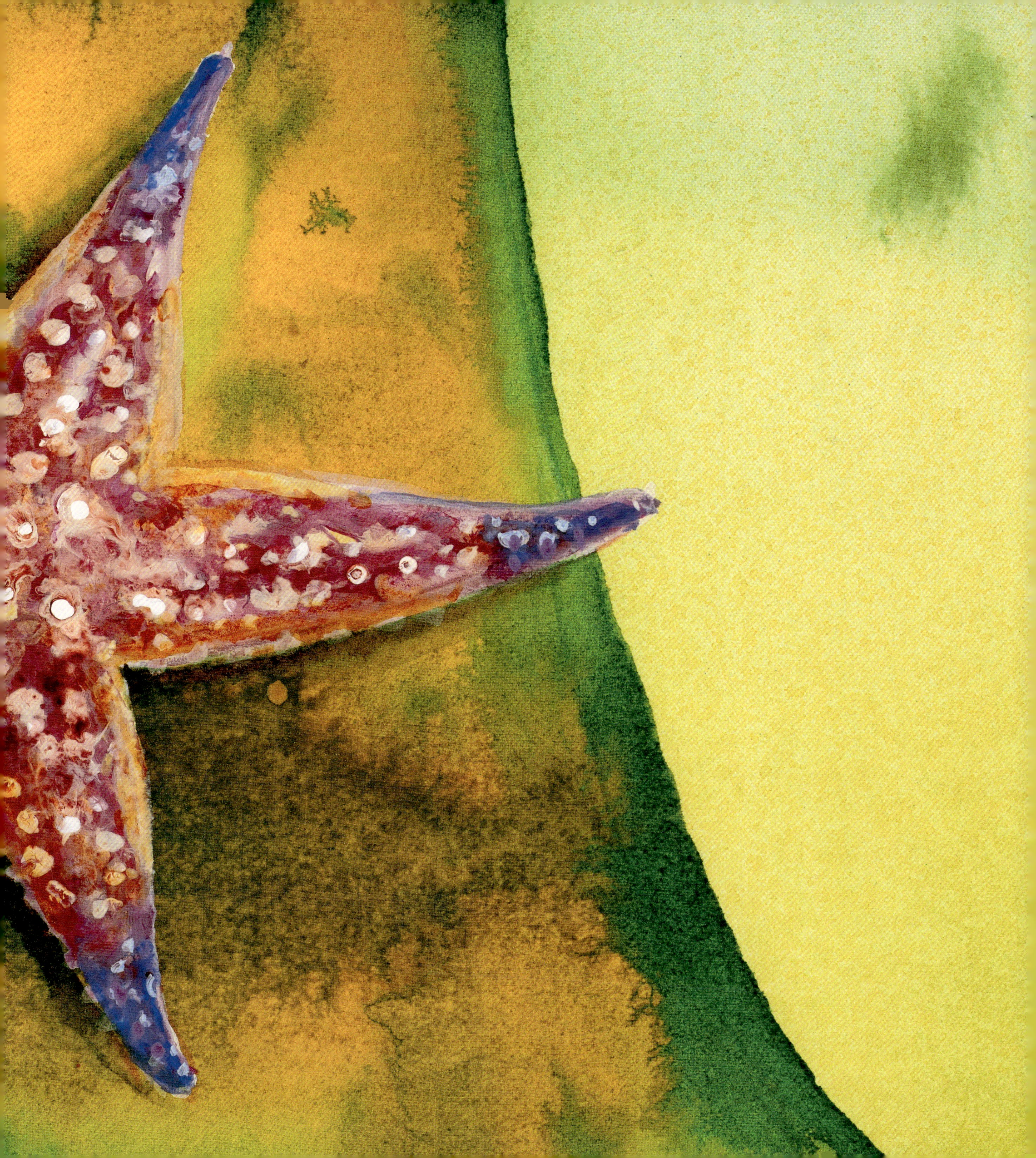

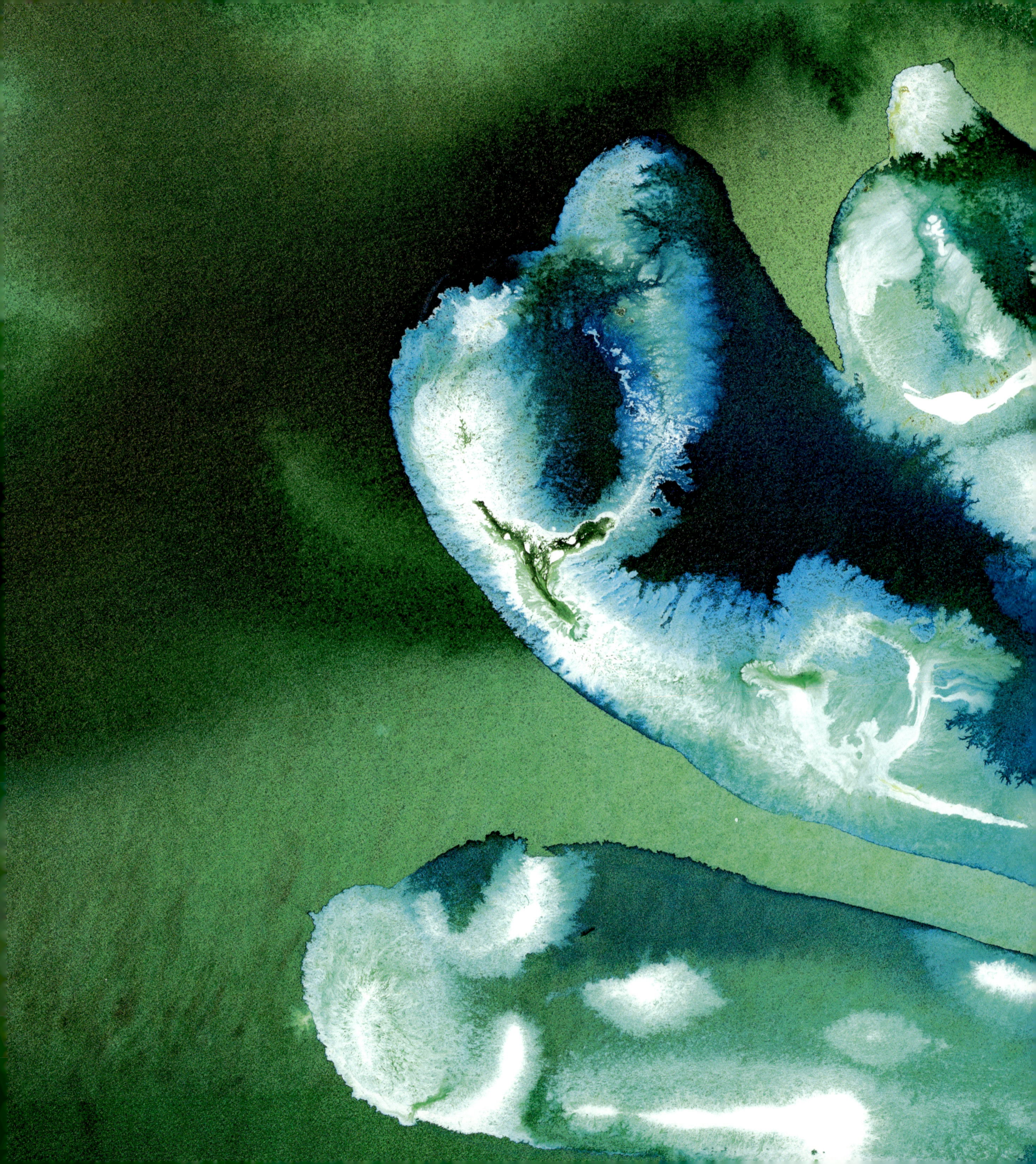

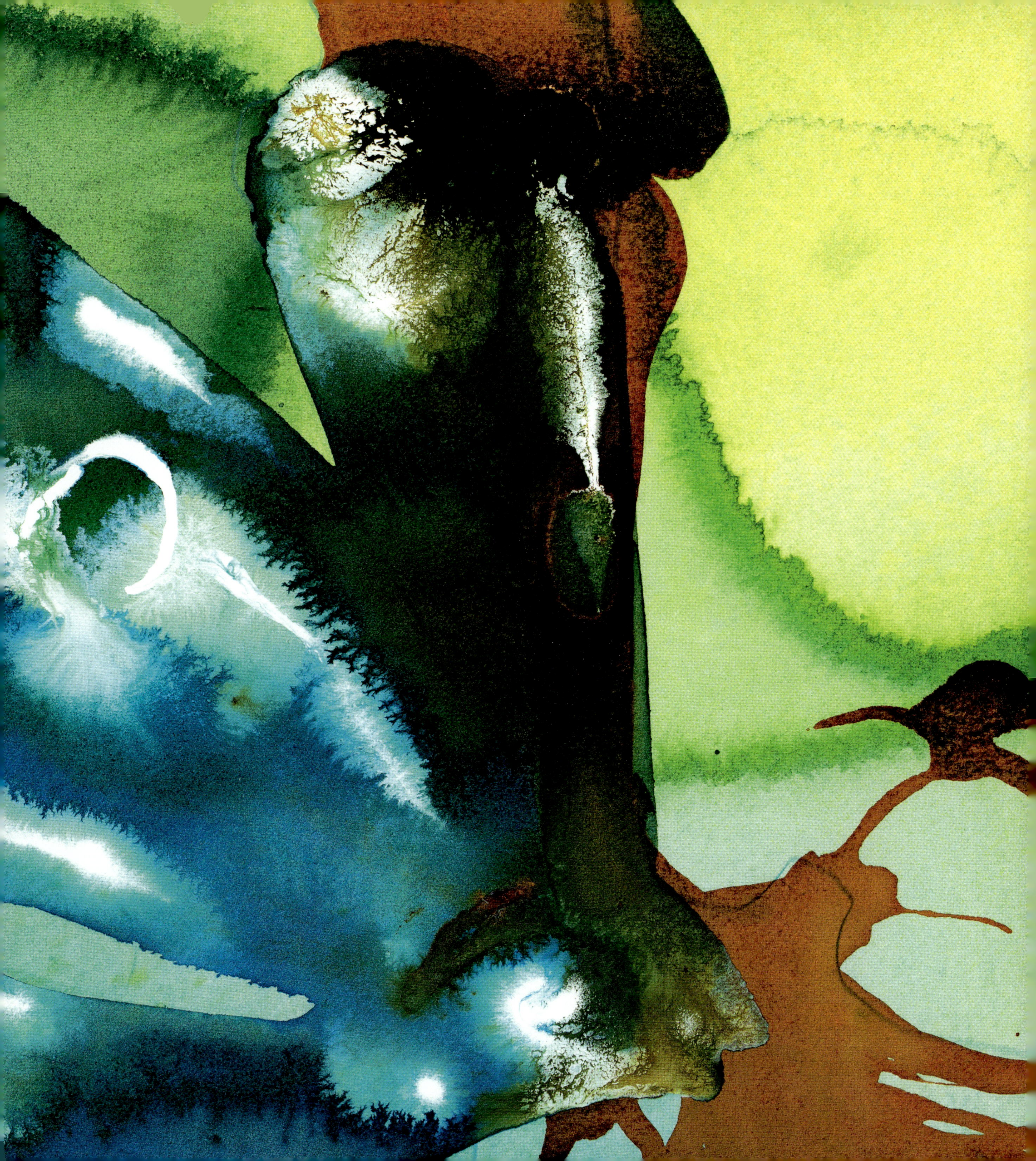

TSUNAMI

Tsunami is a play on Hokusai's famous woodblock print *The Great Wave Off Kanagawa* (1831). However, in my work I chose to depict the tsunami-driven rafting of invasive ecology from the Japanese coast catapulted across the Pacific from the energy generated by the Tōhoku earthquake (2011). Inspired by the monumental gesture and momentum of Hokusai's image, I imagined the scale and energy it must have taken to move these creatures and plants across the vast expanse of the Pacific, and I used research by the marine ecologist Jim Carlton and his colleagues as a reference. These plants and animals hitch a ride either freely or attached to detritus—in one case an unmoored boat, in another, a piece of dock dislodged from the Japanese coast—hitching a ride to new opportunities in the Hawaiian islands and the Pacific Coast of North America, Mexico, and Canada. Carlton and team discovered that an unmoored dock alone harbored over 100 Japanese species and they counted more than 280 species of Japanese hitchhikers on just 600 pieces of debris. Reports had confirmed that there was extensive damage to endemic nesting sites, hatcheries, and adult foraging habitats due to the tsunami.

—AR

Tsunami, 2021. Watercolor and acrylic on paper,
52 × 74 inches (132.1 × 188 cm)

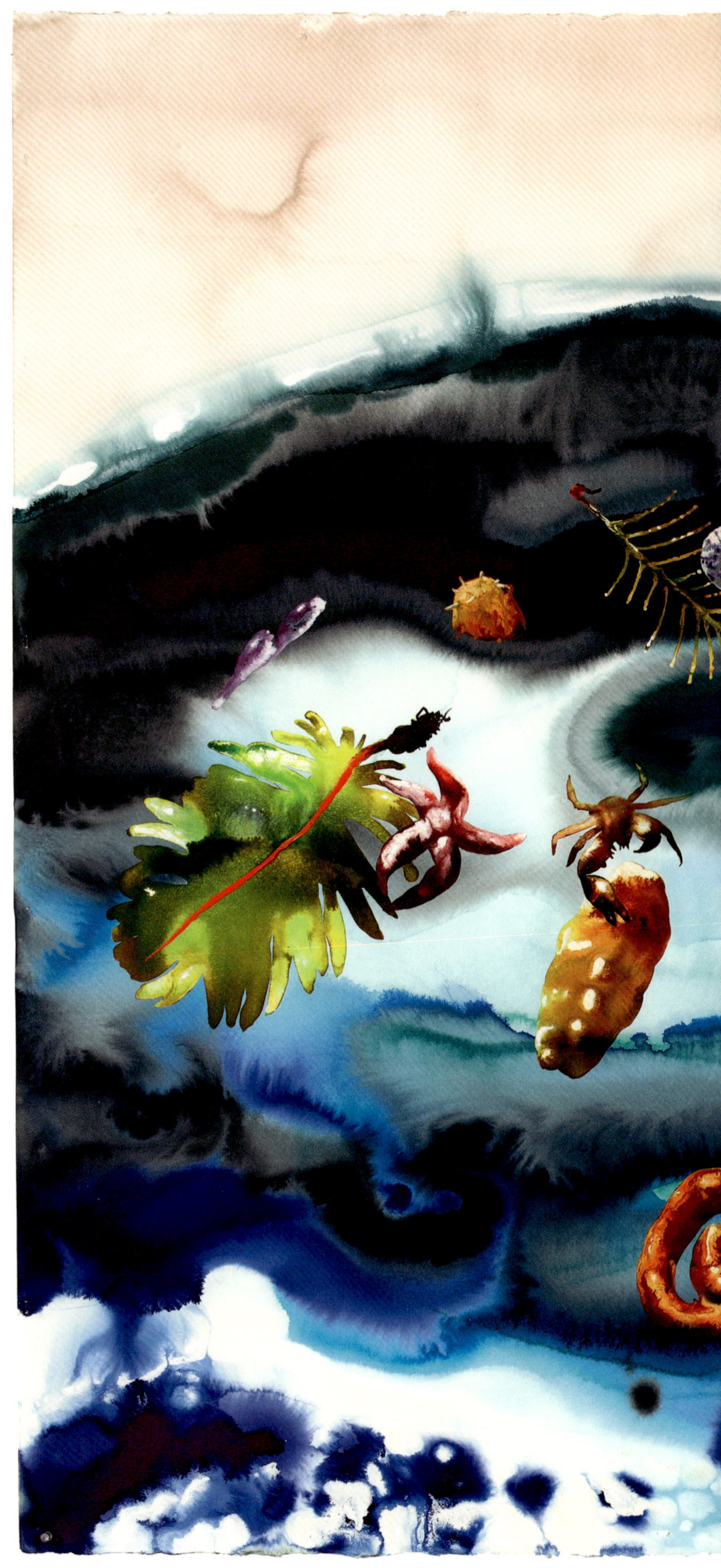

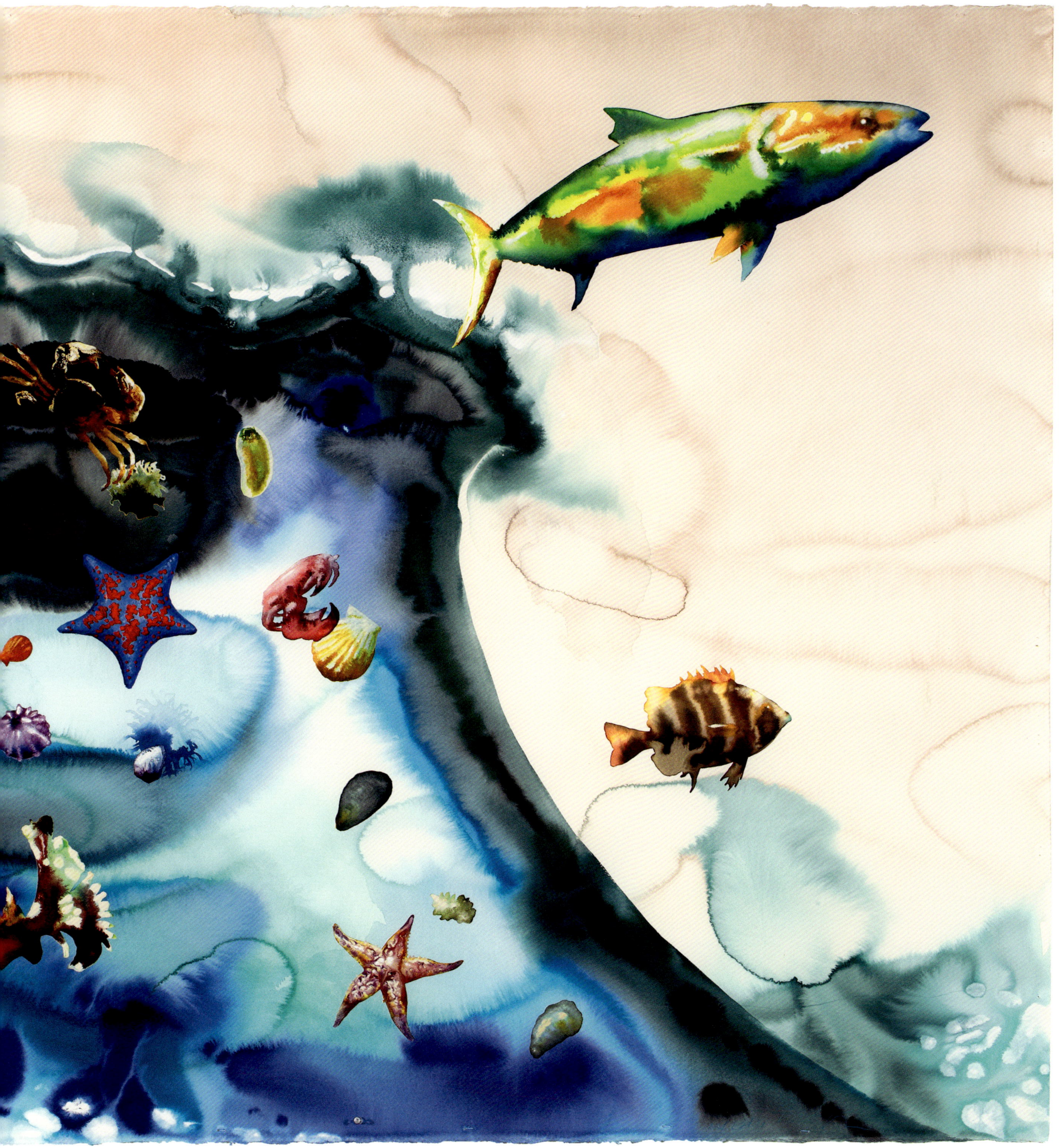

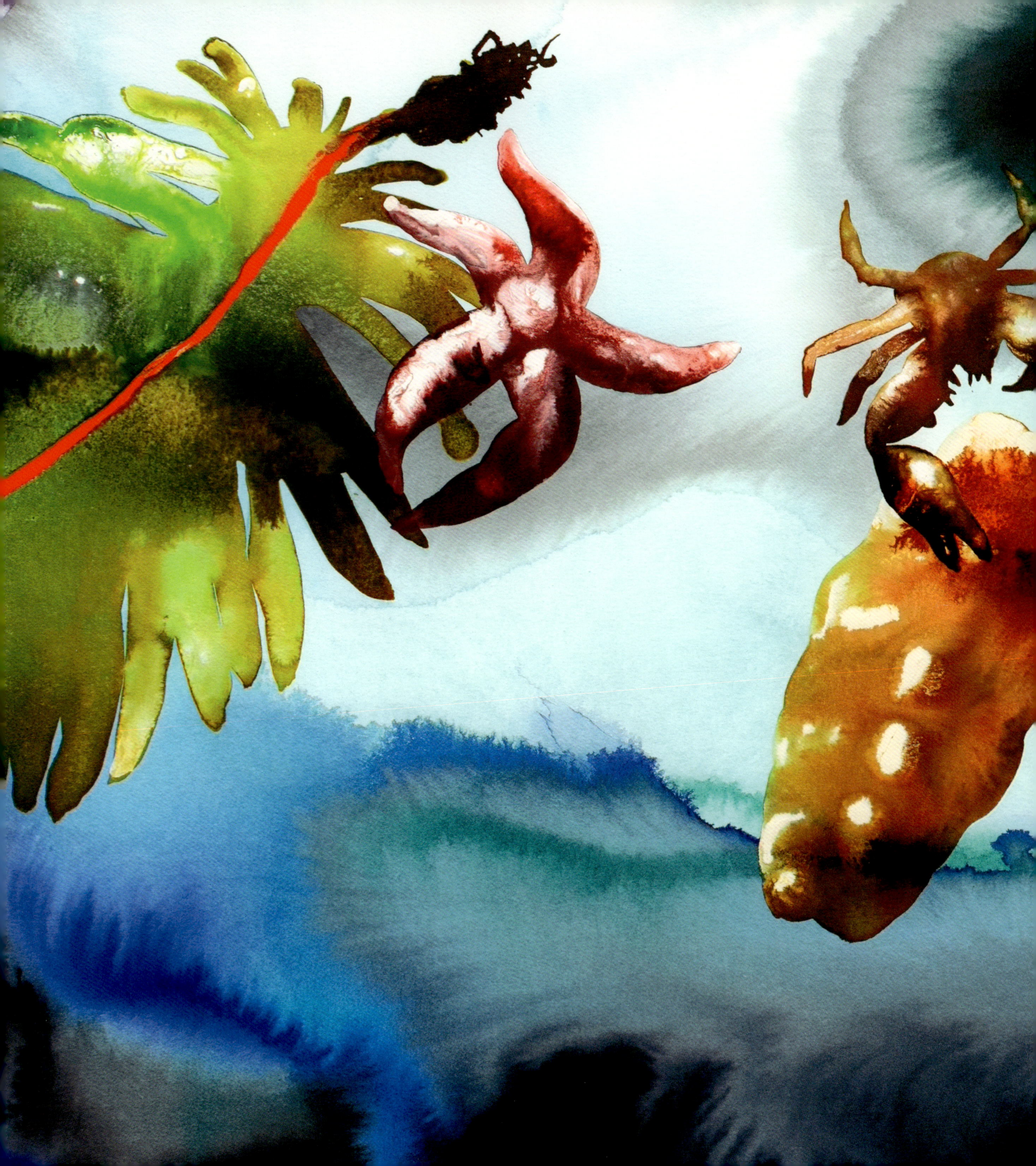

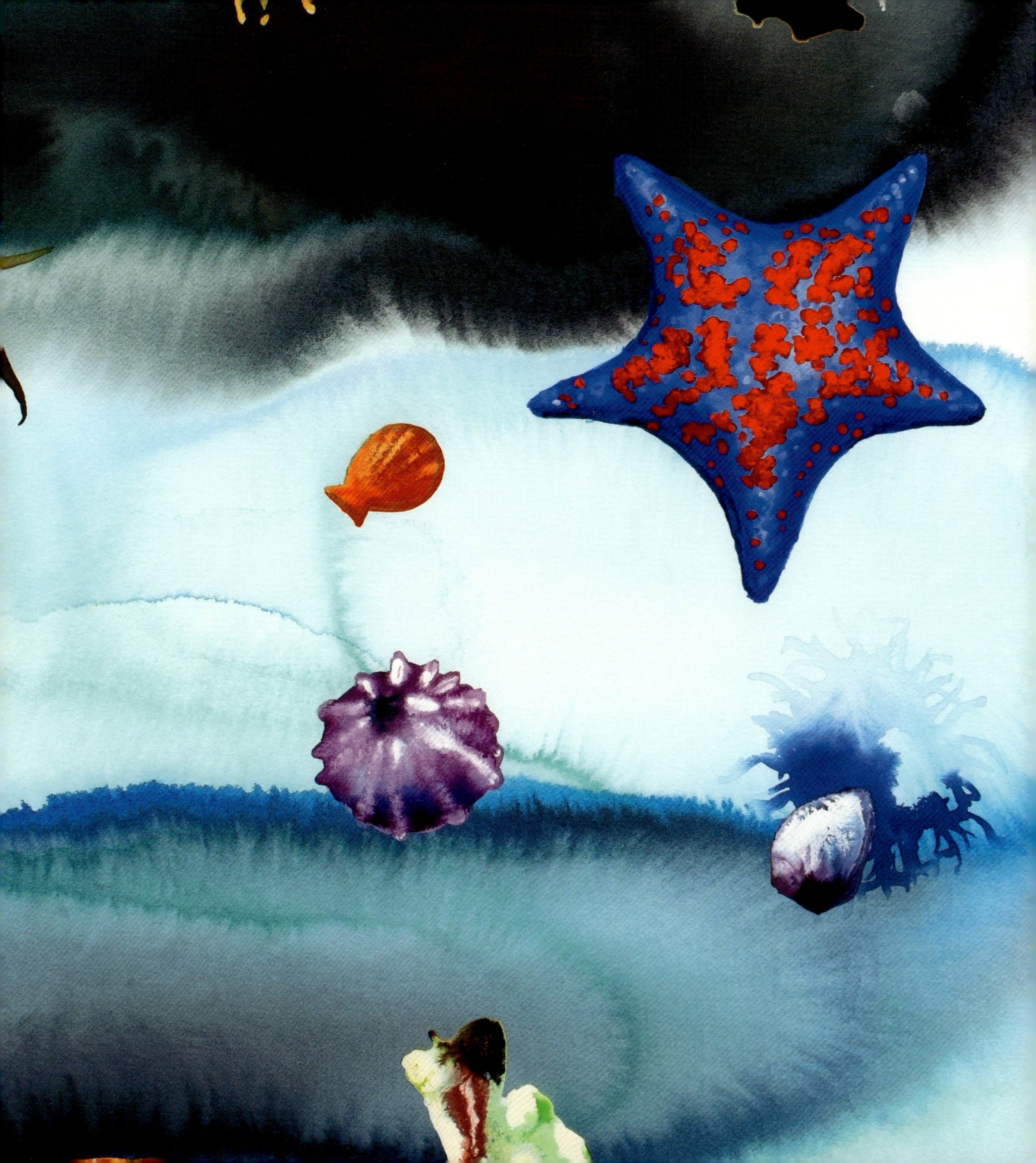

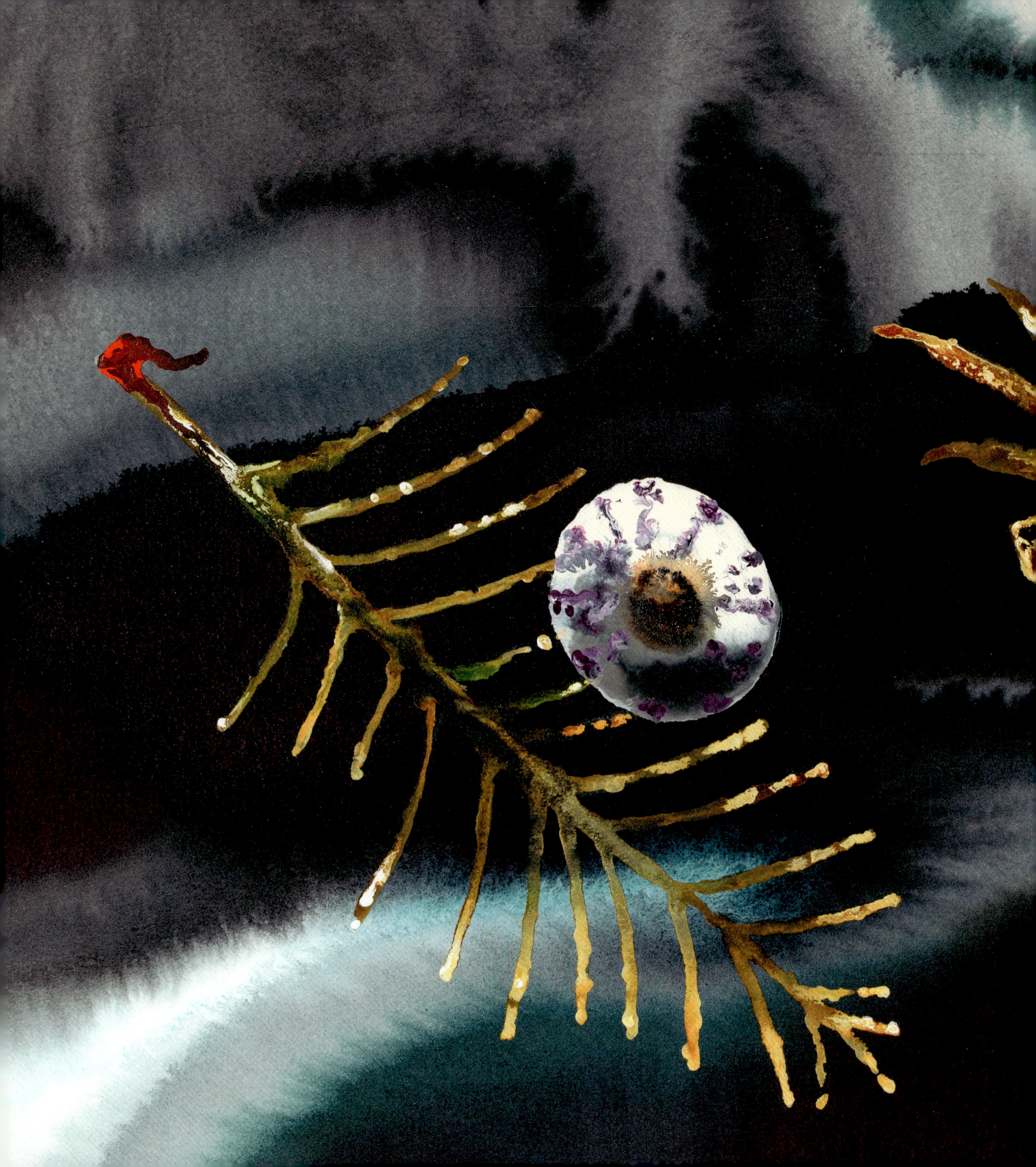

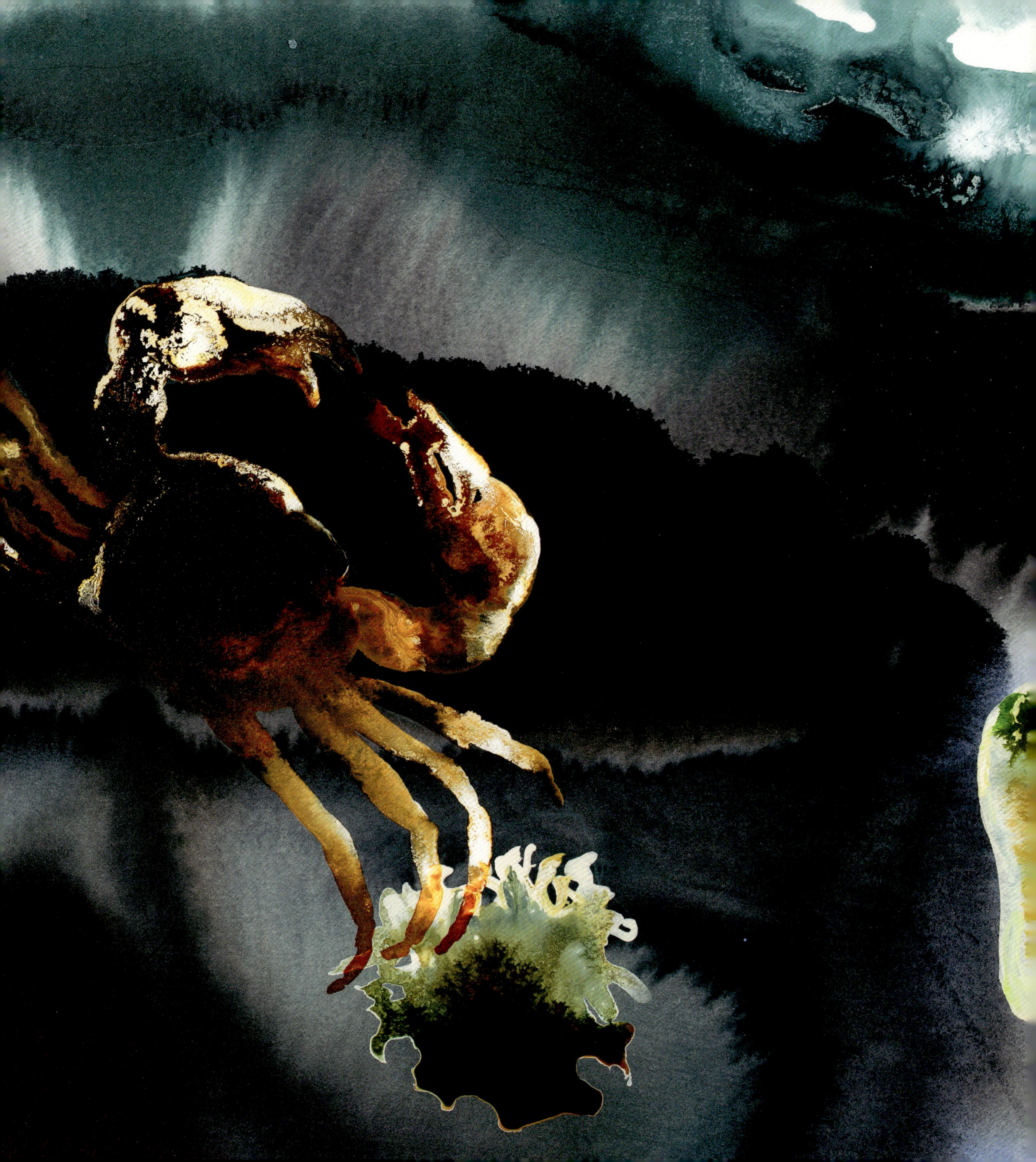

BENTHOS

Benthos continues my fascination with the lightless world at
the bottom of the ocean, which began in 2009–12 when I
collaborated with Ang Lee on his movie *Life of Pi* (2012).
My role was that of "inspirational artist," which involved creating several hundred watercolors that set the visual tone of the
movie. My focus was on designing the carnivorous island and
the Tiger Vision sequence that takes the viewer inside the
minds of Richard Parker, the tiger, and Pi, and to the lightless
world at the bottom of the ocean. This dazzling underwater
world wasn't even conceivable before Jack Corliss, Tjeerd van
Andel, Bob Ballard, and others made the astounding discovery
in 1977; to their amazement, while exploring an oceanic
spreading ridge near the Galápagos Islands, they found that
the hydrothermal vents were surrounded by large numbers of
organisms that had never been seen before and that only lived
in these unique conditions. Sadly there's now a race to mine
and exploit minerals and other resources with remotely operated vehicles. The destruction of these natural landforms, the
compaction of the sea floor, and the creation of sediment
plumes all disrupt aquatic life. Other impacts include noise,
electromagnetic effects, disruption of the larval supply,
contamination, and fluid flow changes. Extractive activities
put these ecosystems at huge risk.

—AR

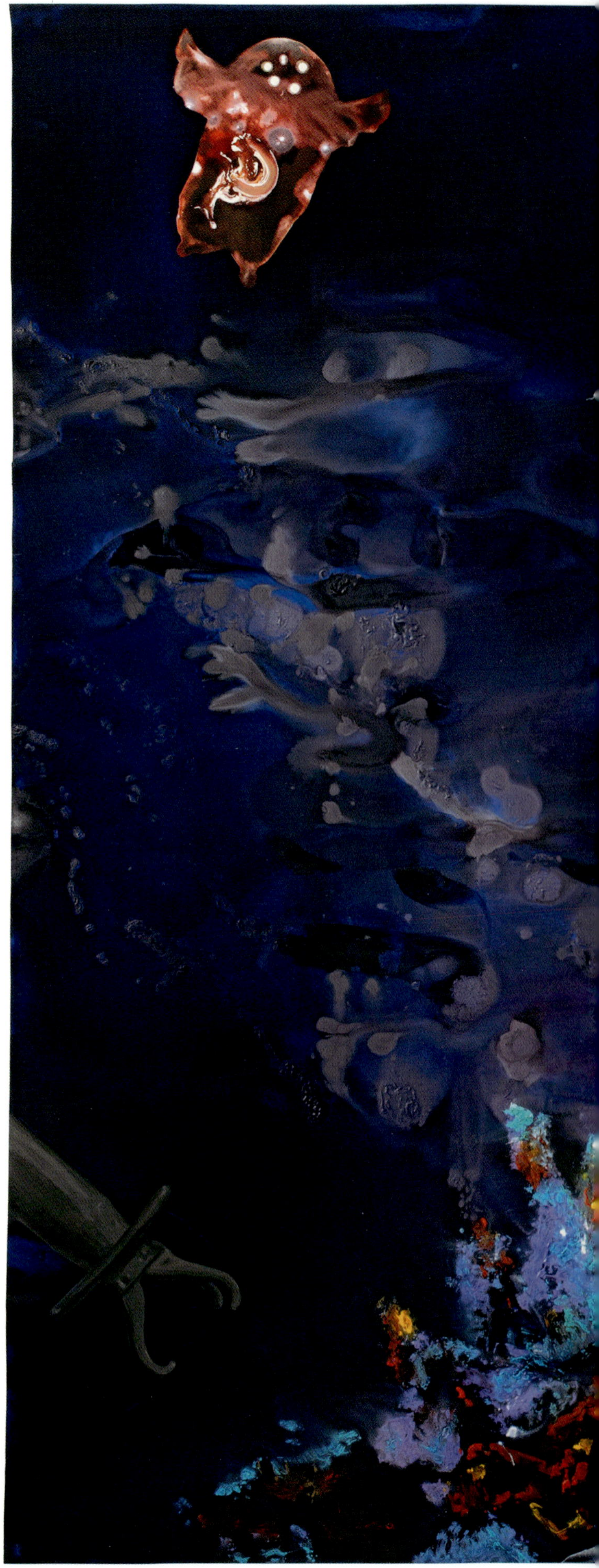

Benthos, 2022. Watercolor and gouache on black paper,
56 × 75 inches (142.2 × 190.5 cm)

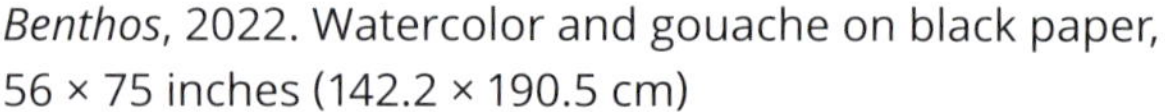

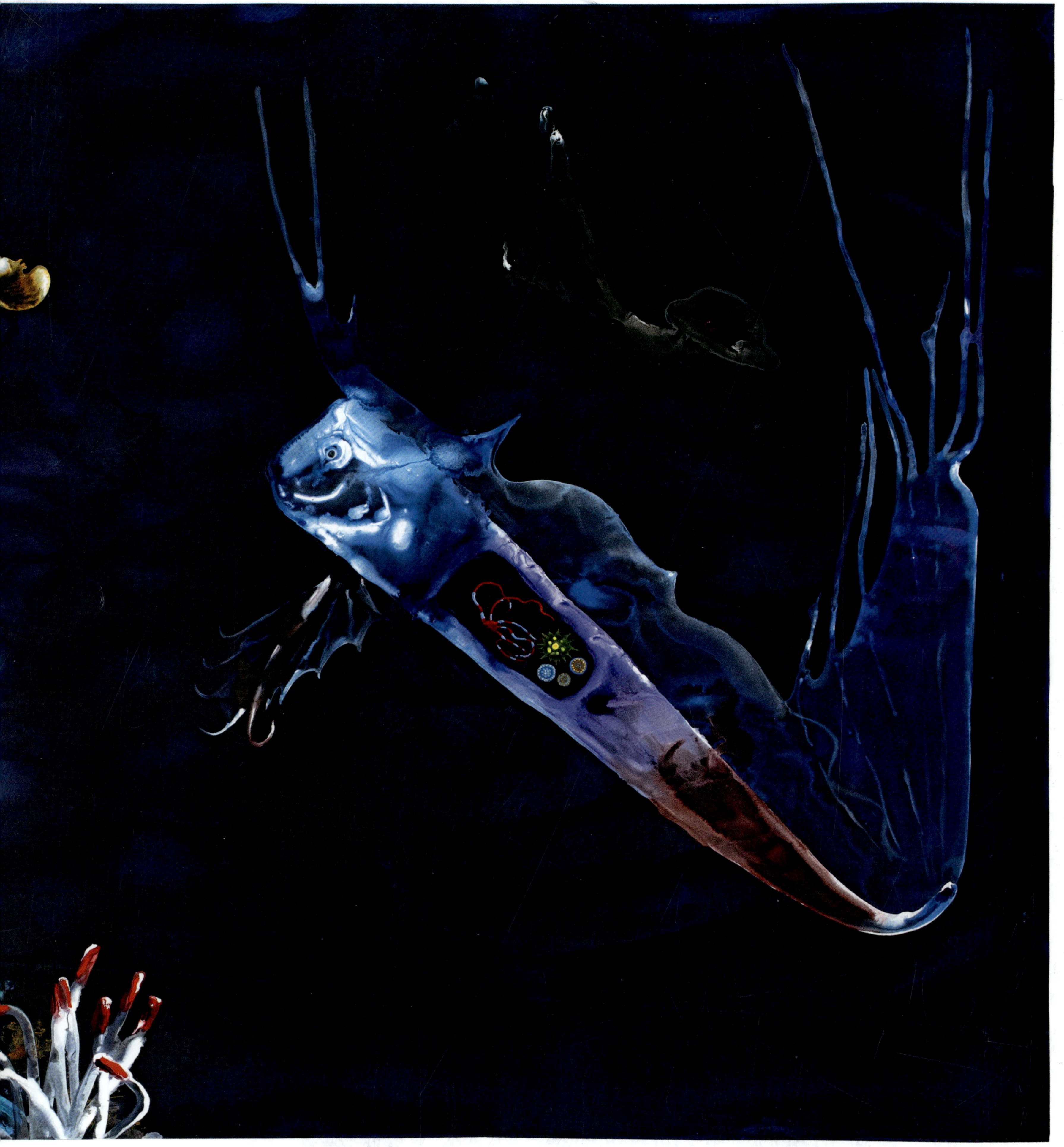

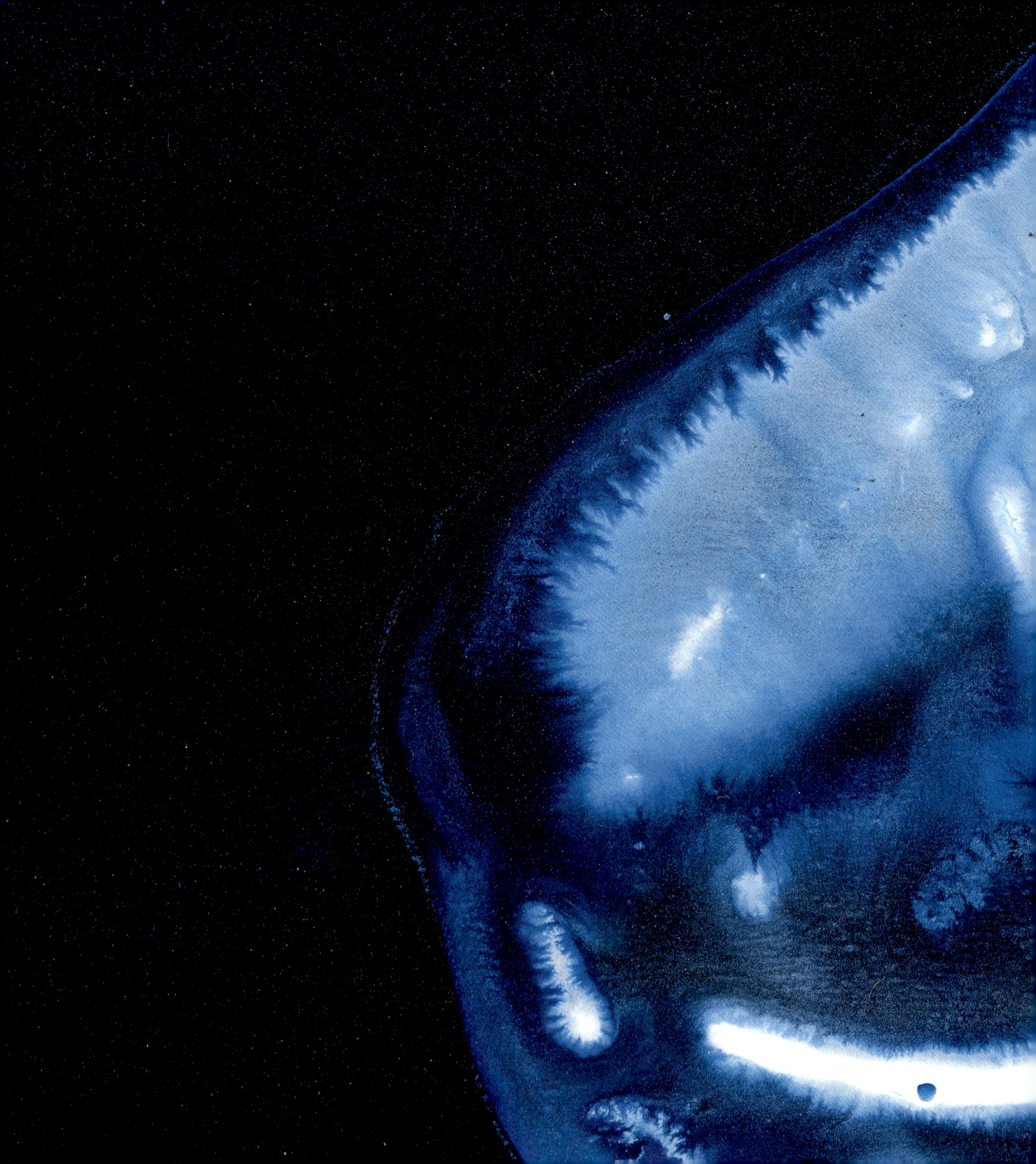

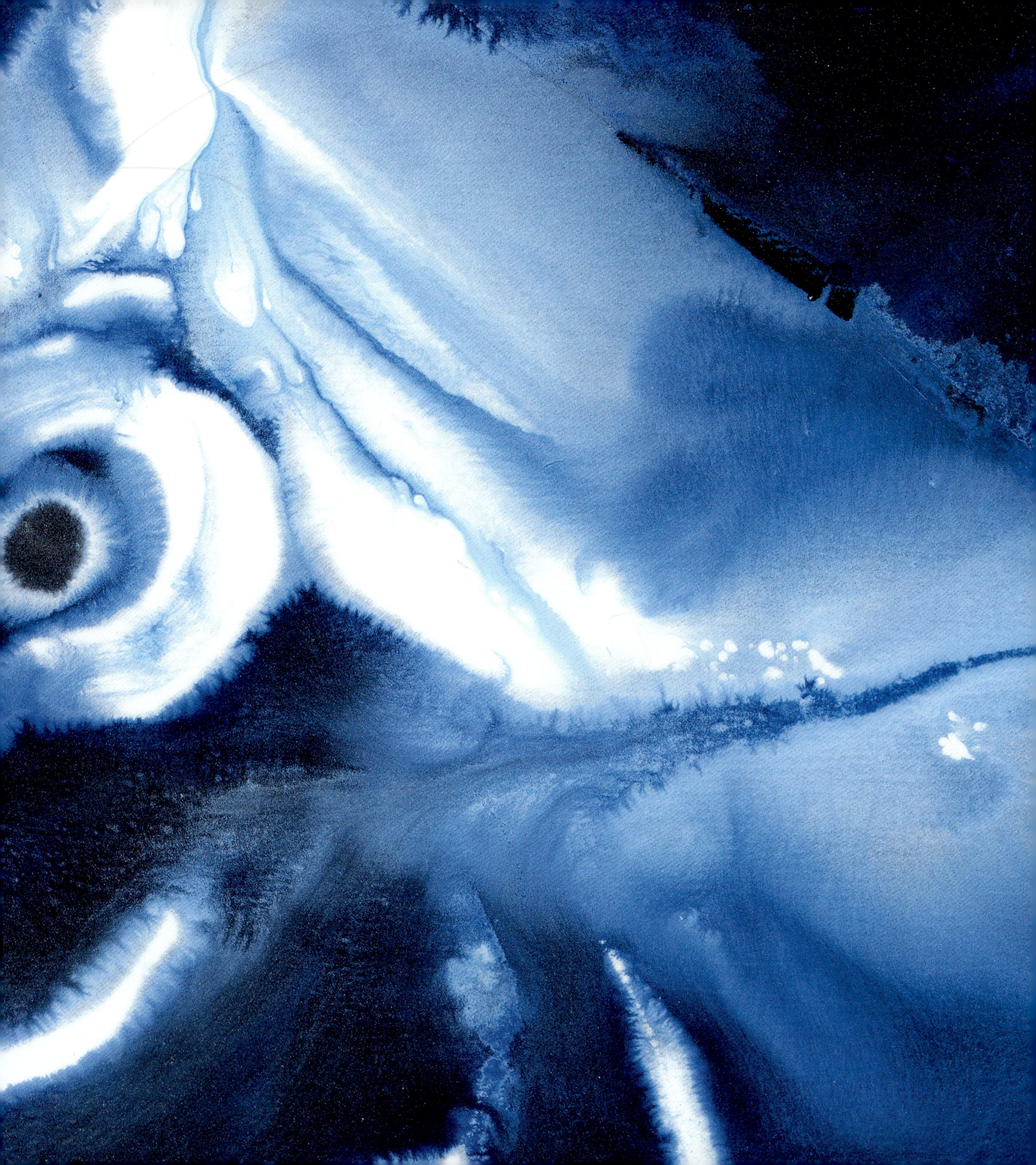

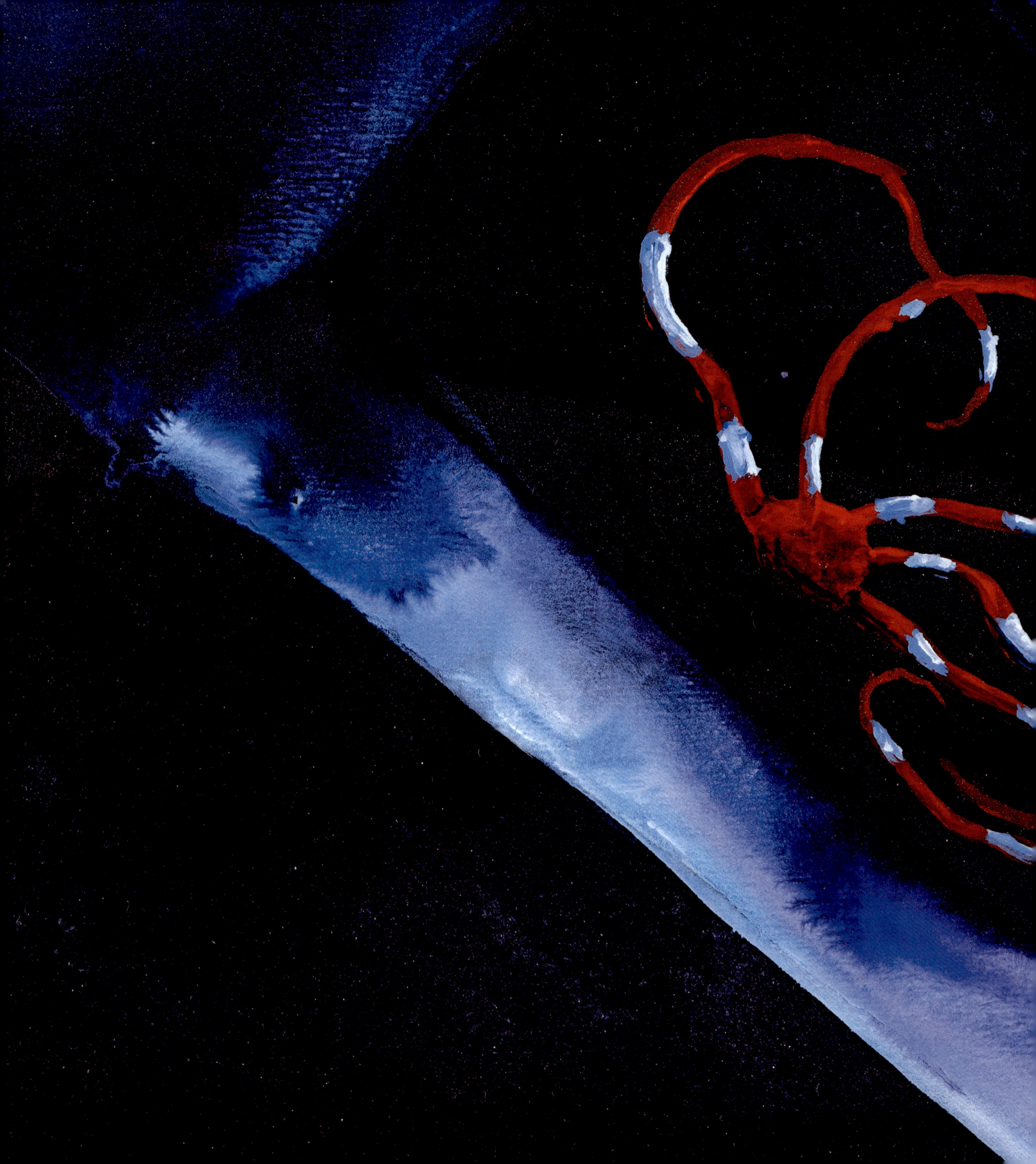

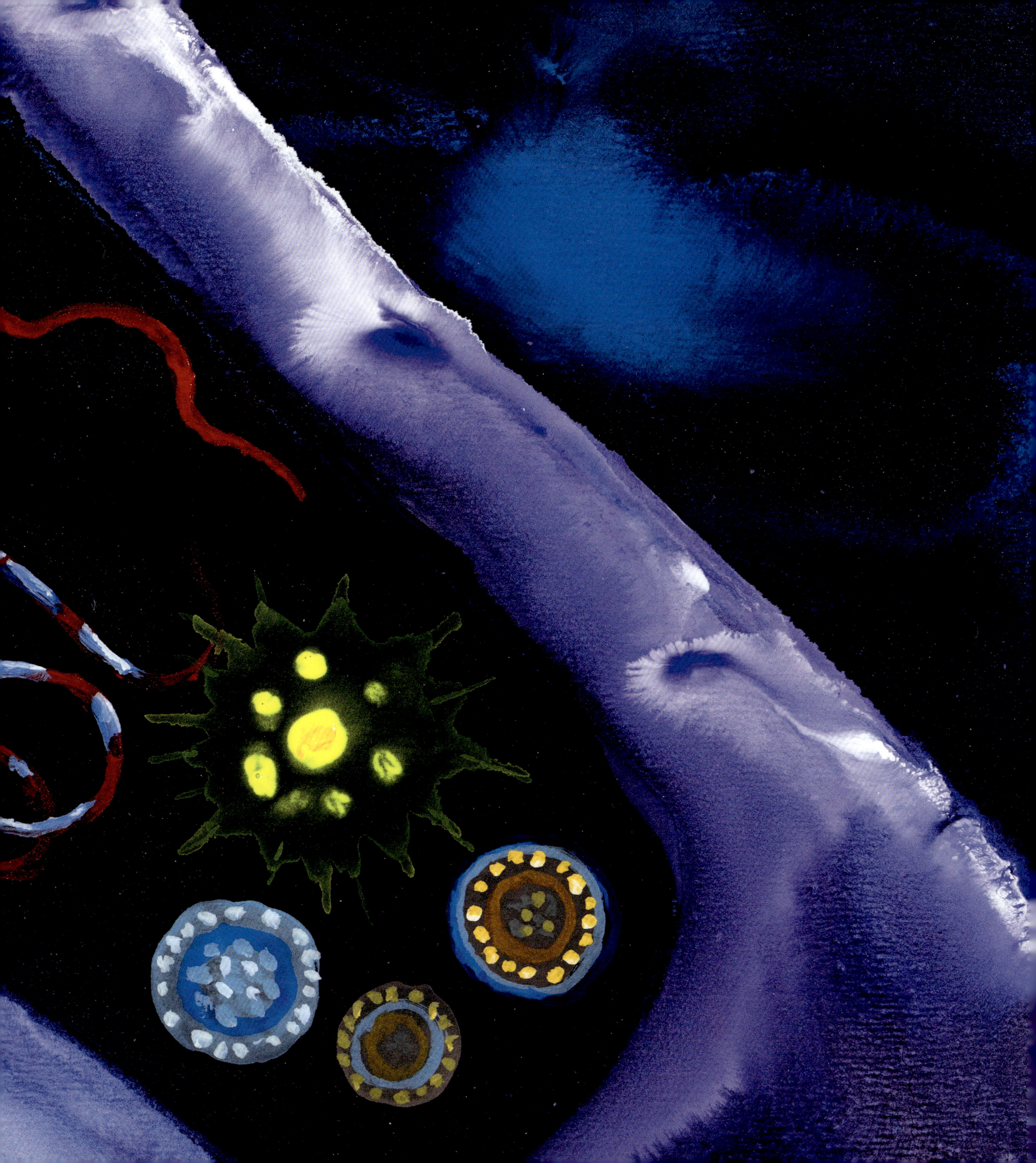

TRANSIENT PASSAGE

Inspired by research on neopelagic ecology by Jim Carlton, Linsey Haram, and Greg Ruiz, *Transient Passage* is about the new branch of science that studies coastal animals that have found a new way to survive in the open ocean by colonizing plastic pollution, which flourishes hundreds of miles out to sea in the North Pacific subtropical gyre, more commonly known as the Great Pacific garbage patch. Plastic will be with us indefinitely, usually wreaking havoc on marine ecosystems. Showing simultaneous views above and below the waterline, and utilizing the blinding light of Winslow Homer's visionary Bahamas watercolors as a springboard for interpretation, my description of this fascinating world just below the open water's surface presents a teeming metropolis of unlikely protagonists right at home in an enormous soup of plastic debris.

—AR

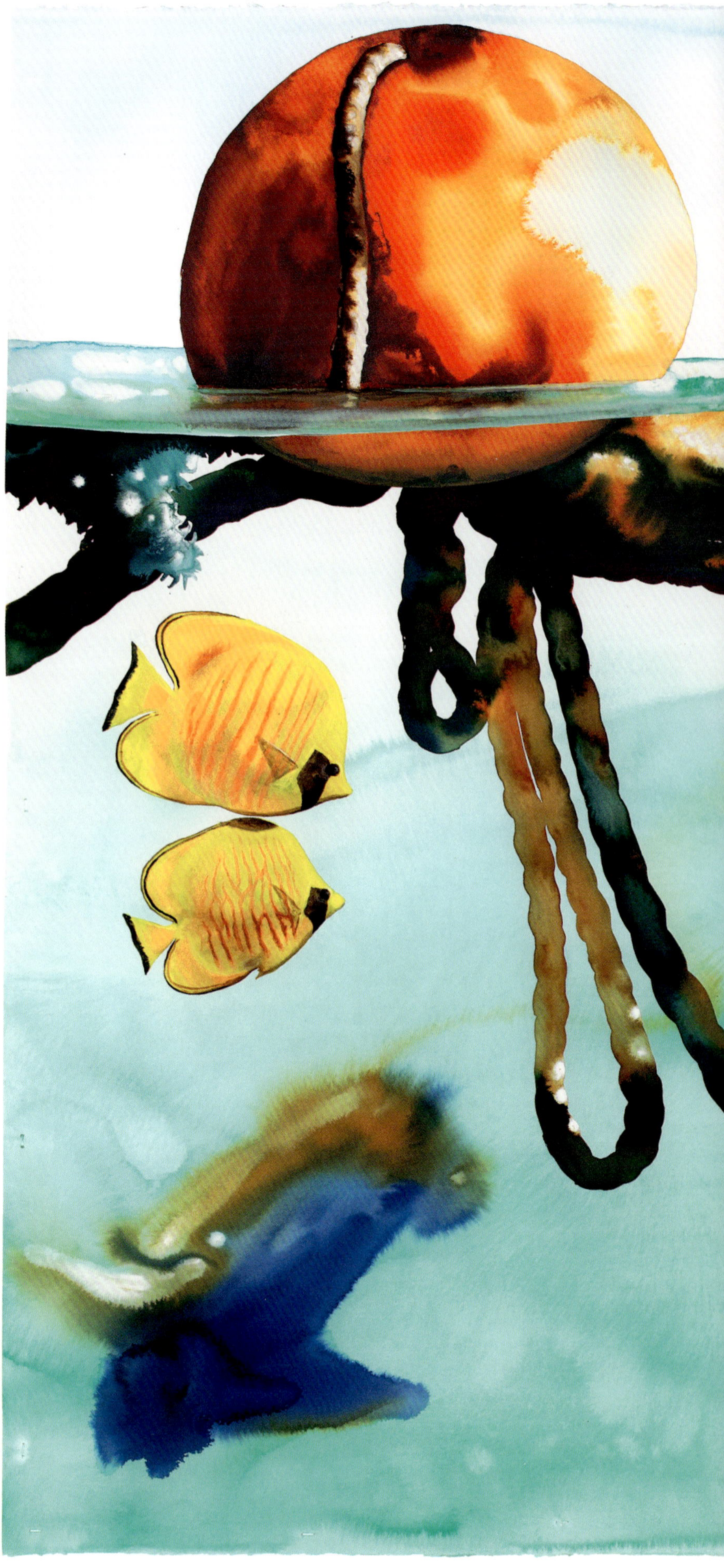

Transient Passage, 2022. Watercolor and acrylic on paper, 52 × 74 inches (132.1 × 188 cm)

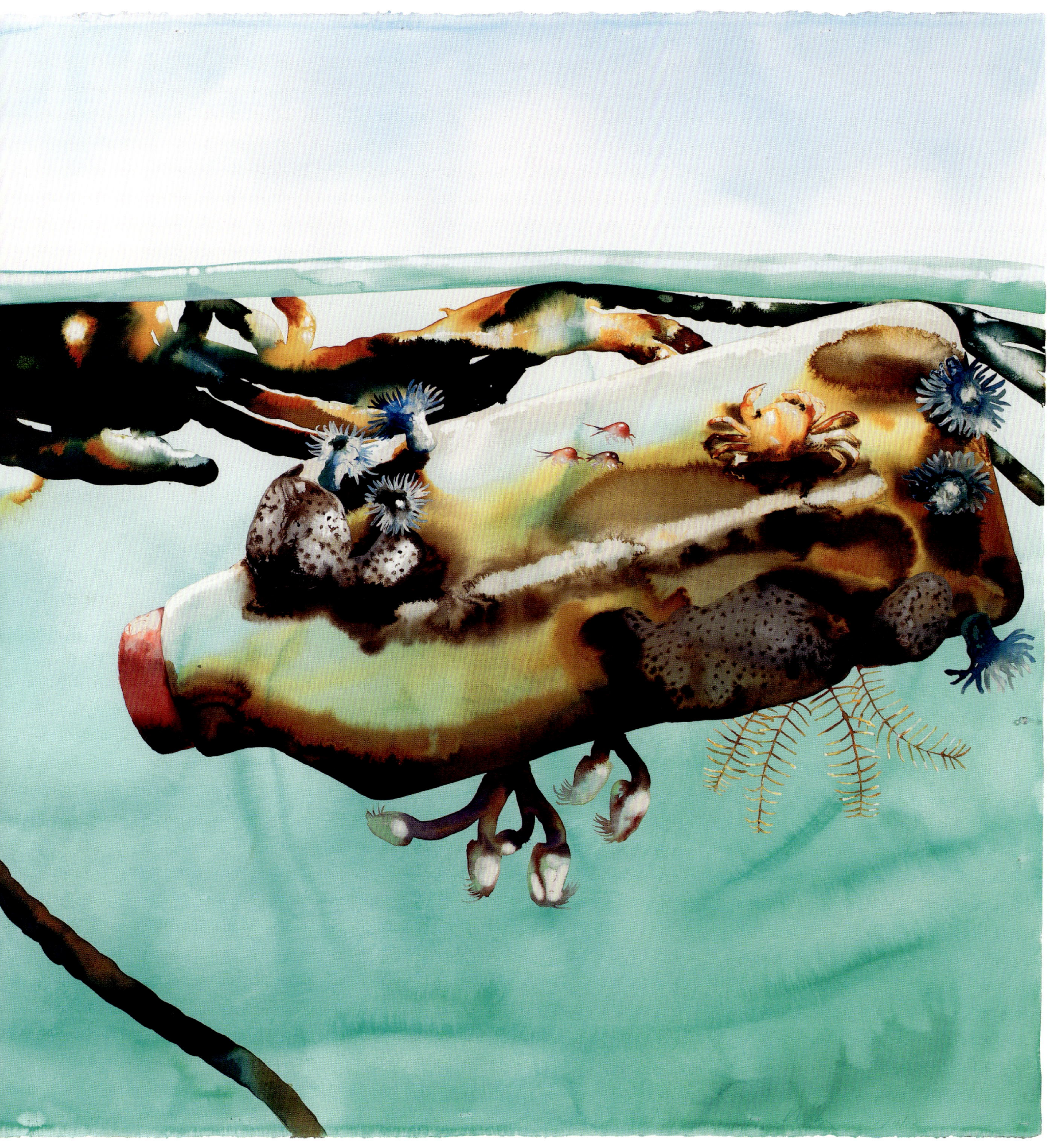

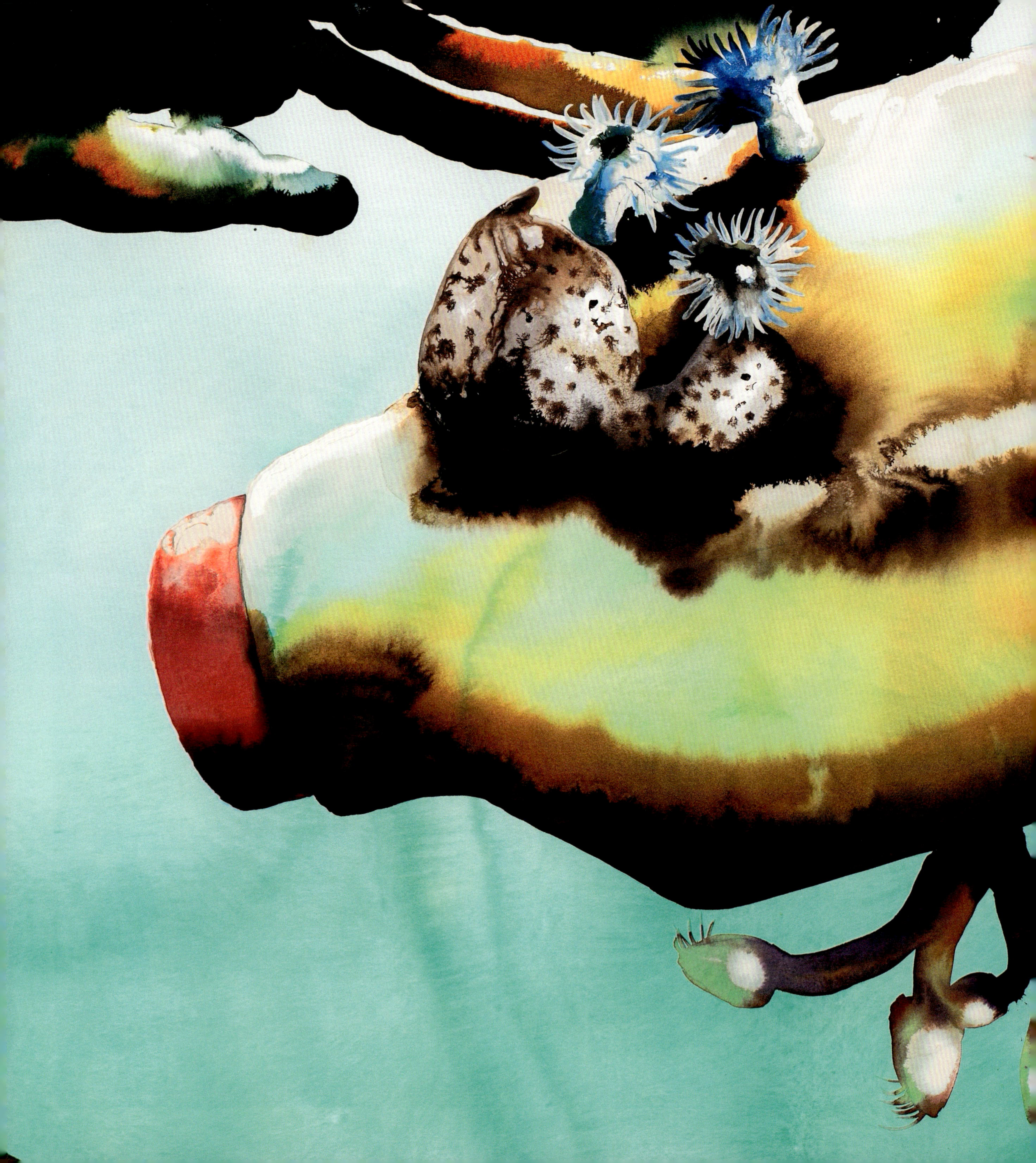

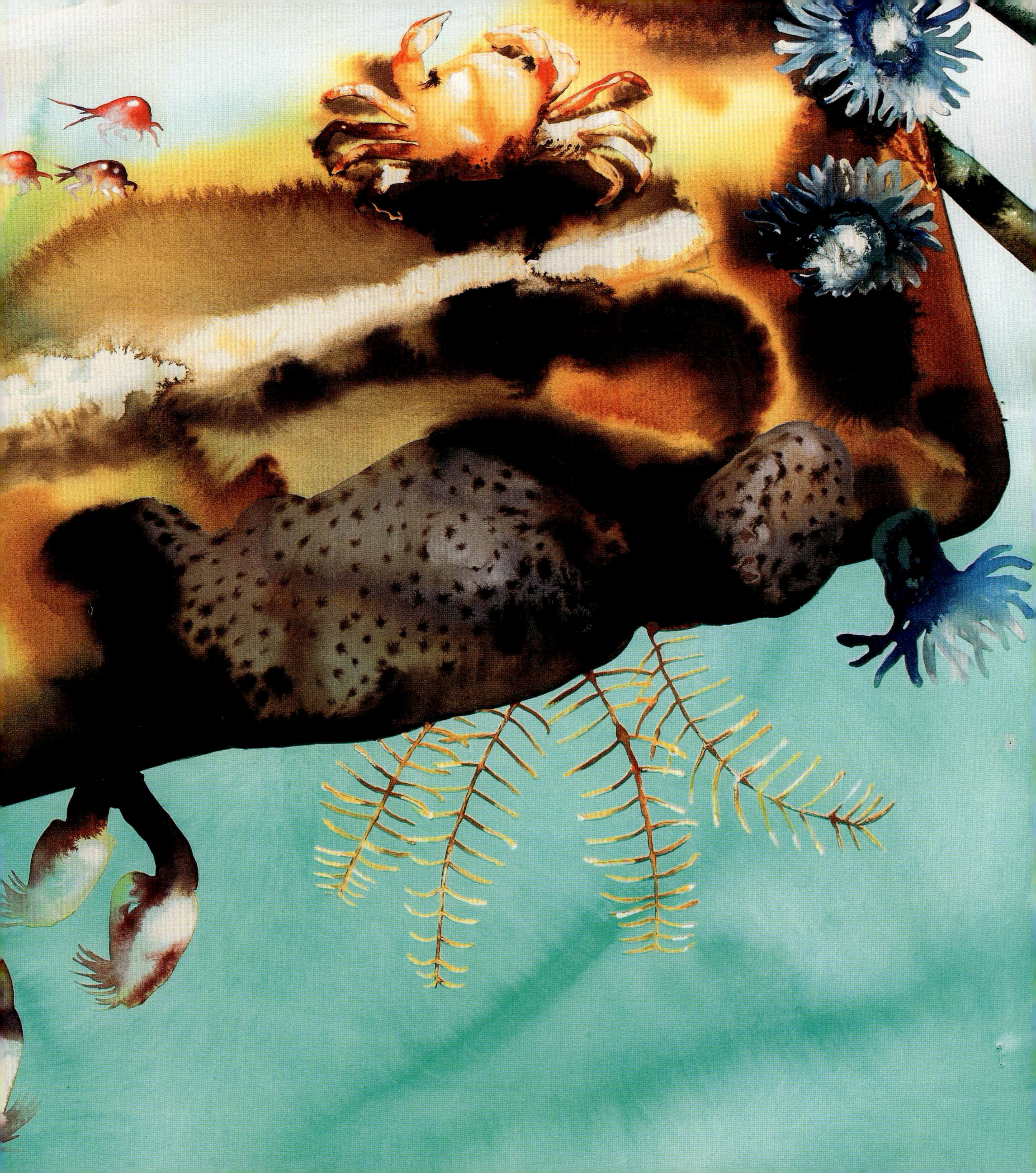

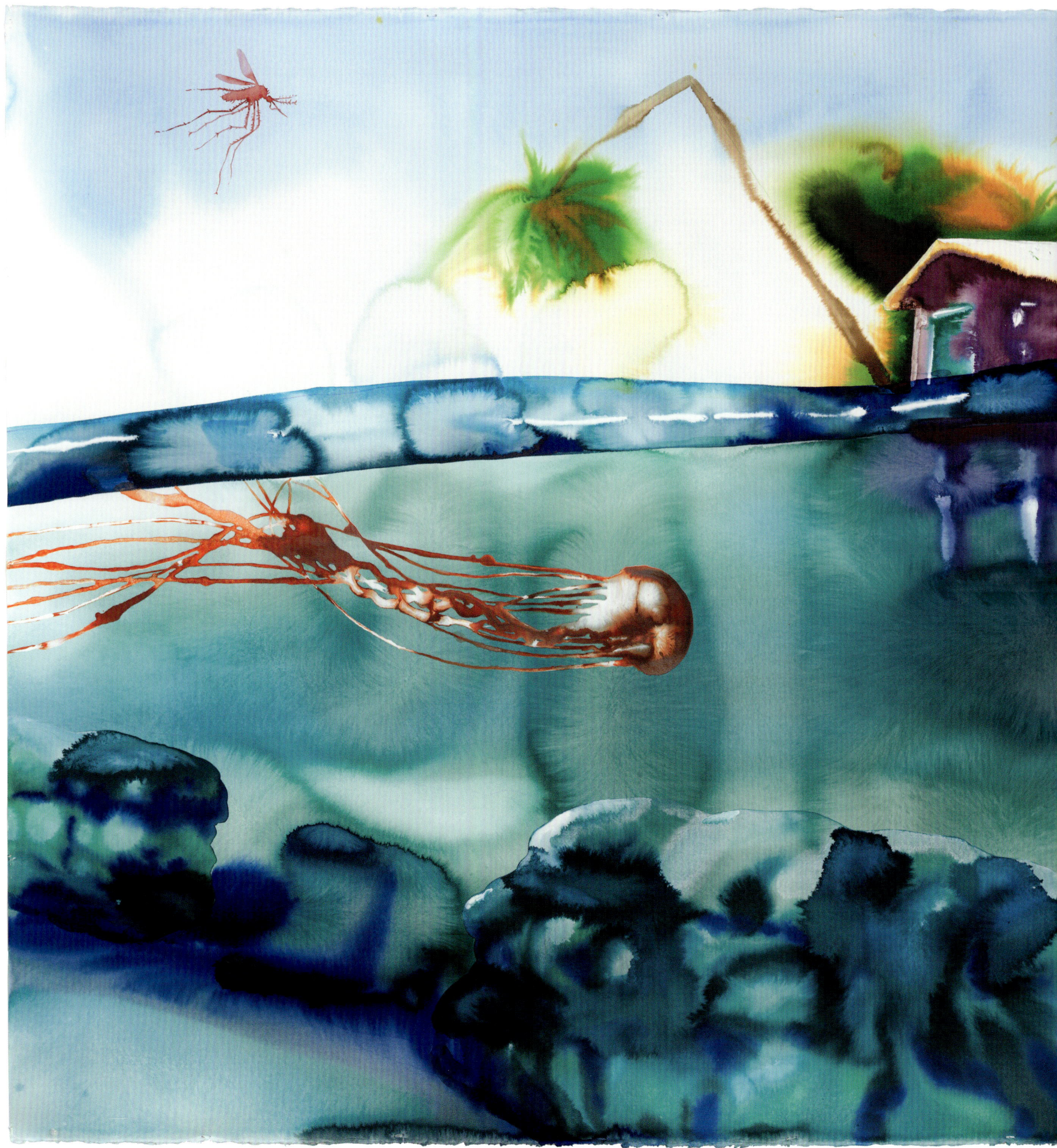

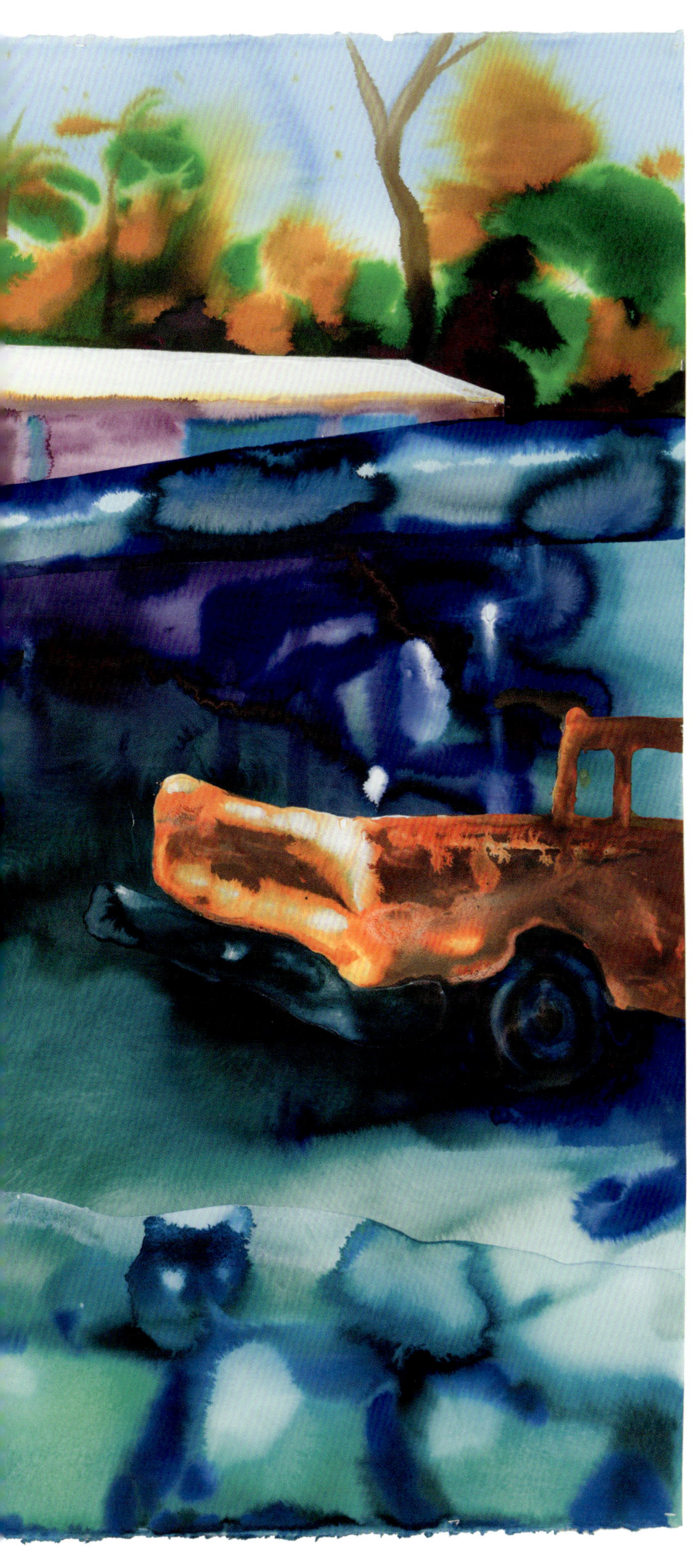

TROPICAL ISLAND

According to the EPA, by 2050, thousands of tropical islands across the globe will be uninhabitable.[1] Many islands are especially vulnerable to the risks of climate change because of their small size, low elevation, remote geographical location, and concentration of human infrastructure along coastlines. Islands are also home to unique ecosystems, including coral reefs, mangrove forests, and diverse populations of native species found nowhere else in the world. Island ecosystems are already stressed from human development and pollution, making them particularly sensitive to additional stresses from climate change. In addition to land becoming swallowed by oceans, drinking water supplies on these islands will be flooded with saltwater as waves become more intense and storms become more frequent. Climate change will affect tourism, an important source of revenue for islands. Sea-level rise, warming water temperatures, and increasing storm surge will make life for humans and endemic plants and animals a challenge.

However, some plants and animals will be able to exploit these new opportunities. In *Tropical Island*—which could depict an island anywhere near the equator—a Pacific sea nettle jellyfish and an *Aedes albopictus* mosquito bring danger from the air and water, while a submerged coastal pile dwelling and a 1973 Ford pickup truck serve as reminders of what was once possible near a shore that was at stable sea level.

—AR

1. See Curt D. Storlazzi et al., "Most atolls will be uninhabitable by the mid-21st century because of sea-level rise exacerbating wave-driven flooding," *Science Advances* 4, no. 4 (April 2018): https://www.science.org/doi/10.1126/sciadv.aap9741.

Tropical Island, 2022. Watercolor and acrylic on paper, 52 × 74¾ inches (132.1 × 192.4 cm)

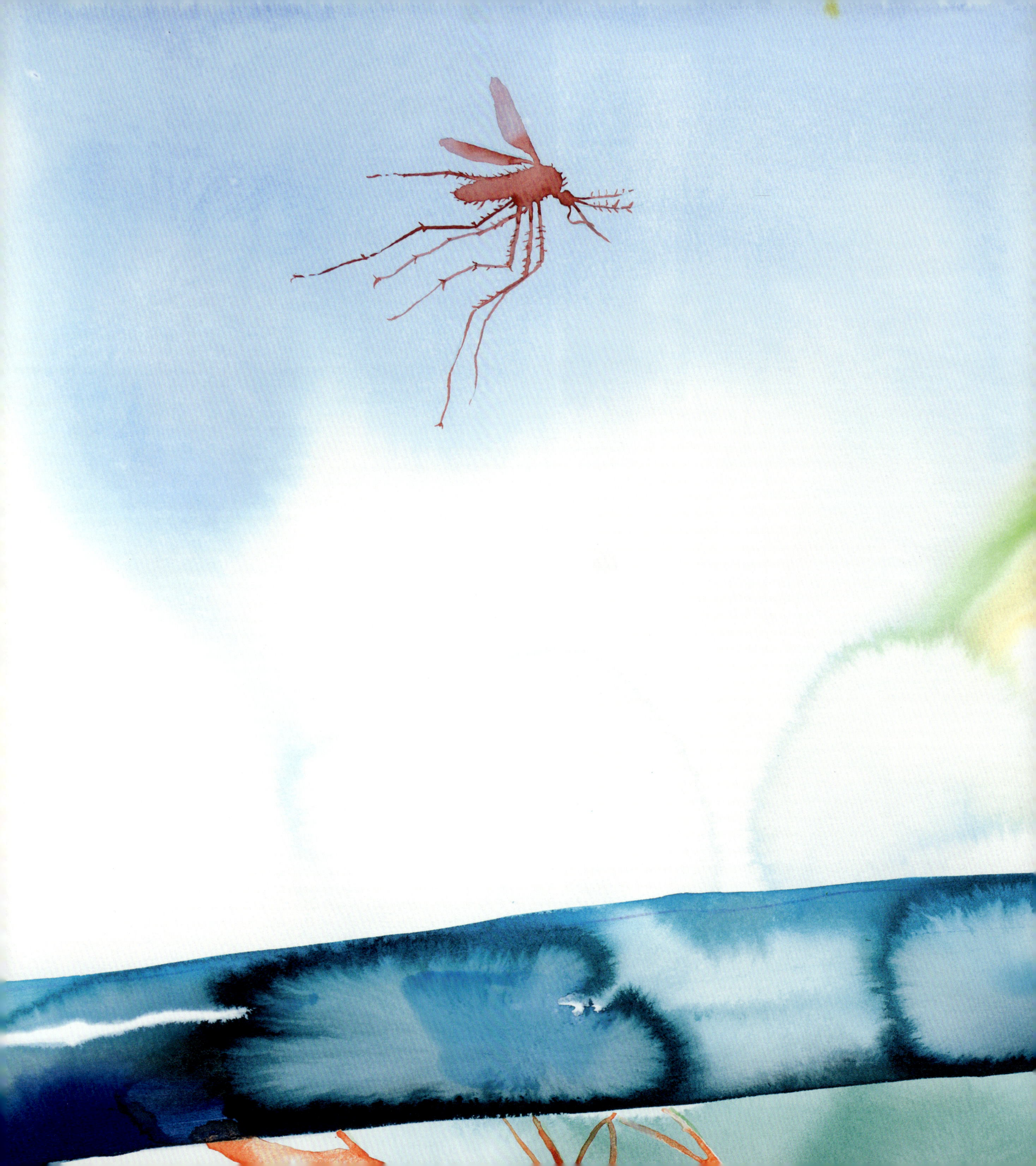

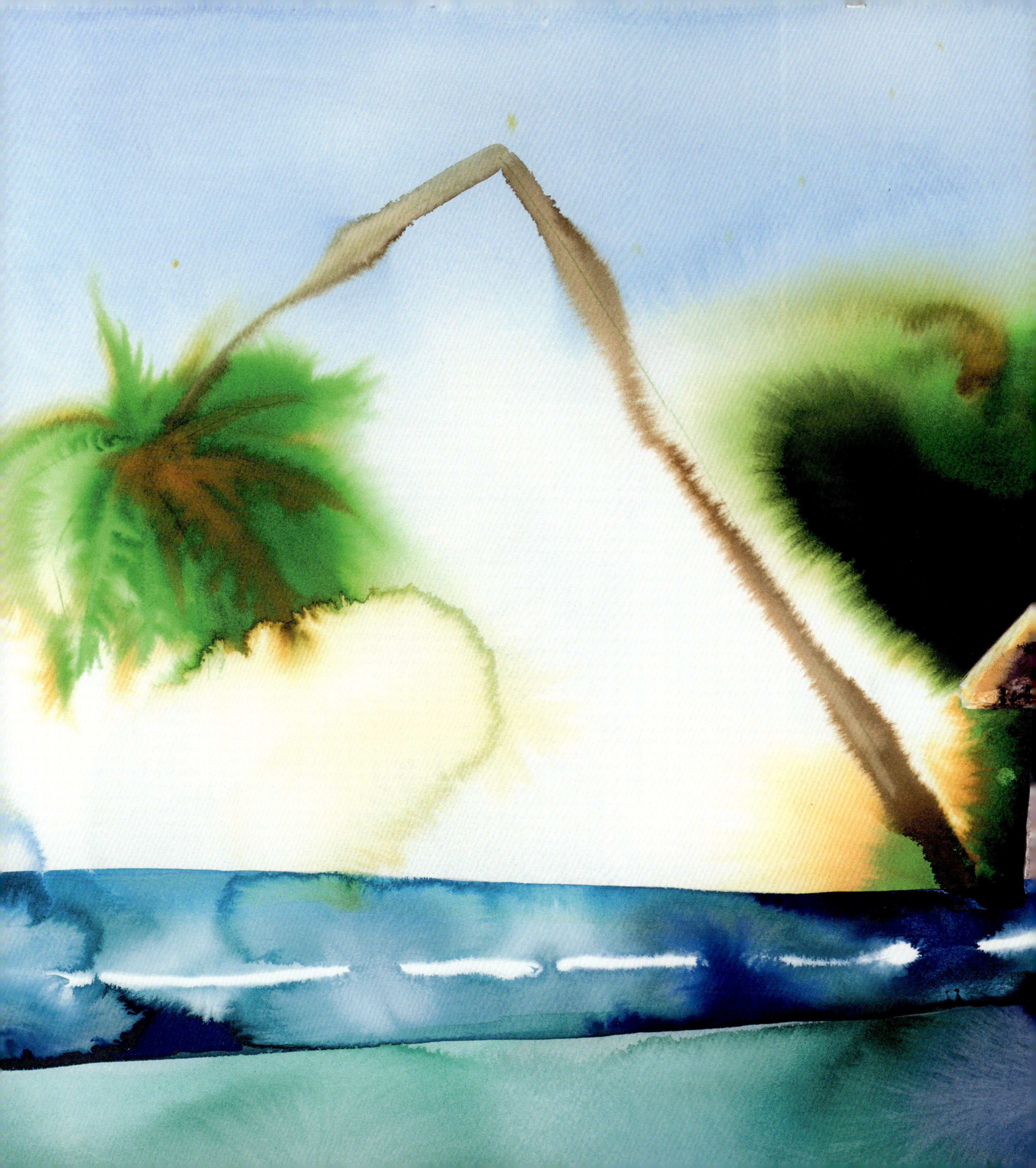

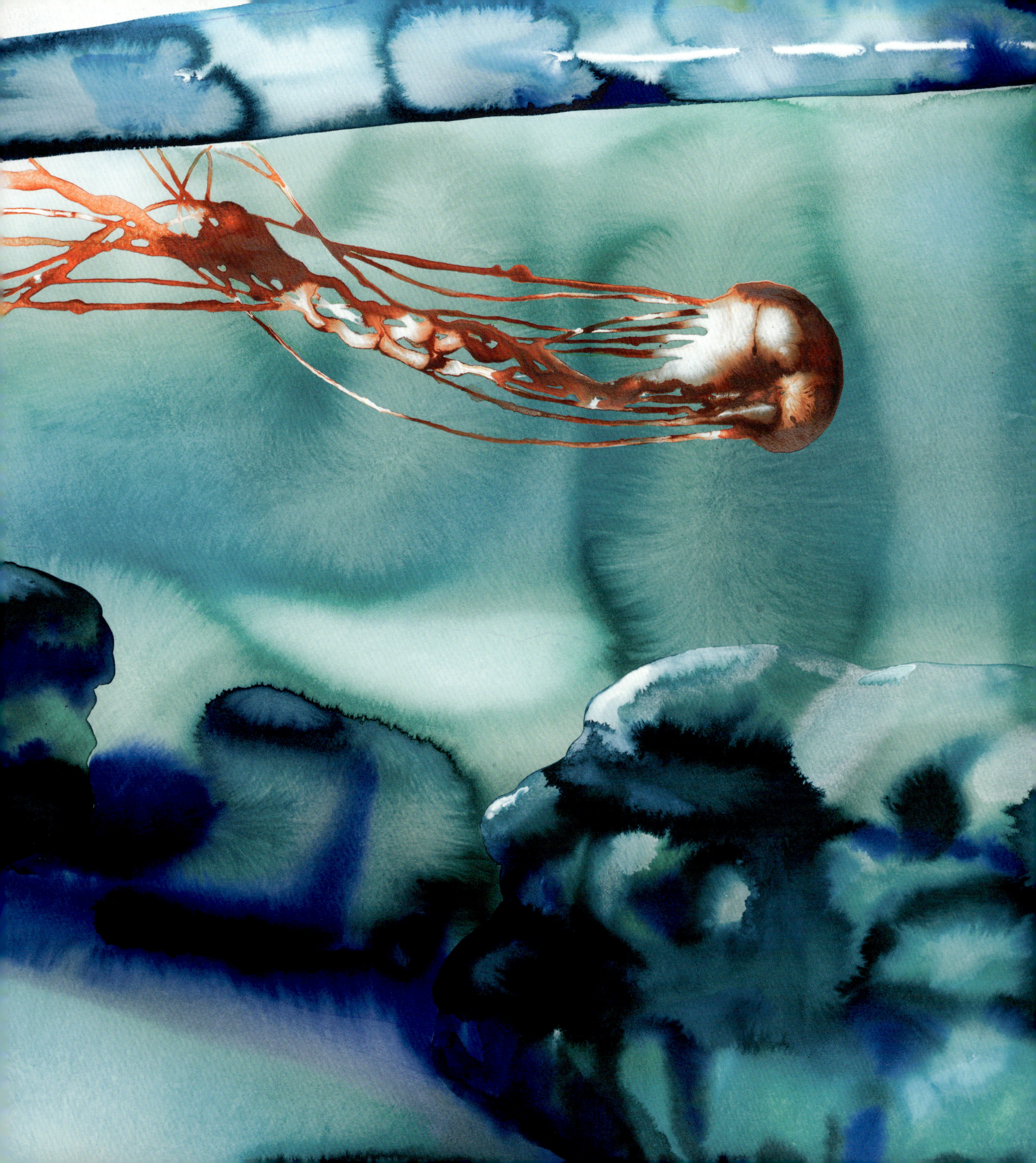

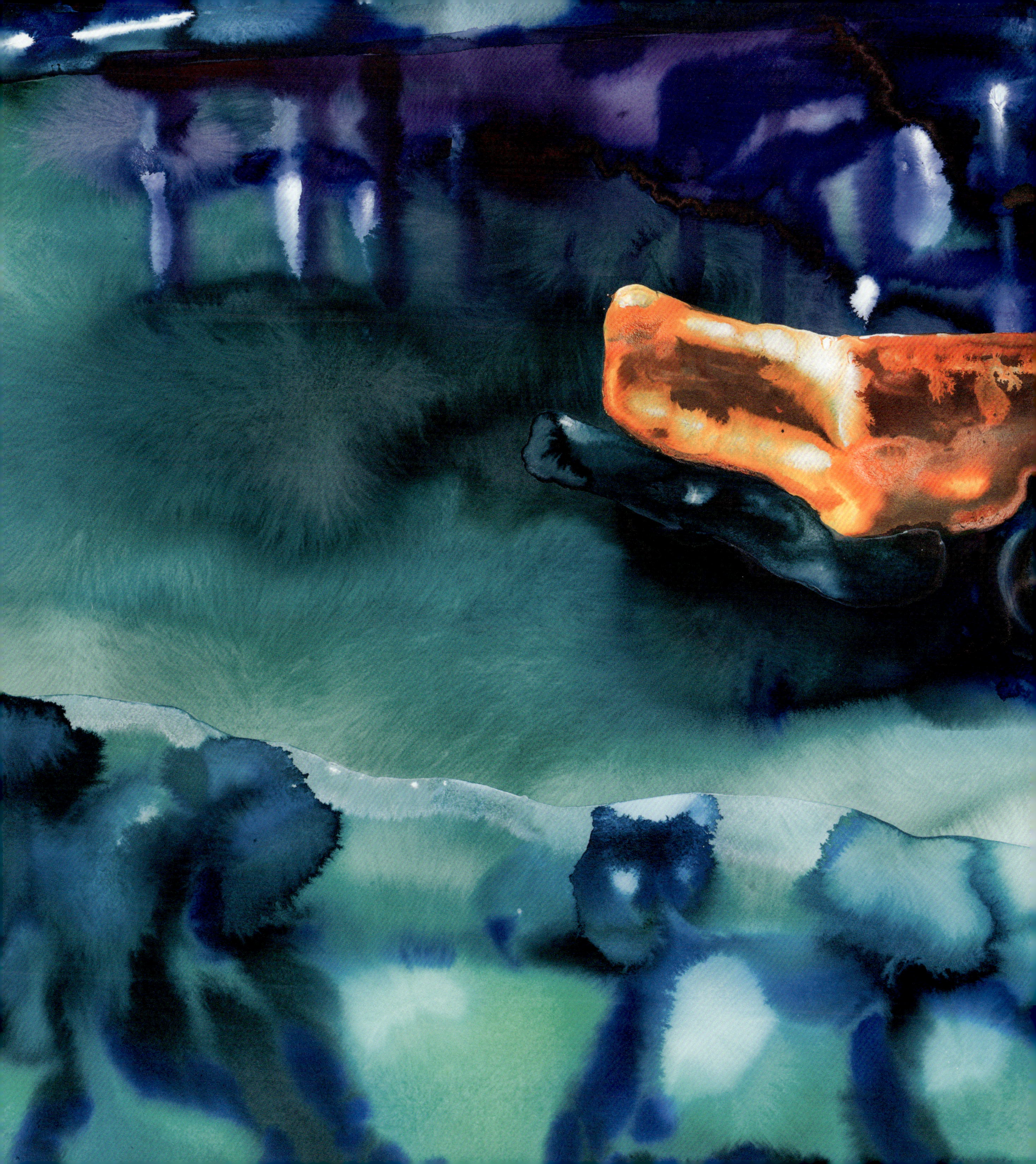

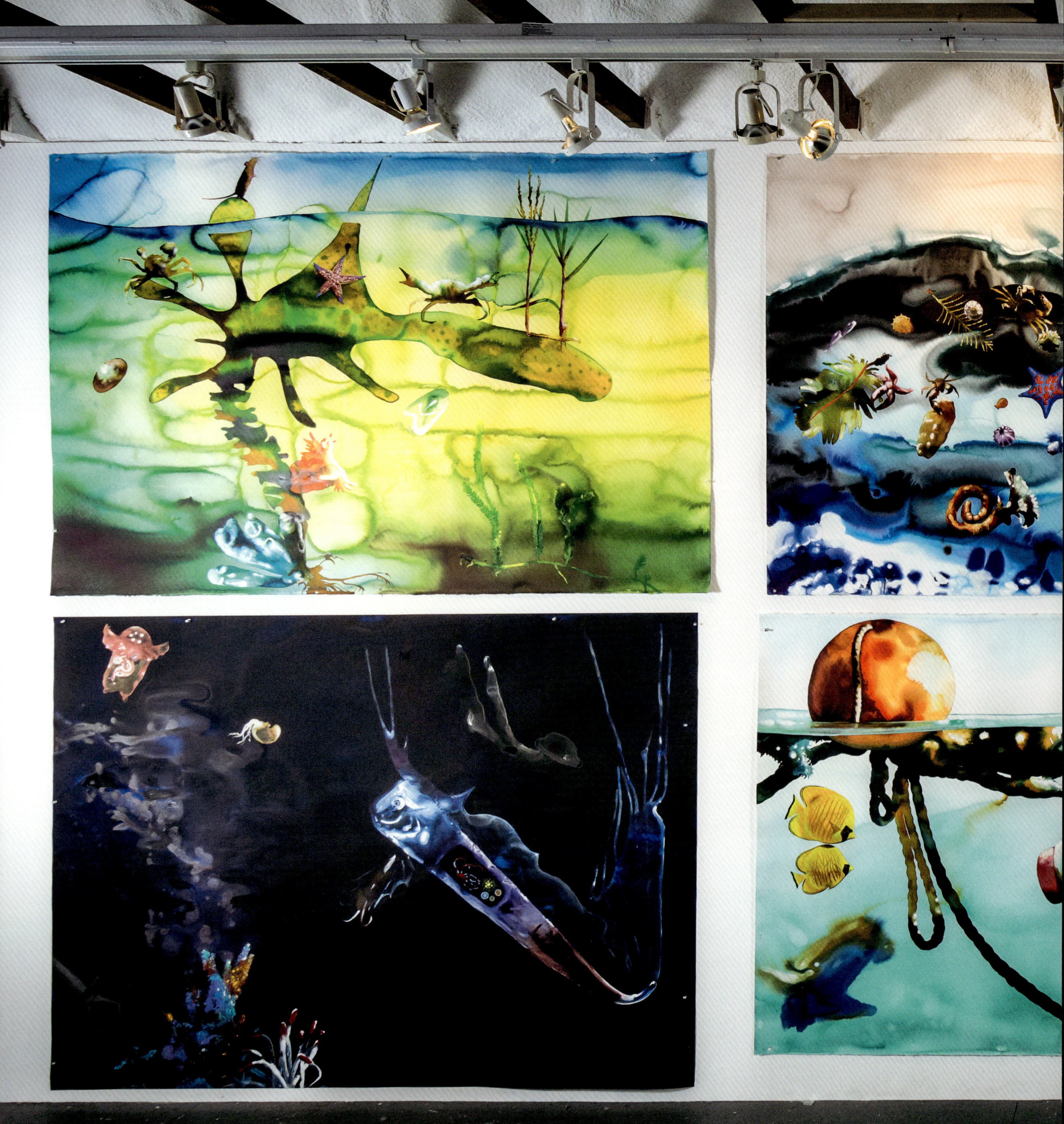

Alexis Rockman's studio, 2022. Clockwise from top left: *Vectors and Pathways*, *Tsunami*, *Reversal of Fortune, Legacy, Transient Passage, Benthos*

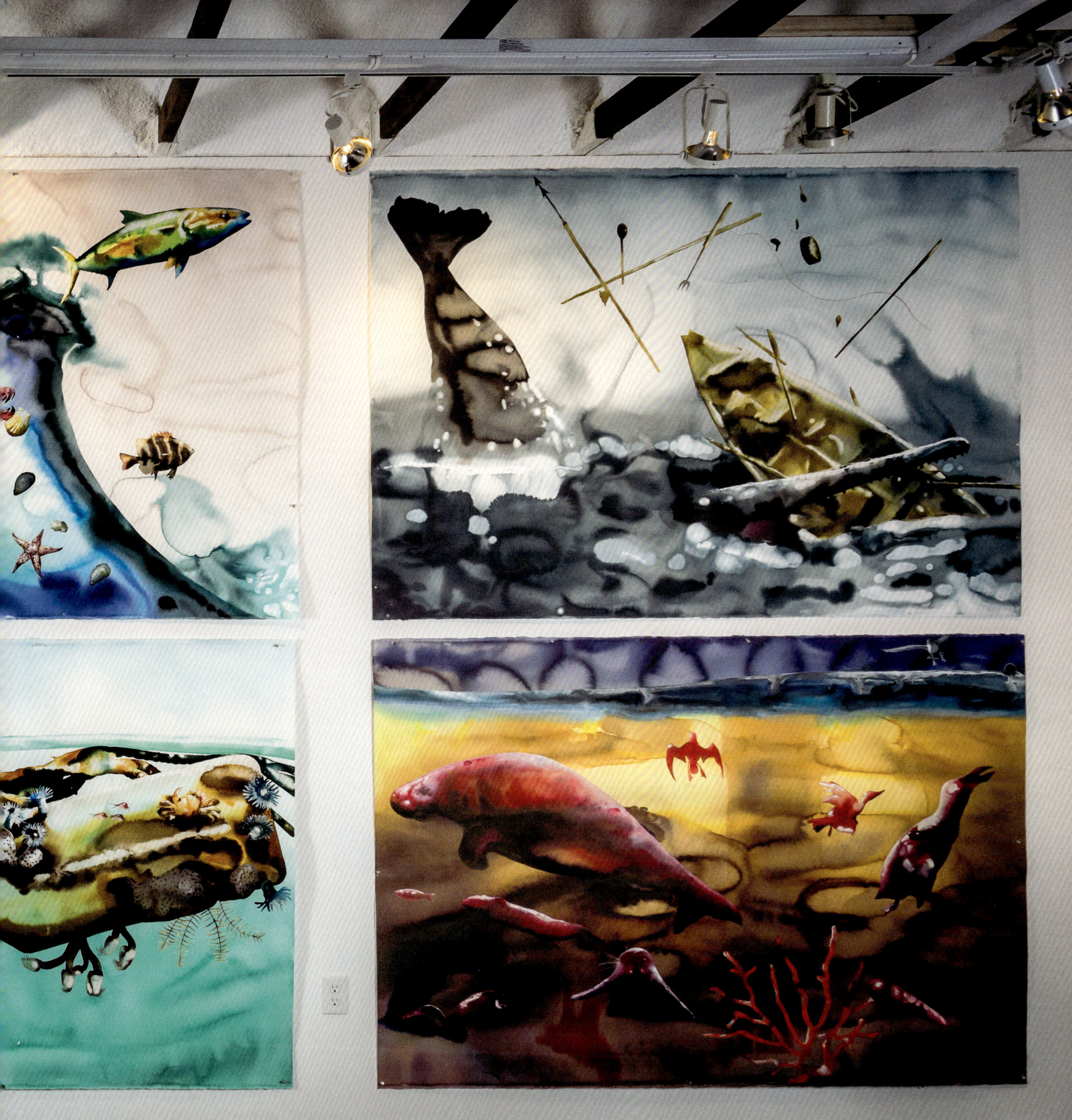

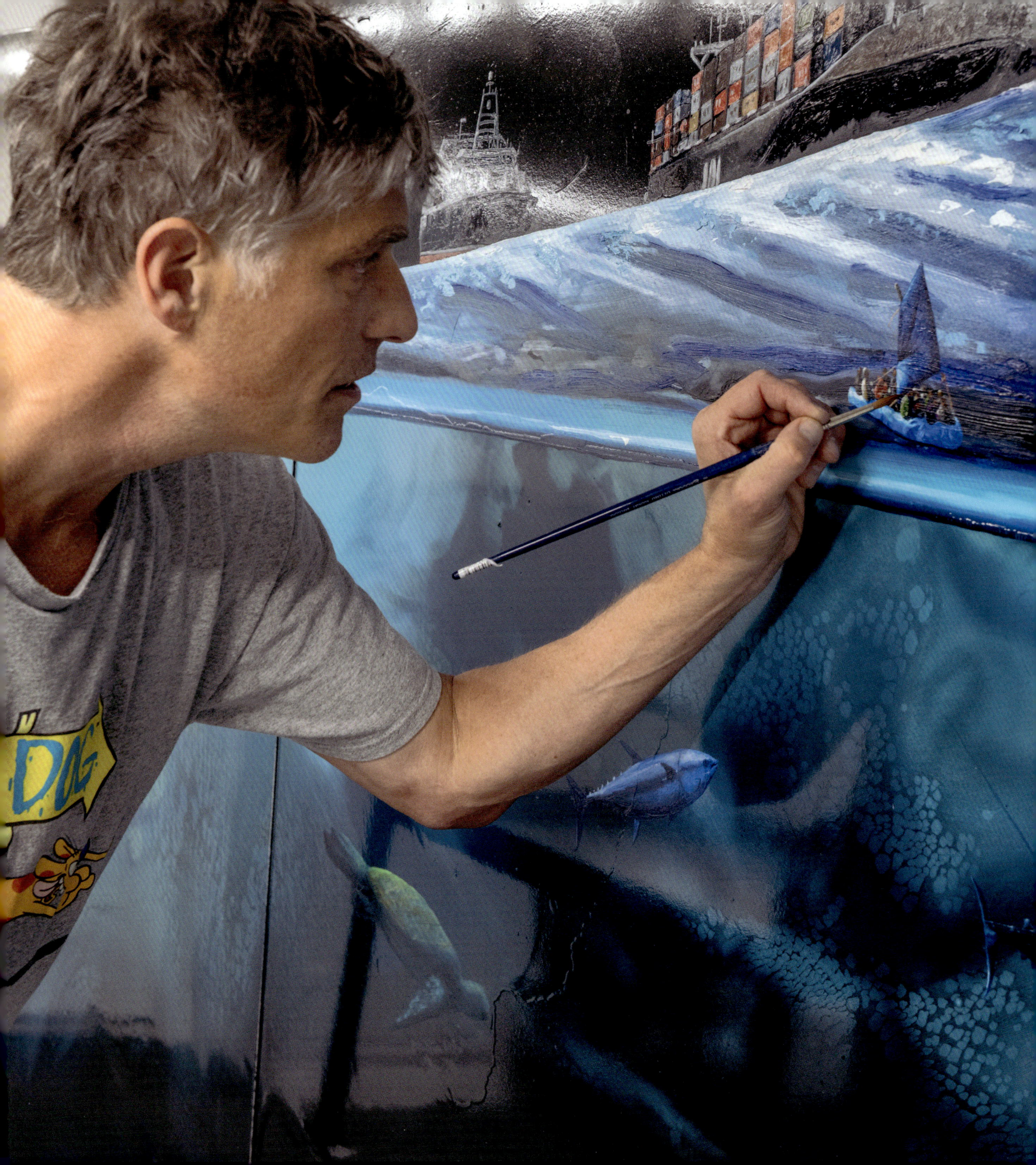

ALEXIS ROCKMAN
IN CONVERSATION WITH
NARI WARD

Alexis Rockman: I've recently been reading some essays and interviews focused on your work. Diana Nawi's essay "Being in the World," in your Perez Art Museum catalogue *Sun Splashed* (2015), was particularly fascinating. What's so moving to me about talking to you now is that we knew each other at SVA [School of Visual Arts] back in the early 1980s. We were good friends, and then we sort of lost track of each other. Since then I've seen your work and was always rooting for you. It's really nice to reconnect here.

Nari Ward: Yes, there was one moment when we did meet, I was working at the art supply store Pearl Paint on Canal Street, and you came by and said, "I'm working as an assistant for Ross Bleckner. Why don't you come by the studio?" So I went by. I remember it was kind of an odd visit. Ross was really kind and he wanted to know more about what young artists were thinking. I wasn't really there yet; I was a student and trying to figure it out. It seemed to me that you were further ahead, and well on your way to figuring things out.

AR: It may have appeared that way. I certainly was driven, but full disclosure: I was terrified of failing.

NW: At least in our professional realm, you seemed locked in. You knew what was going to feed your vision immediately.

AR: It must have been 1984 because I was working for Ross on White Street and that was right after we got out of SVA.

NW: You're right. I didn't actually graduate from SVA—I ran out of money, so I was working to try to stay in New York. What I'm saying is you seemed to have a line on what you were interested in. I couldn't be as efficient because of all the economic pressure that was coming down on me. In any case, I was really taken aback that you offered to have me come by and Ross was generous with his time. I remember one question he asked me and I laugh at it now, because you kind of bailed me out. He asked, "What do you think of this artist Jean-Michel Basquiat?" and I didn't know who the fuck Jean-Michel Basquiat was. I said, "I don't know of this artist. I don't know who you're talking about," and you were like, "Oh yeah, no, Nari's not into the *regular* art world." I was glad you stepped in and cleaned it up for me.

AR: I'm glad you have a good memory of that experience. As young artists we're so fragile. Every word matters so much and a word of encouragement is so valuable. What I think is fascinating about our careers is that there are many parallels. Even though you were born in Jamaica, I consider you a New Yorker, right, because New York is the place of immigration and the diaspora of the Caribbean and we've both managed to take the idea of diversity—mine with biodiversity, yours with cultural and usage diversity—and create a career that's given us not only a way to survive and make a living but we've also managed to have an emotional relationship to those ideas. It's a rare privilege to be an artist and have these opportunities.

NW: Yes, and the other through lines are our early pursuit of illustration at SVA and our roles as storytellers. That was the key thing early on for both of us and then over time we figured out what kind of stories we wanted to tell.

AR: Right! What's fascinating about you is that you take the idea of formal traditions, and you imbue it with a vernacular. I think we both have a love–hate relationship with formal traditions. There's nothing more elegant than minimalism, yet it's also the vessel of the industrial revolution and genocide and all these things about capitalism and the power of technology, which has basically brought us to our knees in terms of climate and politics. That's an interesting parallel relationship.

NW: Yes, it's also kind of inevitable in a sense. I teach sculpture at Hunter College. Within the camp of the university setting—in academia—there are groups of media-specific disciplines that sort of evolve, as ridiculous as it might seem. Nevertheless, I always tease the painters by saying they're much more reflective of the oppressive capitalist regime. Painting as a craft thrived with the rise of the merchant class. Basically, it left the walls of the church architecture and became this portable commercial endeavor, and evolved from there. In my work I address issues that are devastating, traumatic, and angst-driven, yet it's also this market object.

As artists, we're always trying to negotiate this reality—especially when trying to hold a mirror up to the status quo. It's like what you're doing, talking about greed and corruption, and profit over lives and our planet, right?

AR: It's really a terrible paradox and an unsolvable mystery in regard to how we reckon with these issues that we both care about so much. But then we have to get on a plane and go someplace and proselytize about our carbon footprint or have an opening. I won't name names, but how many times have we sold work to people whose politics are diametrically opposed to what we believe in?

NW: Yes, and at the same time we're blessed to be in this position. It's one of the conundrums that feeds my decision to continue teaching, trying to figure out how to give back.

AR: Education is our only hope. My mother, Diana diZerega Wall, is an urban archaeologist and was the chair of anthropology at City College for a couple of decades. As much as we don't want to be influenced by our parents, I find my own interests converging with hers more and more as I get older. At first, I said my work will not be about archeology; well, now I'm painting people and the history of boats!

Since we last spoke things have gone terribly bad for many things that we care about: women's rights, the Supreme Court, the environment. I don't know about you but sometimes it's hard to get up in the morning.

NW: Yes. It can get overbearing. I think you work the same way I do, where the work is a ritual of communing. You're rolling these anxieties, these thoughts, these questions around in your head and you're trying to manifest them in a kind of visual prayer.

AR: Creating is a form of coping, right?

NW: Yes, it's one way to deal with it, because in some ways it's giving form to the monster, and by doing that you're actually in some small way exorcizing it, and getting it into the world so you can see it, also pushing it away from yourself. So in that way you're maybe able to engage a realm of control. Humankind has done it all through our existence—control through religion, control through ritual, and some of it is healthy, and meaningful. I think that's how we function and it gives us a sense of agency over our lives. My work is just that—it's survival, man. It's survival for me.

AR: We're both interested in craft—the refuge and excellence of craft. It's really a place of comfort, because it gives you something to do every day with your time. I've always wondered about artists who do a drawing on a napkin and then go off to lunch while someone else fabricates it. Something we share is an interest in finding objects or images of things that are unlovable—things that aren't considered, discarded things in the neighborhood. We go around finding meaning in things that don't normally have any value. And then there's my attraction to plants and animals that make a living despite humans—rats, pigeons, cockroaches, ailanthus. They're dealing with adversity, because of humans who want to destroy them.

NW: Right, I think we share a similar through line of things that aren't the center. The things that you see, they sort of exist on a periphery of people's everyday lives. I remember reading an interview where you spoke about your work and who your audience is, and you said, "I don't only want to just talk to the art aficionado and art academic; I'm interested in regular people, both audiences," and I think that was really a humble statement, but it meant a lot to hear that, because I agreed. I've always half-jokingly called myself a Social Realist sculptor, because I'm really starting with this thing that everybody recognizes, and then figuring out how to fracture it conceptually. How to add other experiences to it, right?

AR: Absolutely, that's the way in. One of the roles for *Oceanus* is to tell a story about human and natural history that's often not considered and might perhaps be challenging to an audience. I composed the painting with twenty-two model boats from the Mystic Seaport Museum collection, with the resources that were exploited below them—fishing, slavery, whaling, and deep-sea mining.

NW: Yes, and how within that populist framework there can still be other moments of discovery. I think that's what's exciting when I hear you talk about this project; it's all the things we know, but then you're creating this scenario that's totally invented, and which allows for the viewer to fill it in with their own experiences. I call this the element of the abstract, because it allows for a varied range of interpretation. You leave things open for the viewer to finish. You use the material seduction for that world's unbuilding, and through that you bring the viewer to another kind of expectation, another kind of reality that you're conjuring.

AR: Exactly. Now I'm going to quote you. You once said, "with the exceptions of science and art, it's only in a time of crisis that labor and faith are brought together." Are we in a time of crisis?

NW: What I was really getting to was the need to create an intensely intimate collective experience that can also be frightening. It reminds me of your *Shipwrecks* series—thinking about that kind of crisis and urgent moments of things breaking down. At that moment you have to then survive and figure out how to reshuffle what you know into a new reality.

AR: Isn't every day like that as an artist? [*laughter*]

NW: I always reference this James Baldwin quote where he states, "Life is more important than art, that's what makes art important." Basically, what he's saying is that artifice is what saves us. Because if we strictly had to deal with living to survive, without storytelling, we wouldn't want to live.

AR: It's so terrifying.

NW: Right. We look at the mirror and see a reflection that allows us to deal with the uncertainties of life. I think that's kind of what you're talking about when you depict this traumatic narrative, and then present it with this majestic approach. There's something really poetic about your use of the figurative painting tradition in this manner, and I'm also trying to navigate that in my work.

When you came to my exhibition you saw the *Peace Walk* series (2022, fig. 1) composed of large copper panels inspired by make-

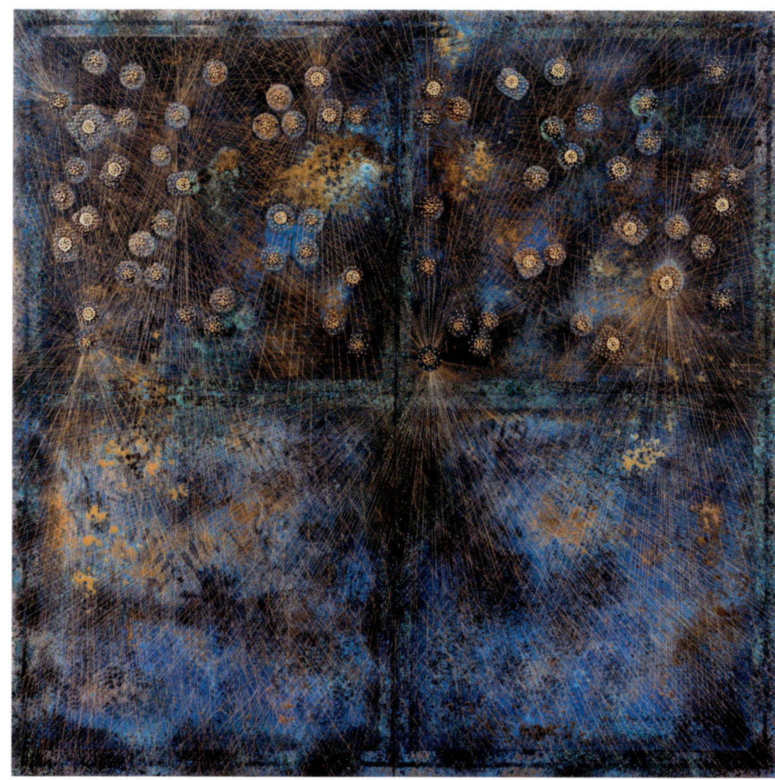

1. Nari Ward, *Peace Walk; ASSEMBLY*, 2022. Copper sheet, copper nails, and darkening patina, 84 × 84 × 3 inches (213.4 × 213.4 × 7.6 cm)

shift street memorials. They reference sidewalk ceremonies of mourning I saw in my neighborhood during the height of the Covid pandemic. Patinated copper panels with marked, outlined evidence of empty liquor bottles and used prayer candles that serve as a collective engagement with death. Someone just lost a friend or family member and they're trying to affirm a kind of nowness. We're all together in the moment, acknowledging our connection to the unknowable, but linked nevertheless.

AR: Do you recall the moment when you started considering yourself a draftsman? You went from illustration to being a draftsman to 3D. What caused that transformation? What was the springboard for that leap?

NW: I think it was Harlem and the urban landscape. I was trying to figure out what stories I wanted to tell and who I was telling them to. And like you I wanted to speak to more than the art-world audience. It was the guy on the street, my neighbor. And someone who has a totally different set of experiences than I do yet perhaps whose diasporic experience was similar to mine. I think I was really interested in the complexities of that, and trying to tell those stories with the objects, those found objects, that I

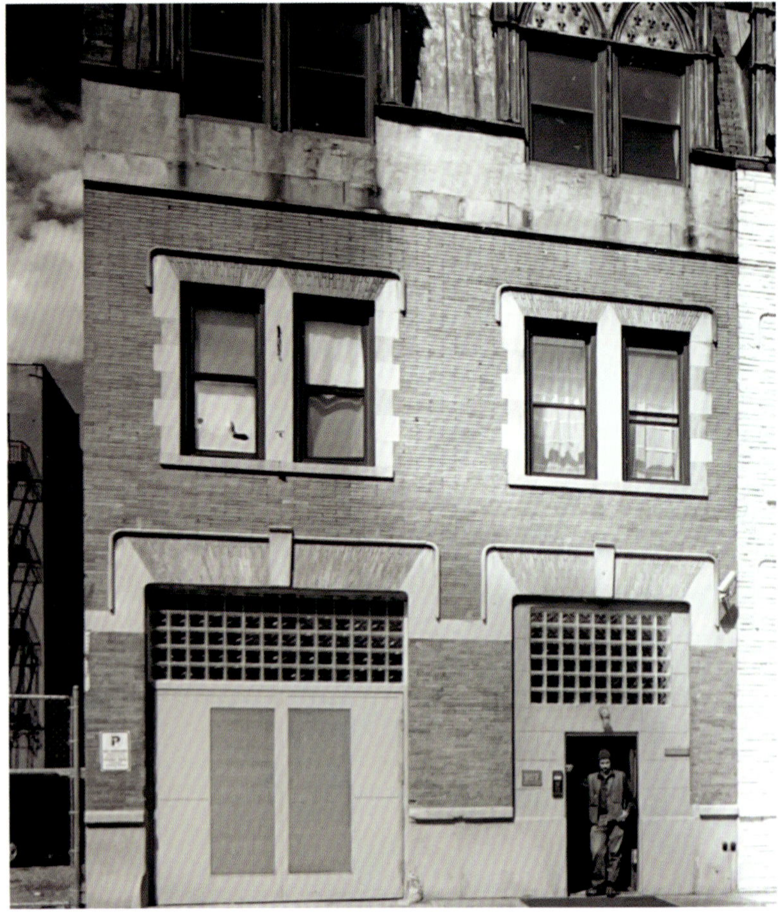

2. Nari Ward in front of his Harlem studio, 2001

to put the stuff I wanted to make. I didn't want to just throw everything away, so that's why, early on, I decided I needed to get my own space. I was renting a firehouse in Harlem and later the owner was looking to sell it so I borrowed, begged, and took out a bank loan to put myself in long-term debt in order to buy it. Now I have a live/work studio space with a grand basement that's packed with collected materials (fig. 2).

AR: What year was this?

NW: This was back in 1999 when I made that jump to do it. That was kind of my strategy—I'll just have to find work to keep the studio space.

AR: Right, and then of course you didn't have to worry as much once you started selling. But in the beginning, when you needed to figure out how it was going to work—that's such a frightening moment.

was collecting in Harlem. I would go into the studio and make these marks that were about the rectangular, and about formal decisions. So, I wanted to figure out how to bring that person I saw on the street into the story I was still thinking about, or some incident I had just experienced, into the rectangle. I think the found objects allowed me to take that on, at least to find a way in, and then figure out how to build around that object.

AR: You were incredibly brave to start out in the art world as a young Jamaican American artist taking a huge economic risk in the 1980s to do that. I think that's fascinating.

NW: I was fortunate to have good teachers and mentors. More than one of them would tell me, "You know, as an artist, especially one of color, you have to figure out how to stabilize your income." Basically, they were saying, don't count on selling work [*laughs*]. You have to figure out how to find work to make the work. So, my mindset was, Well, OK, that's fine; if I really want to do this, that's just what I'm going to have to do. And the biggest challenge in my mind was storage—I had to figure out where I was going

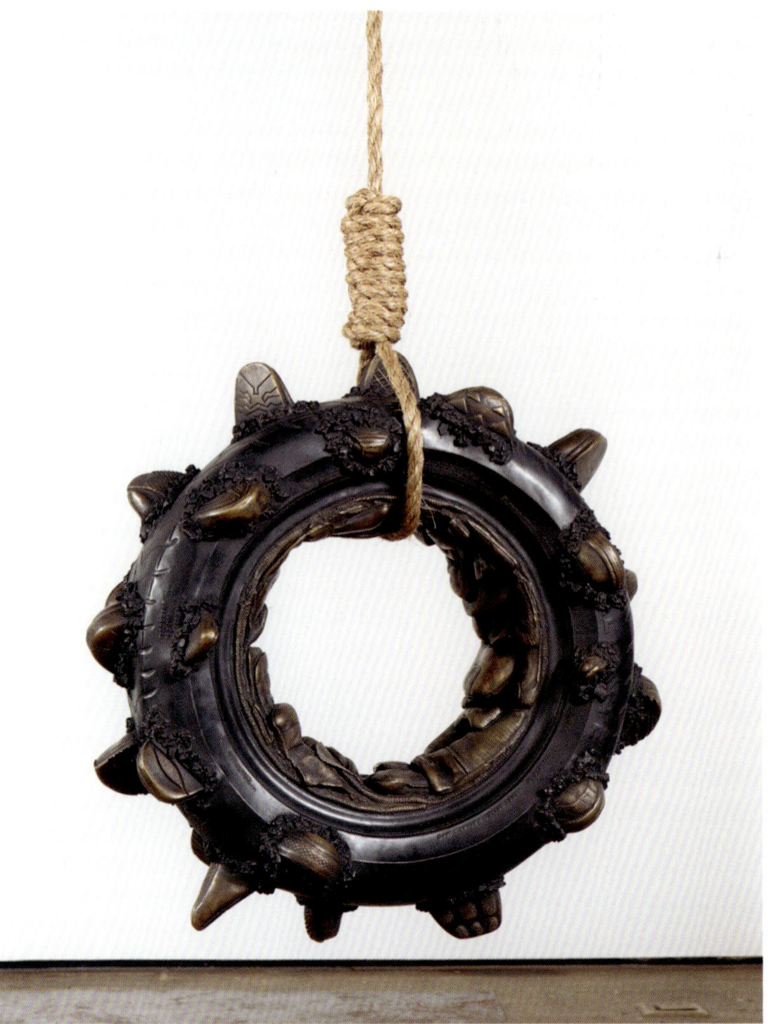

3. Nari Ward, *Swing Low*, 2015. Bronze, rope, 28 × 27 × 13 inches (71.1 × 68.6 × 33 cm)

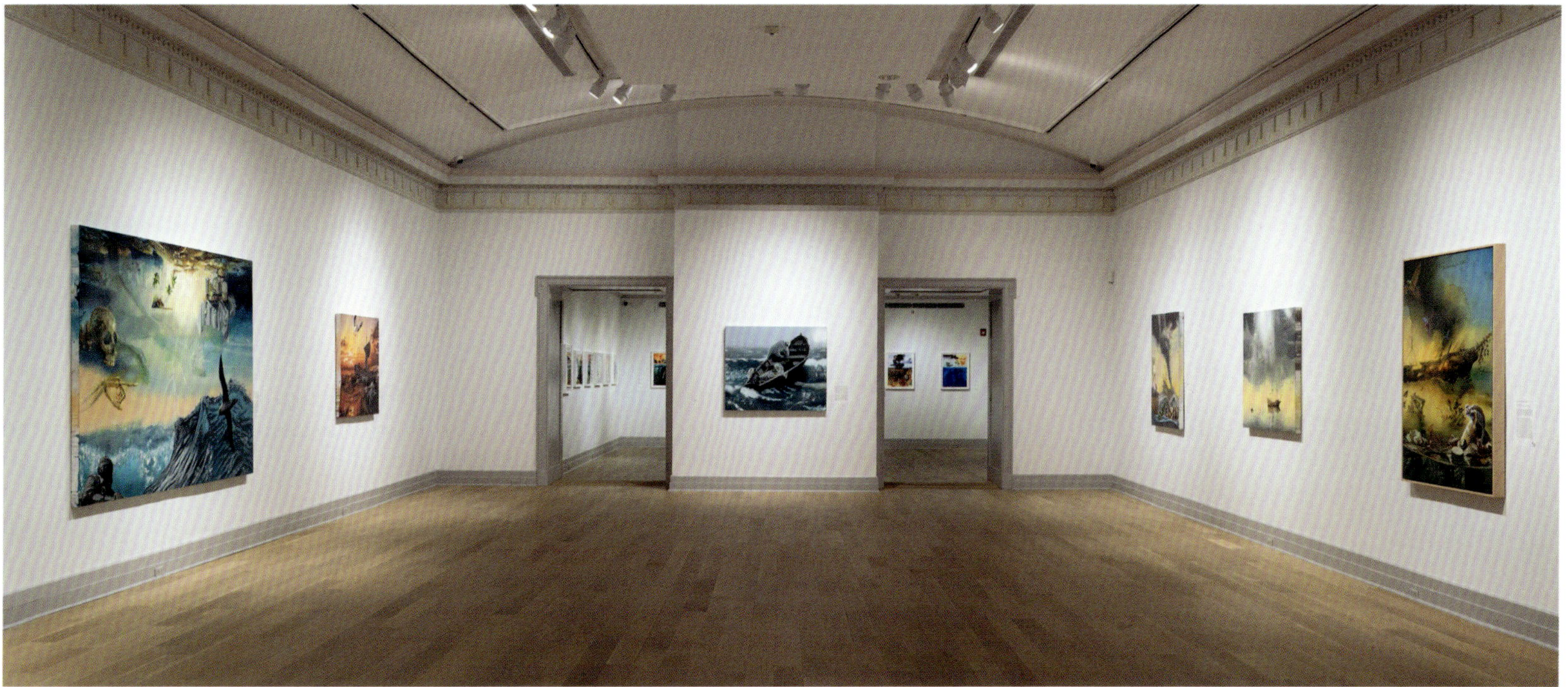

4. *Alexis Rockman: Shipwrecks*, Guild Hall, East Hampton, New York, 2021

NW: Exactly, and every artist has to figure it out for themselves. The irony is that my teaching gig was the necessary benchmark to purchase the building, because as a young struggling artist the bank would never give me a loan. I needed to show that I had a regular income, which wasn't possible earlier in my career.

AR: There's a sculpture of yours, *Swing Low* (2015, fig. 3), that I was looking at this morning. It consists of a hanging tire and has pieces of shoes and sneaker soles sticking out of it. It's such a beautiful and poignant sculpture.

NW: That work brings us back to this idea of depicting crisis— how to deal with trauma while using craft. Presenting upsetting narratives in a way that people don't or can't turn away from. The viewer is confronted with a kind of visual seduction while processing the pain of a history they normally would turn away from or log in a prescribed emotional category, right? Like, "I don't want to deal with that, don't show me that." I'm exposing something, which is actually problematic, because the tire is connected to the rope by a hangman's noose. It's this lynched tire that's hanging there, but then it's also a swing. It's a tire swing that kids would play on and go back and forth. I really wanted to collapse these distinctly different moments and make a new kind of realization. I don't want to proselytize and I think you're the same way, you're not interested in preaching and saying, "Oh, you know, what we're doing is bad for the earth." Yeah, we know that, but it's really how to have them rethink their role in imagining something.

AR: Yes, I see the lynching connection, but it also has associations with both the rural and urban joys of the summer with a tire that's connected to a tree that kids use to get out over the lake and jump off of it.

NW: Right, it's all of that and the terrorizing history of racism. I think we're so accustomed to redacting the negative and only centering the things that make us comfortable. We have to really deal with the uncomfortable things if we want to make change happen, and figure out how those things can be addressed head-on. So instead of just, "Oh, don't tell me about that; I don't want to deal with it," how do we deal with it together? And that's the thing about getting back to the work of viewing—the collective experience. We look at the work, we look at each other; how does the work manifest in what we do after we look at each other?

I'm really fascinated by your *Shipwrecks* series. Chanda Laine Carey's essay in the exhibition catalogue is a really engaging dialogue with the transcultural aesthetics of the shipwreck. I wanted to ask you about that body of work because it really resonates with me, especially in the works I'm doing with street memorials. I'm curious how it came about.

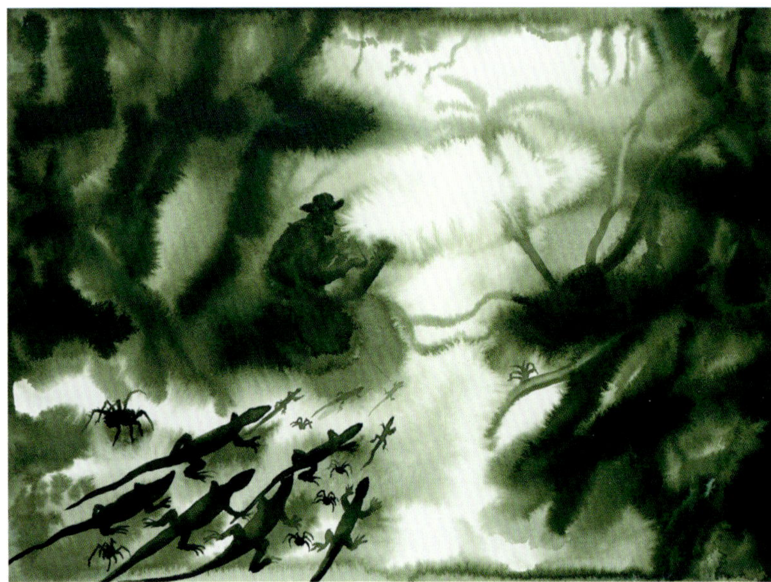

5. Alexis Rockman, *The Interview*, 2018. Watercolor and ink on paper, 18 × 24 inches (45.7 × 60.9 cm)

AR: The *Shipwrecks* project and my interest in natural history go hand in hand. Until the 1940s anytime humans would travel to study ecology they would go by boat. They would have to get there by ship, and chances were that the boats would sink. The idea for *Shipwrecks* emerged while I was working on *Wallace's Line* (fig. 5), a project about the Victorian naturalist Alfred Russel Wallace, who co-authored the theory of evolution through natural selection, independently of Darwin. In 1852, Wallace was coming back from four years in Brazil where he had been collecting specimens for a living, when his ship, the brig *Helen*, caught fire and he lost everything except for a couple of notebooks. I wanted to make a painting of that moment, and it became the first one in that body of work (fig. 6). As there are no photographs, these moments are all about anecdote and eyewitness accounts; there's no other actual evidence of them.

Later on, Andrea Grover, the director of Guild Hall, offered to organize the *Shipwrecks* exhibition (fig. 4, previous page). I said, "Please give me two and a half years to do it." Andrea got the Peabody Essex Museum involved. Its two wonderful curators, Trevor Smith and Dan Finemore, really contributed support for some of the content in these forty-five works. It was a rough period with Covid and they were really great.

NW: The *Shipwrecks* catalogue is just brilliant. It's interesting—you're going from shipwrecks to actual sailing ships in *Oceanus*. However, these ships aren't sinking, they're floating.

AR: Don't worry, they'll all be shipwrecked too, sooner or later. Yes, they're doing their thing, and the way that I frame it psychologically is that the wreck is really the ecology below the ocean waterline, it's what happened to all the fisheries. All these big fish that are still hanging around. You go into Citarella and you see swordfish and bluefin tuna—these fish will be extinct in fifty years.

NW: Wow, it's scary to consider.

AR: The boats in *Oceanus* are the vessels of capitalism. People left the safety of the port to face the terrifying ocean. They're either chasing food, resources, or money, or escaping persecution, or have been bought against their will.

NW: How do you see it in terms of the boats on top and then the viewer's perspective that has them submerged below the waterline? You've done a number of paintings with that compositional device and fish's-eye view (fig. 7, overleaf).

AR: Absolutely. I realized in the mid-'80s that one of the ways I might distinguish myself from our peers, so to speak, was to consider and utilize pictorial languages that were available to us as young artists that hadn't been beaten into the ground by every other artist. When thinking about my love of natural history I remembered the illustrations from the Golden Field Guides, issues of *National Geographic*, the Natural History Museum dioramas, and the New York Aquarium. In them you can often see under the water, beneath the ground, or inside something; there's a wonderful opportunity to see simultaneous views and really understand the idea of time, as they reveal the past, present, and future simultaneously.

NW: I was trying to place that idea of time in the paradigm of my own process. I think about the notion of the remnant, and how things no longer become about the past when they're given the role of protagonist. They're no longer the secondary thing; they occupy the central topic, and shift the expectation for things that aren't meant to be lived through again, becoming reactivated to tell new stories.

Speaking of new stories, you talk about activists, illustrators, and the research and ideas that generate the dialogue. That's why *Oceanus* is in a museum, to better facilitate an educational component, right?

AR: Yes, working with the Mystic Seaport Museum was such an incredibly positive experience. Christina Connett Brophy and her

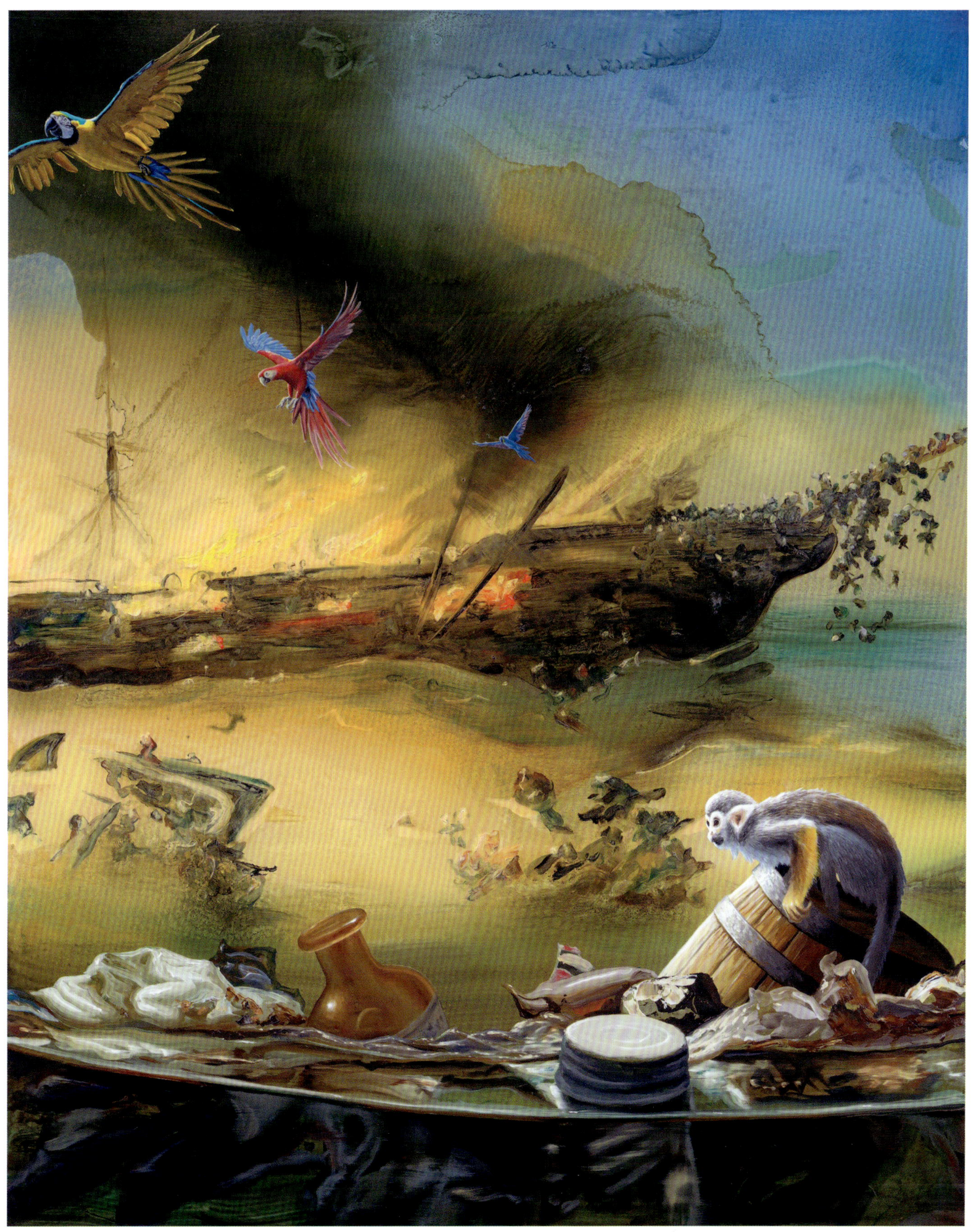

6. Alexis Rockman, *The Sinking of the Brig Helen*, 2017. Oil on Dibond, 56 × 44 inches (142.2 × 111.8 cm)

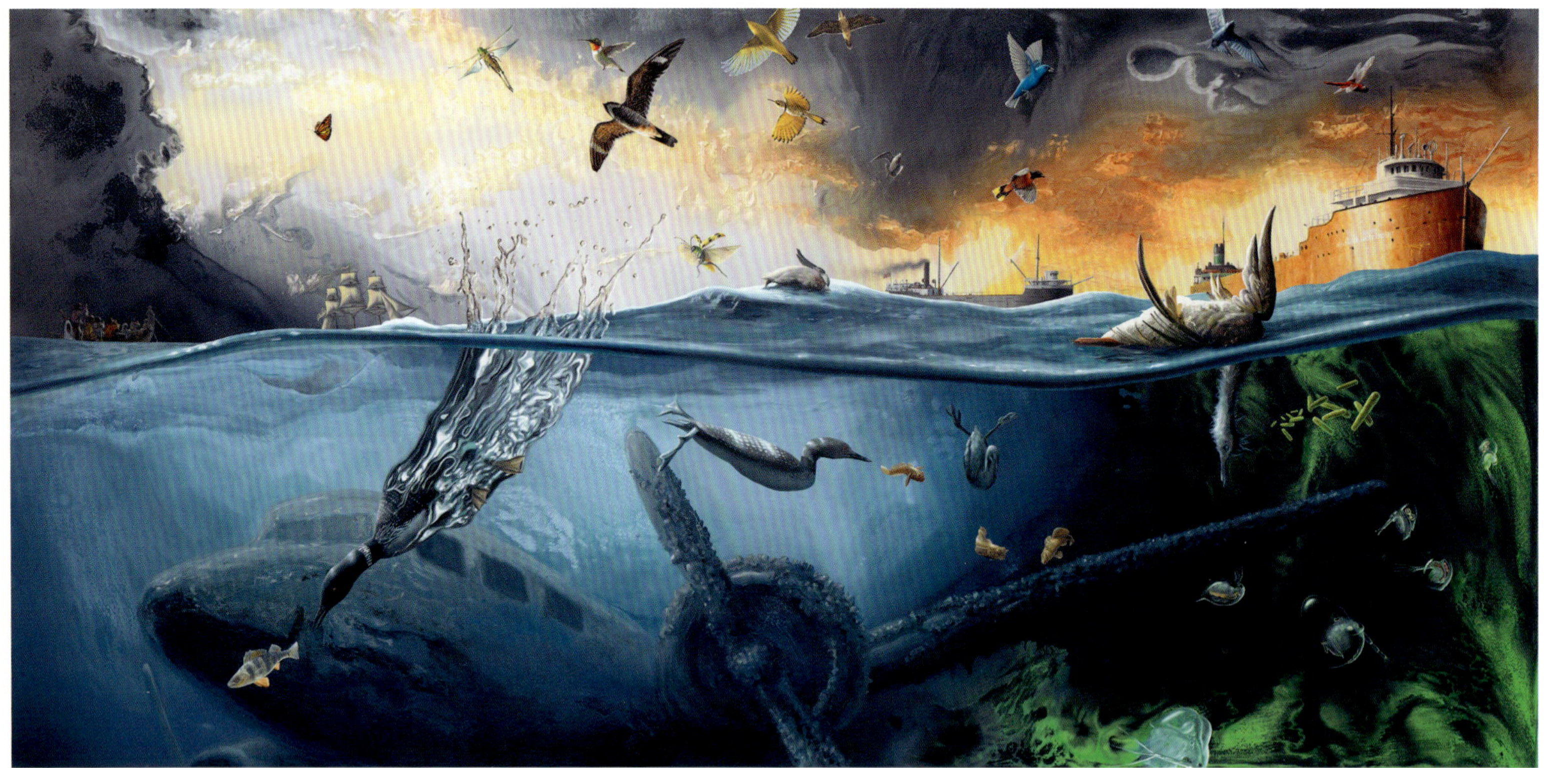

7. Alexis Rockman, *Spheres of Influence*, 2017. Oil and alkyd on wood panel, 72 × 144 inches (182.9 × 365.8 cm)

staff, especially Krystal Rose and Wilson Lawrence, were invaluable in getting me all the names and photographs of the ship models, as well as solving some issues with the painting itself. They made the educational side of the project so much more fun.

NW: I kind of feel like a large part of your focus is on the educational aspect, letting the public know, informing them through exhibitions or even your books and catalogues. I realized while reading them that this all makes total sense. You choose to tell the story through all available channels, to let people know what's happening today and why.

AR: Activism and education are really our only hope. I grew up aware of the Enlightenment and believing that whatever we were going to do with our lives, we would be building on the shoulders of knowledge and the achievements of our ancestors. I didn't understand until recently that there's a strain of tribalism in the human condition that's so strong even self-preservation would be thrown under the bus to support it. There's a powerful and very vocal part of the population that has an investment in challenging facts and science that are perceived as threatening to their short-term bottom line.

NW: Yes, I've thought about that. Strangely enough, *Oceanus* had

me thinking about the way our brains are wired as humans, and, because of your reinterpretation of nature, what would have happened if we didn't decide to profit—if humans didn't decide that it was OK to own the land. What I was getting at was what you said about us being wired in a certain way, predisposed to certain actions, which got me thinking about this book *Vibrant Matter* by Jane Bennett. She's a political theorist who writes about the relationship between humans and nonhuman forces. Considering the extraordinary age of the universe, humankind's existence is just a small blip. It's kind of liberating to try to get away from the anthropocentric thinking about the world. But it's also dangerously nihilistic too.

AR: Often when I speak in public, people come up and say, "Why should I care? Humans aren't going to be here forever, nature will be fine," and so on. That line of thinking really lets us off the hook, morally speaking. We don't live in geologic time. Do we want to make sure our children see elephants, tigers, and tree frogs in the wild? If we aren't careful, they'll be extinct and taxidermied in museums. From the viewpoint of our moral responsibility, we have to be caretakers of what's left of biodiversity. What type of planet do we want to leave for our children?

Opposite: Alexis Rockman, *Endurance*, 2022. Detail

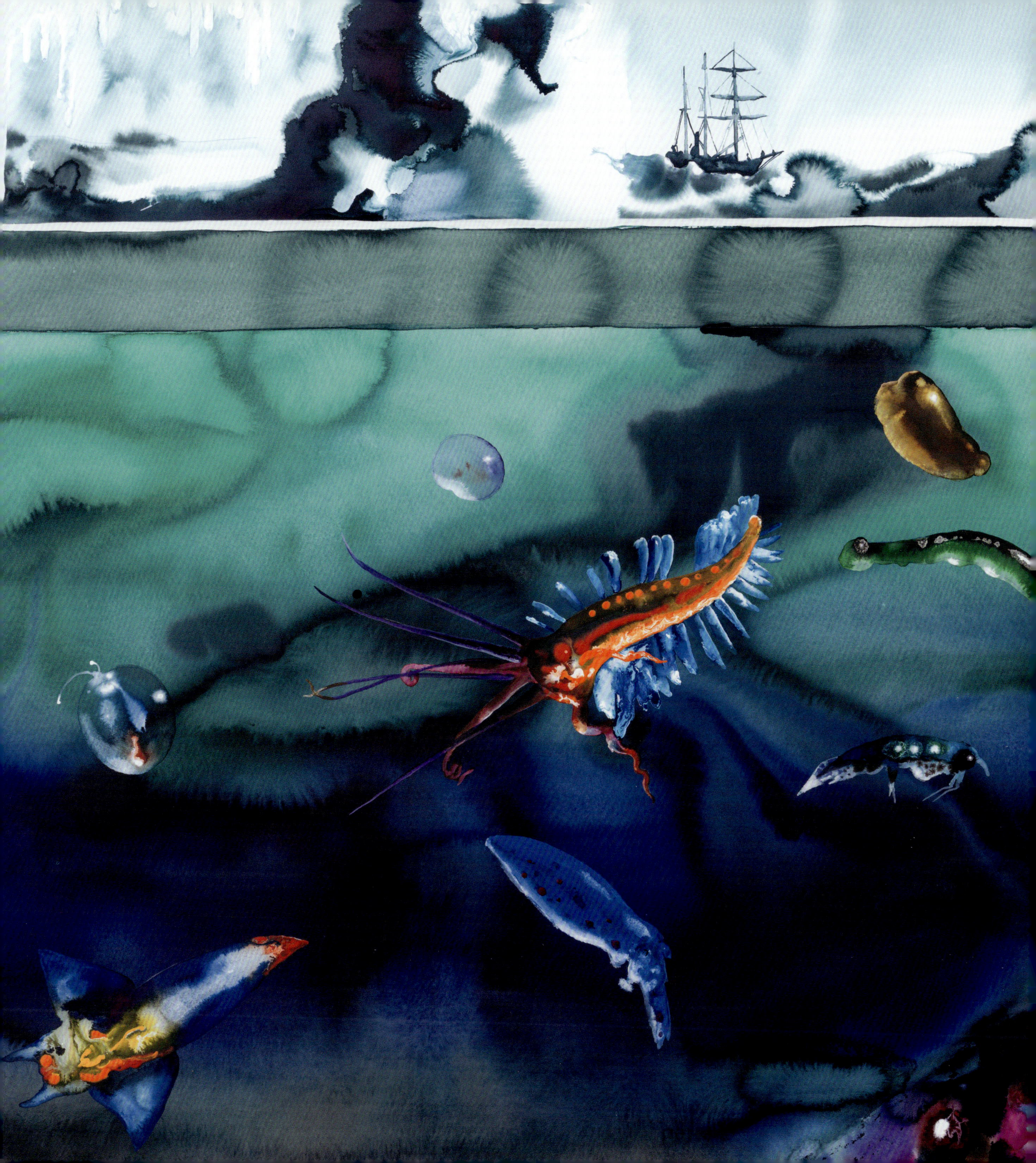

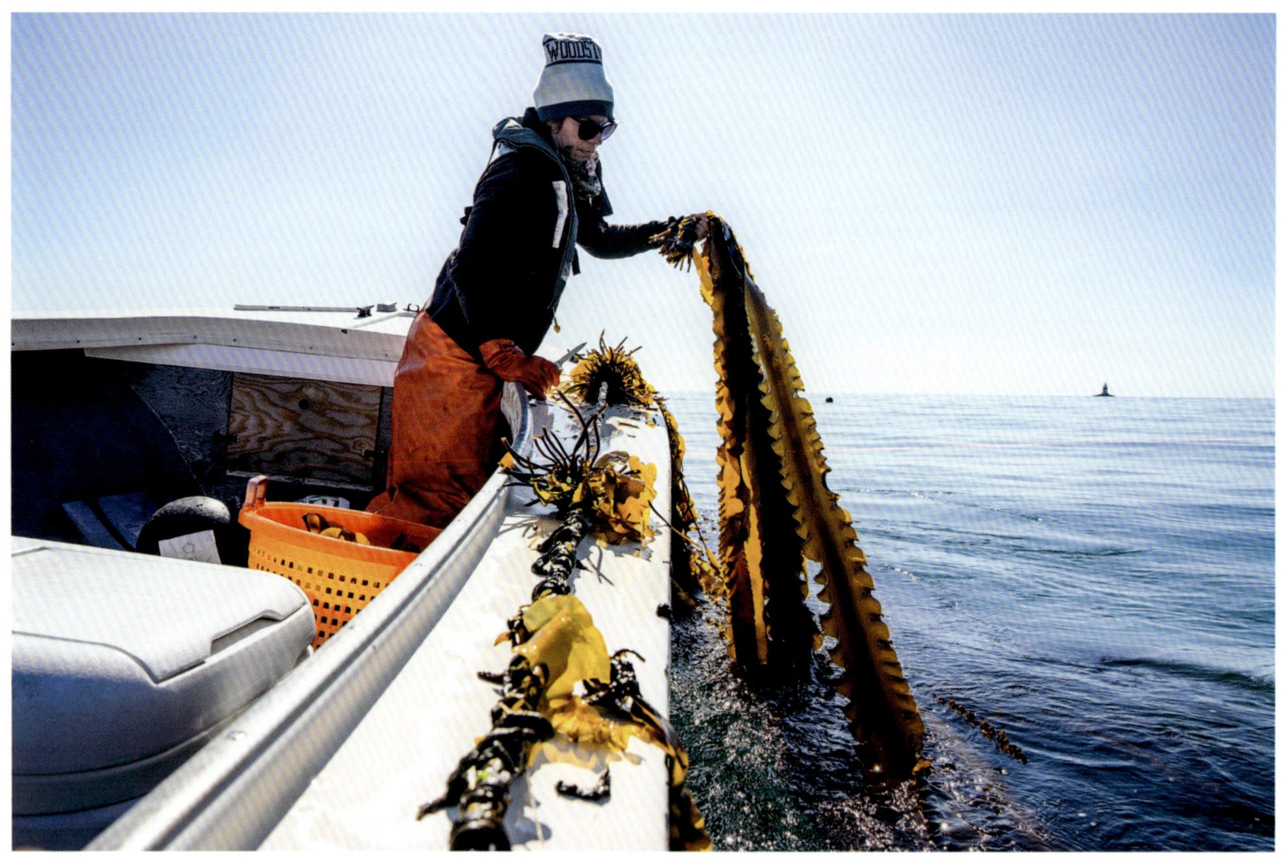

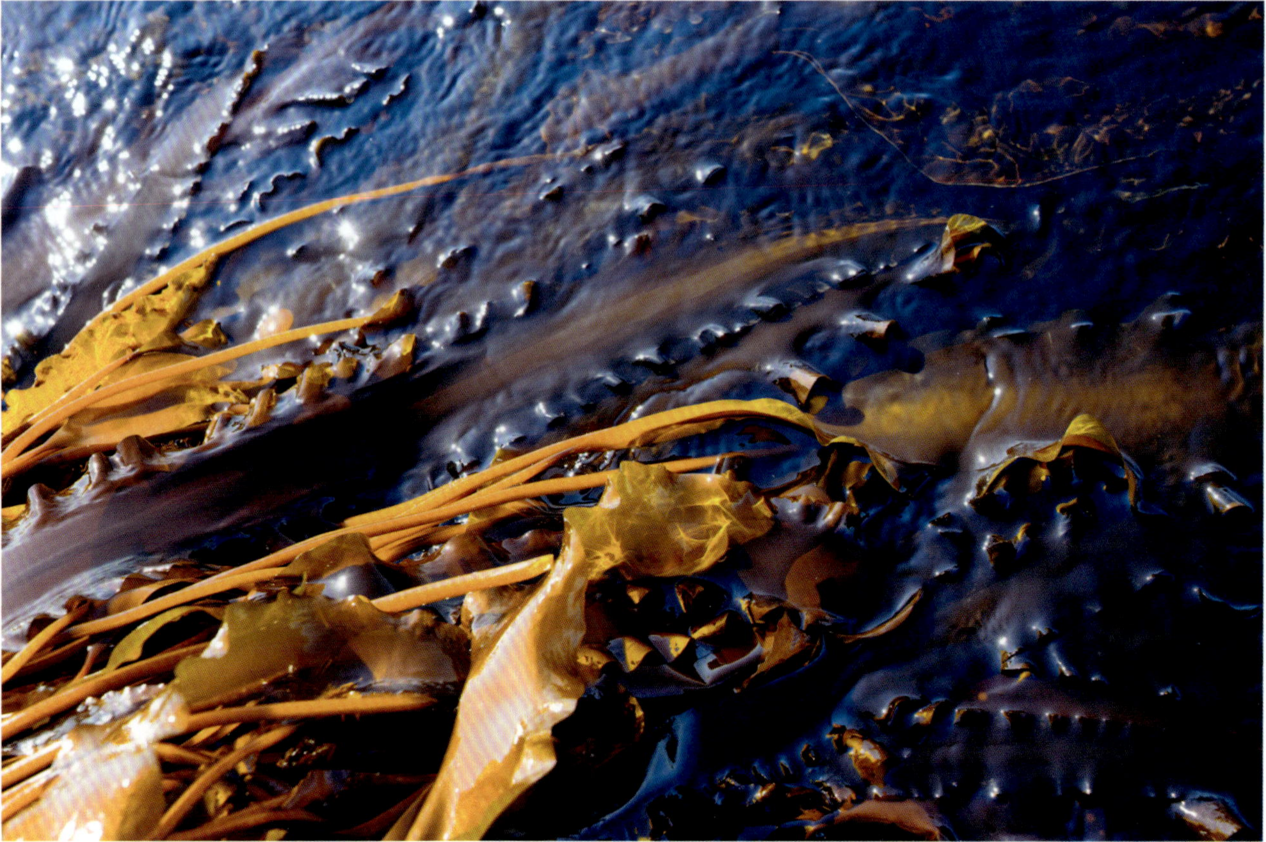

1. Suzie Flores, co-owner of Stonington Kelp Co., harvesting kelp off the Connecticut coast

INNOVATORS AND ENTREPRENEURS: THE FUTURE OF BLUE ECONOMY

CHRISTINA CONNETT BROPHY

Senior Vice President of Curatorial Affairs and Senior Director of Museum Galleries at Mystic Seaport Museum

WHILE THE THEMES OF ALEXIS ROCKMAN'S series are tough, the works provide an opportunity to highlight and explore innovative solutions to some of the most critical problems addressed in the series. Some of these are addressed in the central work, *Oceanus*, which includes species that have been exploited in aquaculture, with positive and negative impacts, including Japanese kelp, the whiteleg shrimp, the Japanese cockle, and Atlantic salmon. Entrepreneurs are working with scientists and policymakers throughout the world to explore sustainable blue economies and remediation strategies for many of our gravest conservation concerns as well as how we continue to exploit one of our greatest resources responsibly for our own survival.

GreenWave is a Connecticut-based incubator nonprofit devoted to encouraging and developing a regenerative sugar kelp industry, one of the quickest-growing global opportunities in the blue economy. Sugar kelp is a fast-growing superfood that absorbs carbon and nitrogen from the water and provides a base for food, beauty, and health products. With a goal of activating and supporting ten thousand new farmers to cultivate over a million acres over the next ten years, GreenWave has inspired new farmers to collaborate and innovate though education and outreach (fig. 1). At the United Nations Ocean Conference in Lisbon in 2022, this industry was mentioned in many sessions as one of the most promising for the sustainability of the global economy and ocean health, bringing new opportunities to coastal communities around the world with low-cost entry.

In rethinking the fish industry, the Iceland Ocean Cluster not only provides incubator opportunities for new start-ups for research and development, but the organization itself has launched an economically sustainable project called 100% Fish (fig. 2).

According to its research, the average raw material utilization rate of cod, one of the most overly exploited fish in the world's oceans and included in the central painting of the *Oceanus* series, is a little over 50 percent, which is a huge loss in the complete value of the fish. By connecting fishers with investors as well as innovators in new product development and new technologies, from fish leather

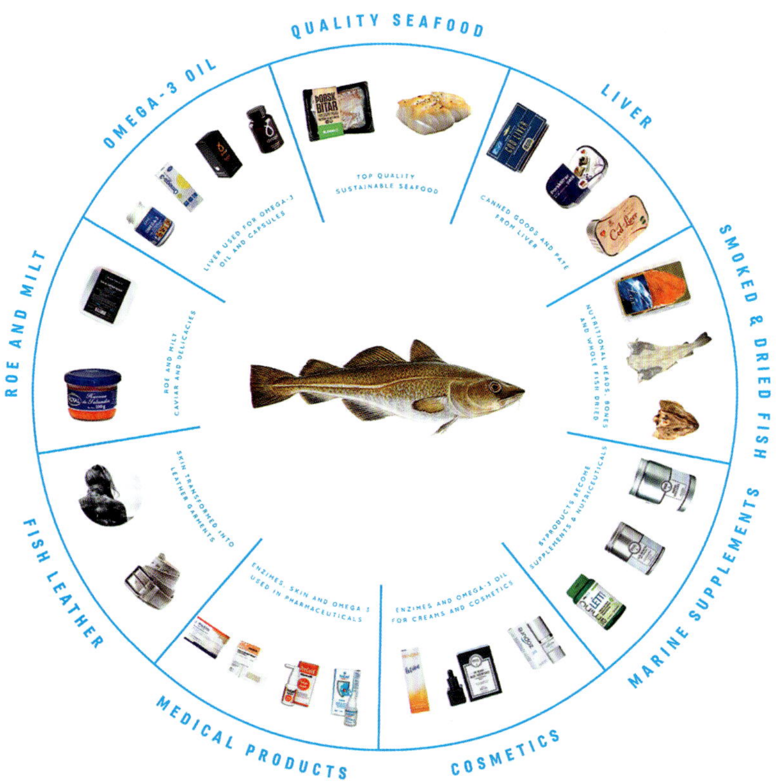

2. The mission of the 100% Fish project at the Iceland Ocean Cluster is to inspire the seafood industry and seafood communities to utilize more of each fish, increase the value of each fish landed, support new business opportunities, increase employment, and minimize waste

to pharmaceuticals to beauty products and everything in between, they are already averaging 80 percent use of each fish. This means fewer fish for greater economic value and less waste.

An essential element for these and many other innovators to succeed is obviously financing, and one of the most promising aspects of new blue economy strategies is the great interest they are garnering from investors worldwide who not only see the positive environmental impacts these entrepreneurs bring to the table but also the financial opportunities. Like Iceland Ocean Cluster, Boston-based SeaAhead is one of these resources, connecting blue-tech start-ups with angel investors and other key stakeholders. Innovate Newport is a community-based organization with surprising reach, connecting local to international entrepreneurs with major players in Rhode Island sustainable energy and other blue-economy-based companies, building partnership and funding opportunities.

Salmon, which is often farmed at some detriment to the environment, is now being raised terrestrially by companies like Ideal Fish, whose stock of salmon, branzino, and other species live in tanks above ground in water free from microplastics and recycled to minimize the carbon footprint. Fish waste is recycled into fertilizer and by-products are used for other industry commodities. BioFeyn, a biotechnology innovator, creates customized nutrient-dense aquafeed for fish farming, which not only increases efficiencies but drastically reduces carbon emissions inherent in more traditional methods of production. Beta Hatch is using biotech to produce immense amounts of insects as a base for aqua and other animal feed, which, in addition to many other advantages, uses only 2 percent of the water needed to produce other forms of protein. In a fascinating use of what is no longer futuristic technology, facial recognition software is being implemented in salmon farming by aquaculture company Cermaq Global to better evaluate individual health of their stock.

In works like *Transient Passage* (pp. 110–13) and *Vectors and Pathways* (pp. 92–97), Rockman focuses on the biological invasions that have plagued the world's oceans as a result of their introduction to non-native ecosystems where they can push out or destroy resident populations. One of the most globally impactful invasives is the lionfish, a venomous top predator originally from the Indo-Pacific, which has spread throughout the Atlantic, Caribbean, and the Mediterranean since its invasion of that hemisphere in the 1980s and wreaked havoc on reef ecosystems. Among many other strategies of remediation, which include promoting their consumption as food (if properly prepared they can be eaten by humans), are entrepreneurs like Inversa, which pays local fishers where lionfish are present for fish pelts for what they call "regenerative" use in the fashion industry, in partnership such companies as the Italian footwear brand P448 (fig. 3) and Teton Leather Co., which makes watch straps, wallets, and other products.

Rockman's *Trophic Web* (pp. 72–75) is about a succession of organisms in an ecological community that are linked to each other through the transfer of energy and nutrients. It looks at the immense damage inflicted upon our reef systems throughout the world through pollution, bleaching, and invasive species like lionfish, among many other factors. According to the National Oceanic and Atmospheric Administration, in 2022, 30 to 50 percent of reefs have already been lost, with a significant reduction in biodiversity and the economic well-being of humans. The loss of reef systems can also be blamed in part for the devastation of coastal communities that rely on these natural buffers from sea-level rise and storms. While there are many fascinating groups working to repopulate reefs globally, one that is particularly interesting is Coral Vita, based in the Bahamas (fig. 4). Relying on new technologies which allow for a fifty times faster growth rate, as well as biotesting species for resiliency to higher temperatures and acidity, Coral Vita outplants corals grown on land-based farms to degraded reefs, restoring life to heavily hit ecosystems. Its model is scalable and its extensive community outreach and education make its solutions sustainable.

Hand in hand with conserving these ecosystems is education and outreach. The SSV *Geronimo* out of St. George's School in Newport, Rhode Island, has tagged thousands of sharks and turtles in the last forty years for the National Fisheries Service and the Archie Carr Center for Sea Turtle Research at the University of Florida. The SSV *Robert C. Seamens* of the Sea Education Association has combined science with the humanities for undergrad-

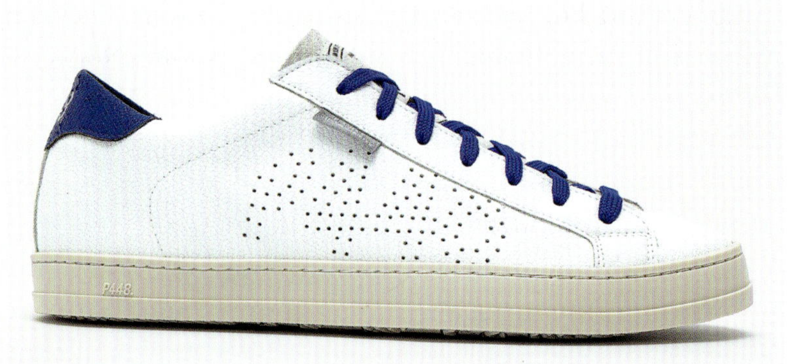

3. P448 sneakers produced with lionfish leather

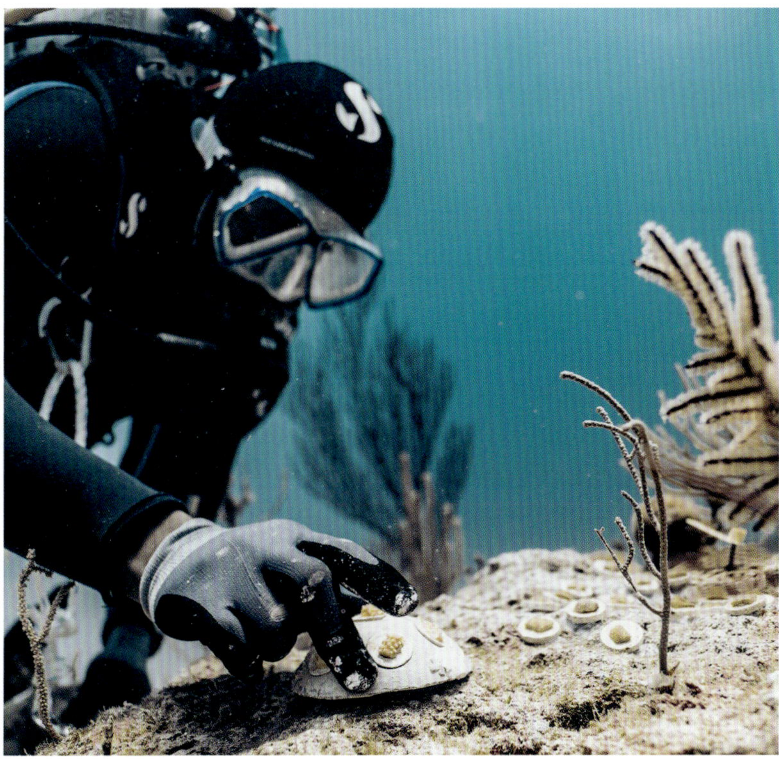
4. Coral Vita technician Tyriq Forbes installing a coral "cookie" on a degraded reef

uates; and the *Foxy Lady* has also tagged thousands of sea turtles for the Archie Carr Center and educated hundreds of Bahamian students (fig. 5). Williams-Mystic, a partnership between Williams College and Mystic Seaport Museum, has run an extraordinary interdisciplinary undergraduate maritime studies program for over forty-five years, focusing on the ocean's most critical issues.

While space exploration fills the media, private philanthropists have invested heavily in state-of-the-art research vessels that are made available at no cost to qualifying scientists. Historically, access to floating laboratories has been a challenge for new research on the deep sea, but that is rapidly changing. The Pink Flamingo Society is a collaboration between over fourteen organizations devoted to getting scientists out on the water, including Wendy and Eric Schmidt's Schmidt Ocean Institute; Norwegian billionaire Kjell Inge Røkke's 183-meter vessel REV *Ocean*, which will launch in 2024; Ray Dalio's *OceanXplorer*, an 87-meter research vessel with an incredible array of media technology and outreach; and the Ocean Exploration Trust, founded by scientist and *Titanic* discoverer Robert Ballard, which runs the E/V *Nautilus*. The opportunities are endless for scientists to have access to the highest level of technology money can buy as well as an infrastructure for support and public outreach.

There are hundreds more examples out there of creative thinkers and collaborators facing issues of sustainability, economy, policy, enforcement, survival, and conservation. The problems are grave and we would be irresponsible to assume there will ever be a return to a baseline that was once normal—what is normal? *Oceanus* presents us with a timeline of the past and an opportunity to talk about a different path to a better future for our oceans.

Resources

Archie Carr Center for Sea Turtle Research: accstr.ufl.edu
BioFeyn: biofeyn.com
Bio Hatch: betahatch.com
Cermac Global: cermaq.com
Coral Vita: coralvita.co
Geronimo: stgeorges.edu/geronimo
GreenWave: greenwave.org
Iceland Ocean Cluster: sjavarklasinn.is/en
Ideal Fish: idealfish.com
Inversa: inversaleathers.com
Ocean Exploration Trust: nautiluslive.org
OceanX: oceanx.org
REV Ocean: revocean.org
Schmidt Ocean Institute: schmidtocean.org
Sea Education Association: sea.edu
SeaAhead: sea-ahead.com
Stonington Kelp Co.: stoningtonkelpco.com
Williams-Mystic: mystic.williams.edu

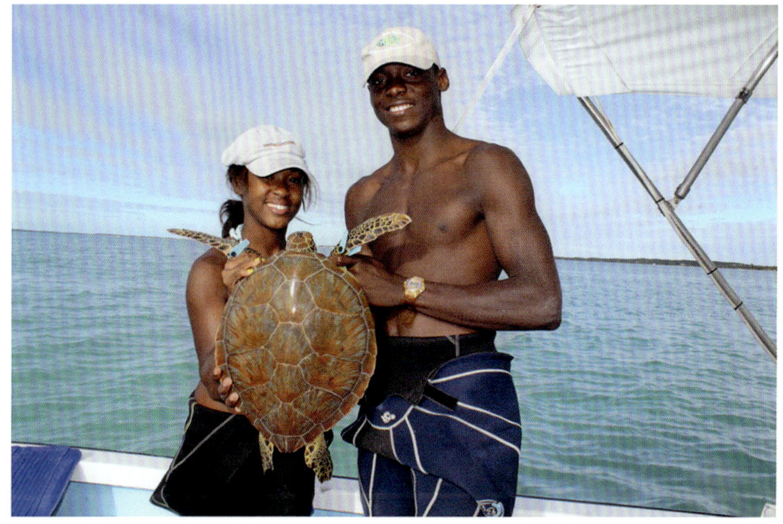
5. Bahamian interns with a tagged green turtle aboard the *Foxy Lady*

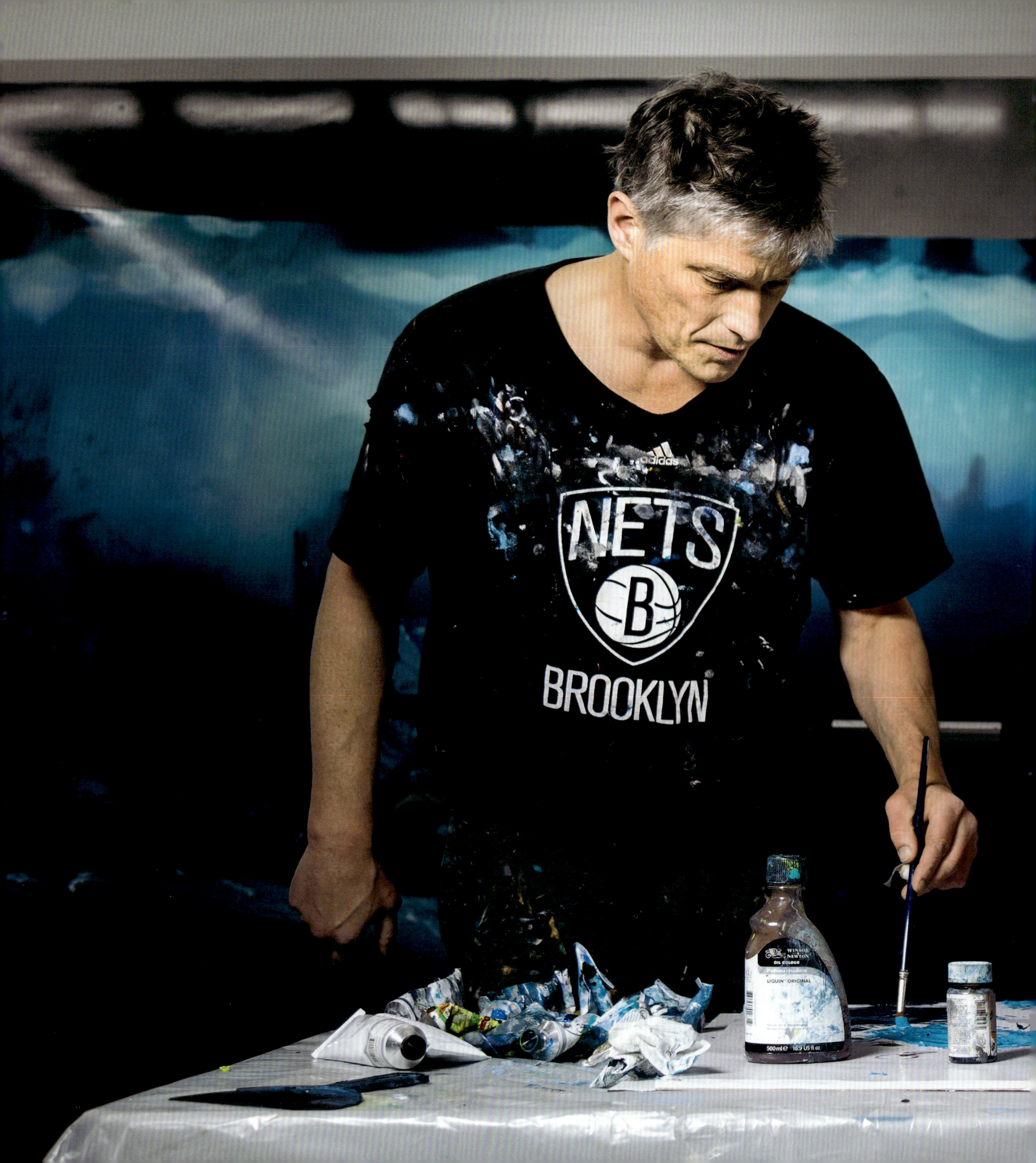

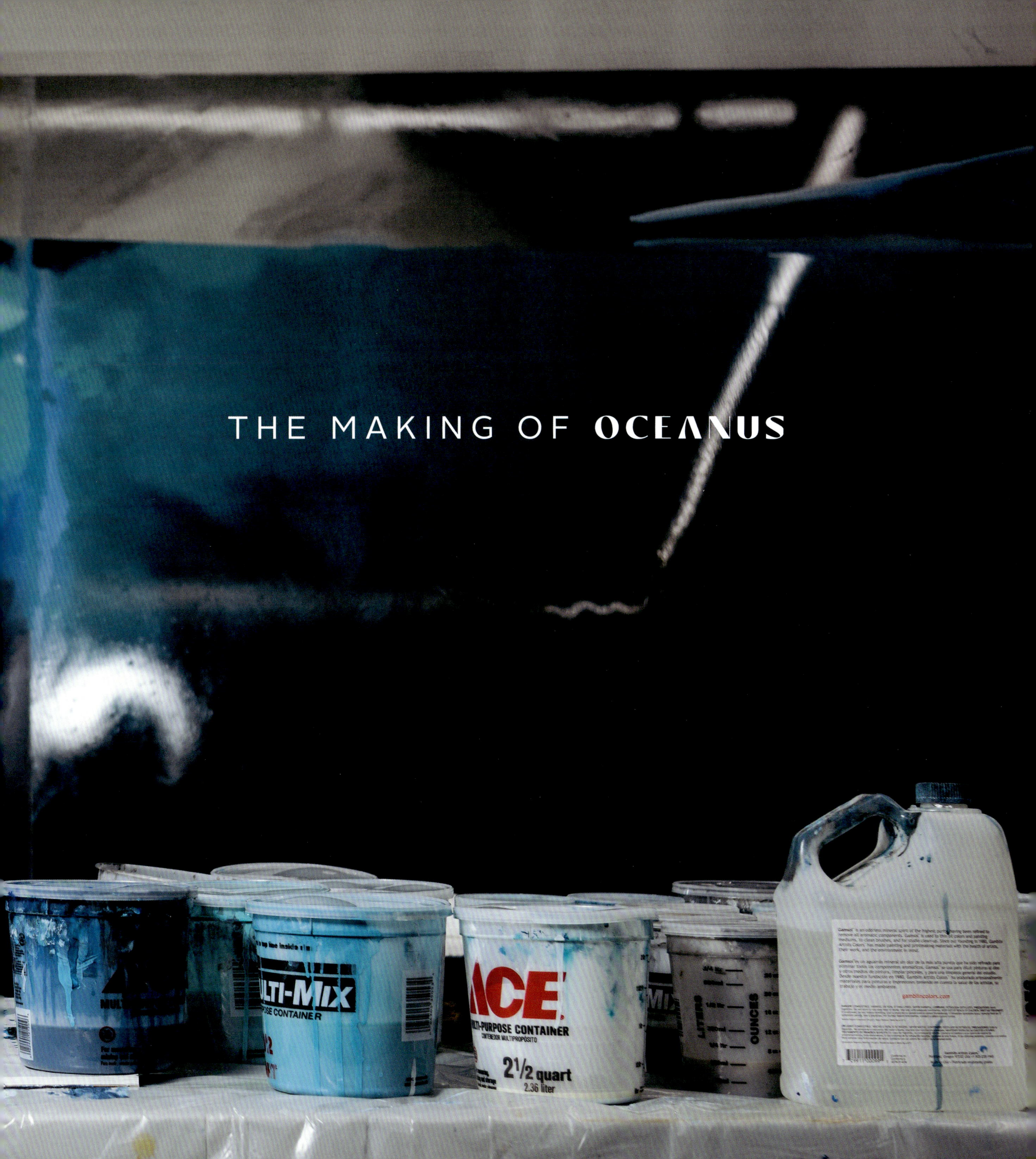
THE MAKING OF OCEANUS

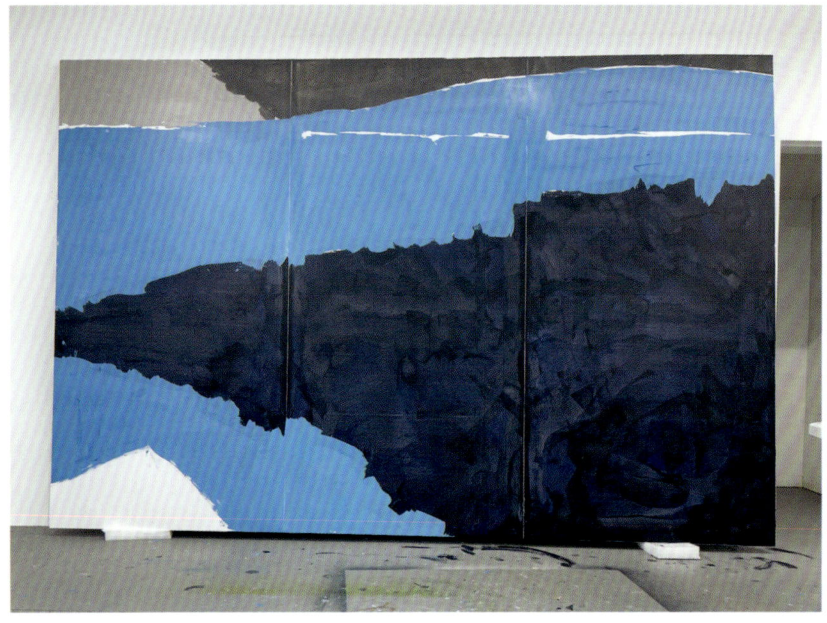
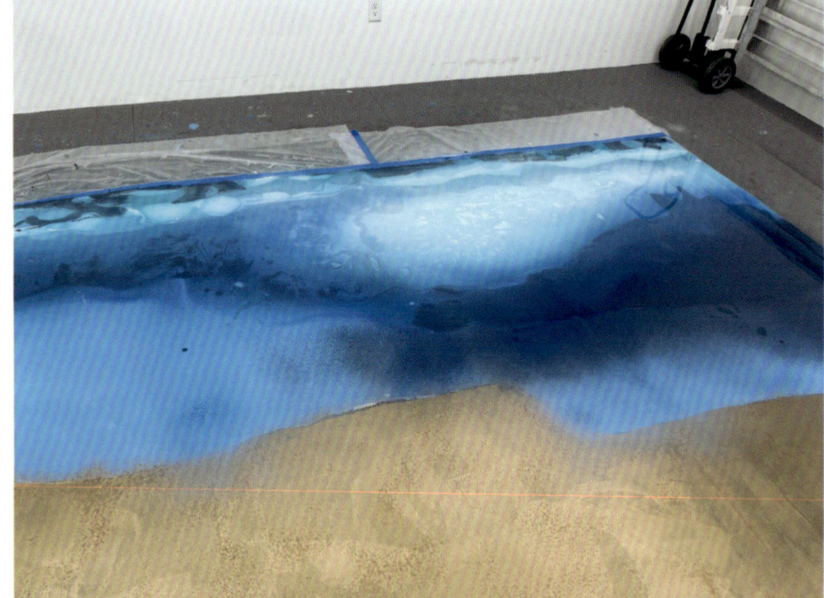
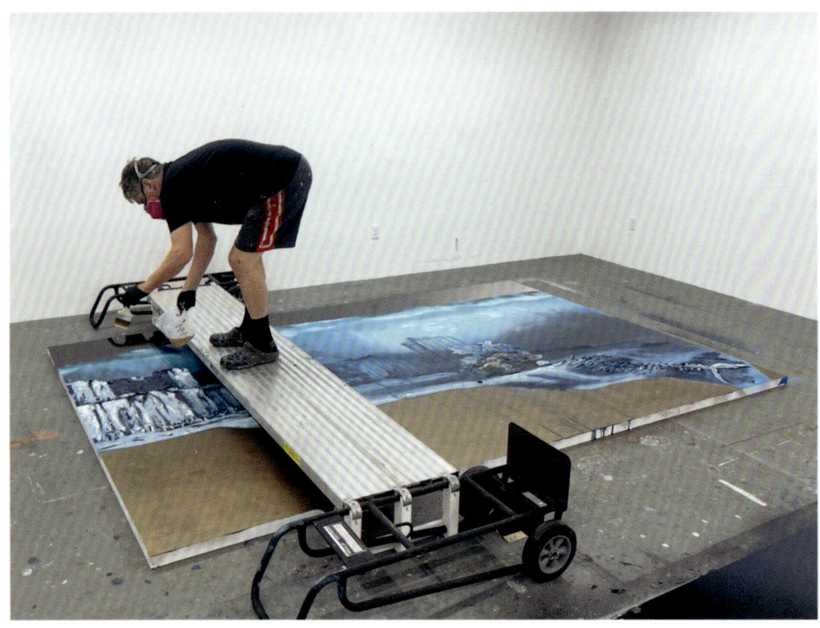
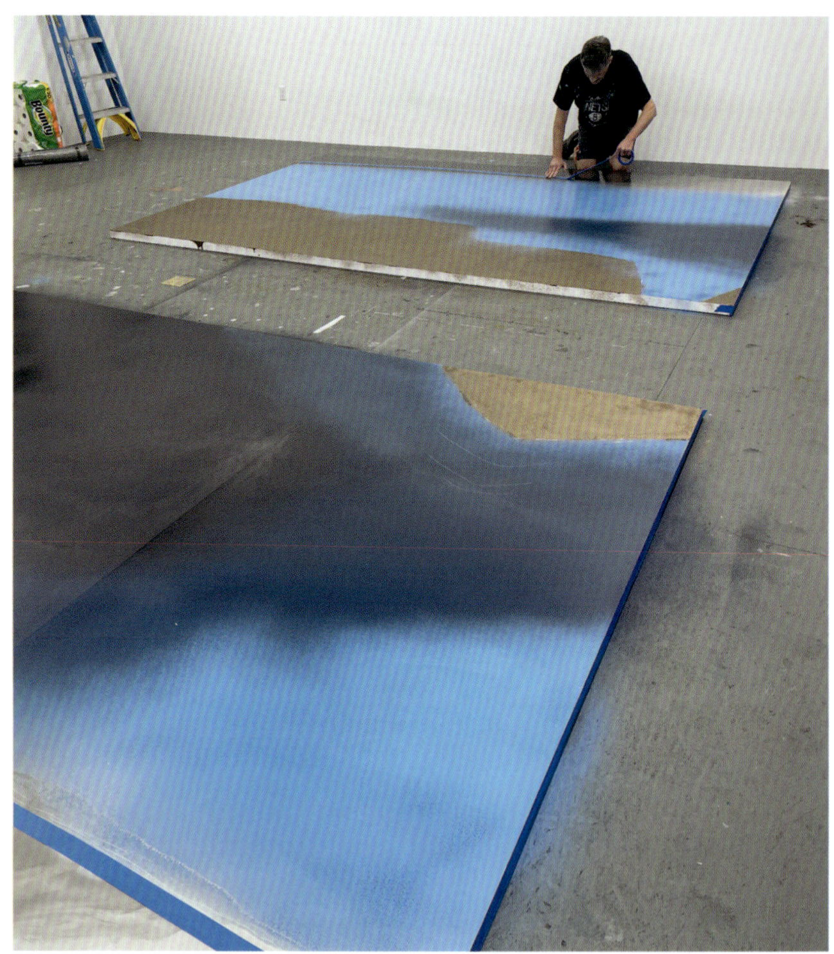
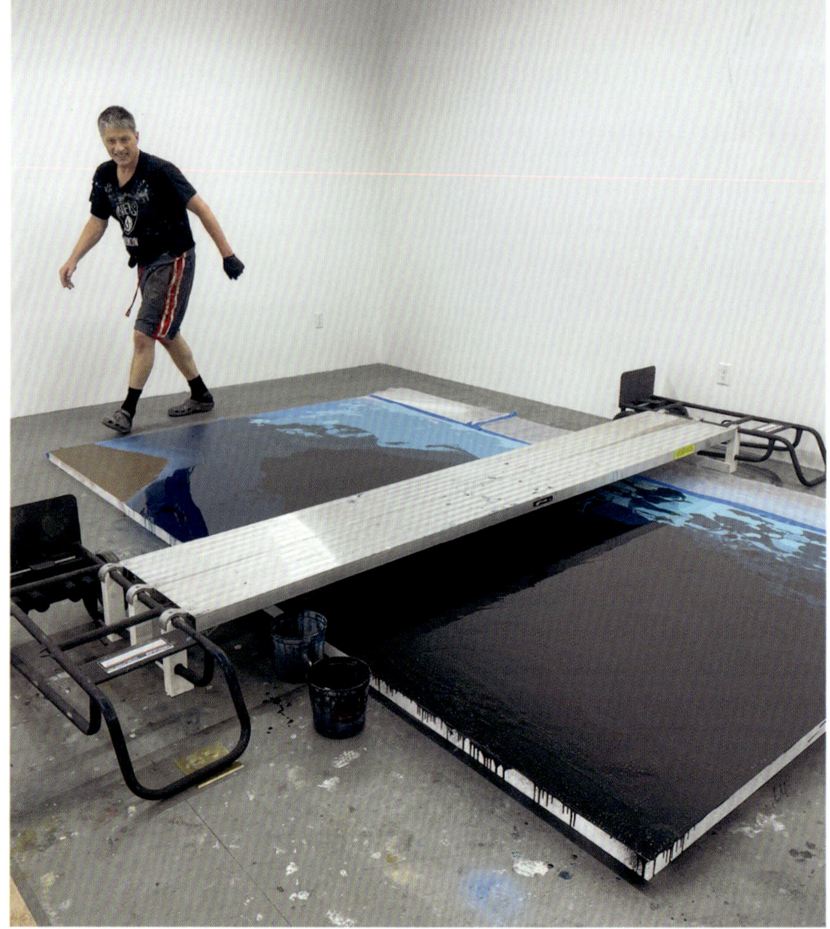

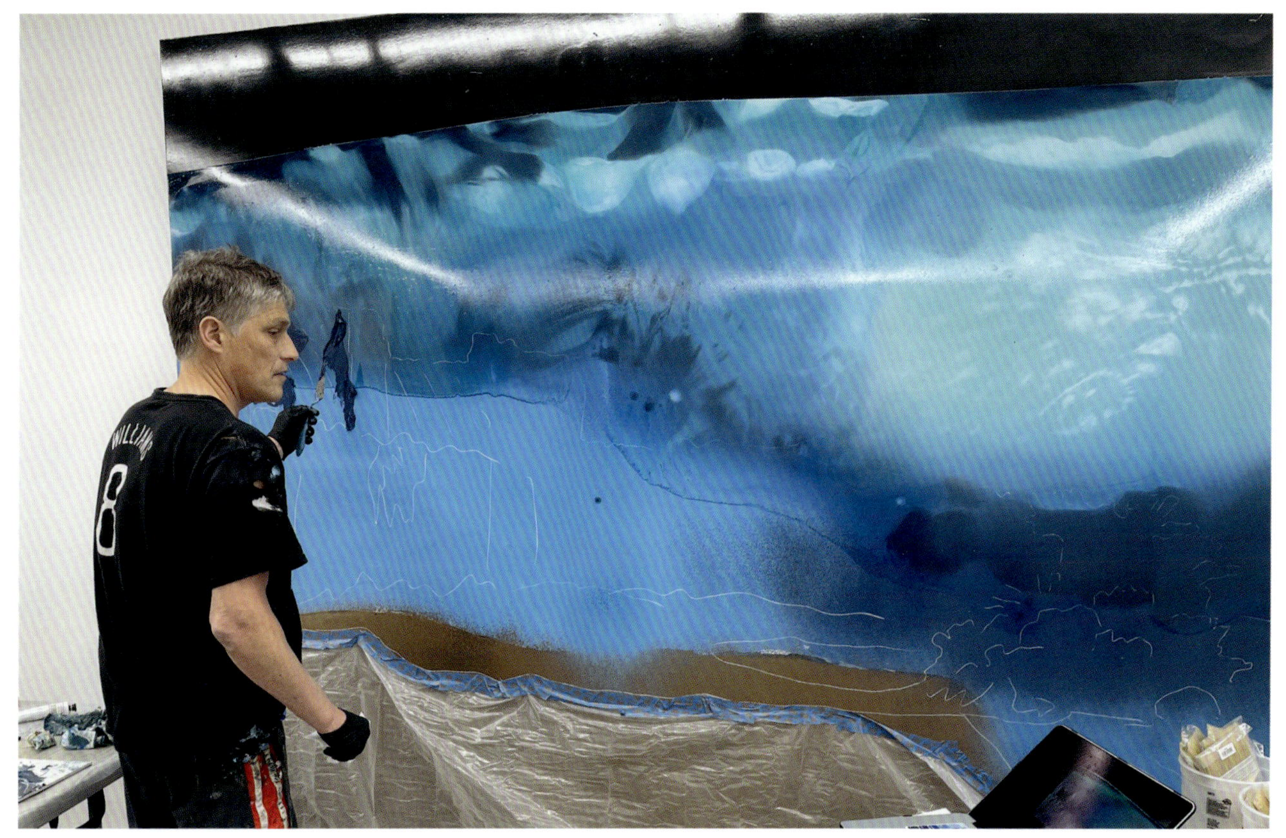

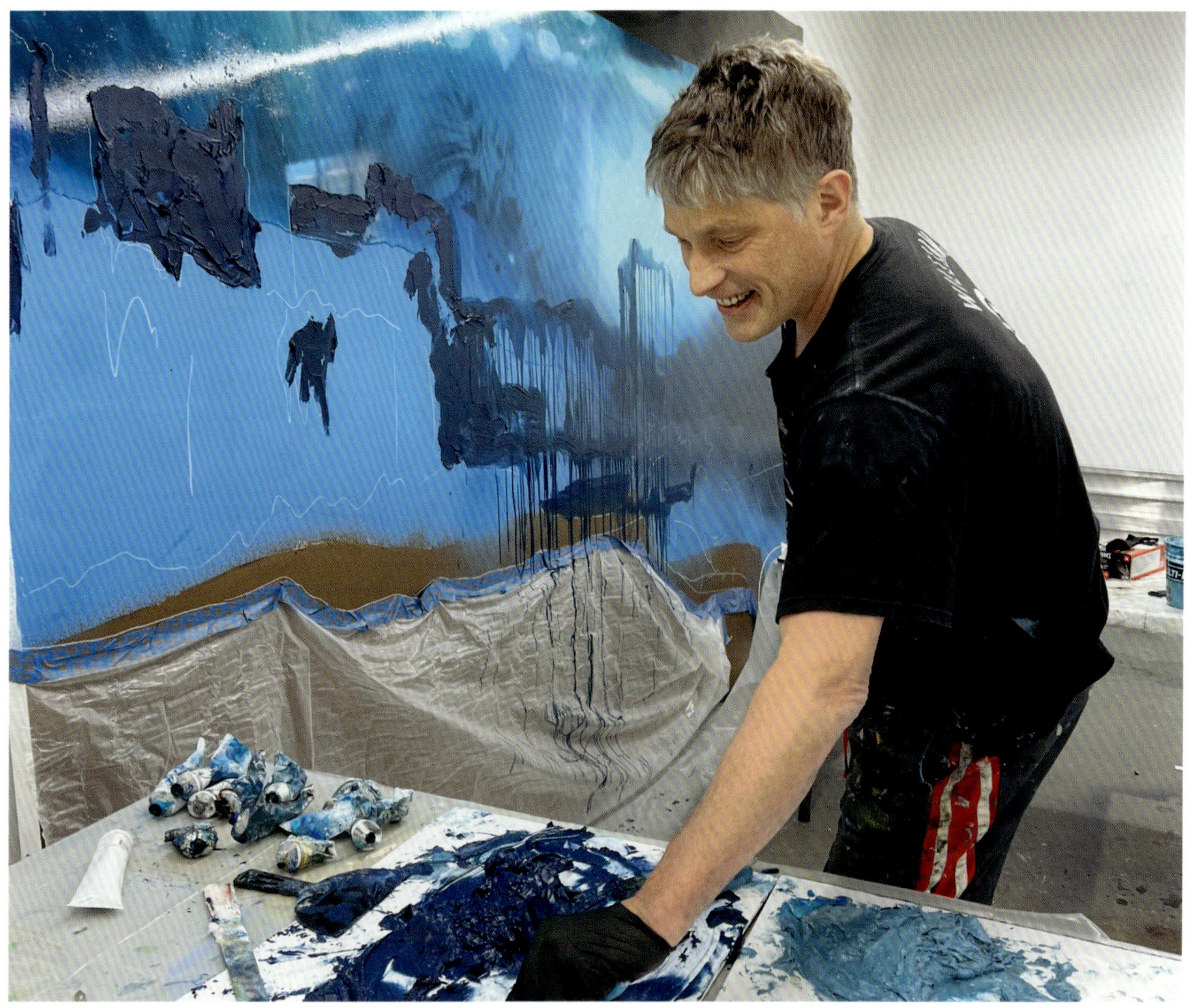

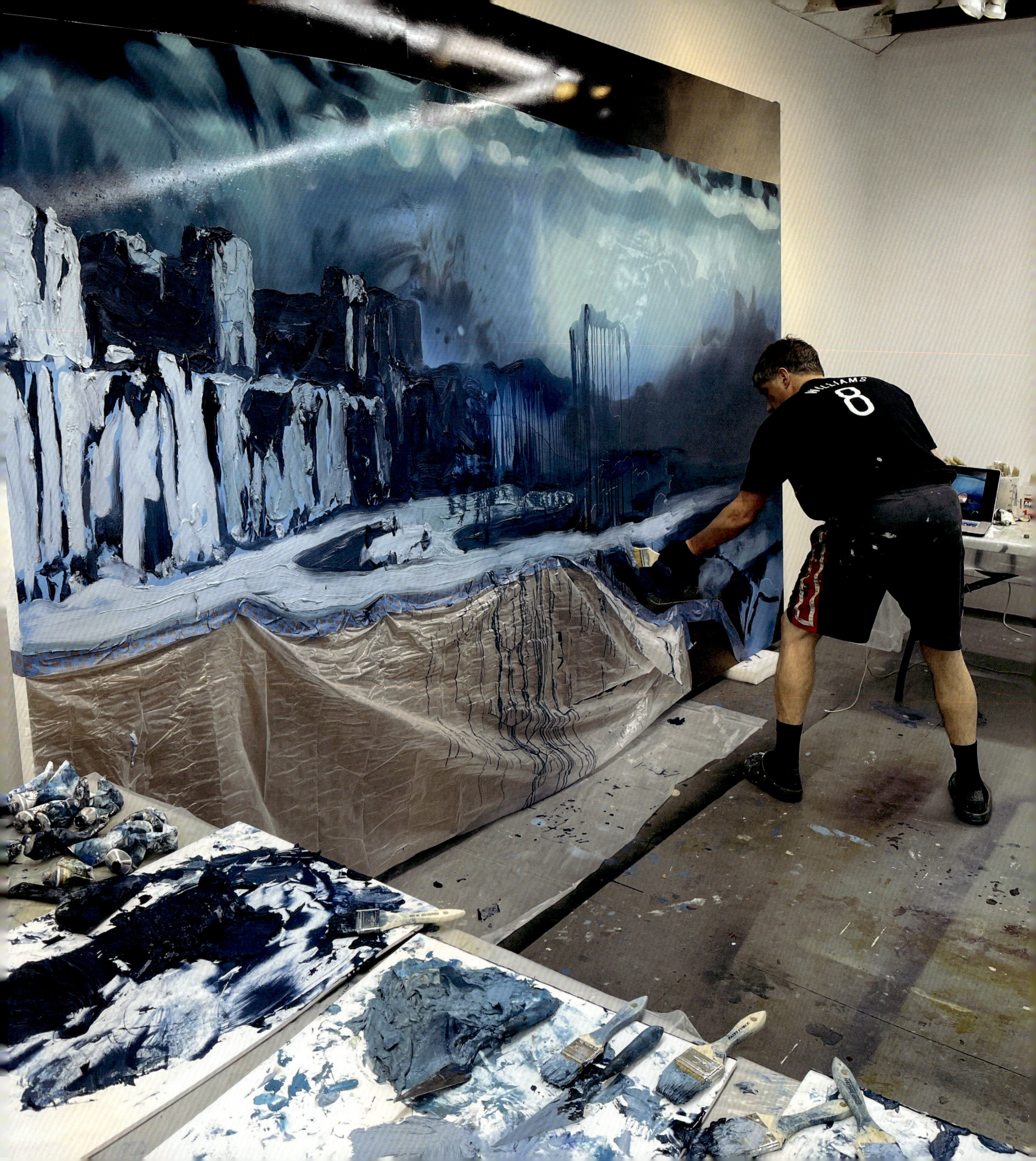

WILLIAMS
8

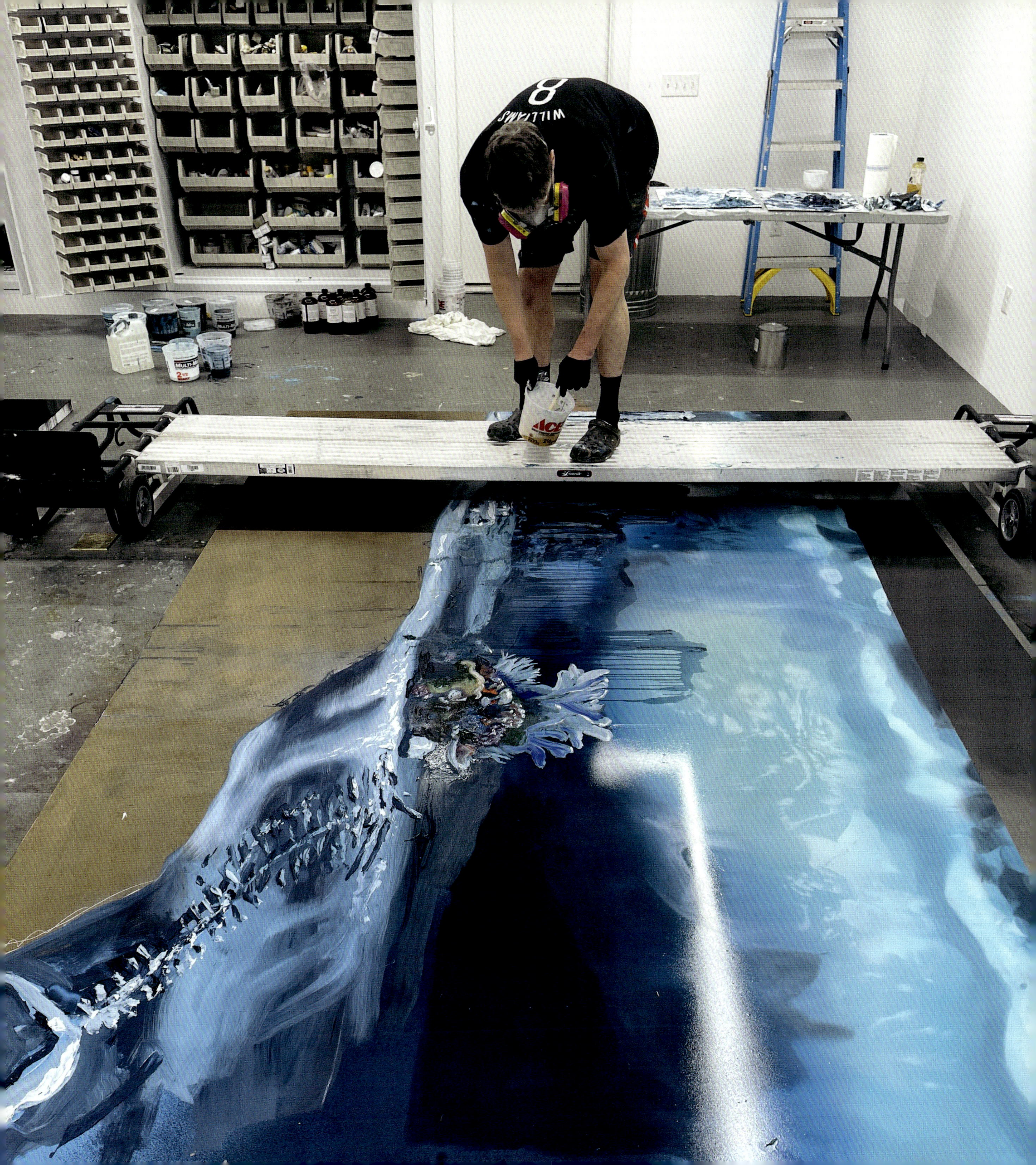

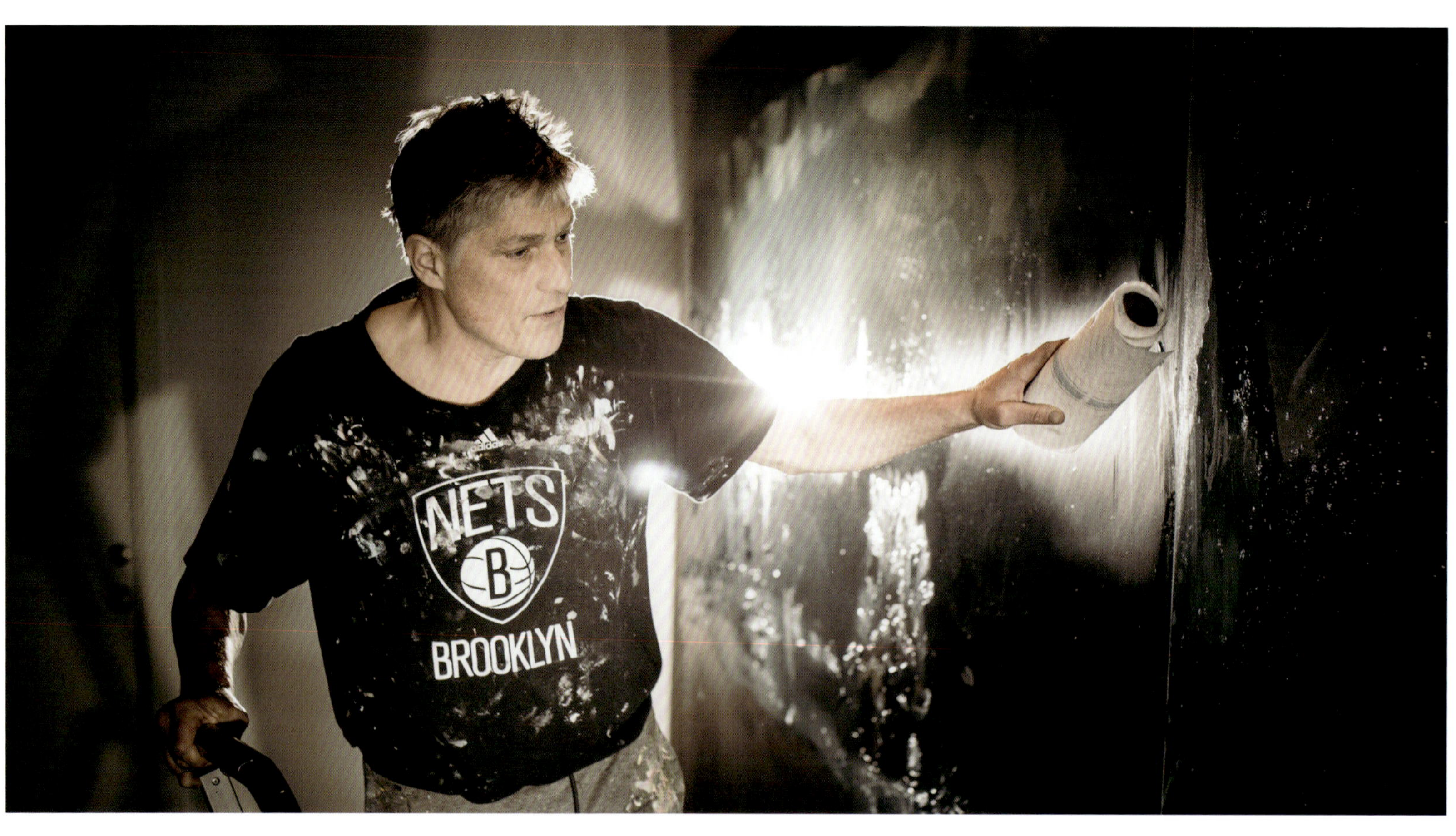

NETS
B
BROOKLYN

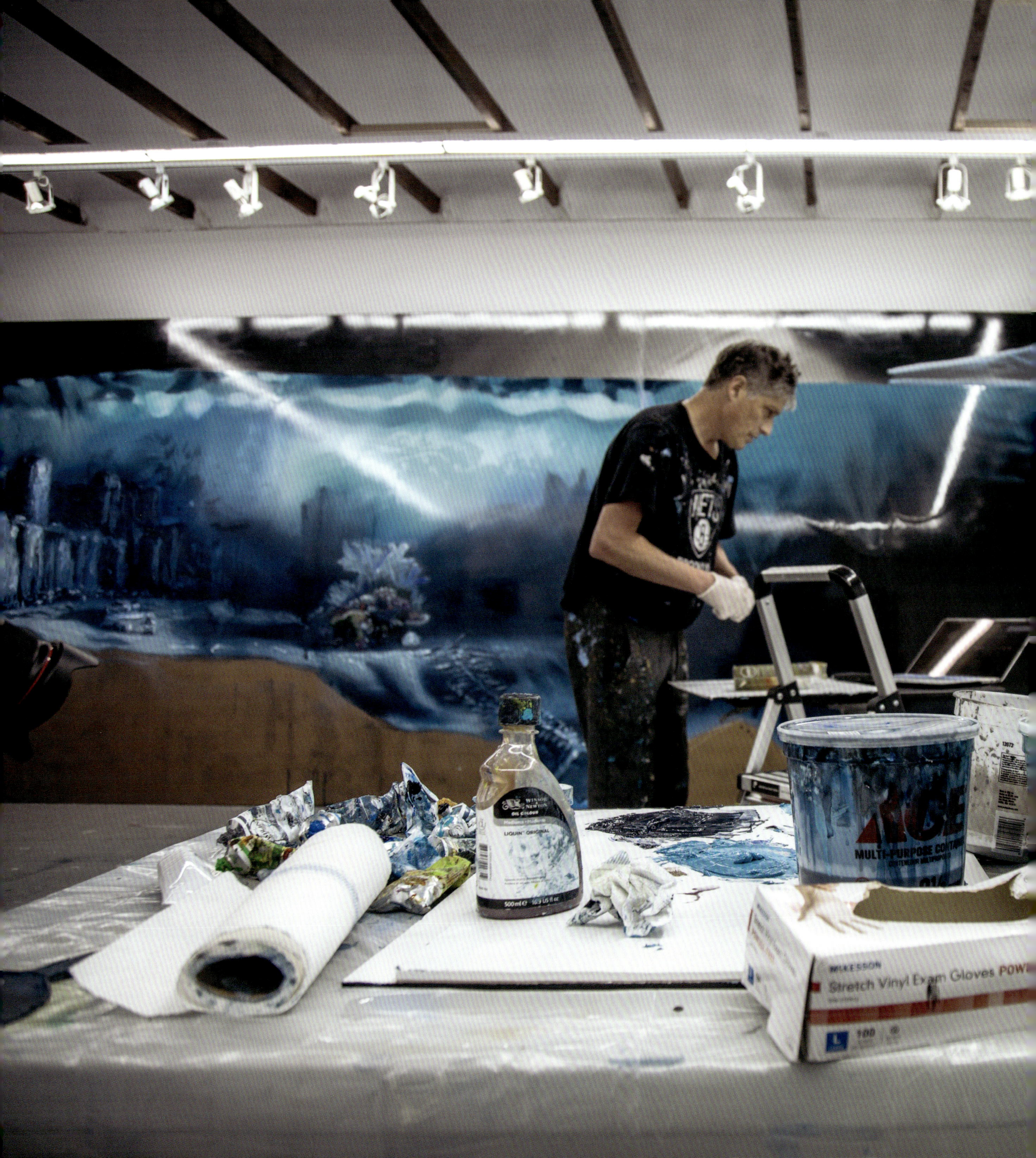

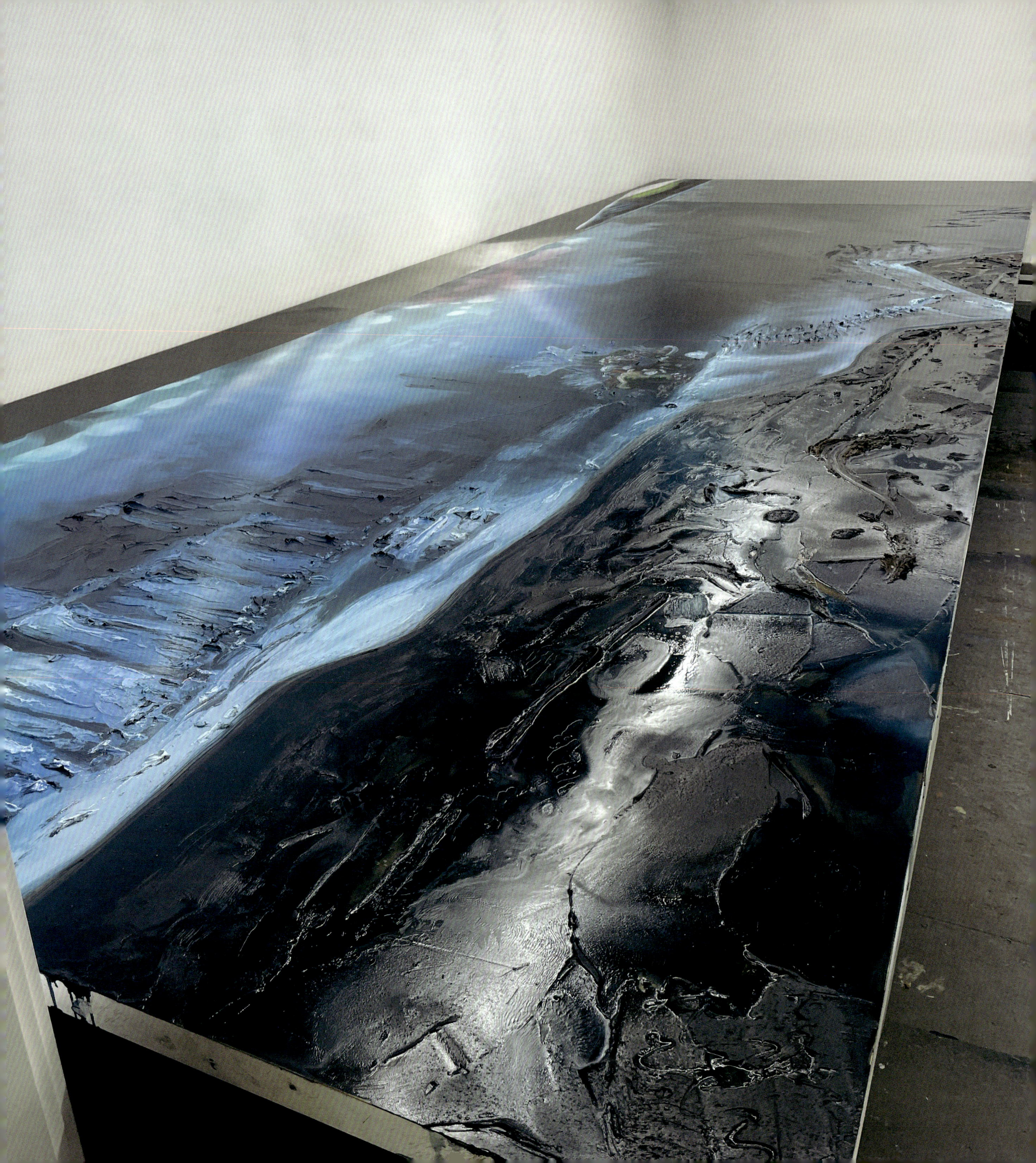

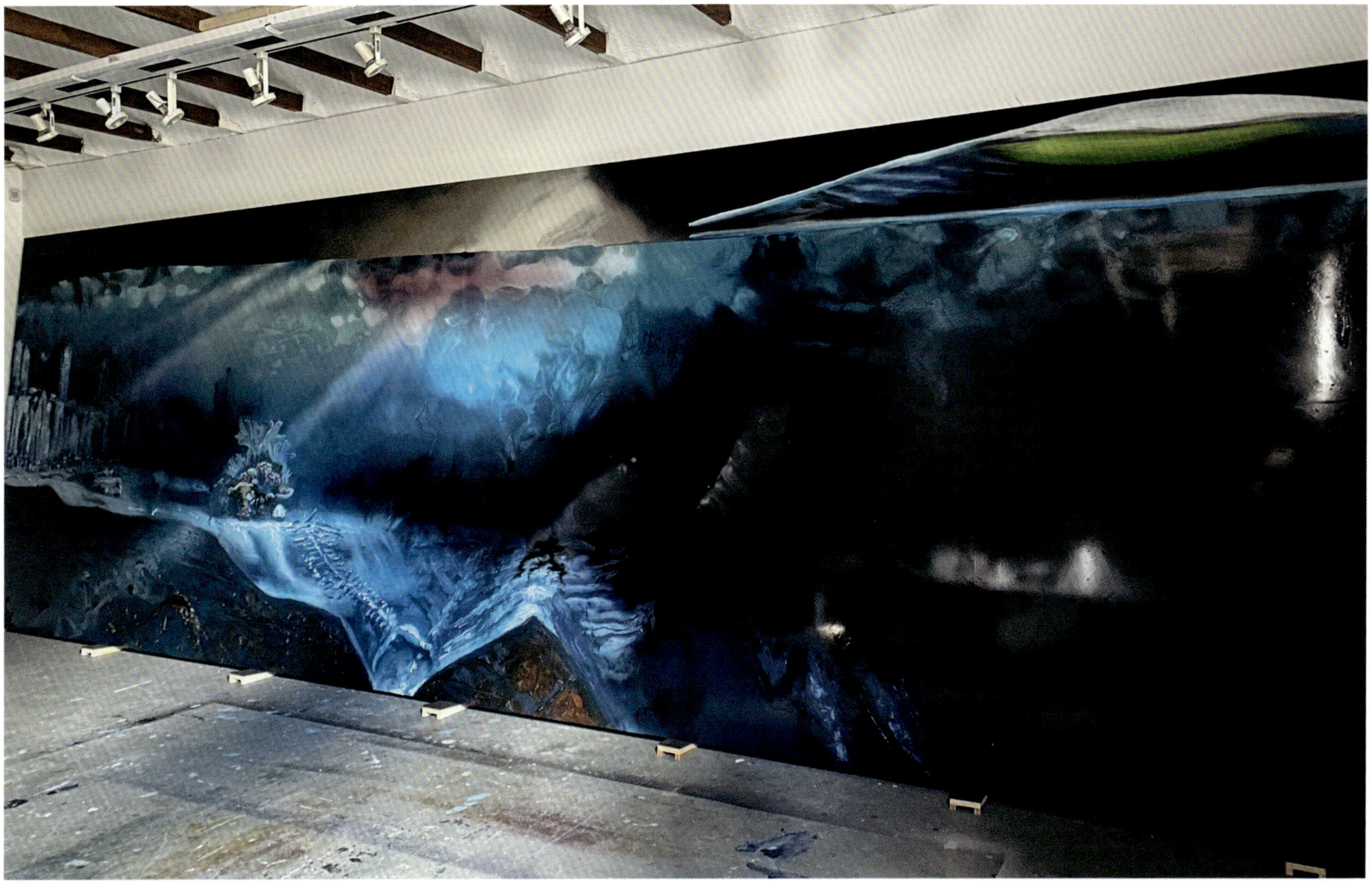

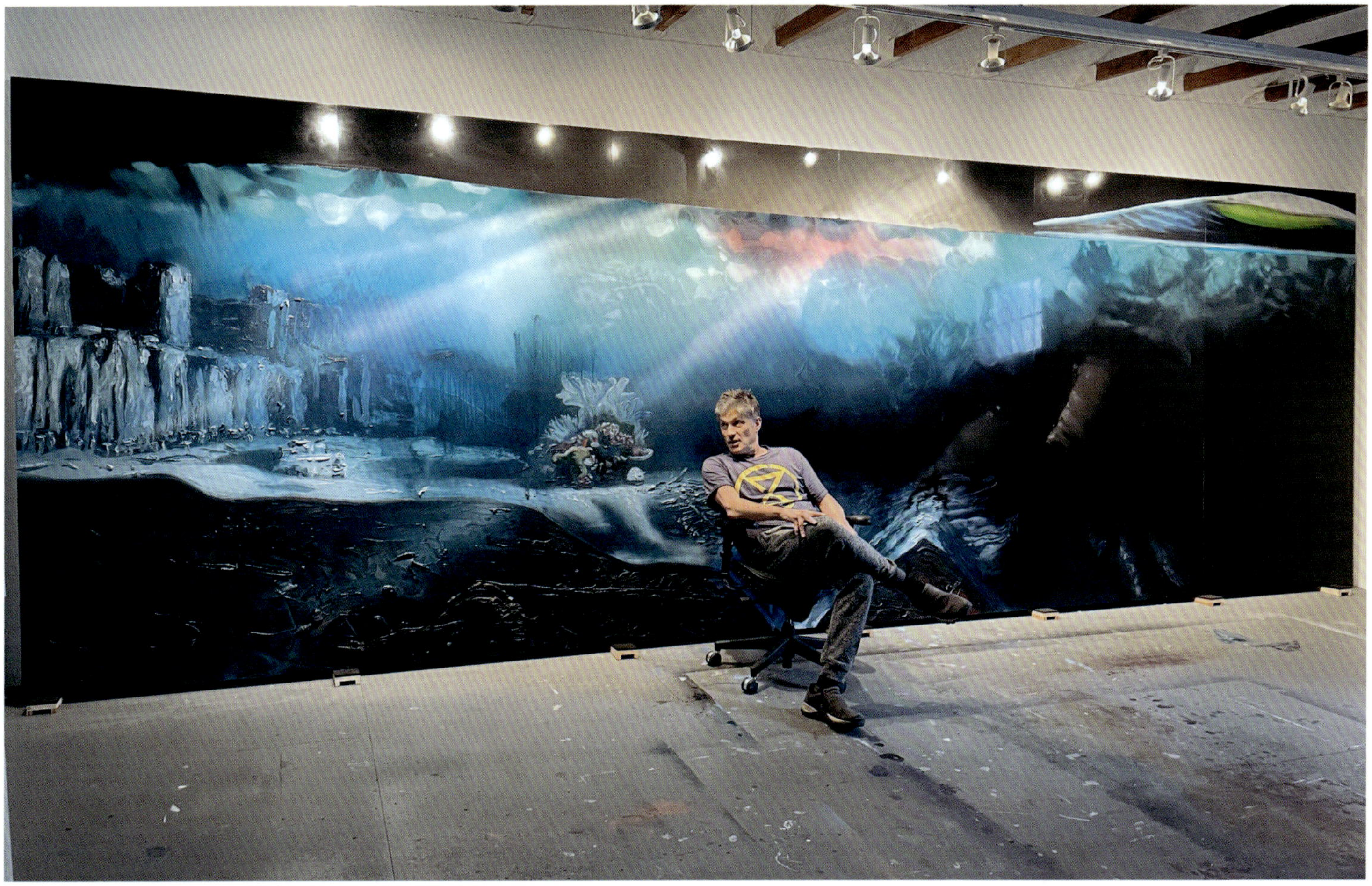

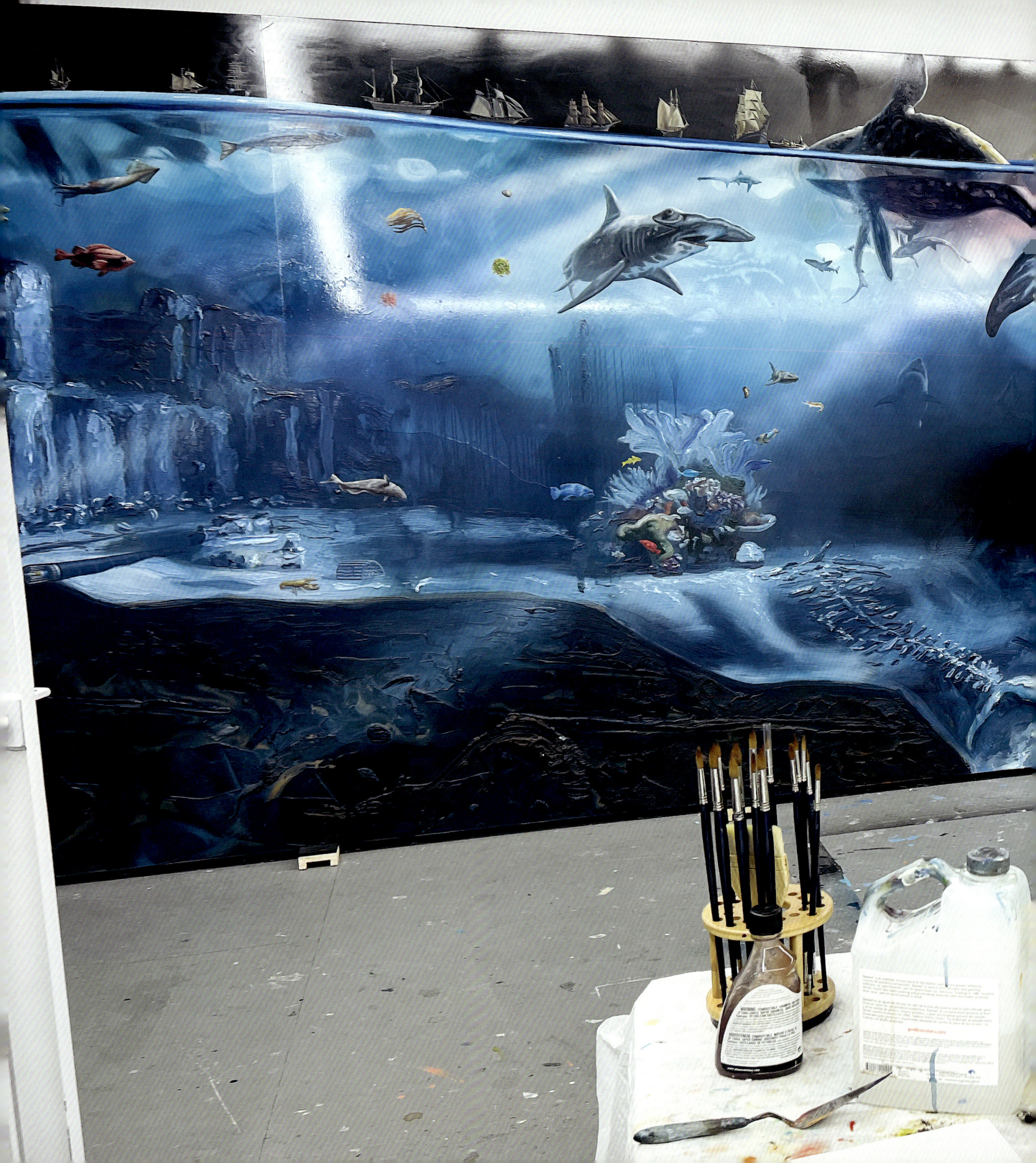

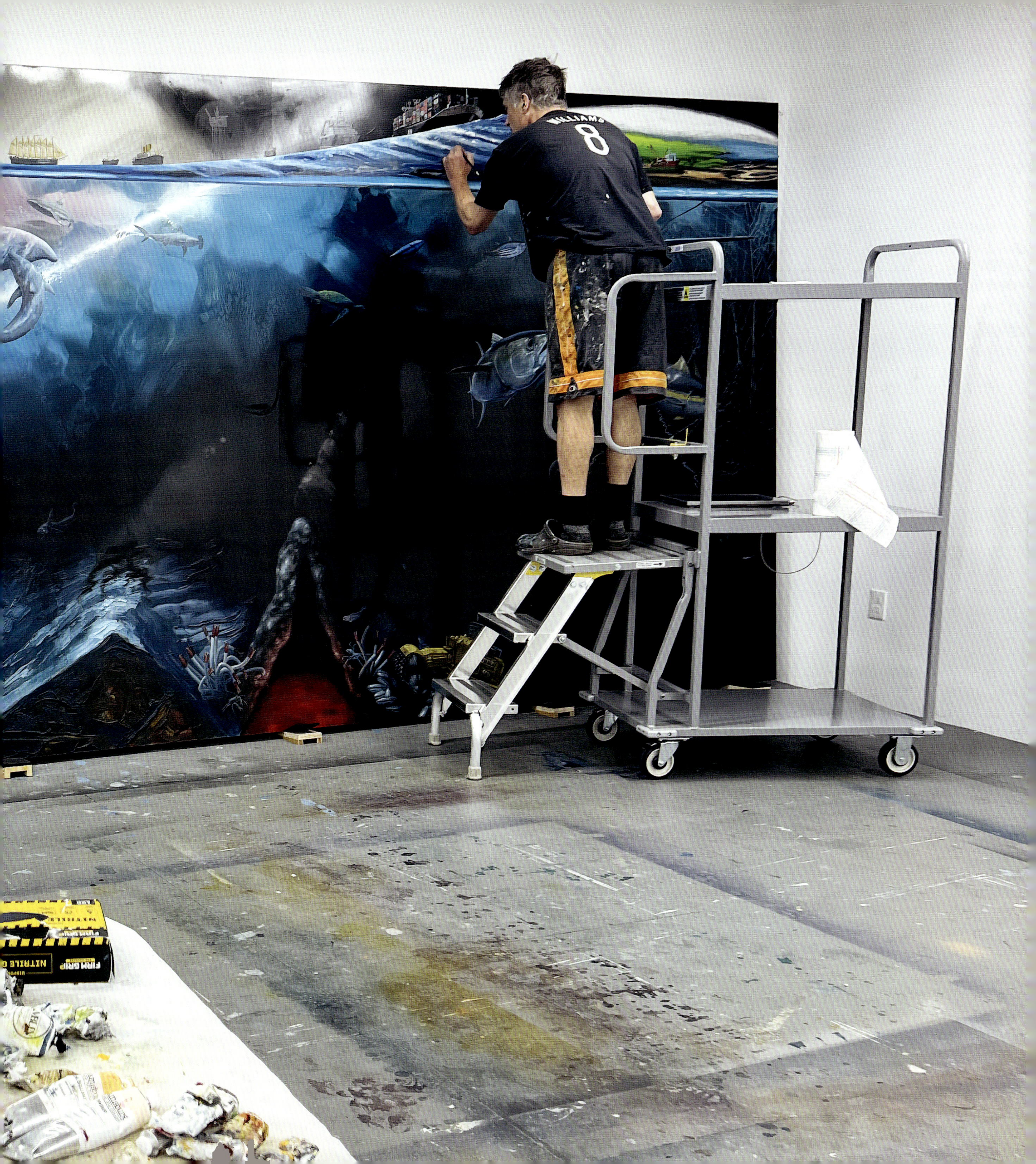

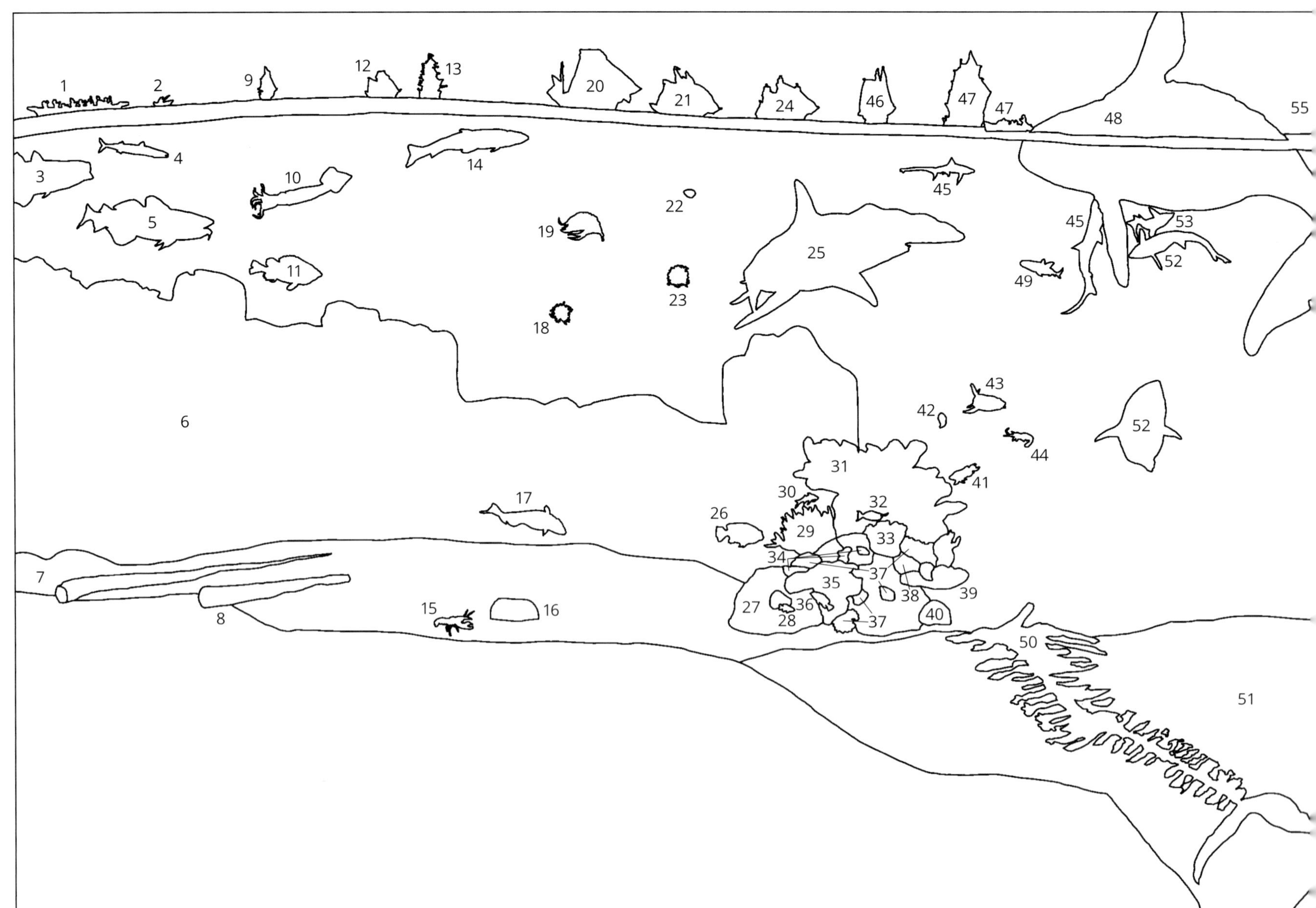

OCEANUS page 50

1. Pequot muhshoon (dugout canoe)
   Nookumuhs (Grandmother)
2. Indigenous Arctic qajaq (kayak)
3. Pollack (*Pollachius pollachius*)
4. Atlantic mackerel (*Scomber scombrus*)
5. Atlantic cod (*Gadus morhua*)
6. Continental shelf
7. 19th-century telegraph cable
8. Fiber-optic cable
9. Marblehead fishing schooner (colonial heeltapper), ca. 1750s–1840s
10. Northern shortfin squid (*Illex illecebrosus*)
11. Beaked redfish (*Sebastes mentella*)
12. Marblehead fishing schooner *Hannah*, ca. 1760s

13. Steam packet *Savannah*, 1819
14. Atlantic salmon (*Salmo salar*)
15. American lobster (*Homarus americanus*)
16. Wooden round-top lobster pot
17. Atlantic halibut (*Hippoglossus hippoglossus*)
18. Red algae (*Gracilaria*)
19. Japanese kelp (*Saccharina japonica*)
20. HMS *Beagle*, 1820
21. Topsail schooner *La Amistad*, 1839
22. Japanese cockle (*Ruditapes philippinarum*)
23. Seaweed algae (*Eucheuma*)
24. Clipper *Sovereign of the Seas*, 1852
25. Great hammerhead shark (*Sphyrna mokarran*)
26. Atlantic goliath grouper (*Epinephelus itajara*)
27. Stony coral (*Echinopora fruticulosa*)
28. Lane snapper (*Lutjanus synagris*)

29. Staghorn coral (*Acropora cervicornis*)
30. Goldsaddle goatfish (*Parupeneus cyclostomus*)
31. Elkhorn coral (*Acropora palmata*)
32. Bluespine unicornfish (*Naso unicornis*)
33. Thin finger coral (*Porites porites*)
34. Smooth dome coral (*Solenastrea bournoni*)
35. Brain coral (*Cyphastrea serailia*)
36. Red grouper (*Epinephelus morio*)
37. Staghorn coral (*Acropora secale*)
38. Finger coral (*Porites divaricata*)
39. Staghorn coral (*Acropora anthocercis*)
40. Brain coral (*Coscinaraea columna*)
41. Rainbow parrotfish (*Scarus guacamaia*)
42. Pacific oyster (*Magallana gigas*)
43. Short-tail nurse shark (*Pseudoginglymostoma brevicaudatum*)

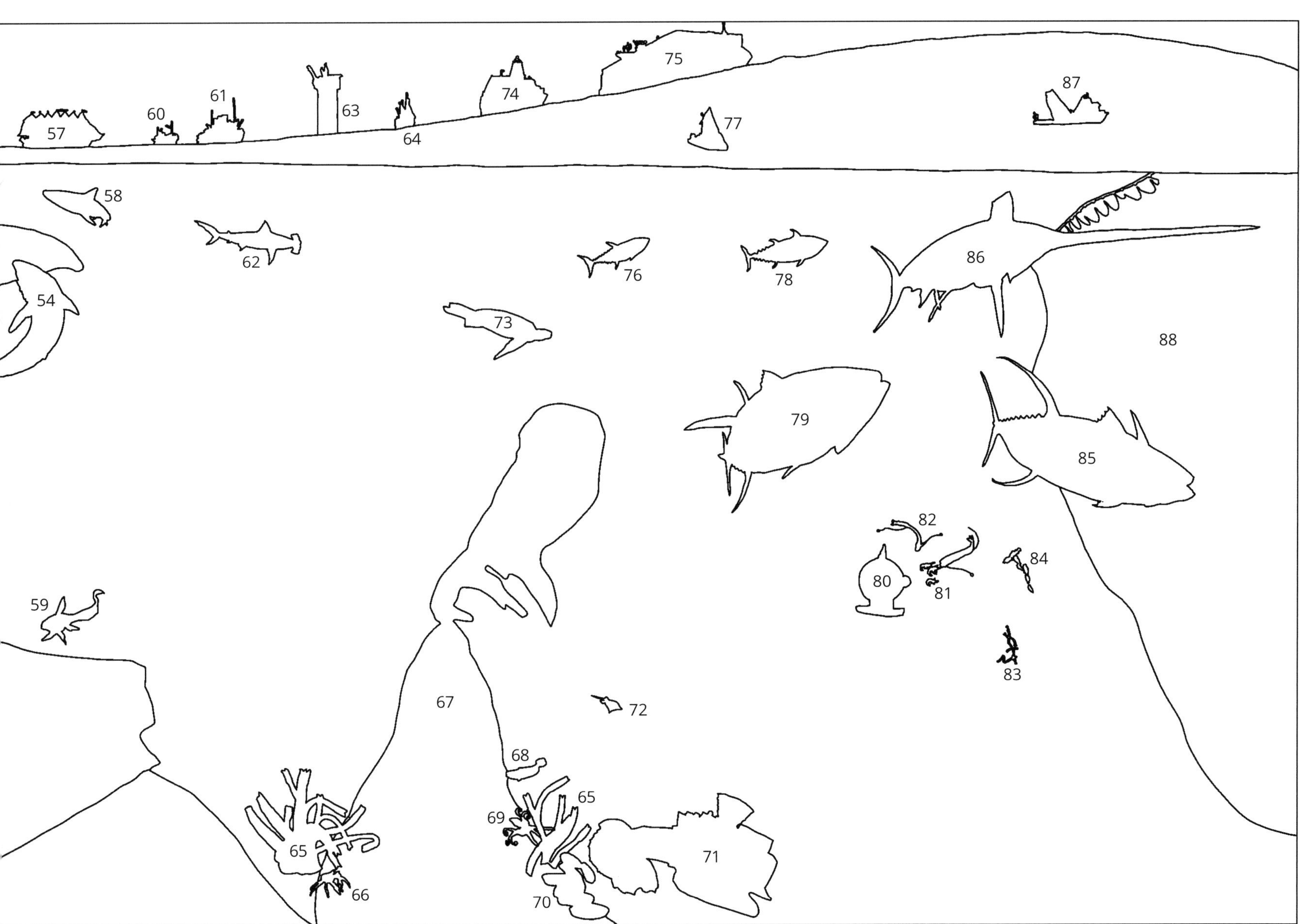

44. Whiteleg shrimp (*Litopenaeus vannamei*)
45. Pelagic thresher shark (*Alopias pelagicus*)
46. Clipper-schooner *Nimbus*, 1872
47. Whaling bark *Wanderer* (with whaleboat), 1878
48. Right whale (*Eubalaena glacialis*)
49. Sandbar shark (*Carcharhinus plumbeus*)
50. Right whale (*Eubalaena glacialis*) skeleton
51. Marine trench
52. Great white shark (*Carcharodon carcharias*)
53. Grey reef shark (*Carcharhinus amblyrhynchos*)
54. Shortfin mako shark (*Isurus oxyrinchus*)
55. Newport fish and lobster boat, 1880s
56. New Haven sharpie
57. Schooner *Thomas W. Lawson*, 1902
58. Oceanic whitetip shark (*Carcharhinus longimanus*)
59. Deep sea rattail fish (*Coryphaenoides acrolepis*)

60. Steam trawler *Surf*, 1911
61. Ocean liner *Imperator*, 1912
62. Scalloped hammerhead shark (*Sphyrna lewini*)
63. Offshore oil rig
64. Steam schooner *Barbara C*, 1920
65. Giant tube worm (*Riftia pachyptila*)
66. Squat lobster (*Shinkaia crosnieri*)
67. Hydrothermal vent
68. Eelpout (*Pachycara matallansi*)
69. Vulcanoctopus (*Vulcanoctopus hydrothermalis*)
70. Giant hydrothermal clam (*Calyptogena magnifica*)
71. Nautilus Minerals deep-sea mining bulk cutter
72. Pacific white skate (*Bathyraja spinosissima*)
73. Kemp's ridley sea turtle (*Lepidochelys kempii*)
74. Catcher-processor *Alaska Ocean*, 1981
75. Container ship *APL China*, 1995

76. Pacific bluefin tuna (*Thunnus orientalis*)
77. Cuban refugee raft
78. Skipjack tuna (*Katsuwonus pelamis*)
79. Atlantic bluefin tuna (*Thunnus thynnus*)
80. William Beebe and Otis Barton in the Bathysphere, 1934
81. Deep sea shrimp (*Oplophorus gracilirostris*)
82. Giant dragonfish (*Bathysphaera intacta*)
83. Gleaming-tailed serpent-dragon (*Idiacanthus fasciola*)
84. Ghostly seadevil (*Haplophryne mollis*)
85. Yellowfin tuna (*Thunnus albacares*)
86. Swordfish (*Xiphias gladius*)
87. Illegal fishing vessel
88. Pelagic drift net

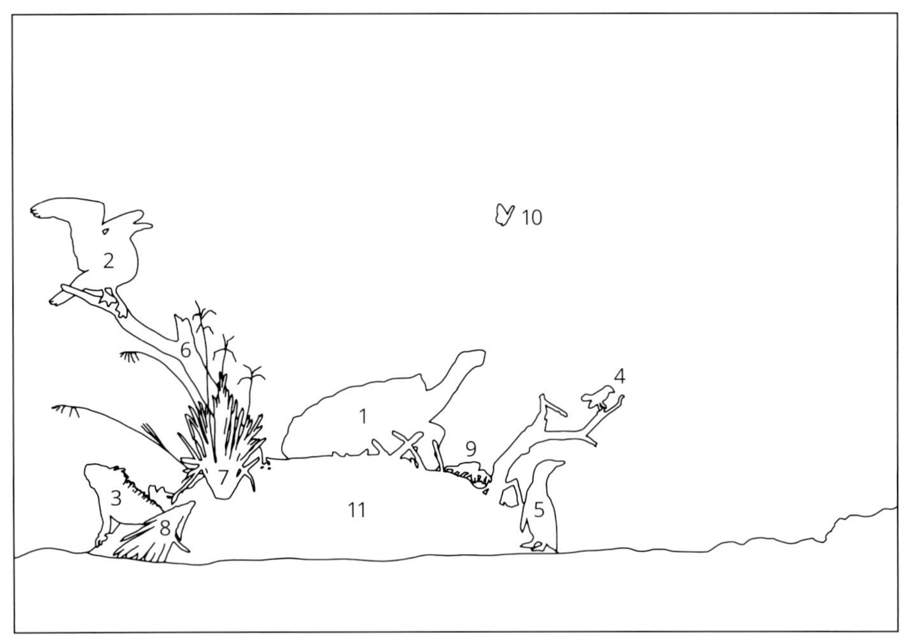

RAFTING THE HUMBOLDT CURRENT page 66

1. Tortoise (*Chelonoidis*)
2. Booby (*Sula*)
3. Iguana (*Ctenosaura*)
4. Blue-back grassquit (*Volatinia jacarina*)
5. Penguin (*Spheniscus*)
6. Tree (*Scalesia*)
7. Bush (*Cryptocarpus*)
8. Plant (*Miconia*)
9. Red rock crab (*Grapsus grapsus*)
10. Cloudless sulfur butterfly (*Phoebis sennae*)
11. Raft of floating vegetation

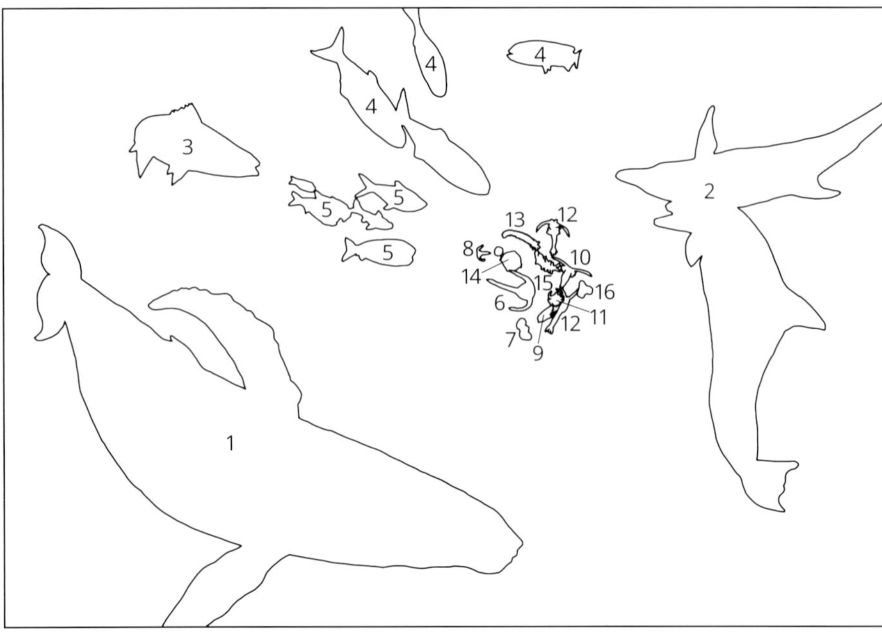

TROPHIC WEB page 72

1. Humpback whale (*Megaptera novaeangliae*)
2. Bottlenose dolphin (*Tursiops truncatus*)
3. Striped bass (*Morone saxatilis*)
4. Bluefish (*Pomatomus saltatrix*)
5. Menhaden (*Brevoortia tyrannus*)
6. Dinoflagellate (*Neoceratium tripos*)
7. Green algae (*Yamagishiella*)
8. Green algae (*Palmella miniata*)
9. Marine amphipod (*Themisto compressa*)
10. Copepods (*Oithona setigera*)
11. Blue crab (*Callinectes sapidus*)
12. Mysid shrimp larvae (*Americamysis bahia*)
13. Bristle worm (*Phalacrophorus pictus*)
14. Dinoflagellate (*Gonyaulax polygramma*)
15. Nudibranch larvae (*Edmundsella pedata*)
16. Anemone larvae (*Cerianthid*)

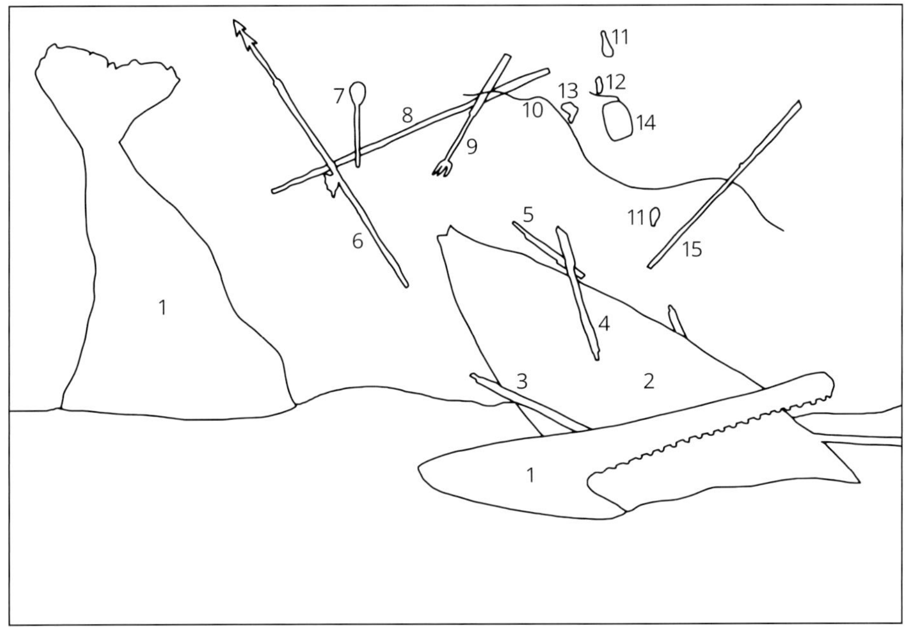

REVERSAL OF FORTUNE page 76

1. Sperm whale (*Physeter macrocephalus*)
2. Whaling boat
3. Blubber pike
4. Strand knife
5. Sheath
6. Provincetown toggle
7. Flensing blade
8. Tail knife
9. Closh
10. Rope
11. Small blubber knife
12. Small blubber knife
13. Sailor's palm
14. Line tub
15. Boarding knife

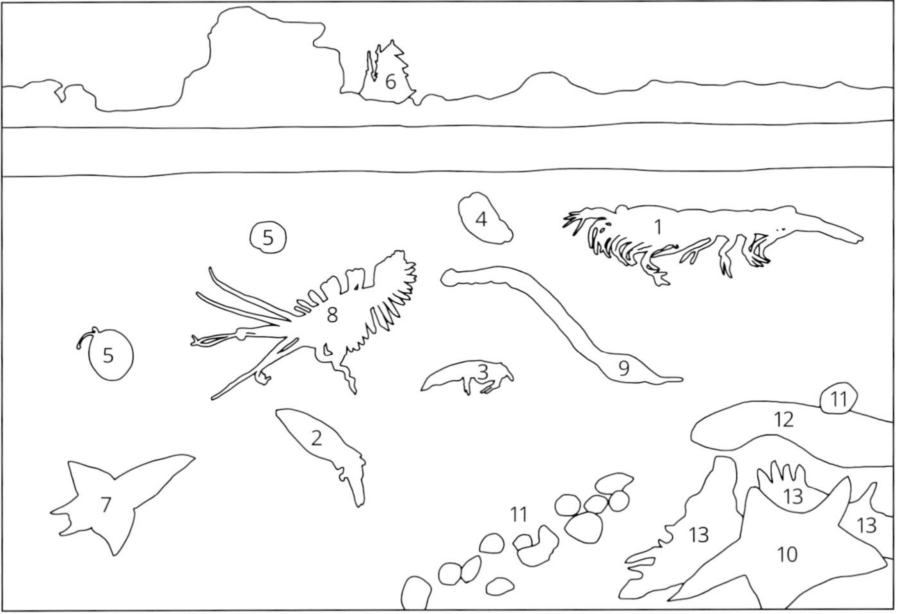

ENDURANCE page 80

1. Antarctic krill (*Euphausia superba*)
2. Glass squid (*Galiteuthis glacialis*)
3. Antarctic amphipod (*Cyllopus magellanicus*)
4. Antarctic pteropod (*Limacina helicina*)
5. Jellyfish (*Calycopsis borchgrevinki*)
6. Three-masted auxiliary schooner barquentine *Endurance*, 1912 (lost 1915)
7. Sea angel (*Clione limacina*)
8. Squidworm (*Teuthidodrilus samae*)
9. Arrow worm (*Pterosagitta draco*)
10. Seastar (*Odontaster validus*)
11. Antarctic sea urchin (*Sterechinus neumayeri*)
12. Ribbon worm (*Parborlasia corrugatus*)
13. Jelly worm (*Flabegraviera mundata*)

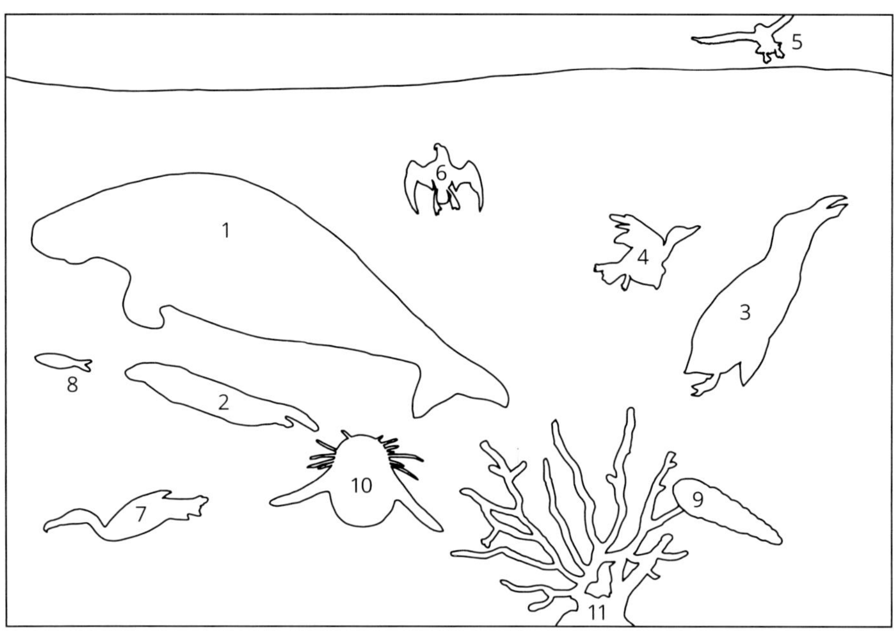

LEGACY page 86

1. Steller's sea cow (*Hydrodamalis gigas*)
2. Sea mink (*Neovison macrodon*)
3. Great auk (*Pinguinus impennis*)
4. Labrador duck (*Camptorhynchus labradorius*)
5. Belarus shearwater (*Puffinus mauretanicus*)
6. Guadalupe storm petrel (*Oceanodroma macrodactyla*)
7. Pallas's cormorant (*Phalacrocorax perspicillatus*)
8. Galápagos damsel fish (*Azurina eupalama*)
9. Salt marsh horn snail (*Cerithideopsis fuscata*)
10. Caribbean monk seal (*Neomonachus tropicalis*)
11. Red coral (*Corallium rubrum*)

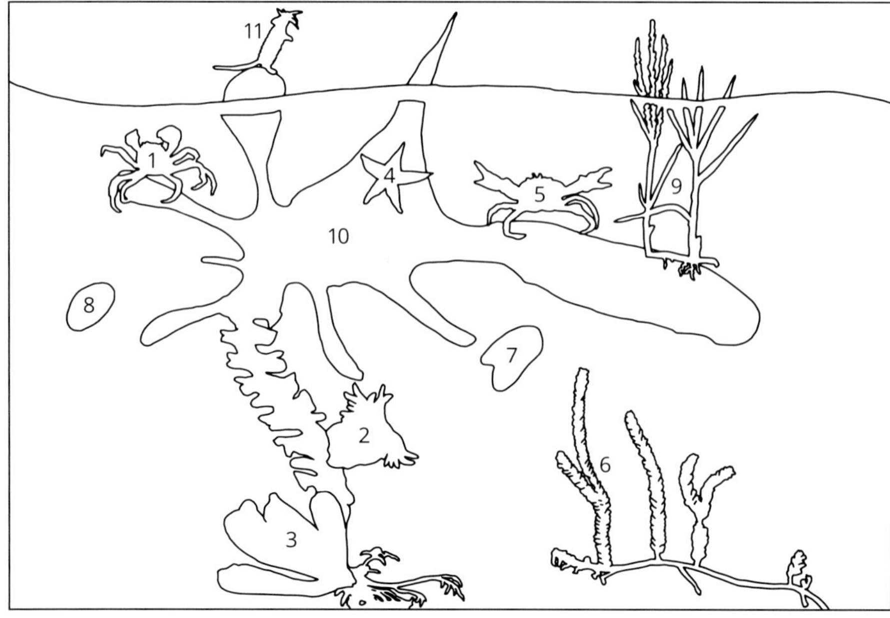

VECTORS AND PATHWAYS page 92

1. Chinese mitten crab (*Eriocheir sinensis*)
2. Red-spotted sea anemone (*Aiptasiogeton eruptaurantia*)
3. Light-bulb seasquirt (*Clavelina lepadiformis*)
4. Northern Pacific seastar (*Asterias amurensis*)
5. European green crab (*Carcinus maenas*)
6. Green seaweed (*Caulerpa taxifolia*)
7. American comb jelly (*Mnemiopsis leidyi*)
8. Mediterranean mussel (*Mytilus galloprovincialis*)
9. Common cord grass (*Spartina anglica*)
10. Wakame kelp (*Undaria pinnatifida*)
11. Black rat (*Rattus rattus*)

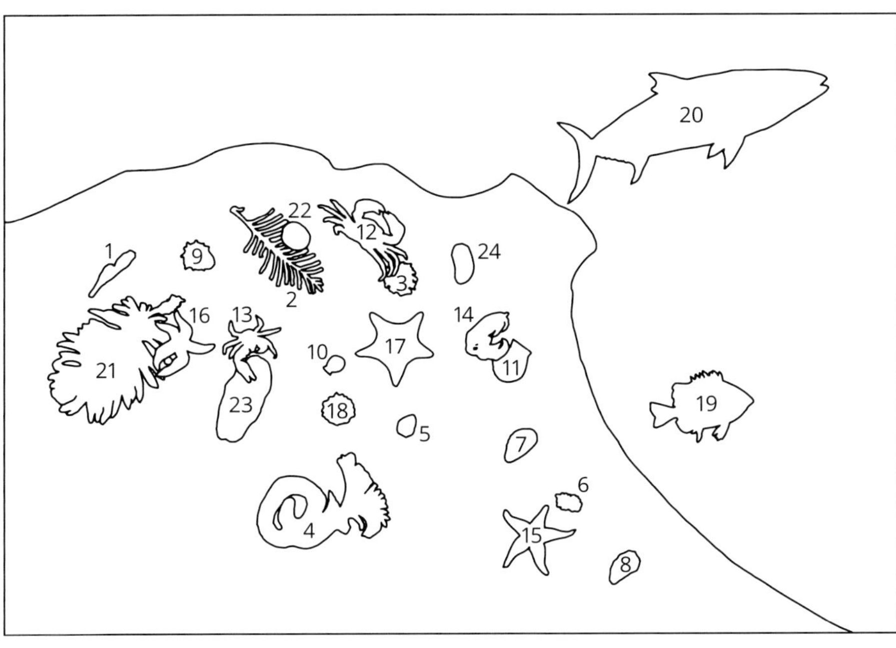

TSUNAMI page 98

1. Sponge (*Sycon raphanus*)
2. Hydroid (*Abietinaria inconstans*)
3. Orange-striped green sea anemone (*Diadumene lineata*)
4. Polychaete tubeworms (*Hydroides ezoensis*)
5. Bumpy limpet (*Lottia dorsuosa*)
6. Carnivorous whelk (*Reishia luteostoma*)
7. Mediterranean mussel (*Mytilus galloprovincialis*)
8. Pacific oyster (*Magallana gigas*)
9. Spiny oyster (*Spondylus cruentus*)
10. Squamous scallop (*Laevichlamys squamosa*)
11. Yesso scallop (*Patinopecten yessoensis*)
12. Asian shore crab (*Hemigrapsus sanguineus*)
13. Granular claw crab (*Oedignathus inermis*)
14. Mud crab (*Sphaerozius nitidus*)
15. Northern Pacific seastar (*Asterias amurensis*)
16. Japanese seastar (*Aphelasterias japonica*)
17. Blue bat star (*Patiria pectinifera*)
18. Sea urchin (*Temnotrema sculptum*)
19. Barred knifejaw (*Oplegnathus fasciatus*)
20. Yellowtail jack (*Seriola aureovittata*)
21. Wakame kelp (*Undaria pinnatifida*)
22. Zebra barnacle (*Megabalanus zebra*)
23. Chiton (*Acanthochitona achates*)
24. Veiled Chiton (*Placiphorella stimpsoni*)

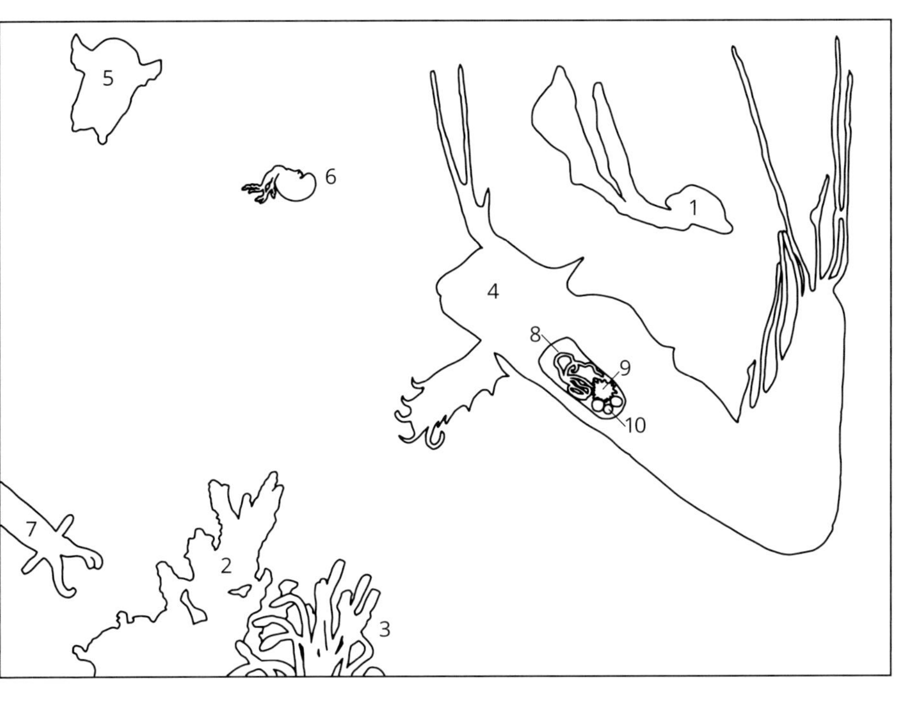

BENTHOS page 104

1. Giant phantom jelly (*Stygiomedusa gigantea*)
2. Hydrothermal vent
3. Giant tube worm (*Riftia pachyptila*)
4. Juvenile king-of-the-salmon (*Trachipterus altivelis*)
5. Headless chicken monster (*Enypniastes eximia*)
6. Paper nautilus (*Argonauta argo*)
7. ROV robotic arm
8. Branded brittle seastar (*Ophiolepsis superba*)
9. Radiolarian (*Acantharia*)
10. Diatom (*Thalassiosira lacustris*)

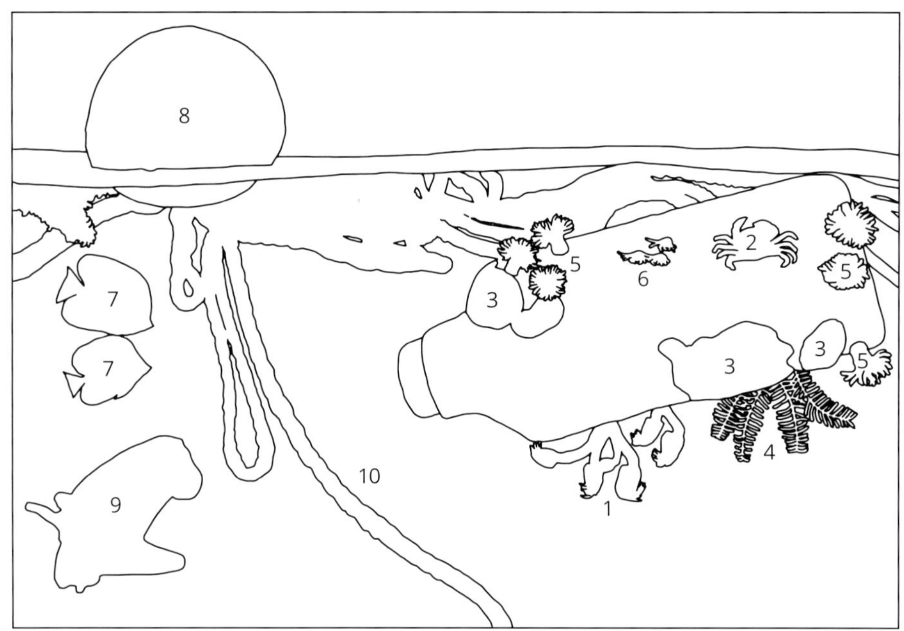

TRANSIENT PASSAGE page 110

1. Gooseneck barnacle (*Lepas anatifera*)
2. Flotsam crab (*Planes major*)
3. Bryozoan (*Jellyella tuberculata*)
4. Podded hydroid (*Aglaophenia pluma*)
5. Anjuna anemone (*Anthopleura*)
6. Amphipod (*Stenothoe gallensis*)
7. Blue-cheeked butterflyfish (*Chaetodon semilarvatus*)
8. Buoy
9. Olive ridley sea turtle (*Lepidochelys olivacea*)
10. Marine rope

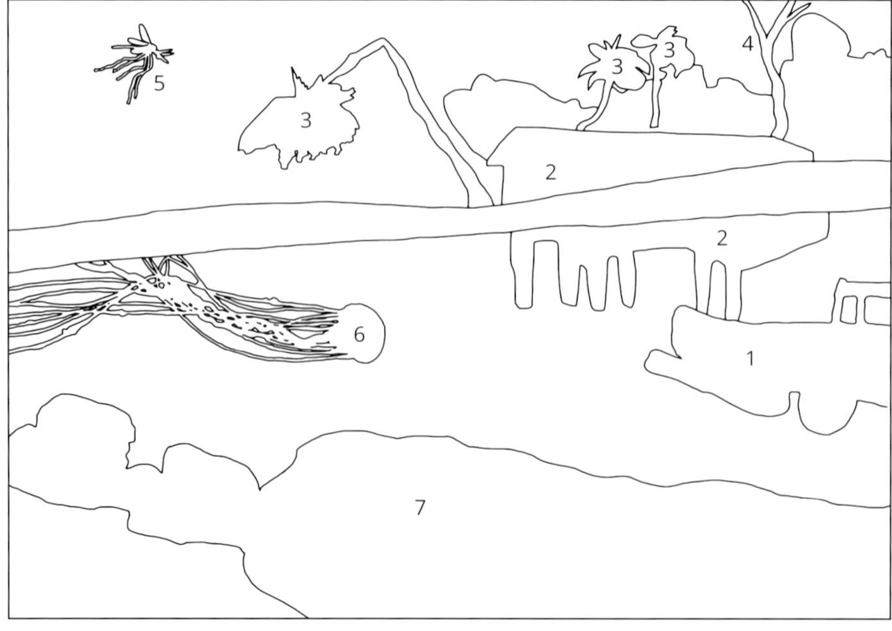

TROPICAL ISLAND page 114

1. Ford F-100 Fleetside/Longbed pickup truck, 1973
2. Coastal pile dwelling
3. Palm (*Areca*)
4. Tree (*Squamellaria*)
5. Asian tiger mosquito (*Aedes albopictus*)
6. Pacific sea nettle (*Chrysaora fuscescens*)
7. Mound seawall

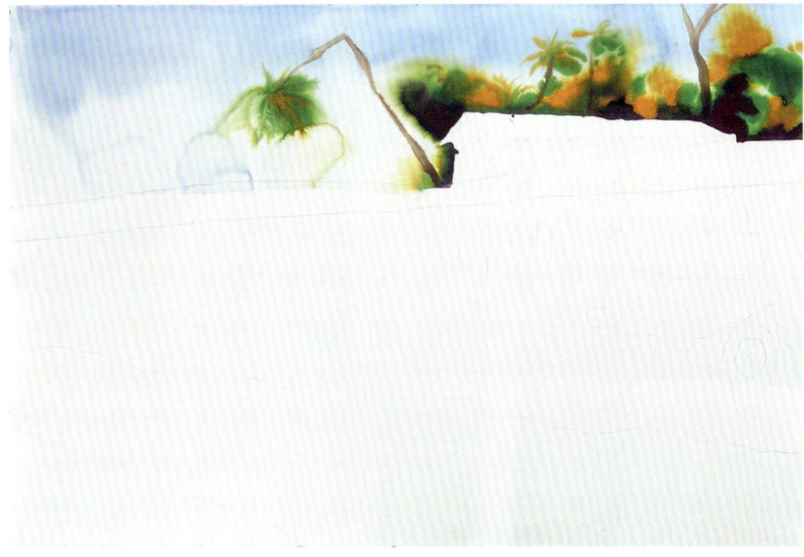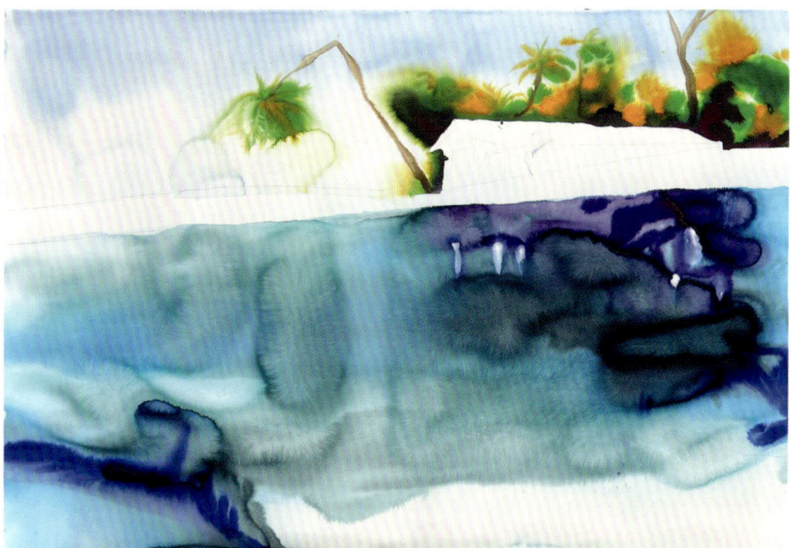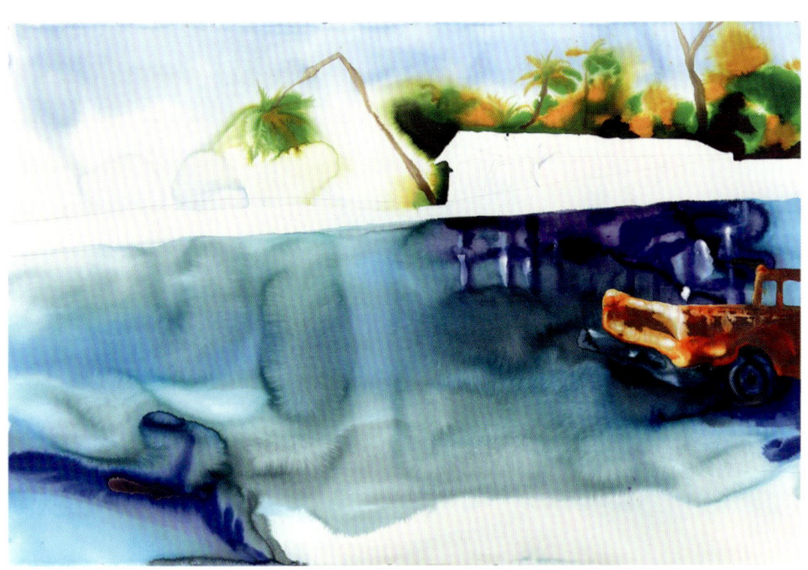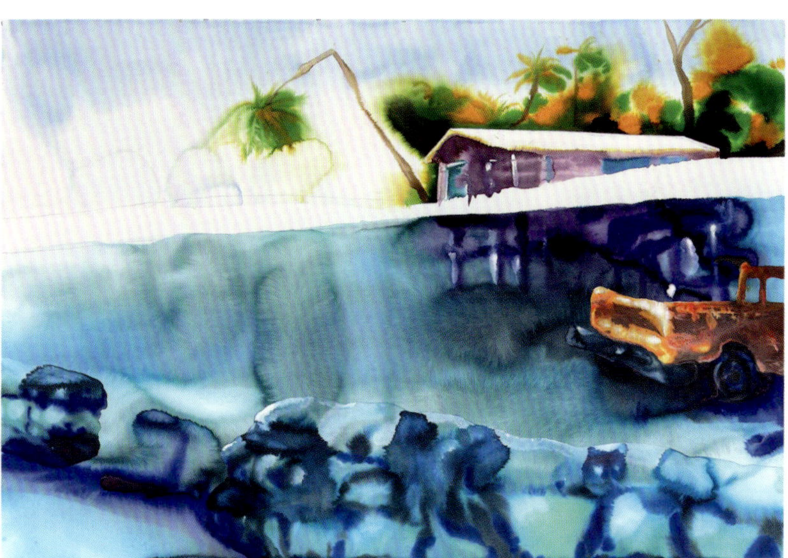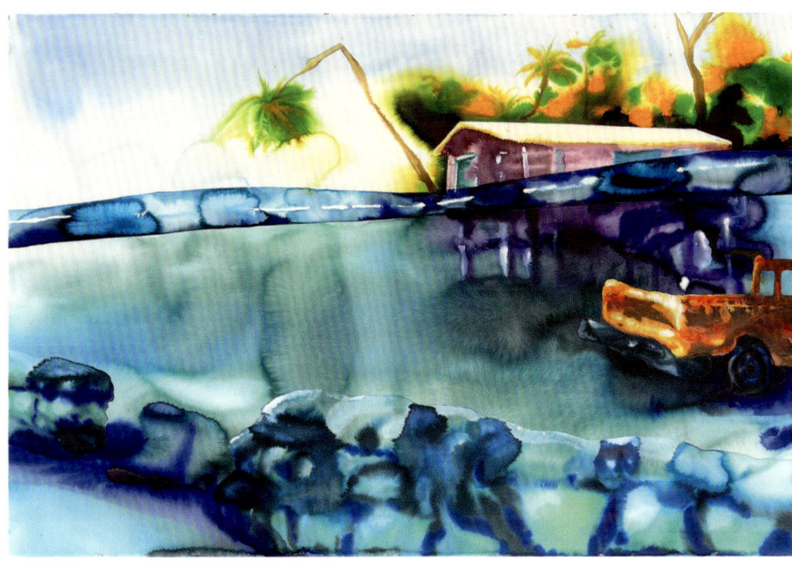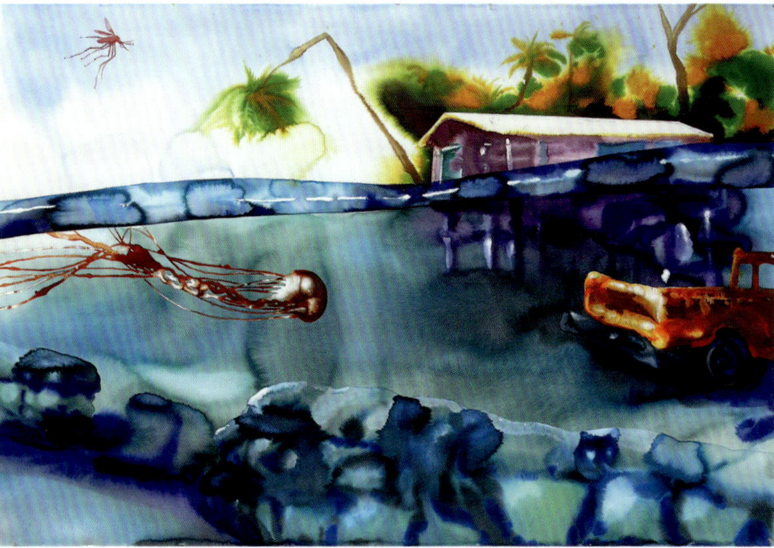

Alexis Rockman, *Tropical Island*, 2022. In progress

Robert D. Ballard is President of the Ocean Exploration Trust and Director of the Center for Ocean Exploration at the University of Rhode Island Graduate School of Oceanography, Explorer-in-Residence at the National Geographic Society, and a Commissioner for the US Commission on Ocean Policy. While growing up, Ballard dreamed of becoming an underwater explorer, which turned into a reality when he went on his first ocean expedition at the age of seventeen. Since then, he has conducted more than 150 deep-sea expeditions, discovering the RMS *Titanic*, the German battleship *Bismarck*, valuable minerals, and oil and gas deposits, as well as new life forms. He served for thirty years in the navy while stationed at the Woods Hole Oceanographic Institution, developing deep-sea submersibles and remotely operated vehicle systems. In 2008 he acquired his own ship, which he named the E/V *Nautilus* after the submarine of his boyhood hero Captain Nemo. The *Nautilus* and its Corps of Exploration, largely made up of women, are presently exploring the 50 percent of our nation that lies beneath the sea. Ballard has received numerous awards for his work, including several from the US Navy, twenty-two honorary doctorates, National Geographic's Hubbard Medal, and the National Endowment for the Humanities Medal. He is a Fellow of the American Academy of Arts and Sciences.

Christina Connett Brophy is Senior Vice President of Curatorial Affairs and Senior Director of Museum Galleries at Mystic Seaport Museum. She is the former Douglas and Cynthia Crocker Endowed Chair for the Chief Curator at the New Bedford Whaling Museum, where she curated over thirty exhibitions and authored and/or edited all related publications on maritime and other subjects, including *De Wind is Op! Climate, Culture and Innovation in Dutch Maritime Painting* (2019), *Whales Today!* (2019), *The Grand Panorama of a Whaling Voyage Round the World* (2018), *Thou Shalt Knot: Clifford W. Ashley* (2017), and *A Wild Note of Longing: Albert Pinkham Ryder and a Century of American Art* (2021). She has secured groundbreaking institutional partnerships with the US Navy, the Smithsonian American Art Museum, and the Consulate General of the Kingdom of the Netherlands, among others, and has worked extensively with the Woods Hole Oceanographic Institution and others on developing exhibitions and programs on whale conservation and ocean health. In addition to her time at Mystic Seaport Museum, she has taught art history and visual culture at Rhode Island School of Design and the University

of Massachusetts, Dartmouth, and lectured extensively in Europe, Russia, the Middle East, and the US on cartography, visual arts, maritime history, and other topics.

James T. Carlton is Professor of Marine Sciences Emeritus at Williams College and Director (1989–2015) Emeritus of the Williams College–Mystic Seaport Museum Ocean & Coastal Studies Program. His research is focused on the environmental history of coastal marine ecosystems, including non-native species invasions and modern-day extinctions. He is Founding Editor-in-Chief of the journal *Biological Invasions*, a Pew Fellow for Marine Conservation, a Fellow of the American Association for the Advancement of Science, and a Fellow of the California Academy of Sciences, and he has been a Distinguished Research Fellow of the University of California at Davis's Bodega Marine Laboratory. He is the only scientist to receive the Interagency Recognition Award from the United States Federal Government for his national and international work to reduce the impacts of exotic species invasions in the sea. Carlton has coedited and authored six books, including *Intertidal Invertebrates from Central California to Oregon* (University of California Press, 2007). In 2007 the James T. Carlton Marine Science Center, an 8,000-square-foot research and teaching facility of the Williams-Mystic Program, was dedicated in his honor. In 2013 he received the Fellows Medal of the California Academy of Sciences, being one of only fifteen marine scientists in the world so recognized in the past fifty-five years.

Sylvia A. Earle is Explorer-in-Residence at the National Geographic Society, Founder of Mission Blue/Sylvia Earle Alliance, Founder of Deep Ocean Exploration and Research (DOER), a Founding Ocean Elder, Chair of the Advisory Council for the Harte Research Institute, Advisor to NTU Earth Observatory of Singapore, and former Chief Scientist of NOAA. Author of more than 230 publications and leader of more than 150 expeditions with 7,500 hours underwater, she is a graduate of Florida State University with MA and PhD degrees from Duke University and thirty-three honorary doctorates. Her research concerns the ecology and conservation of marine ecosystems and the development of technology for access to the deep sea. She is the recipient of more than 150 national and international honors and awards, including the Netherlands Order of the Golden Ark, the Princess of Asturias Award for Concord, the TED Prize, the Explorers Club Medal, the Royal Geographic Society Patron's Medal, and the National Geographic Society's Hubbard Medal. She was *Time* magazine's first Hero for the Planet, and has been recognized as a Living Legend by the Library of Congress.

Michael R. Harrison is Chief Curator and Obed Macy Research Chair at the Nantucket Historical Association. He has held curatorial positions at the National Building Museum, the Smithsonian's National Museum of American History, and the Riverside Museum in Glasgow, Scotland. He is the author of *Collecting Nantucket: Artifacts from an Island Community* (NHA, 2018), coauthor of *Glasgow Museums, the Ship Models: A History & Complete Illustrated Catalogue* (Seaforth, 2019), and has written nearly seventy historical reports on maritime, architectural, and engineering topics for the US National Park Service's Heritage Documentation Programs. He is a graduate of the University of Pennsylvania and the George Washington University.

Alexis Rockman is an artist based in Warren, Connecticut, who has exhibited extensively worldwide since 1985. He has been the subject of many international solo and group exhibitions, including the solo museum shows *Dioramas* at the Contemporary Arts Museum, Houston (1996); *A Recent History of the World* at the Aldrich Museum of Contemporary Art, Ridgefield (1999); *Manifest Destiny* at the Brooklyn Museum (2005); *The Weight of Air* at the Rose Art Museum, Waltham (2008); the mid-career survey *A Fable for Tomorrow* at the Smithsonian American Art Museum, Washington, DC (2010); *East End Field Drawings* at the Parrish Museum of Art, Water Mill (2015); *The Great Lakes Cycle*, organized by the Grand Rapids Art Museum and traveling to five museum venues (2018–20); and his most recent exhibition, *Shipwrecks*, at Guild Hall, East Hampton, and traveling to Peabody Essex Museum, Ackland Art Museum, and Princeton University Art Museum, which featured works depicting the world's waterways as a network by which all of world history has traveled (2021). His work is included in public and private collections around the world, including the Brooklyn Museum, New York; Carnegie Museum of Art, Pittsburgh; Solomon R. Guggenheim Museum, New York; Moscow Museum of Contemporary Art; Whitney Museum of American Art, New York; and Yale University Art Gallery, New Haven. From 2009 to 2012, Rockman collaborated with director Ang Lee on the prize-winning film *Life of Pi*, serving as "inspirational artist" and creating one of *Pi*'s most captivating sequences, Tiger Vision, in which Pi discovers the world through a tiger's eyes while journeying to the bottom of the ocean.

Helen M. Rozwadowski is Professor of History and founder of the Maritime Studies program at the University of Connecticut. Her most recent book, *Vast Expanses: A History of the Oceans* (2018), was published by Reaktion Books. She was awarded the History of Science Society's Davis Prize for best book directed to a wide public audience for *Fathoming the Ocean: The Discovery and Exploration of the Deep Sea* (Belknap Press, 2005). She has also coedited three volumes on the history of oceanography, most recently, *Soundings & Crossings* (Science History Publications, 2016). Her recent work includes a virtual exhibition, "Oceans in Three Paradoxes," an outgrowth of a fellowship she held at the Rachel Carson Center for Environment and Society in Munich, Germany. Her work has contributed instrumentally to the rise of ocean history, and she is coeditor of the University of Chicago book series Oceans in Depth.

Nari Ward is an artist known for his sculptural installations composed of discarded material found and collected in his neighborhood in New York City. He has repurposed objects such as baby strollers, shopping carts, bottles, doors, television sets, cash registers, and shoelaces, among other materials. Ward recontextualizes these found objects in thought-provoking juxtapositions that create complex, metaphorical meanings to confront social and political issues surrounding race, poverty, and consumer culture. He intentionally leaves the meaning of his work open, allowing the viewer to provide his or her own interpretation. Recent solo exhibitions of his work have been organized at the Contemporary Arts Museum Houston (2019); New Museum, New York (2019); Institute of Contemporary Art, Boston (2017); Socrates Sculpture Park, New York (2017); Barnes Foundation, Philadelphia (2016); Pérez Art Museum Miami (2015); and Savannah College of Art and Design Museum of Art (2015). Ward's work is in numerous international public and private collections, including the Albright-Knox Art Gallery, Buffalo, NY; the Brooklyn Museum, New York; Museum of Contemporary Art, Los Angeles; Museum of Modern Art, New York; Pérez Art Museum Miami; Smithsonian American Art Museum, Washington, DC; and the Whitney Museum of American Art, New York.

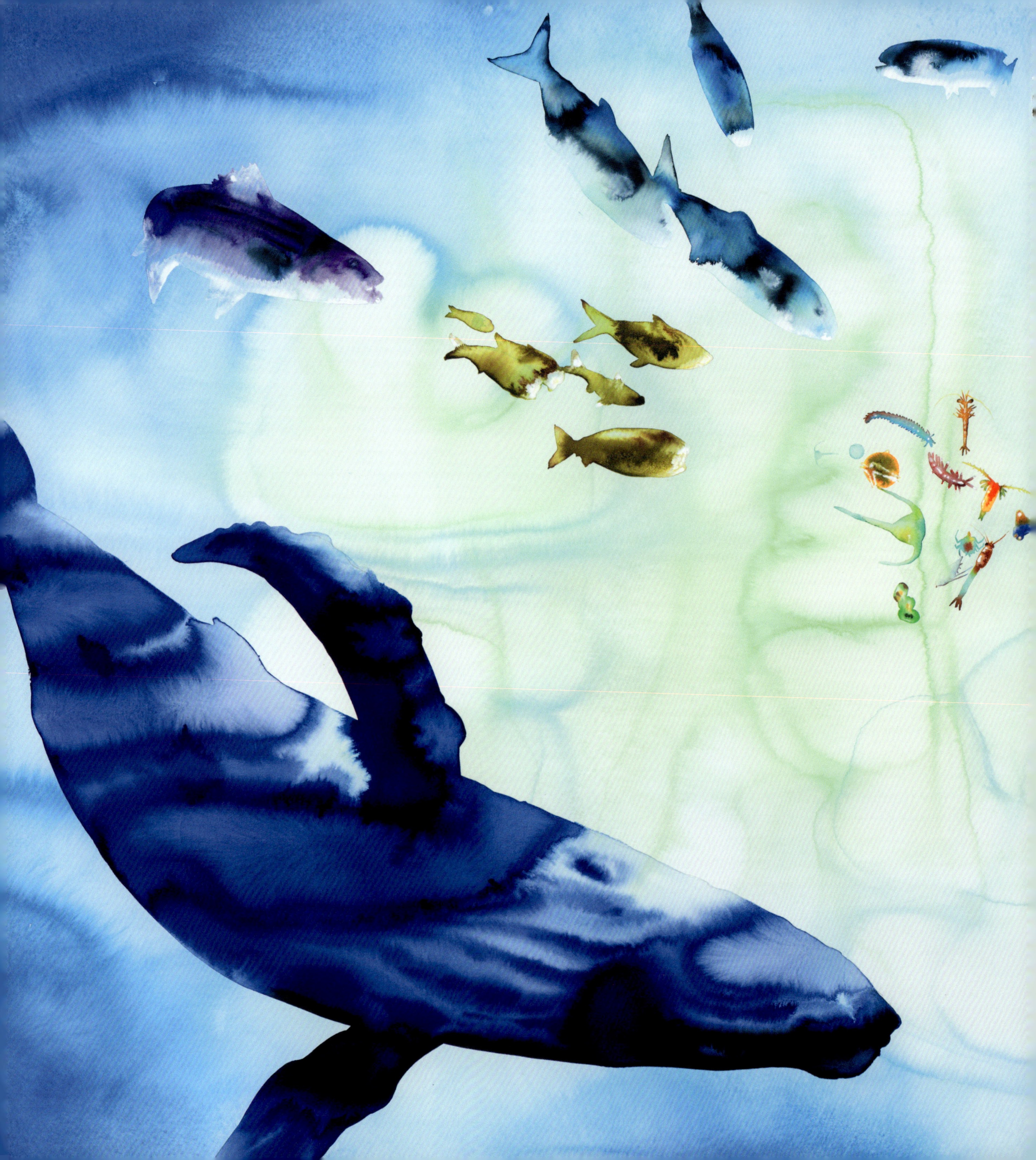

ACKNOWLEDGMENTS

I want to thank Dr. Elizabeth Broun, Director Emerita of the Smithsonian American Art Museum, for introducing me to Alexis Rockman and his extraordinary work as he was doing research for an exhibition on shipwrecks. As I explored contemporary and relevant projects which would connect our collections, site, and mission with the impact of maritime activities on global ocean health and sea-level rise, I kept coming back to Rockman as the perfect fit. I was absolutely thrilled when he said yes to work on this new series of paintings for the permanent collections of Mystic Seaport Museum (MSM).

In presenting this concept to the MSM President, Peter Armstrong, and to the Board of Trustees, I was immediately met with excitement and support, and I want to thank all of them for helping to get this project off the ground, particularly Michael Hudner, J. Barclay Collins II, and Alexander Bulazel for their forward thinking and enthusiasm.

Alexis Rockman: Oceanus, while a companion to the exhibition series, can also stand alone, with a suite of multidisciplinary essays by some of the greatest thinkers, historians, activists, and explorers of our time. Their words connect the themes of Rockman's paintings with our own long history of exploitation in ways that we hope will inspire action and collaboration as we look toward a sustainable future. We are very honored be able to include Dr. Robert Ballard, Dr. James Carlton, Dr. Sylvia Earle, Michael Harrison, Dr. Helen Rozwadowski, and Nari Ward in this exquisite publication.

Margaret Rennolds Chace, Associate Publisher at Rizzoli Electa, has been an extraordinary leader in the creation of this beautiful volume, and Todd Bradway brought his calm expertise and thoughtful management to its execution. Tony Morgan has created an elegant design that captures the glorious essence of Rockman's work while allowing the book to perform at its highest level as a work of art in its own right. Miles Champion was responsible for the excellent copyediting.

In the creation of this series, Rockman worked extensively with our team on the content and production, a collaborative process managed by Krystal Rose, Curator of Collections. Leading the content research on ship models, invasive species, and other themes related to MSM were Krystal Rose and Dr. James Carlton, Director Emeritus at Williams-Mystic. In addition, each of the contributors to this volume spoke with the artist about the themes of their essays and provided guidance on content within their respective areas of study. I thank them profusely for their time in these discussions.

Additional thanks go to Wilson Lawrence, Lead Exhibits Fabricator and Installer; Joe Michael, Museum Photographer and Master Printer; Dan Harvison, Creative Services Producer; Paul O'Pecko, Vice President for Collections & Research; Chris White, Collections Manager; Jenny Carroll, Cataloguer; Laura Nadelberg, Registrar; Suki Williams, Associate Director for Production, Associate Curator, Film & Video; Walter Carroll, Exhibits Fabricator; and Sophia Terry, intern, for her transcription work. Their hard work and dedication were integral to the success of this project.

We also wish to thank the Mashantucket Pequot Museum & Research Center, for the use of its muhshoon, *Nookumuhs*, for inspiration in *Oceanus*.

It is with my deepest gratitude that I thank Alexis Rockman for his dedication and devotion to this remarkable project, his professionalism, his extraordinary talent, and his immense integrity and authenticity in all that he does. It has been my honor.

—Christina Connett Brophy

Alexis Rockman would like to dedicate this project to Dorothy Spears. He extends his thanks to Dr. Christina Connett Brophy, Dr. James Carlton, Wilson Lawrence, Krystal Rose, Joe Michael, Todd Bradway, Tony Morgan, Alexander Winch, Bryan Lebouf, Mark Mennin, Dr. Jill Leonard, J. Barclay Collins II, Alexander Bulazel, and John Koegel.

Mystic Seaport Museum would like to thank the following for their generous financial support of this exhibition and publication:

Capital Group

Philip E. Galluccio

The River Branch Foundation

In honor of Professor James T. Carlton
From his students

This project was produced with a grant from
Hartford Foundation for Public Giving
publication of the global nation

Published on the occasion of the exhibition
Alexis Rockman: Oceanus, organized by Mystic Seaport Museum
and held there May 27, 2023–Spring, 2024.

Copyright © 2023 by Mystic Seaport Museum, Inc., Mystic, Connecticut

Library of Congress Control Number: 2022948524
ISBN: 978-0-8478-9944-9

First published in the United States of America in 2023 by

Rizzoli Electa
A Division of Rizzoli International Publications, Inc.
300 Park Avenue South
New York, NY 10010
rizzoliusa.com

in association with

Mystic Seaport Museum
75 Greenmanville Avenue
Mystic, CT 06355
mysticseaport.org

For Mystic Seaport Museum:
Christina Connett Brophy, Curator and Editor
Todd Bradway, Managing Editor
Miles Champion, Copy Editor
Mór Madden, Image Researcher

For Rizzoli Electa:
Charles Miers, Publisher
Margaret Rennolds Chace, Associate Publisher
Alyn Evans, Production Manager

Book design: Tony Morgan/Step Graphics, Inc.
Exhibition title design: Lakuna Design
Keys rendering: Alexander Winch

Cover: *Oceanus*, 2022 (detail): see p. 50
Front endpaper: Alexis Rockman working on *Oceanus*, 2022
Rear endpaper: Alexis Rockman's Connecticut studio, 2022
p. 2: Alexis Rockman, *Tsunami*, 2021 (detail): see p. 98
p. 4: Alexis Rockman, *Vectors and Pathways*, 2021 (detail): see p. 92

2023 2024 2025 2026 2027 / 10 9 8 7 6 5 4 3 2 1

Printed in Italy

Photography credits: Front endpapers, 2, 4, 9, 24, 26, 27, 28, 29, 30, 76–79, 86–113, 120–21, 136–37, 142, rear endpapers: Photos: © Mystic Seaport Museum, Joe Michael; pp. 6, 10, 21, 39, 42, 48–75, 80–85, 114–19, 122, 128–31, 159: Photos: © Adam Reich; p. 12 (top): Courtesy of the Bodleian Library, University of Oxford, Bodleian Library MS. Bodl. 264, pt. I; p. 12 (bottom): Courtesy of the Barry Lawrence Ruderman Map Collection and Stanford University; p. 13 (left): © Amgueddfa Cymru – Museum Wales; p. 13 (right): Courtesy of the Biodiversity Heritage Library and Cornell University Library; pp. 14 (left), 32–34, 37–38, 40–41: © Mystic Seaport Museum Collection; p. 15 (right): Courtesy of the National Museum of American History and the Library of Congress; p. 16 (top): © Martha Delzell Memorial Fund, Courtesy of the Indianapolis Museum of Art at Newfields; p. 16 (below): Courtesy of the Metropolitan Museum of Art, Gift of Mr. and Mrs. Erving Wolf, in memory of Diane R. Wolf, 1977; p. 17: Courtesy of the University of Toronto Library and the Internet Archive, archive.org/details/allredlineannals00johnuoft; p. 18 (left): Courtesy of the Universal Film Manufacturing Company and the Internet Archive; p. 18 (right): Courtesy of the Travel Film Archive; p. 19 (right): Courtesy of Columbia Pictures; p. 22: Courtesy of Kate Sutter and the Ocean Agency Image Bank; p. 35: Courtesy Division of Work and Industry, National Museum of American History, Smithsonian Institution; p. 36 (top): Nantucket Historical Association Collection, gift of the Friends of the NHA, 1989.126.4; p. 36 (bottom): Photo: © Caryn B. Davis; p. 40 (top): Courtesy of Historic New England; p. 43: Courtesy of Harvard University Library; p. 44: Photo: Juan Jose Valdes and Rosemary Wadley, National Geographic Magazine and the NOAA Center for Coastal Mapping; p. 45 (top and bottom): Courtesy of Robert Ballard and the Ocean Exploration Trust; p. 46: Courtesy of Robert Ballard and the Ocean Exploration Cooperative Institute; p. 47: Photo: © Bryce Groark; p. 125: Courtesy of the artist and Lehmann Maupin, New York, Hong Kong, Seoul, and London. Photo: Elisabeth Bernstein; p. 126 (top): Courtesy of Nari Ward; p. 126 (bottom): Courtesy of the artist and Lehmann Maupin, New York, Hong Kong, Seoul, and London; p. 127: Courtesy of Guild Hall © Gary Mamay; p. 132 (top and bottom): Photos: © Elizabeth Ellenwood; p. 133: Courtesy of Iceland Ocean Cluster; p. 134: Courtesy of Inversa; p. 135 (top): © Coral Vita / Harry Lee; p. 135 (bottom): Courtesy of Stephen Connett; pp. 138–41, 143, 146–47: Photos: Dorothy Spears; pp. 144–45: Photos: © Mystic Seaport Museum, Krystal Rose; pp. 148–55: Courtesy of Alexis Rockman.

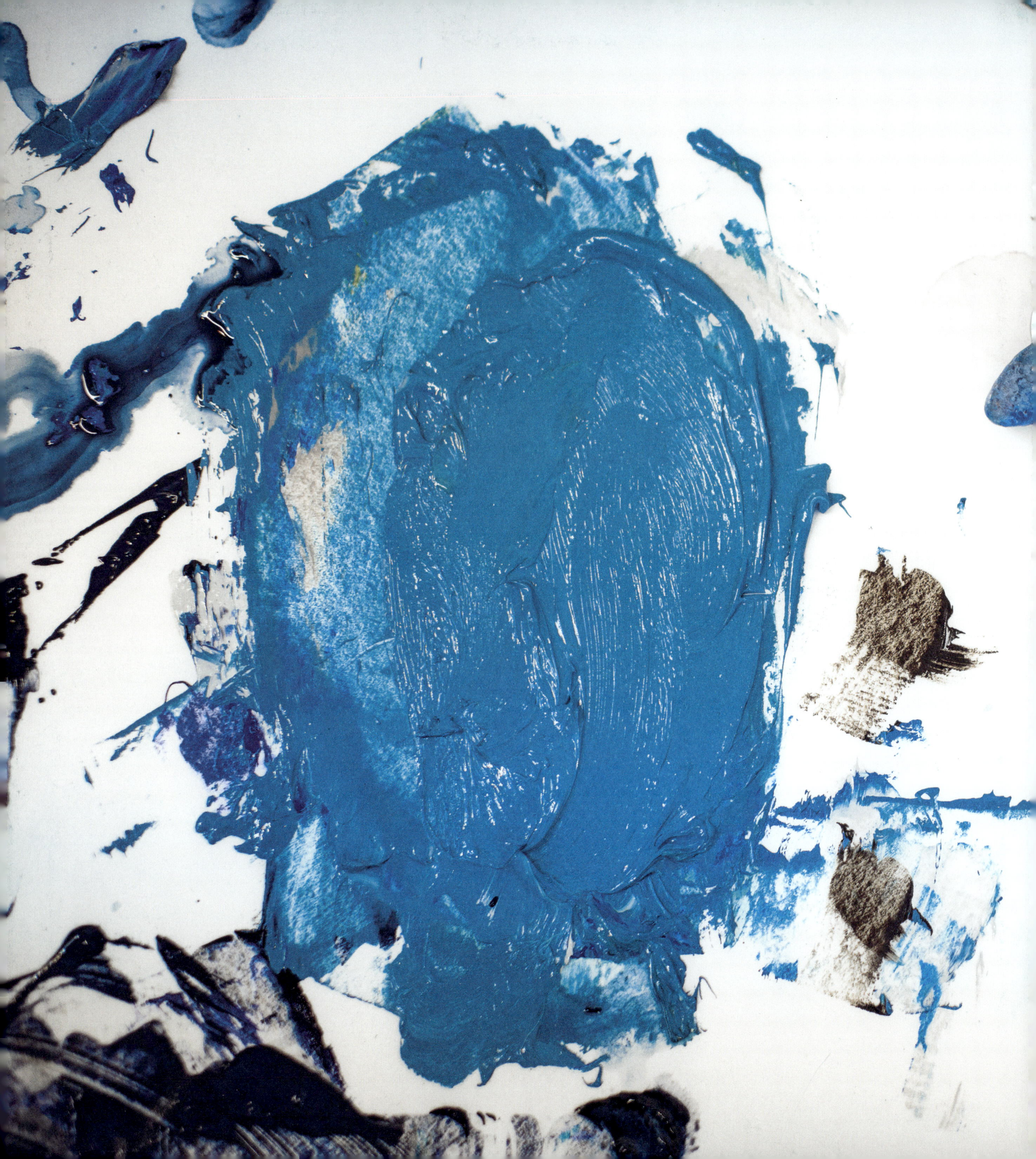